Exploring
with Custer

The 1874 Black Hills Expedition

STEREOGRAPHS OF THE BLACK HILLS.
Photographed by W. H. Illingworth.

PUBLISHED BY W. H. ILLINGWORTH.
No. EAST SEVENTH STREET, ST. PAUL, MINN.

No. 854. Custer's Expedition.

by *Ernest Grafe & Paul Horsted*

Golden Valley Press

Exploring with Custer

The 1874 Black Hills Expedition

by Ernest Grafe & Paul Horsted

In Memory of Doug Horsted, 1963-2000.

First page: W.H. Illingworth stereoview No. 854, "Gen. Custer's Expedition." (Minnilusa Pioneer Museum)
Pages *ii-iii:* The mass of men, animals and equipment that was the Black Hills Expedition spreads out across the plains of Dakota Territory, in this scene enlarged from the stereoview on the first page. Elk antlers picked up in the Black Hills, seen on top of several wagons, tell us the photograph was taken as the Expedition made its way home to Ft. Lincoln. Gen. Custer is thought to be the figure in front at left. (Minnilusa Pioneer Museum)
Pages *iv-v:* W.H. Illingworth's panoramic view of the Permanent Camp of the Black Hills Expedition, about three miles east of the present town of Custer. (Devereaux Library Archives)

Exploring With Custer: The 1874 Black Hills Expedition is published by Golden Valley Press, an imprint of Dakota Photographic LLC, Custer, South Dakota. If you have knowledge of original diaries, letters, other documents or photographs from the 1874 Black Hills Expedition, especially if not published in this book, please drop us a line. Email us at editor@goldenvalleypress.com; or write to Golden Valley Press, 24905 Mica Ridge Road, Custer, SD 57730. You can also contact the authors through the web site **www.custertrail.com.** This site will contain occasional updates and other information about this ongoing project. You may also order additional copies of this book and related Black Hills Expedition items such as maps and prints through the web site. If you have information on the Expedition's route in or near the Black Hills, please contact Ernie Grafe at erniegrafe@aol.com or (605) 391-9303, or by mail through the publisher. Thank you.

Photographs (if not credited elsewhere) and related text are ©Paul Horsted.
Trail guide and text are ©Ernest Grafe.
Biography of W.H. Illingworth is ©Don Schwarck.

The information contained in this book is accurate to the best of the authors' knowledge. The authors and publisher assume no liability whatsoever for errors or omissions of any kind. Boundaries and land ownership change often in the Black Hills; you should check with local offices of the U.S. Forest Service or county planning agencies for the latest maps and information. This book may depict areas that are privately owned; such depiction does not mean these areas are open to the public. Always obtain permission from the owner before entering or crossing any private property.

Trail guide design by Ernest Grafe.
Photography section design by Camille Riner.
Cover design by Paul Horsted.
Copy editing by Norm Nelson.

Produced and published in the United States of America by Dakota Photographic LLC. Printed in the Republic of Korea by Doosan Printing.

First Edition, July 2002.

Library of Congress Catalog Card Number: 2002102921

ISBN (hard cover limited first edition) 0-9718053-0-X
ISBN (soft cover) 0-9718053-1-8

Please see pages 284-285 for a complete list of sources and collections who graciously provided material for this book.

Contents

Acknowledgements

More than three years of research and field work have gone into this book, but in many ways it is a collaboration with earlier authors, editors, scholars and researchers who built the foundation that made *Exploring with Custer* possible.

The authors would particularly like to thank Joe Sanders and Jack McCulloh, who, along with the late Larry Owen, began studying the Expedition a decade ago. They shared with us their enthusiasm and friendship and many rewarding hours on the trail. They also deserve credit for discovering a number of Expedition ruts within the Black Hills. We are all indebted, in turn, to Dr. Donald R. Progulske, whose groundbreaking 1974 book *Yellow Ore, Yellow Hair, Yellow Pine,* published by South Dakota State University, has been the bible on the Custer Expedition for more than 25 years. And Cleophas C. O'Harra, a former president of the South Dakota School of Mines and Technology in Rapid City, made perhaps the earliest effort to map and mark the Expedition trail, beginning in the 1920s.

Exploring with Custer could not exist in its present form without original Illingworth stereoviews that were generously loaned by the Minnilusa Pioneer Museum (part of The Journey in Rapid City, South Dakota) as well as prints of the 1874 photographs loaned by the Devereaux Library Archive at the South Dakota School of Mines and Technology (also in Rapid City). The authors would especially like to thank Robert Preszler, director of the Minnilusa Pioneer Museum, and Donna Neal, archivist at the Devereaux Library, for their help.

Blaine Cook, Forest Silvilculturist for Black Hills National Forest in Custer, South Dakota, enthusiastically supported the project in many ways. BHNF provided financial support for the early phase of re-photographing the 1874 photo sites, for which we are very grateful. BHNF Historic Preservation Officer Dave McKee also assisted us with advice on issues of preservation of cultural resources. Todd Mills, Interdisciplinary GIS Specialist, helped us with digital scans of USGS topographic maps, which are used extensively in the trail guide. We'd also like to thank John Twiss, Forest Supervisor for Black Hills National Forest, for providing the preservation message on the opposite page, and for his support of this project.

Steve Baldwin, executive director of the Black Hills Parks & Forests Association, was a key player in bringing together a number of parties interested in the 1874 Expedition, the outcome of which is the book you hold in your hands.

We are appreciative of research assistance from a number of individuals and institutions in South Dakota: Jessie Sundstrom at the 1881 Custer County Courthouse Museum, Custer; Brian Bade of Storyteller West in Rapid City; Bob Kolbe of Kolbe's Clock Shop in Sioux Falls; Rocky Boyd, via the Hearst Library in Lead; Dr. Harry F. Thompson of the Center for Western Studies at Augustana College, Sioux Falls; Marvene Riis, Jeanne Kilen Ode and Nancy Tystad Koupal of the South Dakota State Historical Society in Pierre; and Bradley Block and Craig Pugsley of Custer State Park. We also relied on the help of Thomas R. Buecker at the Ft. Robinson Museum in Crawford, Nebraska; the University of Minnesota Archives in Minneapolis; Sarah Heiman, via the Beinecke Rare Book and Manuscript Library at Yale University; John Doerner and Kitty Deernose of the Little Big Horn Battlefield National Monument in Montana; the Old Military and Civil Records Branch of the National Archives in Washington, D.C.; Richard Wood of Alaskan Heritage Bookshop in Juneau, Alaska; Mark Kenneweg and Kevin Kirkey of Ft. Lincoln State Park in Mandan, North Dakota; and Jim Davis of the North Dakota State Historical Society in Bismarck.

We are publishing for the first time the location of an Illingworth photo site in Wyoming that was discovered and shown to us by Russell Tracy and George Whalen.

Some of the journals we quote were readily available in book form thanks to the diligent persistence of editors like Dr. Lawrence Frost, John M. Carroll and Wayne R. Kime. Other journals and newspaper reports were collected by Herbert Krause and Gary D. Olson in the tremendously useful book *Prelude to Glory,* published by the Center for Western Studies at Augustana College. Individuals who own the originals or publishing rights to several 1874 Expedition diaries graciously granted permission to quote from their material or earlier books. These individuals include Jill Frost Merke, Sandy Barnard, Kirk Budd and Bob Aldrich. David Rambow, modern-day wet-plate photographer, provided valuable insights on this 19th-century photographic process. Charles Cochran advised us about Expedition guns, ammunition and other equipment of the U.S. Cavalry.

Bev Pechan assisted us by verifying published newspaper accounts of the 1874 Expedition. Attorney Todd Epp helped us with copyright issues. Don Schwarck wrote the biography of W.H. Illingworth. Kim Hadd and Teryl Cruse of Graphic City consulted on design issues. Manuscript pages were read by Bob Martin, Steve Baldwin and Brian Bade. Norm Nelson served as copyeditor.

Any mistakes that remain are of course due entirely to our inability to make the corrections they carefully pointed out to us.

Paul Horsted would like to specially thank his wife Camille Riner and daughter Anna Marie for their support, love and understanding as this project took over our lives the last six months before publication. Burt and Gladys Horsted, Paul's parents, and Al and Linda Riner, Camille's parents, also helped us in too many ways to count. Thank you.

Ernie Grafe would like to thank Claudine Bach, who contributed her gifts for color and language. He would also like to thank Jeffrey Rogers Hummel for always knowing the answer, Todd Schweiger for the clipping that made this possible, Mike Forrette for setting the example, and Larry Emmert for rescuing a sore-footed hiker in Floral Valley.

Many people gave up their valuable time to talk with us and sometimes guide us in the field, including Orville "Pete" Harper, Chester Hejde, Margaret Hobart, Paul Hobart, John Honerkamp, Ivan Hovland, Doris Vore Lake, Bill Lei, John Lienemann, Marshall "Bink" Nussbaum, Ivan Reynolds, Leonard Reynolds, Nels Smith, Bill Whalen and John Whalen.

There were still other friends, businesses, landowners, family members and public service employees who helped and supported our efforts: Dan Horsted; Dave Strain of Dakota West Books; John & Nancy Gausman; Gerald and Carol Veldhuizen of Staple and Spice Market; Nancy Gellerman of Sage Creek Grille; Greg and Jodi Latza of PeopleScapes, Inc.; Dan and Ardelle McPherson; Bob and Sharon Martin; Denise Thompson and Barry Rivera; Bill Goehring; Everett Akam; A Walk in the Woods Gallery; ArtForms, Inc. Gallery; Smatterings Gallery; Pat Boyd and George Prisbe, Wet Edge Gallery; The Journey Museum gift shop; Custer Business Enterprises; Custer Area Chamber of Commerce; Norma and Charley Najacht, *Custer County Chronicle;* Deb Holland, *Rapid City Journal;* Bob Bosse and Kyle Mork, S.D. Public Broadcasting; Mike Wolforth, Light Images; Linda Geyer; Bill Honerkamp, Black Hills, Badlands and Lakes Association; Warren Crawford; Perry Livingston; Garrett Smith; Jim Wainright; Cameron Ferweda; Homestake Mining Company; Jerry Brown, Pete Lien & Sons, Inc.; Kevin Casey, Bear Country USA; Dave Nielsen; John D. McDermott; Roy Alexander; Eric and Melissa Nelson; Karen Anderson; Ina Davis; James Bruch; Paul Bruch; Lee Dueker; Todd Teahon; David Moore; Keith Johnson; Mary "Toots" Soholt; Robert Schmitz; Arlo "Sonny" Fobaire; Jesse Driskill; Bob Cronn; Mary Garman; Scott Christensen; and Betty Necklason.

A heartfelt thank you to all who have helped make this project so enjoyable and rewarding—and to Donald "Pete" Peterson and Norma Eckmann for tending the graves of Privates John Cunningham, George Turner and James King.

Paul Horsted *Ernie Grafe*
Custer, S.D. *Rapid City, S.D.*

Historic Preservation in the Black Hills National Forest

Heritage resources are not only the physical remnants of history—the artifacts, art and ruins —but also the settings and landscapes that provide a link to our past. The route of the Custer Expedition is an excellent example of a heritage resource and it should be protected for the enjoyment of current and future generations. Physical vestiges of the trail, artifacts discarded or lost by Expedition members, and the locations of campsites as well as other activities are all part of this unique resource located on private and federal land in the Black Hills.

On federal land, the National Historic Preservation Act (NHPA) and the Archaeological Resource Protection Act (ARPA) protect heritage resources from destruction by federal projects, unauthorized excavation, looting, artifact collecting or vandalism. Members of the public can become active participants in federal historic preservation programs and activities. To learn about preservation opportunities or to report vandalism, please contact the nearest federal land management agency or your State Historic Preservation Office.

The authors of this publication have provided a gift to current and future generations by bringing the past to life. Please enjoy this treasure from our past but take care to leave the trail segments, photo sites, camp locations and associated artifacts undisturbed for future generations.

John Twiss, Forest Supervisor
Black Hills National Forest

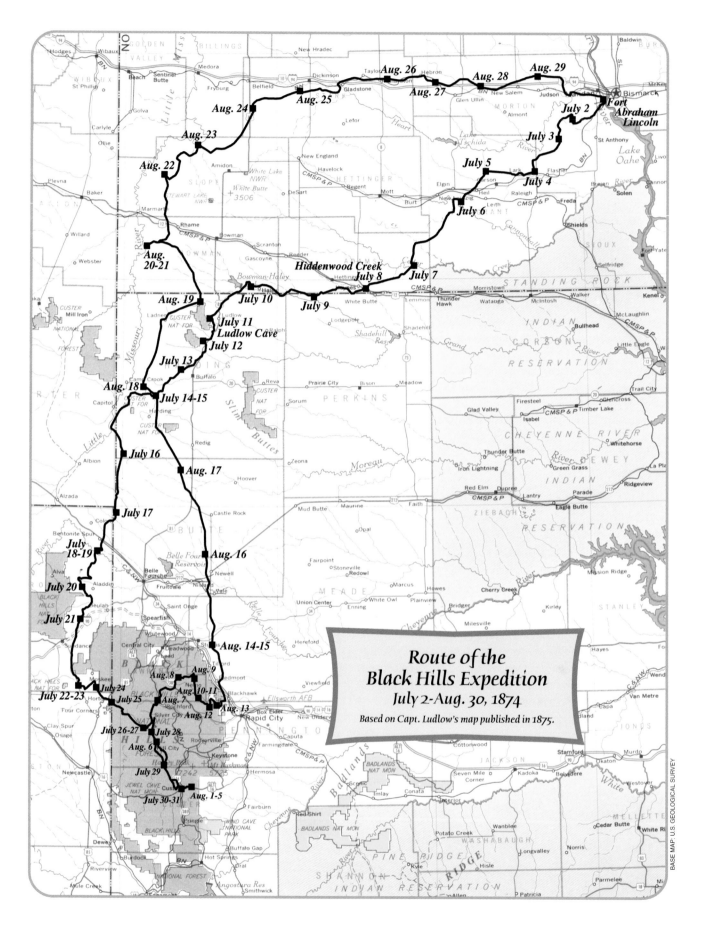

Route of the Black Hills Expedition
July 2–Aug. 30, 1874

Based on Capt. Ludlow's map published in 1875.

Preface

The presence of George Armstrong Custer has always been hard to ignore, and his name as well as his image are prominent on our cover. But the Black Hills are the true heart of this book, which grew out of a fascination with those three weeks of summer in which the Hills were photographed, mapped and written about for the first time.

We have drawn from all of these records and documents to turn the Black Hills Expedition of 1874 into an active, stimulating experience. William Illingworth's photographs, reproduced here with new clarity, present glimpses of trail life that are embellished by first-hand narratives of the time. Diarists and newspaper writers with the Expedition left us a wealth of picturesque prose, the best of which is woven together in these pages for an intimate view of day-to-day life. The explorers speak to you in their own voices, as if they were crouched around a campfire and interrupting with their versions of the story.

We also probed the accounts for every nuance of detail about Custer's path within the Hills, correlating those clues with the Expedition's map—and sometimes with very old ruts—to produce an extremely accurate guide designed for both the casual reader and the weekend adventurer. You can easily ignore the trail instructions to follow the unfolding story of each day in the Hills. If you take our book into the field, however, it will lead you to the very places you read about or see in the Illingworth photographs. You might almost hear the rattle of wagons and bray of mules echoing down through the years.

As rich as we hope the experience will be, there is much more to discover in the original Expedition sources listed in our bibliography (page 284). The published diaries and narratives of Theodore Ewert, James Calhoun, John Ryan and Fred Power provide many details—particularly about the trail beyond the Black Hills—that we were not able to include here. The collection of newspaper accounts and selected journals in *Prelude to Glory* is a treasure in itself. Nothing would make us happier than a surge of new interest in these publications, many of which have gone out of print.

We would like to acknowledge that while the Expedition holds a deep fascination for us today, it resulted in a terrible loss for the Lakota people. We never talk of "discovering" the Black Hills because they were in everyday use at the time, part of a territory guaranteed to the Lakota by the Fort Laramie Treaty of 1868. There are those who argue that a military reconnaissance was permissible under the treaty, but it is hard to argue that the *intent* of the Expedition was strictly military—not with its photographer, practical miners and newspaper correspondents. "As carried out by Custer," historian Donald Jackson wrote in the book *Custer's Gold,* "the expedition was a treaty violation in spirit if not in fact." Those of us who live in and enjoy the Black Hills cannot escape the reality that we benefit from what happened in 1874.

We do not intend to glorify Custer. He has provoked equally strong feelings of admiration and disdain among the people who knew him in his lifetime and the people who still argue about him today. Those divergent opinions are reflected—fairly, we hope—in these pages.

This book represents more than three years of research and field work, and we hope it is just the beginning. Two new documents surfaced during that time (geologist Newton Winchell's field notebook and Sgt. John Ryan's memoir), but so much more might still be out there. Private Ewert said "several" photographs were taken at the Aug. 12 camp near Custer Gap, but the group photo is the only one we know about. Where are the others? Where are the letters sent home to loved ones? Where is the miner W.T. McKay's diary, mentioned but never found? We hope some of you will join in this collaboration, perhaps uncovering material that we could include—with appropriate credits—in the next edition of *Exploring with Custer.*

Below: Detail from W.H. Illingworth's stereoview No. 852 "Custer's Expedition" shows the formation of four lines of wagons used for plains travel.

Gen. Custer and several men pose in front of his tent, a gift from former West Point classmate Thomas L. Rosser, chief surveyor for the Northern Pacific Railroad. (Note the "N.P.R.R." on the tent.) The two men had worked together during the Yellowstone Expedition of 1873, but this photograph is thought to have been taken by W.H. Illingworth in 1874 due to the presence of the Colt's Model 1873 revolvers and the 1873 Springfield breech-loading carbine. These were the new weapons delivered to Fort Lincoln just two days before the Black Hills Expedition departed. John Doerner, chief historian at Little Bighorn Battlefield National Monument, identifies the other men (from left) as chief scout Bloody Knife, interpreter Louis Agard (uncertain), and Arikara scouts Little Sioux and Goose. Two of Custer's beloved stag hounds rest in the foreground. The bottom of the photo shows the edges of the wet-plate emulsion.

Prologue
A journey to the last unknown place

General George Armstrong Custer had no idea how to enter the Black Hills when he arrived at the head of a massive reconnaissance expedition in 1874. The Arikara and Santee Sioux scouts insisted it would be useless to continue with the wagon train, and available maps revealed nothing of the interior canyons, creeks or dark pine forests. "Maps might be packed away," Private Theodore Ewert wrote in his diary. According to the *New York Tribune,* "The only authentic map of that section is a piece of blank paper."

The Black Hills had been a mysterious presence at the center of a country the white world had been exploring and occupying for a long time. Lewis and Clark had gone home 68 years earlier, while the discovery of gold at Sutter's Mill was already a quarter of a century in the past. Now roads and telegraph lines connected forts and mining towns all across the West. Steamboats proliferated on the Missouri, homesteaders were proving up on their claims not far away, and the Union Pacific Railroad made its regular runs along the Platte River—less than 200 miles to the south. Andrew Hallidie had tested his cable car in San Francisco the year before. Yellowstone National Park was getting ready for the first tourists. And the invention of the telephone was less than two years away. Yet the Black Hills of Dakota Territory were still "a piece of blank paper."

They had been protected in part by their distance from the most-used travel routes—the Platte and North Platte Rivers to the south and the Missouri River to the north. The men and women who traveled those roads quested after a dream shimmering just over the horizon. Trappers sought beaver in the Rocky Mountains, Mormons longed for their Promised Land, and farmers were drawn to the fertile river valleys of Oregon. These steady migrations turned into a flood during the California Gold Rush, which led to other rushes in Nevada, Oregon, Idaho, Colorado and Montana. Travelers might have cast a curious eye toward the Black Hills, but they had already marked their destinations at the other end of the trail.

It wasn't entirely an accident, however, that pioneers didn't know enough about the Black Hills to make them a destination. The western (Teton) Sioux, or Lakota, fiercely resisted any encroachment on the Hills as they were surrounded by an ever-tightening network of forts, military roads and gold rush trails. If the so-called Thoen Stone can be believed, a party of seven men dug up gold in the Black Hills as early as 1833, but were killed by Indians before they could leave. There are any number of similar ghost-like reports of an early presence—stories of skeletons and dated notebooks and old sluice boxes—none of them yet verified in a way that satisfies historians. All we can say for sure is that if any white men did enter the Black Hills before 1874, they left no solid record or artifact (with the possible exception of the Thoen Stone) that survives to this day.

The Lakota did not attack scientific expeditions that began to appear in the Badlands, but when a hunting party under English sportsman Sir Saint George Gore approached the Hills in 1856 it was stripped of horses and ordered out

Left: A well-worn horseshoe found at an Expedition campsite on private land. (Paul Horsted Collection)
Above: Michael Smith, wagon master for the Black Hills Expedition, poses for photographer W.H. Illingworth. (Devereaux Library Archives)
Below: Ft. Lincoln, Dakota Territory, located near present-day Bismarck, North Dakota, was the departure point of the Expedition. W.H. Illingworth photo, probably taken before the Black Hills Expedition. (Minnesota Historical Society)

of the area. In the same year, negotiating a treaty with General William S. Harney at Fort Pierre on the Missouri, the Sioux agreed to permit travel along the Platte and White Rivers but insisted on keeping the Black Hills to themselves.

That treaty was cited the following year by Lakota hunters who confronted an Army mapping party under Lt. G.K. Warren. He found a "very large force" at Inyan Kara—an outlying peak on the northwest edge of the Black Hills—waiting for a nearby herd of buffalo to grow their winter coats. The hunters said they were prepared to fight, if necessary, to keep the buffalo from being scattered. Warren turned back and was later joined by a chief named Bear's Rib, who offered his protection as the soldiers skirted the Black Hills to the south and east. In return he asked Warren to tell the President that white people could not be allowed to come into his country. Feelings were so strong among his people, he said, that they would turn away members of another band who were thinking of selling land to the whites.

Warren's small party crossed French Creek where it emerges from the Black Hills, continued north to another outlying peak known as Bear Butte, then explored to the south and east as far as the south fork of the Cheyenne River, which they followed to the mouth of French Creek. Thus it was that a young geologist attached to the expedition, Dr. Ferdinand V. Hayden, had two opportunities to examine French Creek—to study the stones and minerals it had washed down from the Black Hills. And when Warren published an account of this and other explorations, it suggested the likelihood that gold could be found in the Black Hills.

It is possible that the reports from 1857 influenced General Custer during his own reconnaissance 17 years later. Once inside the Black Hills his every choice of direction seemed bent on reaching French Creek. And of course it was there that he went into permanent camp with his practical miners and newspaper reporters—there that gold was duly discovered and its presence made known to the world.

Pressures to explore the Black Hills had been growing for many years, although blunted for a time by the Civil War and by the lure of more certain gold strikes in the Rocky Mountains and Montana. By late 1867, however, two private exploring parties were being formed at Yankton in Dakota Territory. They were stopped in their tracks by the Fort Laramie Treaty of 1868, which included the Black Hills in a large reservation for the Lakota. The Army would now be charged with enforcing the terms of the treaty, and

800   Our first crossing of an Alkali Valley

through strong letters and the threat of troops it discouraged several other exploring parties before they ever got started from Cheyenne or from towns along the Missouri. The Black Hills remained untouched a while longer, despite a growing clamor among frontier editors, legislators and businessmen for exploration of the Hills.

This isolation finally came to an end in 1874 when General Custer was ordered to lead a reconnaissance south from Fort Abraham Lincoln, recently built across the Missouri from Bismarck, Dakota Territory—temporary end of the line for the Northern Pacific Railroad.

Lieutenant General Philip H. Sheridan, commanding the Division of Missouri, took credit for the idea in his annual report for 1874. He had been contemplating for two or three years, he said, the idea of establishing a fort near the Black Hills to control hostile Indians who were raiding frontier settlements to the south, in Nebraska. "With this view," wrote Sheridan, "I mentioned the subject in the presence of the President, the honorable Secretary of the Interior, the honorable Secretary of War, and the General of the Army."

It would be extremely interesting to have a full and true transcript of that conversation, since it is hard to believe that the reason for Custer's reconnaissance was the construction of a fort—or at least the only reason. Like any decision it was probably influenced by a number of hidden agendas and underlying causes. Most often mentioned is the Panic of 1873 and the severe depression that followed. Farm prices plunged, jobs were scarce, crime was up, and bankruptcies were far more common. President Ulysses S. Grant faced hard times. He was certainly aware of the calls for opening the Black Hills, not to mention the effect a gold rush would have on the economy.

A larger view of the causes might include the Northern Pacific and Union Pacific Railroads, which needed new business and the freedom to continue laying rails without disruption. The Seventh Cavalry's infamous attack on Black Kettle at the Washita, after all, had been part of a military campaign to clear a path through Kansas for construction of the Union Pacific. Now the Seventh was in Dakota

Territory, about to mount a provocative exploration of the Black Hills. Much later, General George Crook reportedly made the situation explicit to Dr. Valentine McGillycuddy, who had worked under him as an Army surgeon in 1876. In the October 1928 edition of *Motor Travel*, McGillycuddy wrote, "Under the pressure of the railroads, Gen. Sheridan, as [Crook] admitted to me, had been forced to send Custer into the Hills in 1874 to find gold, and thus start up a mining excitement which would force the miners into the Hills and split the reservation open."

In 1874, of course, the Army stuck by its original explanation as the country was caught up in a heated debate over the merits and validity of the Expedition. When Bishop William H. Hare of Chicago learned in early June that rumors of the reconnaissance were true, he wrote: "We are the marauders in this case." A special commissioner to the Sioux, Bishop Hare worried that the Expedition would produce "serious and disastrous results." The commander of the Department of Dakota, General Alfred H. Terry, responded that he was "unable to see that any just offense is given to the Indians by the expedition to the Black Hills. . . . From the earliest times the government exercised the right of sending exploring parties into the unceded Indian Territory . . . . It is a large party, it is true . . . . It was made large for the purpose of *preventing* hostilities."

Preparations for the Expedition had begun in mid-May of that year. Custer ordered company commanders to report any need for new equipment. He replaced morning drill with target practice, and asked Terry to assign two infantry companies as a rear guard for the wagon train. He hired guides and teamsters and a large contingent of Indian scouts. William Illingworth was hired in St. Paul as a photographer. Custer did not stint on the engineering department (see page 13), but worked to line up scientists on a limited budget. The University of Minnesota agreed to send Newton Winchell as a geologist. When Sheridan asked O.C. Marsh of Yale if he would like to collect fossils, Marsh sent George Bird Grinnell, who was accompanied by the scout Luther North as an assistant. Aris Donaldson signed on as botanist, subsidized by the *St. Paul Pioneer*, for whom he would write stories.

Four other newspapers sent correspondents of their own. Nathan Knappen reported for the *Bismarck Tribune*, Fred Power the *St. Paul Press*, Samuel J. Barrows the *New York Tribune*, and William E. Curtis the *Chicago Inter-Ocean*.

Opposite page, top: W.H. Illingworth stereoview No. 800, "Our first crossing of an Alkali Valley," probably showing a noon rest period on the Expedition's route across the plains. (Minnilusa Pioneer Museum)
Bottom: U.S. Army button from an Expedition campsite on private land. (Paul Horsted Collection)
This page, above: .50 caliber cartridge from an Expedition campsite on private land. (Paul Horsted Collection)
Below: A sketch from the field notebook of Expedition geologist W.H. Winchell shows what is now known as the Buckhorn Range north of Custer, S.D. Overlays show a passage from the notebook and a modern-day photo of rock formations seen in the sketch.

Curtis was the one practicing journalist in the crowd (although several others wrote extremely well) and he moonlighted for the *New York World,* which also printed Custer's reports. As the stories by these five correspondents were published and reprinted by other newspapers around the country, General Custer and his Black Hills Expedition could be certain to stay in the limelight for weeks and months to come.

While the population of Fort Abraham Lincoln swelled through June, Custer was finishing *My Life on the Plains.* "As I pen these lines," the last paragraph begins, "I am in the midst of scenes of bustle and busy preparation attendant upon the organization and equipment of a large party for an important exploring expedition, on which

I shall start before these pages reach the publishers' hands. . . . Bidding adieu to civilization for the next few months, I also now take leave of my readers." He was forced to delay a while longer, awaiting arrival of new .45 caliber breech-loading Springfield carbines as well as the improved Colt's .45 pistol. They were delivered on the last day of June, and on July 2 the command finally left the post.

It must have been a grand procession. Custer led the way, of course, accompanied by his headquarters staff as well as the reporters and scientists. Sixteen musicians were close on their heels, riding white horses as they played "The Girl I Left Behind Me." The band was followed in turn by the main body of Indian scouts, an artillery contingent of

Exploring with Custer

three Gatling guns and a Rodman rifled cannon, several ambulances, and a train of more than 100 wagons. Geologist Newton Winchell made a sketch of the order of march, which is reproduced on page 101.

Out on the plains the Expedition became a sprawling traveling machine. It threw out scouts in front and on the sides to be alert for trouble while Custer went ahead to choose the best route for his wagons. A "pioneer" party— a rotating company of cavalry— would go to work building the road itself, when necessary, using an assortment of picks, shovels, axes and other tools. The wagon train traveled single-file in the Hills but divided into four columns on the prairie, protected at all times by five companies of cavalry on each flank as well as two companies of infantry bringing up the rear. Also trailing behind was a small herd of cattle, in case the hunters couldn't supply enough meat.

Two experienced miners, Horatio N. Ross and William T. McKay, had joined the Expedition. It may never be known exactly how they came to be there. Some sources insist Custer hired the men himself, even paying them out of his own pocket. Others say Ross and McKay signed on as teamsters and were more or less tolerated but certainly not official.

There were more than a thousand men in all, and one woman, a black cook named Sarah Campbell—"Aunt Sally" to the men. Everyone endured terrible water, searing sun and blowing alkaline dust that stung like salt in open wounds or on sunburned skin. The Expedition marched south across the Cannonball and Grand Rivers to enter what is now the northwestern corner of South Dakota, where on July 11 it stopped at a cave that was named for the engineer, Capt. William Ludlow. The column continued west across the border into Montana territory, to the Little Missouri River, dropping south from there to reach the Belle Fourche River on July 18.

South of the Belle Fourche was a countryside completely different from the dry plains endured by the explorers during the previous two weeks. Some of them would describe it as an earthly paradise. Here they were poised at the edge of the "piece of blank paper" known as the Black Hills.

In just a few days they would see a landscape no white men had ever seen before. ❖

Opposite page: Top, two rock carvings, believed to be authentic, survive from the Expedition's visit to the Black Hills area. One carving, a "74" over "G Custer," is on top of Inyan Kara mountain, west of the Black Hills. Newspaper accounts of the time (see pages 28-29) describe the carving of Custer's name when he and a detachment visited the mountaintop. The other carving, a faint "GC" over a "US 74," is on a rock outcrop overlooking the Permanent Camp east of Custer, S.D. Although partially defaced, it appears to be George Custer's initials. Whether he carved it himself, however, is not documented.

Bottom, a groove in the earth marks the area where a wagon rut was formed in virgin soil. This rut is located not far from Deerfield Lake (see page 65). Like other ruts scattered across the Black Hills, this groove is believed to be original to the Expedition, though it may have seen later wagon or stagecoach traffic. Core samples from large trees growing in the rut date the trees to the early 1880s, so this is a very early trail indeed.

This page: Left, A harness buckle found at an Expedition campsite on private land. (Paul Horsted Collection)

Above, Ludlow's Cave in 1874, photo by W.H. Illingworth (Minnilusa Pioneer Museum) and in 2001 (©Paul Horsted). The Expedition camped near Ludlow's Cave enroute to the Black Hills, at an area now known as the Cave Hills in northwestern South Dakota.

Part I: Life on the Black Hills Trail
by Ernest Grafe

Map labels

July 20

JULY 21
Guide: 18-22
Photo: 164-165

July 21

John Cunningham died of dysentery here. George Turner was shot the next morning and died during the day's march.

JULY 22-23
Guide: 22-29
Photos: 166-169

JULY 24
Guide: 30-37
Photo: 170-171

(B)
July 22-23

July 24

Black Hills National Forest Map, 60% actual size

INTRODUCTION

How to use the guide

Finding historic sites and reading first-person accounts of the dramas that unfolded exactly where you stand is an exciting way to experience the Black Hills Expedition of 1874 — but not the only way. The selections included here are so vivid and written with such force that they bring the adventure to life wherever they are read. How you use these pages will depend on whether you read them only for the story or as a guide to the trail.

READING FOR THE STORY

The title of each chapter is the time period it covers, while the subtitle describes briefly the area in which the Expedition traveled. You will then find a selected quote from one of the participants, followed by a summary of events for the day (or days).

Feel free to bypass the box labeled *Taking the trail*. You may also ignore the excerpt from the Expedition map, unless you have an interest in the way it depicts a specific area of the Black Hills. In the remainder of each chapter, all directions and commentary related to tracing the trail have been confined to shaded boxes that can easily be disregarded.

If you would like to follow the Expedition's progress, the map sections at left and on the following pages will be the easiest to use. They are reproduced (at 60 percent of original size) from the popular Black Hills National Forest map you may already be familiar with. The maps within the Trail Guide itself are portions of U.S.G.S. topographic quadrants that allow a more detailed understanding of the landscape, but make it difficult to keep track of where you are in relation to the rest of the Black Hills. Overlooking the topo maps and shaded boxes will let you focus on the story of the Expedition as revealed in seven journals, the dispatches from five newspaper correspondents, the final reports, and two reminiscences recorded many years later. You will hear the voices of very different personalities: a geologist, a Prussian trumpeter, an engineer, reporters, officers, and Custer himself. They wrote with deep feeling about their immediate experiences, and sometimes contradicted each other in illuminating ways. More often they reinforced each other, adding new details to a rich and intimate portrait of life in a 19th-century exploring party.

The voices of 1874 as well as occasional editorial remarks are blended together in a continuing narrative. To keep it flowing, original material is differentiated from commentary only by a change in the style of type, while the source of each quote is identified in parentheses at the end of the paragraph. Please read the text in the example below for further clarification.

⌇Excerpts from journals and dispatches are printed in text that looks like this. Each new section or theme is marked by the blue ornament. *(The name of the source in parentheses is keyed to a list beginning on page 14)*

Each new "speaker" on a subject or event follows immediately in an indented paragraph. *(Source)*

Editorial comments and any additional information or explanations are printed in text that looks like this.

The excerpts contain a number of eccentric **spellings** and lapses of **grammar**, all of which appeared in the original newspapers or diaries.

You will soon become acquainted with the personalities of the writers through their points of view and the style in which they express themselves. Brief biographies are also provided in the list of sources (page 14), which identifies the publications where it is possible to learn much more about the explorers and about the Expedition.

FOLLOWING THE TRAIL

You can reach a new level of involvement with history by following in the Expedition's footsteps—visiting the camps, springs, rock formations and even many of the photo sites you read about. The Illingworth photo locations are marked on the maps and cross-referenced to his views, while the views (and their modern-day versions) are cross-referenced to the pages in the Guide that disclose their locations.

At a minimum, all you really need to get started is this book and a sturdy vehicle with an odometer. The directions in each shaded box will lead you to a point discussed in the text above or below it, as outlined in the example at left.

A **Global Positioning System (GPS) receiver**, while not required, is a very good idea. They are fairly inexpensive, user-friendly and enjoyable to use. A GPS receiver relies on radio signals from satellites to pinpoint (within a few feet) your latitude and longitude. It will remove any guesswork from following the directions, and a few places cannot be found any other way. Finally, hikers will always be able to find their way back if they record the latitude and longitude of their point of departure.

Carrying your own **topographic maps** is also a good

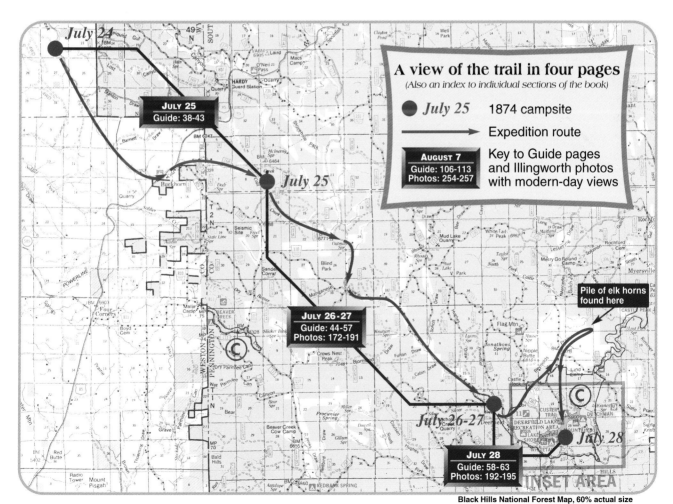

A view of the trail in four pages
(Also an index to individual sections of the book)

● **July 25** 1874 campsite

→ Expedition route

AUGUST 7	Key to Guide pages
Guide: 106-113	and Illingworth photos
Photos: 254-257	with modern-day views

JULY 25
Guide: 38-43

JULY 26-27
Guide: 44-57
Photos: 172-191

JULY 28
Guide: 58-63
Photos: 192-195

Pile of elk horns found here

Black Hills National Forest Map, 60% actual size

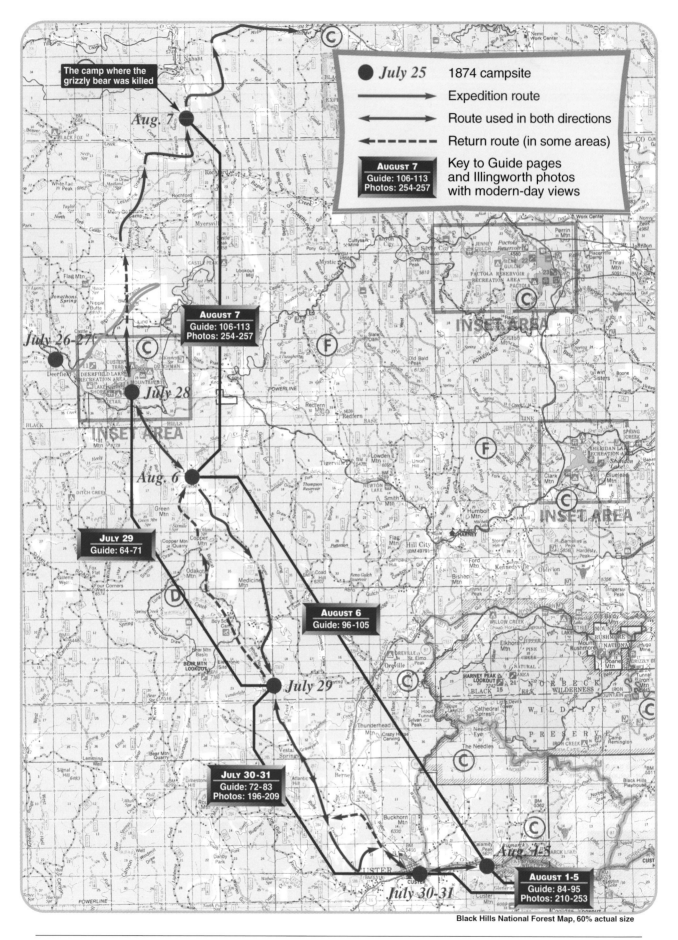

The camp where the
grizzly bear was killed

Aug. 7

● *July 25*   1874 campsite

Expedition route

Route used in both directions

Return route (in some areas)

AUGUST 7
Guide: 106-113
Photos: 254-257

Key to Guide pages
and Illingworth photos
with modern-day views

July 26-27

AUGUST 7
Guide: 106-113
Photos: 254-257

July 28

INSET AREA

INSET AREA

INSET AREA

Aug. 6

JULY 29
Guide: 64-71

AUGUST 6
Guide: 96-105

July 29

JULY 30-31
Guide: 72-83
Photos: 196-209

Aug. 1-5

JULY 30-31

AUGUST 1-5
Guide: 84-95
Photos: 210-253

Black Hills National Forest Map, 60% actual size

idea. They provide a larger overview of an area, and you may want to make notations as you go along. The maps required for each portion of the route are listed in a box called *Taking the trail* at the beginning of each chapter (along with other useful information), and each map within the Guide is labeled according to the topo maps it draws from.

A NOTE ON THE MAPS: The topo quadrants reproduced in the Guide were provided in digital form by the Black Hills National Forest, and will look slightly different than commercially available topo maps. There are two major variations:

- The quadrants in the Guide lack the green shading that, on a normal topo map, represents forest growth.
- Instead, on *most* maps you will see outlined areas shaded in grey. The light grey color denotes private land (as do the white areas on the BHNF map below), which helps us avoid violating the property rights of our neighbors.

(Continued on next page)

Black Hills National Forest Map, 60% actual size

SYMBOLS AND COLOR: With very few exceptions, anything appearing in red is either on the Expedition route or related to it in some way.

 Pointers like these are used on the maps to designate a specific place that is on or near Custer's trail.

 44 13 06.7   The number in the pointer box (above) will 104 11 23.4   generally correspond with a number in one of the shaded direction boxes, accompanied by its latitude (the top reading: 44 degrees, 13 minutes, 6.7 seconds) and longitude (the bottom reading: 104 degrees, 11 minutes, 23.4 seconds). If your GPS does not display tenths of a second, simply round up or down.

Exception: GPS coordinates will *not* be displayed when the designated location is on private land. In that case, look for an extra-bold reference to **Point 6** within the text—either in one of the direction boxes or in the editorial remarks.

Also appearing in these boxes will be directions, historical information and descriptions of what you might find.

Pointers like these are used primarily for navigation points that are off the trail. They may also pinpoint related sites of interest.

E 44 15 32.7   If there is any chance for ambiguity, navi-
103 37 49.2   gation points will be associated with GPS coordinates in one of the direction boxes.

Exception: If a point is permanently established and easily found, such as the intersection of two highways, **Point E** will be referred to only within the text, as seen here.

 The places where Illingworth stood to take his photographs are marked by these symbols.

B 43 45 58.1   The GPS coordinates for each photo site
103 32 16.3   are given (unless the site is on private land, in which case a reference to **Point B** will be included in the text). You will also find Illingworth's number for each photo, if available; a title; and the number of the page on which the photo is printed in this book. With the photo will be text that indicates how closely the site can be determined—whether the modern-day view was shot within inches or yards or only in the general area of the place where Illingworth set up his tripod in 1874.

OTHER SYMBOLS: The general area of the Expedition trail is indicated, with varying degrees of certainty, by a red arrow on the topographic maps. In valleys or constricted areas of level land—much of the time, in other words—the route is a near certainty. Elsewhere it appears that the trail has been followed by roads that are still in use today. There are a few cases where doubts exist, however, and they are described in the accompanying text.

The engineering staff recorded the latitude and longitude of most camps, and those readings are usually marked on the topo maps. Sometimes the longitude is not within a map section, however, because it is wrong by a factor of one or two miles (see below). Only the latitude will be shown in that case, using this symbol.

Ludlow's latitude: 44 07 46

A word on the Expedition map

The general route of the Expedition through certain areas in the Black Hills has been known for a long time, but there were just as many places where no one has ever been able to say for sure how the Expedition got from point A to point B. I hope to fill most of those gaps in the Guide, presenting evidence that other researchers can confirm or disprove in an ongoing effort to define the first trail made by white men in the Black Hills.

As you will see, some of the evidence came from newspaper reports and diaries that described direction, distance and/or topography. In a few cases it was physical, in the form of ruts that appear to have been left by the wagon train. And some conclusions were inductive—a reasonable assumption that a present-day road (for example) had its roots in the trail engineered by General Custer.

The source used by far the most often, however, was a map of the Expedition's travels created during the following winter in St. Paul, Minnesota, and published with the official report in 1875. The map is cited time and again in these pages, and sometimes it led me to conclusions that

I realized—with regret—were contradictory to beliefs held by other people or even published elsewhere.

It was a hard choice to make: the map versus apparently reliable but anecdotal evidence dating back to a time when some of Custer's contemporaries were still alive. Each kind of evidence had its strong points, and each its flaws. But the story told by the 1875 map is hard to ignore if you consider the way it was made and if you work very carefully with its clues. This section is for those who have an interest in the Expedition map, in the reasons I relied on it so heavily, and in how I used it to reach my conclusions.

The underlying framework for the map was a series of latitude and longitude readings recorded at all but 10 of the camps, requiring instruments that Capt. William Ludlow, the Expedition's engineering officer, described in his report:

Two chronometers (mean solar, 1362, Arnold & Dent, and sidereal, 202, Bond & Sons) were carried . . . in

a basket . . . . Additional instruments were a small Würdemann transit, No. 94, and a Spencer, Browning & Co. sextant, No. 6536.

The chronometers were treated with such care because precise time was required to compute longitude. In fact, this was the area in which Ludlow had the greatest difficulty. It may be that the chronometers were affected by changes in altitude within the Hills. Whatever the reason, the engineer's longitude readings tended to be inaccurate. As demonstrated in the Guide, they were usually half a mile to two miles too far west. (The error was generally much smaller when the Expedition remained in camp for more than one day.)

Latitude was a different matter. Wherever we have other evidence of a camp's location—either through photographs or inferences drawn from the confinements of geography—Ludlow's latitude slices through the heart of the camp. If there is an error, it never seems to be more than a few hundred yards. As a point of reference for mapping the trail, then, the latitude readings were far more reliable than longitude.

The trail itself was drawn from meticulous measurements made by two two-man teams, as described by Ludlow.

The two sergeants, Becker and Wilson, each with one man as an assistant, kept separate trails with prismatic compass and odometer—one with an odometer-cart, a two-wheeled vehicle specially constructed for the purpose, the other in an ambulance. Two odometers were read on each vehicle, and the compass-notes made as full as possible.

In other words, each team recorded the exact distance and direction of each leg in the day's journey. The wagon train might travel, say, six-tenths of a mile on a bearing of 175 degrees (slightly east of south), then cross a stream and continue a tenth of a mile north of east (80 degrees). The measurements were carefully noted, averaged, and plotted as a "meander line" to connect the camp locations. Sometimes the engineers either grew lax or faced obstacles. No crossings of Negro Creek are shown on July 29, for example, even though the journals say it happened (page 69). In general, however, you need only examine the course of the trail on Ludlow's map to appreciate how carefully it was drawn. The example above (shown at 200 percent) depicts the crossing of Loues Creek on July 30 (page 72).

Human beings make mistakes, of course. A compass bearing might be misread by a degree. (Two or three such errors in a row would compound the problem.) Notes could be smudged, or wrong, or misread later at St. Paul. In places it almost seemed as if someone forgot to correct for magnetic North. Worst of all, Sergeant Becker had to squeeze or stretch his trail between erroneous longitude readings. He must have suffered a certain amount of frustration back in the mapping room.

The result is that we cannot rely on the Expedition map taken *as a whole.* We cannot simply place it over a modern map of the Black Hills and be done with things. But the map is wonderfully *suggestive* when studied section by section, particularly because it includes yet another element—the shapes of surrounding hills and valleys. "The general topography during the day was taken as thoroughly as possible," wrote Ludlow, "by my assistant, Mr. W. H. Wood, and myself." It appears the two men made notes and sketches during the day that would later be incorporated by Sergeant Becker. There was even a man assigned to take readings from a thermometer as well as an aneroid barometer, which relies on a sealed chamber instead of mercury to record changes in air pressure. Barometer readings were translated into the altitude measurements recorded at each camp.

Ludlow's attention to detail gives us an invaluable tool. The section below (from page 19) shows the trail crossing Redwater Creek along Highway 111 south of Aladdin, Wyo., then turning west over what are known locally as the Red Buttes. It seems inconceivable to some that Custer tackled the Buttes, and yet there they are on the map, in the right place, drawn beneath the trail. It is just as inconceivable to me that Ludlow and his men could have made a mistake of this magnitude—that  they could show the trail moving straight west when it really continued south, or show it going over hills if it stayed in the valley. In this case we are fortunate to have the corroboration of several journals. Said Forsyth: "Passing over . . . a very high ridge, we came into our present camp."

These were the kinds of clues I looked for in the map—not only relationships *between* landmarks and the trail, but also any possible correlations between the shape of the trail as drawn and the topography of that immediate area. As part of the research I enlarged sections of the scanned map on a computer by 792 percent, matching the 1:24,000 scale of the U.S.G.S. quadrants (2.64 inches = one mile). These sections of the Expedition map were printed on clear film that could be overlaid on the topo maps.

The overlays were extremely helpful in suggesting areas of the route that had never been understood before. If Becker's trail made a sudden turn, for example, the line might fall on a draw that worked well with the rest of the trail. In most cases (whenever the route was on public land), I then walked or drove the area to confirm that the wagon

The enlarged overlay of Ludlow's map at left made it clear that the explorers passed along the west side of Gillette Prairie on their way home.

train could have passed through it without great difficulty. This kind of evidence is presented in several places in the Guide, which I hope will lead to further study and exploration.

Other researchers have tried to work with the Expedition map in the past, as revealed by notes in the archives described below, but today we have technology that could not even be imagined 70 years ago. We also have the advantage of published, easily accessible journals and dispatches that either hadn't yet been discovered or were hard to find in their original form. Thanks to the dedicated work of many other people, this is the first time that all available resources—the map and the accounts—have been brought together in an effort to solve the riddles of Custer's trail.

—Ernie Grafe

A key to the sources

Except for the Expedition map, each excerpt or paragraph of information in the Guide is followed by a name in parentheses that matches one of the sources below. In [brackets] at the end of each source is the publication or location on which we relied. Please consult the bibliography on page 284 for more information.

(Bismarck Tribune) of Bismarck, N.D. ◆ Correspondent Nathan H. Knappen had filled in for the editor of the *Tribune* during the winter of 1873-74, then sold life insurance in Bismarck as well as "White's Portable Fly and Mosquito Net Frames." But not for long. When the Black Hills Expedition left Fort Abraham Lincoln, just across the river, Knappen was there as the youngest of its reporters. (He turned 19 in August.) Knappen quit the *Tribune* just two weeks after his return, and bought or managed three newspapers over the next two years in Minnesota. Each venture failed, and Knappen died early in 1878. [From *Prelude to Glory*]

(Calhoun) ◆ The diary of James Calhoun reflects the point of view of a man born (in 1845) to a well-off merchant family in Cincinnati, Ohio, with the freedom to travel widely in Europe. He enlisted in the Army at the age of 19 and became a lieutenant in 1867. Assigned to the Seventh Cavalry in January of 1871, he had married General Custer's sister Margaret by March of the next year. Calhoun became acting assistant adjutant general for his brother-in-law, serving in that capacity during the Yellowstone Expedition of 1873 as well as the Black Hills Expedition. He also died with Custer, at the Little Big Horn, in 1876. [From *With Custer in '74*]

(Cartwright) ◆ Born in Terry, Montana, R.G. Cartwright was for many years a Physical Education teacher at Lead, South Dakota. There he met Charles Windolph, a former sergeant with the Seventh Cavalry (a private in H Company in 1874). Cartwright's larger interest was in the Battle of the Little Big Horn, but he recorded some material on the Expedition that is preserved in the Cartwright archives at the Hearst Library in Lead.

(Custer) ◆ The field reports of General George A. Custer were published by several newspapers of the time, providing us with an idea of his thoughts and reactions—both in what he wrote and what he left out. He was 34 at the time of the Expedition, and of course would never reach his 37th birthday. He remains perhaps the most written-about figure of the era. [From *Prelude to Glory*]

(Dodge) ◆ When the federal government authorized a scientific study of the Black Hills in 1875 (to settle the question of whether gold could truly be found there), Col. Richard Irving Dodge was chosen to head the expedition. He kept a journal that refers to crossing Custer's path a number of times, throwing further light on the location of the trail. Born in North Carolina, Dodge was writing a book during the Expedition that would later be published as *The Plains of North America and Their Inhabitants*. [From *The Black Hills Journals of Colonel Richard Irving Dodge*]

(Ewert) ◆ Born in Prussia in 1847, Private Theodore Ewert came to America at the age of ten and joined the Army in time for the Civil War. He was 15 by then, and four feet, eight inches tall. Promoted to 2nd lieutenant in the artillery, he was court-martialed for drinking on duty and gambling with enlisted men. His sympathy for the enlisted man is very clear in the diary he kept during the Black Hills Expedition. He had signed up with the Seventh Cavalry again, as a private, but left in April 1876. He later married, had two children, held other military posts for most of his life, and died in November of 1906. [From *Private Theodore Ewert's Diary Of The Black Hills Expedition Of 1874*]

(Expedition map) ◆ The first page of each chapter contains the relevant section of a large fold-out map (one of three; see pages 281-283) that was included at the back of the official report. The map, covering the Black Hills portion of the route, was scanned into the computer and proved to be invaluable in preparing the guide. [From *Report of a Reconnaissance of the Black Hills of Dakota made in the Summer of 1874*]

(Forsyth) ◆ An acting aide-de-camp to General Philip Sheridan, Major George A. "Sandy" Forsyth was asked to command the left column of the Expedition. George Bird Grinnell wrote that he was "looked up to with enormous respect" for his role as commander in the Beecher Island fight of 1868. Forsyth was wounded three times in the fight, and twice had to have his leg re-

broken and stretched. Sheridan ordered Forsyth to keep a diary during the Expedition. [From *Prelude to Glory*]

(Grant) ◆ Son of the President, Lt. Colonel Fred Dent Grant (a brevet rank) had also been an acting aide-de-camp to General Philip Sheridan, and was also directed to keep a journal. In theory, he was on the Expedition as an aide to Custer. He was 24 at the time. [From *Prelude to Glory*]

(Grinnell) ◆ Born of an old New York family, George Bird Grinnell would go on to an illustrious career as a writer and naturalist. He played a large role in preserving Yellowstone and Glacier National Parks, and in organizing the Audubon Society. At 24 he was the Expedition's zoologist and paleontologist, with the assistance of his friend Luther North, the well-known scout. Grinnell later wrote a number of articles and reminiscences that add several details to the overall picture. [From *The Passing of the Great West*]

(Inter-Ocean) ◆ Correspondent William E. Curtis was born in Ohio in 1850 and joined the *Chicago Inter-Ocean* in 1872. Quickly establishing a reputation for enthusiasm and literary ability, he interrupted the courtship of his future wife to join the Expedition—during which he moonlighted as a correspondent for the *New York World*. After 1874 Curtis became one of the finest newspaper correspondents in the West, and later traveled much of the world. When he died in 1911 he was the Washington correspondent of the *Chicago Record-Herald*. [From *Prelude to Glory*]

(Ludlow) ◆ The Chief Engineer for the Department of Dakota was Capt. William A. Ludlow (sometimes referred to by his brevet rank of colonel). He had been a contemporary of Custer's at West Point, and was involved in the fistfight that Custer failed to stop—for which Custer was disciplined. Ludlow kept a journal that he reproduced in the official report. [From *Report of a Reconnaissance of the Black Hills of Dakota made in the Summer of 1874*]

(New York Tribune) ◆ Correspondent Samuel J. Barrows, a native New Yorker, began working for the *Tribune* in 1866, when he was 21. Five years later he enrolled in the Harvard Divinity School, but continued to serve as the newspaper's correspondent in Cambridge. He joined the Yellowstone Expedition in 1873, affording him an acquaintance with Custer before the Black Hills Expedition was mounted. Barrows became a Unitarian minister in 1876, served as a Congressman for one term, and later became involved in prison reform. He died in 1909. [From *Prelude to Glory*]

(O'Harra) ◆ Cleophas C. O'Harra, then-president of what is now the South Dakota School of Mines and Technology in Rapid City, was one of the earliest researchers of the Expedition. In the 1920s he developed a map of the route and collected first-hand information. His papers are preserved in the Devereaux Library Archives at the School of Mines.

(Pioneer) ◆ Aris B. Donaldson, a teacher in his native Ohio, was hired in 1869 as one of the original faculty members of the University of Minnesota. He was professor of rhetoric and English literature, but resigned to become the Expedition's botanist—and a correspondent for the *St. Paul Daily Pioneer*—at the age of 43. After 1874 he bought a newspaper, which he edited until his death in 1883. [From *Prelude to Glory*]

(Power) ◆ Refers to a recently discovered journal kept by Fred W. Power, correspondent for the *St. Paul Daily Press*. Power was born in Virginia in 1847, but virtually nothing else is known about his life, either before or after the expedition. [Courtesy of Kirk Budd]

(Press) ◆ Refers to the dispatches of Fred Power published in the *St. Paul Daily Press*. [From *Prelude to Glory*]

(Ryan) ◆ Born in West Newton, Massachusetts, in 1845, John Ryan began a 14-year military career during the Civil War. He served with the Seventh Cavalry during much of that time, surviving the Little Big Horn and mustering out a few months later. He returned to West Newton and became a police officer (later a captain), and wrote about his experiences in the West. The manuscript came to light in 2000 and was published the following year. While much of the material on the Black Hills Expedition borrows from other published reports, Ryan added some original material about his own experiences. [From *Ten Years with Custer*]

(Snow) ◆ An ambulance driver during the Expedition, Fred Snow wrote his reminiscences 20 years later. [From *Prelude to Glory*]

(Winchell) ◆ Newton M. Winchell had been a professor of geology at the University of Minnesota as well as the state's geologist since 1872, and was given leave to join the Expedition. He was 34 at the time. Most of his detailed daily journal was included in the official report. [From *Report of a Reconnaissance of the Black Hills of Dakota made in the Summer of 1874*]

(Winchell notebook) ◆ Paul Horsted discovered that field notebooks carried by Newton Winchell during the Expedition were preserved in the University of Minnesota Archives at Minneapolis. They contained several anecdotes and sketches not included in the official report (above).

(Wood) ◆ William H. Wood, a civilian assistant with the engineering corps, wrote a brief reminiscence in 1927. [From *Prelude to Glory*]

CHAPTER 1

Saturday through Thursday, July 18-23

From the Belle Fourche River to Inyan Kara

This is better country than I expected to find. What endless enjoyment for the finite mind to contemplate the wonderful works of nature. (Calhoun)

After a two-day layover on the Belle Fourche River, Custer and his men entered the Bear Lodge Mountains and moved south toward Inyan Kara in search of a usable entrance to the Black Hills. They made one camp on Hay Creek, west of present-day Aladdin, Wyoming, and another just a few miles east of Sundance. It was here—now almost within sight of an interstate highway—that one soldier died of dysentery while a second was shot during an early-morning argument. The wounded man died on the trail, and both soldiers were buried at the very edge of the Black Hills, due east of Inyan Kara. Distance traveled from the Belle Fourche to Inyan Kara: 54.8 miles.

Taking the trail

MAPS: Instead of the usual topographic quads, this chapter uses the "Devil's Tower" and "Sundance" Bureau of Land Management (BLM) maps.

CAUTIONS: None. Roads are paved or smooth gravel.

TO START: On Interstate 90, drive 11 miles *east from Sundance* or 18 miles *west from Spearfish* to Exit 199. Turn north on Highway 111 and travel 8.4 miles to its end at Highway 24. Turn left and drive another 3.2 miles, to a county road on the right, and pull to the side. Had you stopped here on July 20, 1874, you would have been directly in the path of wagons coming out of the gap in the ridge to the north. Pause here a moment to catch up with the command and to understand how it got here.

This is how Capt. Ludlow and his engineers saw their entrance to the Black Hills area, passing through the eastern foothills of what we now call the Bear Lodge Mountains. After more than two weeks on the open plains, the explorers felt they had entered a kind of paradise. Chicago reporter William E. Curtis vividly described for his readers (next page) what the Expedition had endured until this time.

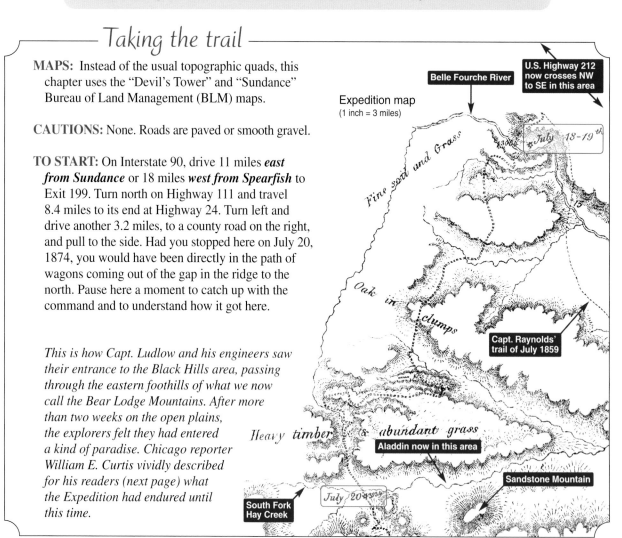

Expedition map
(1 inch = 3 miles)

Belle Fourche River

U.S. Highway 212 now crosses NW to SE in this area

Fine soil and Grass

July 18-19th

Oak in clumps

Capt. Raynolds' trail of July 1859

Heavy timber & abundant grass

Aladdin now in this area

July 20

South Fork Hay Creek

Sandstone Mountain

Prelude

Arriving at the Black Hills

☞People who sit in cool, dark parlors and shaded offices may envy us, but if they consider seven and eight and ten and fourteen hours in the saddle, under a sun that raises the mercury a hundred degrees on a parched, dusty plain, an experience to be envied, four days such as we have spent would convince them to the contrary. . . . The ambulances are full of poor soldiers who have fallen out by the way. The animals feel the heat and the want of sufficient water even more than the men, and whenever the train stops the air is hideous with the braying of the poor, thirsty, tired mules. *(Inter-Ocean)*

This is a taste of what the Black Hills Expedition had already experienced in the seventeen days before it came to the Belle Fourche River on July 18, 1874. The explorers had covered 292 miles and endured an average high temperature of 89 degrees since leaving Fort Abraham Lincoln.

☞The most of the 'bottom lands' in this region are covered with a sediment of alkali, which is as fine as the finest powder, and sifts through veil or any other protections a person can wear, and sifted through is very painful, getting into the pores of the skin, and burning and smarting till one imagines himself in the process of cremation. The heat and wind parches and cracks our lips and faces, and this dust settling on the blistered flesh is about as serious torture as the strictest disciplinarian can desire. *(Inter-Ocean)*

It was almost suppertime when the command set up camp on the Belle Fourche about four miles west of the Wyoming-South Dakota border (due south from the Bentonite plant on U.S. 212 at Colony). Horses, mules and a herd of trailing cattle were put out to graze along the river, while ten companies of cavalry and two of infantry pitched their tents. Each cavalry company had its farrier, saddler and blacksmith. There were teamsters for the 110 wagons that carried supplies. There were more than 70 Indian scouts, a scientific corps, three doctors, and a photographer. Four reporters had come along, as well as two practical miners hired by the leader of the Expedition, Lt. Col. George Armstrong Custer—usually called General Custer for his brevet rank during the Civil War. In all there were more than a thousand men. There was also one woman, a black cook named Sarah Campbell, known to the men as "Aunt Sally."

They were not yet in unknown territory, having just crossed the trail of an exploring party led by Capt. William F. Raynolds in 1859. (See Ludlow's map at left.) Soon they would be camped near Inyan Kara Mountain, where another expedition under Lt. G.K. Warren had been turned back by a Sioux hunting party in 1857.

The primary focus of this guide is the Expedition's journey though the unmapped heart of the Black Hills, beginning at Inyan Kara on July 24. But the stage is being set a few miles back along the trail, and two men will die between the Belle Fourche and Inyan Kara.

SATURDAY, JULY 18

☞Captain Raynolds's trail of 1859 passed along the crest of the hills in rear of camp. *(Ludlow)*

I think it was Ludlow who said, "Look at that!" There were two rows of sunflowers, just the gauge of the wagon apart, and as far as we could see, just an unbroken line of sun-flowers. *(Wood)*

After crossing the bad lands we came in to a beautiful valley just beyond which we are glad to see timber. This [is the] first since leaving the Mo River. *(Power)*

The guides continued to proclaim the uselessness of attempting to take the wagons further . . . . They have hitherto supposed we would skirt the hills without seriously attempting an entrance. *(Ludlow)*

SUNDAY, JULY 19

☞Commenced raining at 1 a.m., and, as there is every prospect of its continuing all day, we will not move until tomorrow. This will give the animals a much needed rest, and enable the men to wash their clothes. *(Forsyth)*

Twice this day did we receive orders to strike tents and prepare to move; twice the rain commenced to fall in torrents; twice we received orders to pitch our tents and remain 'till the next morning; twice we were drenched to the skin . . . . You may ask, "Did not the officers stand exposed to these storms and rains as well as the rank and file?" I answer emphatically "No!" As soon as a storm was seen approaching, four six or eight men were called upon to stretch the captain's or lieutenant's tent, and as soon as the first pins were driven these would step inside dry and comfortable while poor Pat, Hans or Dick could stand in the storm and finish driving the pins, and then already wet through and through, he could go and pitch his own little dog-tent. *(Ewert)*

Here you can see two kinds of discrepancy. One is factual (Forsyth makes it sound as if there was never any intent to leave camp, while Private Ewert indicates that Custer tried to) and the other has to do with point of view. Officers and enlisted men saw this day in very different ways.

☞It rained until 4 o'clock . . . built a fire at the entrance of my tent and read the day through. *(Forsyth)*

The command lay in camp to-day and built a crossing over the Belle Fourche. *(Grant)*

About four o'clock in the evening the teamsters were ordered to hitch-up and the entire train crossed the creek the same evening, the companies, except "L" (who had been out all day selecting a road for tomorrow) remaining in the old camp. *(Ewert)*

The precaution was taken . . . in view of a possible rise during the night. *(Ludlow)*

. . . the Infantry Battalion following as guard. *(Calhoun)*

MONDAY, JULY 20

On the 20th we . . . began, as it were, skirmishing with the Black Hills. We began by feeling our way carefully along the outlying ranges of hills, seeking a weak point through which we might take our way to the interior. *(Custer)*

We crossed the Belle Fourche and marched directly into the Black Hills. The country was quite poor at first, with large quantities of hematite iron ore. Burr-oak at different places. Crossed over the hills and got on a long divide which looked like a large meadow — the grass as thick as in any hay field I ever saw. *(Grant)*

The high table narrowed to a ridge and suddenly turned to the left; the trail descended into a valley thickly wooded with oak and pine. *(Ludlow)*

This valley, especially in comparison with the "hot, dry, burned-up landscape north of the Belle Fourche," inspired the engineer to lyrical rapture:

The temperature was delightful; the air laden with sweet wild odors; the grass knee-deep and exceedingly luxuriant and fresh; while wild cherries, blueberries and gooseberries abounded, as well as many varieties of flowers. All these advantages, combined with that of an abundance of pure cold water, were ours, with rare exceptions, until the final departure from the hills. *(Ludlow)*

As I gaze upon this particular spot, I think that it is a great pity that this rich country should remain in a wild state, uncultivated and uninhabited by civilized men. Here the wheel of industry could move to advantage. The propelling power of life in the shape of human labor is only wanting to make this a region of prosperity. . . . Man is the promoter of earthly happiness. He is the divine instrument, pre-ordained from primitive existence to diffuse this beneficence upon the earth. Man is the noblest work of God. In this wild region man will ultimately be seen in the full enjoyment of true pleasure, in the possession of happiness ordained by honest labor. For the hives of industry will take the place of dirty wigwams. Civilization will ere long reign supreme and throw heathen barbarism into oblivion. Seminaries of learning will raise their proud cupolas far above the canopy of Indian lodges, and Christian temples will elevate their lofty spires upward towards the azure sky while places of heathen mythology will sink and rise no more. This will be a period of true happiness. *(Calhoun)*

Happiness for white men, at least. Lt. Calhoun, who was Custer's brother-in-law, provides an excellent expression of one rationale the nation used for taking Indian land: It was underused, and we—the late arrivals—were the ones who could make it work.

Over a narrow ridge into a small grassy park, thence into another and another, the trail led to camp facing a lofty sandstone range of hills through which a narrow pass had admitted us. *(Ludlow)*

Tuesday, July 21
To Government Valley, northeast of Sundance — The death of Private Cunningham

1 44 39 10.6 This is the starting place, at the mouth of 104 15 18.2 the "narrow pass" referred to by Ludlow in the last passage above. A county road runs north through the gap where the wagons would have started appearing a little before 5:00 o'clock the previous evening. To get a better view of the campsite that was the starting place on July 21, turn around and drive three tenths of a mile east on Highway 24, pulling to the side when you can do so safely.

A 44 39 04.6 From the highway you can see the land 104 14 59.6 on your right sloping down to the south fork of Hay Creek, which is marked by a line of trees. Beyond that is a wide and fairly level expanse (on private land) that served as a campground on the night of July 20. Take note of a small knoll (**Point 3**) that lies near the center of the flat.

This is the first camp in the Black Hills and our tents now stand on ground never trodden by any of the white race. . . . Our work of exploration commences and strict energy, perseverance and endurance called into play. Maps might be packed away as the space for the Black Hills is blank, and scouts without any knowledge of the country. *(Ewert)*

Excellent pasturage, a spring of cold water. Not much water for the public animals. *(Calhoun)*

*Local lore places this camp on a specific flat west of Aladdin, Wyo. Ranchers George and Bill Whalen, whose family has deep roots in the area, say a man named John Pearson told them that a knoll on the flat (**Point 3**) had been the center of camp. It is tantalizing to try to imagine what Pearson found or saw there, because he arrived in the area in 1885—just eleven years after Custer. He apparently never said why he reached the conclusion he did, but the Expedition's reading for the camp (**Point 2**) is very close.*

2 44 38 35 This is the latitude and longitude reading 104 15 27 recorded by Capt. Ludlow, just 300 yards south and 400 yards west of the knoll.

🖎 Our friend Illingworth took photos of this camp & surroundings. *(Power, July 20)*

Broke camp at 4:30 a.m. and shaped our course in a southeasterly direction through a gap in the hills. *(Forsyth)*

*Power's journal entry was a clue to the location of an Illingworth stereoview that had never been publicly identified, **Photo 807**, "View from our first camp in the Hills, looking north" (page 164). We were searching for the site west of Aladdin when we learned that Russell Tracy of Sundance had already showed the photo to rancher George Whalen. He said it looked familiar, and took Tracy to what is known locally as Red Hill (**Point C**). Despite the title of the stereoview Illingworth was actually looking east, while Power's remark leaves open the possibility that Illingworth exposed another photo—one that included the camp.*

You can see Red Hill from **Point A**, about a mile to the east and south. If you look almost straight south, you can see the low hills over which the wagons moved before dawn.

Continue east on Highway 24. (If you see an historical sign referring to deep ruts left by the Expedition's wagons, take it with a grain of salt. We have been told by local residents that the sign refers to remnants of an old county road.) Stop after nine-tenths of a mile

B 44 38 46.4 South of the road here is a saddle between
104 13 50.8 two hills. Illlingworth's **Photo 807** was taken above the saddle to the right (**Point C**), on private land.

Return to Highway 111 (**Point D**). If you care to make a side trip in time to another historical era, continue 1.5 miles east on Highway 24 to an interpretive site at the Aladdin Coal Tipple, a relic of the extensive coal mining that occurred here in the 1890s and into the Twentieth Century. You may also want to stop at the Aladdin general store.

Otherwise turn south on Highway 111 and drive 2.1 miles.

🖎 An hour after daybreak the headquarters came to an abrupt halt. Immediately in front was a steep banked creek and on either side the hills arose like walls. . . . Some of the scouts who had been sent ahead to reconnoiter and select a road, had returned and reported that none could be found where the train could possibly get along. *(Ewert)*

This may have happened in Section 36 on the flanks of Little Table Mountain, where Ludlow's map shows a sharp left turn at a drainage. Compare the route with this description.

🖎 General Custer, unused to being foiled even by nature, now mounted his little pony, Dandy, and started to find a

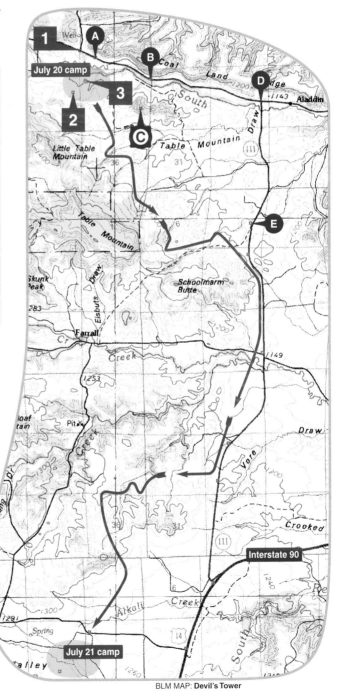

BLM MAP: **Devil's Tower**

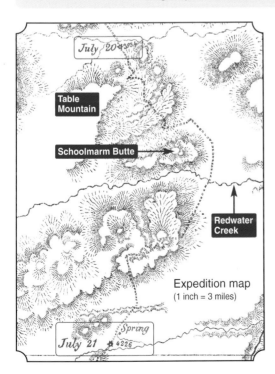

Expedition map
(1 inch = 3 miles)

water, delightful from its clearness and coldness, proved to have been impregnated by the gypsum-veins, and to be endowed with highly medicinal properties. *(Ludlow)*

I had a chance to see the specimens and curiosities gathered by General Custer. He had the trunk of a tree petrified, two prairie owls, one hawk, one porcupine, several beautiful horned toads and three live rattlesnakes and for the transportation of these he selected the best ambulance on the expedition. The sick men, for whose benefit all the ambulances were taken, had to ride in a rickety, broken-springed concern whose joltings were scarcely a degree easier than an army wagon. *(Ewert)*

Private Hoener, Company B, 7th Cavalry, accidentally shot himself. *(Calhoun)*

. . . through the leg while mounting. The shot did not do any very great damage. *(Power)*

This would be foreshadowing if the story were fiction. That gypsum-impregnated water could be dangerous, and another gun will go off within 24 hours.

To reach the evening's campsite, drive south on Highway 111, noticing the deeply eroded washes you cross almost immediately. Imagine how they looked before the roadbed was built up, and whether you would cross them in a wagon. That will make it easier to understand why the whole wagon train turned up the ridge just north of the washes.

At the stop sign (**Point F**) check your odometer and turn right on the service road. Drive 1.2 miles to a graveled ranch road (**Point G**) and turn right. In a mile or so you should start to see unusually large rocks in the pasture on your left.

On the surface of the valley in which we are camped, sometimes half a mile from the range of sandstone bluffs formed by the Lower Cretaceous, are seen very large quartzite bowlders. *(Winchell)*

These massive boulders are still impressive today, particularly where ranchers have piled them in windrows that might remind you of Stonehenge.

8 44 30 51.2 At 1.7 miles from the service road is the 104 15 15.0 entrance to the former Pete Harper ranch, which encloses Custer's camp of July 21. Note that some of the boulders have been gathered up and placed along the entrance like forbidding sentries. The camp itself was on the flats to the south, beyond ranch headquarters.

9 44 30 18 This is Ludlow's recorded latitude and longi-104 15 52 tude for the camp.

A beautiful spring of hard water . . . is situated within the camp. It is so copious that it furnishes water for nearly one thousand men, with their horses, and six hundred and fifty mules. The water, however, has a cathartic effect on those who drink freely. *(Winchell)*

The former owner of the ranch, Orville "Pete" Harper, knows the "cathartic" effect of that spring, which bubbles up from a gypsum outcropping just

Poor Cunningham . . . died, purely through the neglect of the men claiming to be doctors, men who were paid by the Government to look after the health of its soldiers.

half a mile behind the ranch headquarters. Harper said he never drank from the spring unless he was very thirsty and didn't have any other choice—and even then only sparingly. The effects were similar to those of milk of magnesia, he said. His horses generally resisted the water as well, but his cows didn't seem to mind.

There is no way of knowing whether water from this spring was given to Private John Cunningham of Company "H," who had suffered for several days from chronic diarrhea—generally referred to at the time as dysentery. Harper wondered, however, if the gypsum-laden water might have sealed his fate.

Being on duty as Orderly Trumpeter made it imperative for me to remain around headquarters, and as one of the men of my company, John Cunningham, was lying ill in one of the ambulances, I went to him to see if any assistance or help could be rendered. . . . Cunningham was taken with acute dysentery about the 13th, and went on the sick report. The doctor? (a civilian contract doctor???) marked him for duty. The disease becoming worse, he went on again on the 17th, when "Butcher" Allen (as the men afterwards called him) marked him for duty again. *(Ewert)*

This was Acting Assistant Surgeon S. J. Allen, one of two assistants to Assistant Surgeon and Chief Medical Officer J. W. Williams—who would prove to be of no greater help.

The 18th, on the line of march, Cunningham, through weakness and loss of blood, fainted and fell off his horse . . . . and now this man lay in the broiling rays of a July sun, dying, crazy through neglect . . . . My first step was to the tent of the Chief Medical Officer, Dr. Williams. I found him lying on his bed in a drunken sleep. I called on him and shook him, but he would not wake up. Then seeing the Adjutant General, Lieutenant Calhoun, I rode up to his tent. I went to him and begged him to get the doctor to come over and see Cunningham. While talking to him the tears came into my eyes as I described to him Cunningham's condition and he, seeing how earnest I took the matter to heart, went immediately and with great effort awoke Dr. Williams. This gent?, after rubbing his eyes and thinking over the matter for fifteen minutes, finally staggered over to the ambulance, with some trouble raised himself on the steps attached to the rear of the ambulance, looked at the dying man for a moment with a drunken stare, then staggered back to his tent, fell on his bed and slept. *(Ewert)*

It is hard to imagine how helpless and dependent Ewert and Cunningham must have felt so far from any resources other than those provided by the army.

I now sent word over to our company that Cunningham was dying and in a very few moments a dozen or more of the boys were with me, and we were discussing the propriety of reporting the doctor to Gen'l Custer when Professor Donaldson stepped up to the crowd and asked us the cause of the excitement, which we told him. He gave us an order on the Sutler for anything that we might need for our poor, dying comrade, then went to Gen'l Custer and reported our case to him. The General sent for Dr. Williams, but finding him under the influence of the flowing bowl, sent him back to his tent, then called for Dr. Allen. This "drunken specimen of Doctorism" came

and claimed that Cunningham was not dying. He prescribed a few opium pills and left. *(Ewert)*

The roster for the Expedition included a third acting assistant surgeon, A. C. Bergen, but for some reason he is not mentioned in this account.

That evening, four of us volunteered to set up with him. At 11:25, poor Cunningham paid the debt of Nature and died, purely through the neglect of the men claiming to be doctors, men who were paid by the Government to look after the health of its soldiers and who only managed to drink the brandy furnished by the same Government for the use of its sick soldiers. *(Ewert)*

Private John Cunningham . . . who has been sick for a few days past, died at 11 o'clock tonight. The General obtained a large piece of petrified wood. *(Calhoun)*

The men who sat up with Cunningham would not get much sleep. Reveille was customarily sounded at 2:45 a.m., followed by a general roll call. Breakfast was taken in the dark, after which the soldiers began to break camp and tend to their mounts.

Wednesday, July 22
A fatal duel — Government Valley to Inyan Kara Mountain

Just as we were in the act of saddling our horses, I heard the report of a carbine in the line of "M" Company tents who were encamped immediately on our right. Ever on the lookout for news, I ran, with a number of others, to "M" Company picket-line where we could see an unusual commotion. *(Ewert)*

If you had been parked in 1874 at **Point 8**, the entrance to the former Pete Harper ranch, you no doubt would have heard this shot echoing across the pastures to the south, beyond the headquarters buildings.

Ewert makes a mistake in referring to a "carbine" (rifle), since every account agrees the shot came from a revolver. The "commotion" involved two soldiers, William Roller of Missouri and George Turner of Texas, who were said to have enlisted together.

They were both pretty good soldiers but rather excitable men. Turner at times was very quarrelsome, and during his service in the company had several quarrels with different men of the company. *(Ryan)*

Prior to their arrival . . . it seems that they had a quarrel and a fight in which Turner got worsted; this kept him, being naturally of a quarrelsome disposition, aching and working for revenge. Through constant taunts and insults he finally prevailed on Roller, who was of a more quiet nature, to go out and fight him again. *(Ewert)*

They both adjourned to the woods at Unionville, South

Carolina, a couple of years previous to this affair. They fought it out with their fists and Turner got the best of Roller. Roller passed the remark to Turner, "Turner, you have been imposing upon me ever since I belonged to this company without any necessity. Now the next time you strike me either one of us has got to die right then and there." *(Ryan)*

This seems to have kept Turner pretty quiet, though he would, whenever an opportunity offered, still persist in belittling Roller. *(Ewert)*

Those two men happened to be on stable guard one night. . . . Privates would stand guard about three or three and one-half hours each over the horses each relief and there were three reliefs. That brought the end of the third relief's tour of duty at reveille in the morning, and on this occasion Roller was on the third relief, and when we went to groom our horses in the morning before daylight, Turner had eaten his breakfast and had gone back among the horses. Soon afterwards, our horses being groomed, and we had breakfast eaten, we were waiting for "boots and saddles" to sound. I was sitting on my saddle at the right of the line of my company. *(Ryan)*

Remember that this is taking place where cattle now graze less than two miles from Interstate 90.

It appears that during Roller's absence from the horses to get his breakfast, some one unfastened one end of the side lines from one of his horse's feet, and twisted the chain around another foot and attached the chain to the third foot, and when the horse started to walk, it was almost impossible for him to do so, as the chain had cut into one of the fetlock joints. *(Ryan)*

Some one had cross-hobbled Roller's horse. Roller, . . . seeing his horse in this condition, swore that he could whip the man that had played this dirty, cowardly trick on his poor horse. *(Ewert)*

Roller . . . let an oath out of him, saying, "The man that did that to my horse is a son of a b." Turner . . . wheeled around to Roller and said, "Did you intend that word for me?" Roller's reply was, "I did not intend it for you particularly but whoever the man was that tied the chain around my horse's foot like that." *(Ryan)*

Turner said that he believed Roller meant him when he used the remark, S_ of a B_, and he intended to take it that way anyhow, etc., etc., at the same time throwing his hand around to his right side where he generally carried his revolver. . . . He had changed his six-shooter from the right to the left side this same morning, and this simple little accident caused him to lose his life. *(Ewert)*

While Ewert has Turner reaching for a "six-shooter" (notice how early that term is already in use), the sergeant of Turner's own Company M offers a different story in a recently uncovered manuscript.

Within an instant Turner made a grab for his carbine which laid across his saddle on the ground but Roller was too quick for him, as he had his .44 caliber Colts pistol in his holster which hung from his waistbelt. . . . He whipped out his pistol and in an instant shot Turner through the body. I sprung off of my saddle and immediately rushed down there. Roller had the pistol still smoking in his hand. I grabbed it out of his hand. If I had not, he probably would have shot Turner a second time. I said, "Roller, what did you do that for?" He immediately answered, "I had to do it. If I hadn't he would have killed me." *(Ryan)*

At the time when the shot was fired, the two men were scarce four steps apart, and then Turner fell; he had his revolver in his hand showing that if his revolver had been in its accustomed place, his right side, he would surely have shot and killed Roller. *(Ewert)*

Those who saw the affray say Turner was trying to draw his revolver. *(Bismarck Tribune)*

It's hard to know who to believe on the subject of Turner's weapon—carbine or revolver—since all surviving accounts are second-hand.

Turner on his deathbed insisted that he did not attempt to draw his revolver until Rollins' [sic] revolver was pointed at him. *(Bismarck Tribune)*

Turner was a little the slower, and, to use his own words, "he got the best of me or I should have settled him." *(Inter-Ocean)*

This is a significant disagreement about the dying man's last words. William Curtis of the Inter-Ocean *was the better reporter, but his accounts of the incident reveal a cynical and unsympathetic view of the rank-and-file enlisted man.*

Both men are unknown, were desperate characters, and it is quite probable were serving under assumed names—a common thing in the army. Before he died Turner ordered his back pay and some effects sent to a man named Hughes in Jeffersonville, Ind., and that, probably, was his true name. *(Inter-Ocean)*

Turner spoke of a brother-in-law in Jeffersonville, Indiana. *(Bismarck Tribune)*

Turner was placed in an ambulance and died on the line of march about two o'clock p.m. this same day. The men in his company expressed no sympathy for him, he having but few, if any, friends among them. *(Ewert)*

DEVEREAUX LIBRARY ARCHIVES

With the luxury of wide-open prairie spaces, the Expedition camps of July 20 and July 21 might have looked much like this one in North Dakota, where William Illingworth took **Photo 801**, "Camp on Hiddenwood Creek." (A large version of this photo is printed at the back of the book.)

I placed Roller under arrest and took him up to the captain of my company. . . . He told me to take him over to General Custer. I did so and General Custer told me to take him and turn him over to Captain Sanger who commanded the Infantry battalion that was with us. I did so and Roller was kept under guard during the balance of that expedition. He was finally brought to Fort Lincoln a prisoner. *(Ryan)*

We came across further details on Roller in the archives of R.G. Cartwright. (See "A key to the sources," page 14.) One hand-written note says

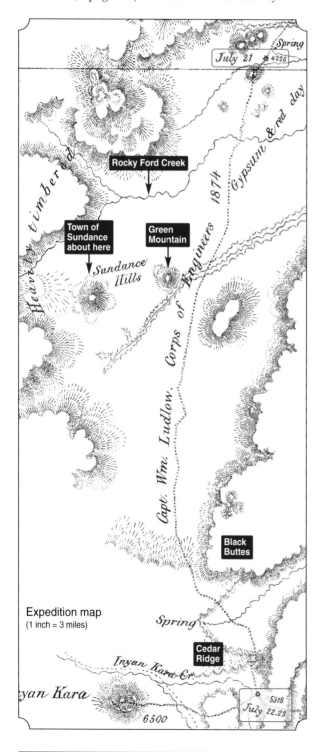

Expedition map
(1 inch = 3 miles)

Roller was *"chained to the back of a forage wagon. While in camp he was shackled to the iron point of a wagon tongue."* Another note specifies Windolph as the source: *"Under arrest, Roller walked during the Expedition. Roller was tried at Yankton [Dakota Territory] and acquitted in twenty minutes."*

The memoir of Roller's sergeant disagrees (not convincingly) on the location of the trial.

Roller was turned over to the civil authorities and was taken to some town in Wyoming Territory for trial but it could not be ascertained in which territory this shooting took place and he was released by the civil authorities and came back to the company, served out his time and received an honorable discharge and went away. Later on in 1876, after the Custer Massacre, we found Roller as an enlisted man again, I think in Co. I of the 7th U.S. Infantry. *(Ryan)*

Finally from the sergeant comes a postscript on the quarrelsome George Turner.

It seems that nobody knew much about Turner, as he said very little about himself while in the company. . . . After coming in off of this campaign to Fort Rice, his clothing and effects were sold at public auction. Some of the men in the company said they thought he had some money stored away among his clothing. At the auction sale, which took place in the company barracks, I examined the box that contained his clothing very thoroughly. . . . I found about three hundred fifty dollars rolled up in a neat little roll and tucked into the finger of this glove. This money with what pay, clothing money, etc., that there was coming to him was entered with his final statements. The captain of my company wrote a letter to this uncle of his in Jeffersonville, Indiana and in the course of time it came back from the dead letter office, no such party having been found there, and I suppose this money is somewhere at Washington waiting for an owner. *(Ryan)*

This all happened much later, of course. On July 22, the command left at its usual time of 4:45 a.m.

Go back to the service road (**Point G**) and set or check your odometer. Turn right (southwest) and drive 4.9 miles.

10 44 27 08.7 You should find a pullout here on the right, 104 16 43.7 just before the service road starts down the hill. Green Mountain is straight ahead, and Sundance Peak beyond that to the right. Ludlow's map makes it clear that the Expedition passed to the east of Green Mountain after crossing somewhere near your parking place.

The course led southward up the Redwater valley, which is from four to ten miles in width. *(Ludlow)*

The trail crossed about four miles east of the "Sundance Hills," as they were shown on Custer's military maps—named for the rituals of self-sacrifice and religious renewal once conducted here by the Lakota Sioux. The town of Sundance was established

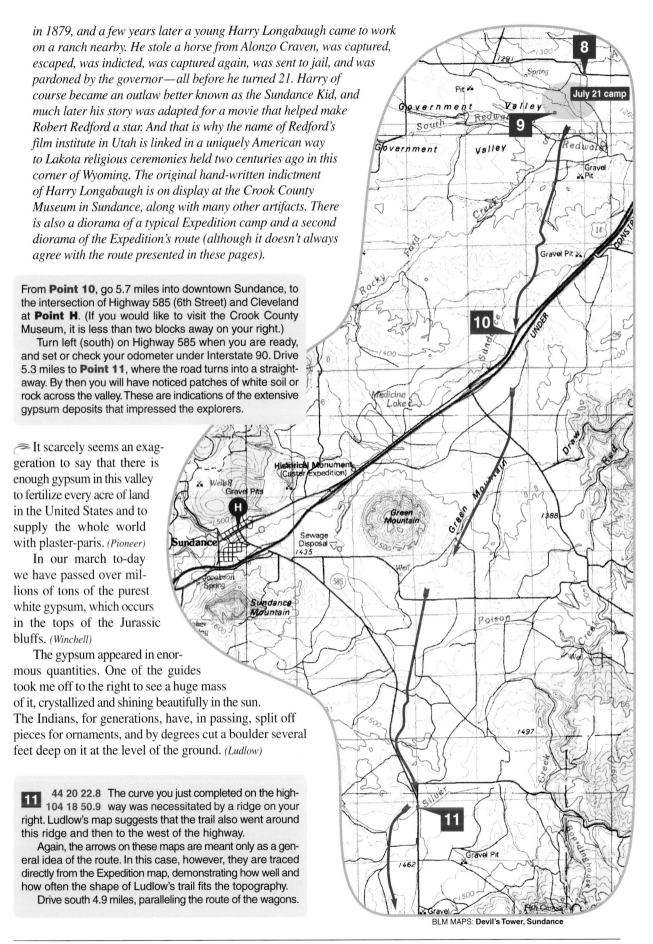

in 1879, and a few years later a young Harry Longabaugh came to work on a ranch nearby. He stole a horse from Alonzo Craven, was captured, escaped, was indicted, was captured again, was sent to jail, and was pardoned by the governor—all before he turned 21. Harry of course became an outlaw better known as the Sundance Kid, and much later his story was adapted for a movie that helped make Robert Redford a star. And that is why the name of Redford's film institute in Utah is linked in a uniquely American way to Lakota religious ceremonies held two centuries ago in this corner of Wyoming. The original hand-written indictment of Harry Longabaugh is on display at the Crook County Museum in Sundance, along with many other artifacts. There is also a diorama of a typical Expedition camp and a second diorama of the Expedition's route (although it doesn't always agree with the route presented in these pages).

From **Point 10**, go 5.7 miles into downtown Sundance, to the intersection of Highway 585 (6th Street) and Cleveland at **Point H**. (If you would like to visit the Crook County Museum, it is less than two blocks away on your right.)

Turn left (south) on Highway 585 when you are ready, and set or check your odometer under Interstate 90. Drive 5.3 miles to **Point 11**, where the road turns into a straight-away. By then you will have noticed patches of white soil or rock across the valley. These are indications of the extensive gypsum deposits that impressed the explorers.

☞ It scarcely seems an exag-geration to say that there is enough gypsum in this valley to fertilize every acre of land in the United States and to supply the whole world with plaster-paris. *(Pioneer)*

In our march to-day we have passed over mil-lions of tons of the purest white gypsum, which occurs in the tops of the Jurassic bluffs. *(Winchell)*

The gypsum appeared in enor-mous quantities. One of the guides took me off to the right to see a huge mass of it, crystallized and shining beautifully in the sun. The Indians, for generations, have, in passing, split off pieces for ornaments, and by degrees cut a boulder several feet deep on it at the level of the ground. *(Ludlow)*

11 44 20 22.8 The curve you just completed on the high-
104 18 50.9 way was necessitated by a ridge on your right. Ludlow's map suggests that the trail also went around this ridge and then to the west of the highway.

Again, the arrows on these maps are meant only as a gen-eral idea of the route. In this case, however, they are traced directly from the Expedition map, demonstrating how well and how often the shape of Ludlow's trail fits the topography.

Drive south 4.9 miles, paralleling the route of the wagons.

BLM MAPS: **Devil's Tower, Sundance**

Belle Fourche River to Inyan Kara

12 44 16 04.9 At 10.2 miles from I-90 you come to a
104 18 42.0 place where Custer's route and the highway converge for a convenient passage between a high point on the left and the head of a draw on the right.
Continue 1.2 miles.

13 44 15 30.5 From this point on the highway, the top of
104 17 30.4 Inyan Kara is visible to the southwest. In line with the peak you should be able to see a cluster of trees and a log structure about half a mile away. Rancher Nels J. Smith (grandson of the former Wyoming governor) told us about a good spring there that corresponds in distance and location with a spring shown on Ludlow's map (page 24).

Illingworth took **Photo 805** from **Point I**. See page 29 for more information.

BLM MAP: **Sundance**

⌐ After traveling about 18 miles we descended into an elegant valley. . . . On entering this valley to our right we discovered a spring of pure water, flowing sweetly from the rocks. *(Calhoun)*

Two miles from camp we crossed a pretty little streamlet, quite well wooded. *(Forsyth)*

The sun poured down its burning heat on man and beast, and as we found no water 'till about three o'clock, we were near perishing. About three in the afternoon my company, who were on duty as rear guard, came to a spring a little to the right of the main trail but found that the companies ahead had so trampled in and around the little spring as to make its waters nearly unfit for drinking. Nevertheless, the men, with dried and nearly blackened tongues, drank water, dirt, sand, bugs, and grass, anything to alleviate the terrible, raging thirst. *(Ewert)*

There certainly were times when your experience depended on whether you were riding up front with headquarters (as were Calhoun and Forsyth) or bringing up the rear. It is tempting to wonder whether Private Ewert was ever content with anything in his life, but in this case there is other testimony about the difficulties of a long march on a day when the temperature reached 91 degrees.

⌐ The ambulances not enough to carry the sick; some of the men very ill indeed. *(Grant)*

A great many of Col Wheatons men *[infantry]* gave out to day on acct of warm weather & no water. I remained back with the wagons—found it rather dusty & think in future that I will try it with Hd Qts. *(Power)*

Check your odometer and continue. In about three-tenths of a mile you will see—if it still stands—a weather-beaten wooden structure up against the tree line on your right. This was once the Inyan Kara post office. A short distance beyond is a ranch headquarters that was once a stage station.
The Expedition's engineer referred to what are now called the Black Buttes in describing this section of the trail.

⌐ Inyan Kara was in sight all day to the southward, approaching which the trail turned to the left around two igneous-looking peaks, and reached camp on Inyan Kara Creek, so called from flowing west past the foot of that peak. A heavy well-marked pony and lodge trail led up the Redwater valley southeasterly to the Red Cloud and Spotted Tail agencies. *(Ludlow)*

14 44 13 39.8 Here, 2.4 miles from Point 13 and 13.8
104 16 29.8 miles from the I-90 overpass, Soldier Creek passes beneath the highway. In *Wyoming Place Names*, Mae Urbanek says the creek was given its name because the Expedition "camped on this creek." It is almost certain that this spot was within the camp, which we believe extended to the south along Inyan Kara Creek. Continue another seven-tenths of a mile to an historical marker on the left.

15 44 13 05.2 This is the location of the historical sign, 104 16 13.7 beyond which is a draw. Note that Ludlow's map (page 24) shows headquarters just west of a break in the ridge that is similar in shape to this draw.

16 44 13 00 This is Ludlow's recorded latitude and longi-104 15 57 tude for the camp of July 22-23.

On the north side of the draw behind the sign you will see a fenced-in plot where two headstones mark what may be the last resting place for the soldiers Cunningham and Turner. You are permitted to walk up the hill to the little cemetery, which would be a good place to read the accounts of the funeral that was conducted here as darkness began to fall.

Upon a little knoll, within the limits of our camp, a broad grave was dug. *(Pioneer)*

At 8 o'clock the funeral cortege assembled in front of Headquarters. The Band played the dead march and the funeral procession moved to a little knoll just below the bluffs where a grave had been dug. *(Calhoun)*

> *The grave site along Highway 585 between Four Corners and Sundance matches these descriptions. It is indeed on a small knoll "just below the bluffs," apparently within the camp. Some ranchers in the area believe the actual grave was elsewhere, but we have been unable to find any written records that show who located the headstones, or when, or what information this location is based on. The true resting place of Cunningham and Turner—like that of Private King near Rapid City—may never be known.*

Just before sundown, Cunningham and Turner were sewed in canvass and the ten companies of cavalry drawn up in line, and as the corpses of the two men were lifted in the ambulance, the band chanted forth the solemn, funeral dirge whose weird tones floated away over the hills with indescribable sadness. . . . Arrived at the grave, the companies formed themselves around the new-dug grave and caps in hand listened to the burial service read very impressively by Michael Walsh of "H" Company, after which the customary three vollies were fired. *(Ewert)*

By the light of a lantern the funeral service was read. A platoon of soldiers then stepped to the edge of the grave and fired three successive volleys. The dead heeded not! A trumpeter then came up, and blew loud and long. No response came! *(Pioneer)*

Just as the twilight was deep-ening into darkness, "Taps" or "Lights Out" [was] sounded by Trumpeter Ewert of "H" Company. *(Ewert)*

The effect of the sound—simply a trumpet strain in the register of five notes—was such the Priests' March in "Athalia," or the "Ruins of Athens" march produces when Rubinstein plays it, and when the last echoes died away men forgot to swear, and chaff, but the camp was as still as if all the pulses in those long lines of tents had ceased to beat. *(Inter-Ocean)*

Returning from the grave the band played a lively quick-step while the fatigue party, detailed for that purpose, filled up the grave and leveled it with the surface of the earth, after which a large fire was built over the spot to obliterate all traces of the ground having been disturbed. *(Ewert)*

Simply human driftwood—men who have committed crime somewhere, and are hiding in the service under assumed names; men who cannot brook the liberties and familiarities of society, and take refuge in military discipline; men who are disappointed, disheartened, and ambitionless, and find the lazy life of a soldier a relief. Cunningham was one of these classes, his own reticence making it difficult to decide which. He was intelligent, well-educated, and, from his silent courtesy to all, and a well-bred indifference to everything, was popular and influential, but let himself lie aimless, the foot-ball of fate, till he was kicked into an unmarked grave in the wilderness. Could any destiny be sadder? *(Inter-Ocean)*

Nothing remained of poor "Cunny" except the remembrance that, with all his faults, he was, or had been, a very excellent man and comrade. Good bye, old man, good bye, rest soft and easy, for we all must, in a few years hence, follow you into that dark and unexplored Hereafter from whose bourne no traveler ever returns. *(Ewert)*

Privates John Cunningham and George Turner lie in a common grave east of Inyan Kara. The Expedition camped in the valley below on July 22-23, 1874.

Thursday, July 23
Climbing and photographing Inyan Kara

We are camped four or four and a half miles east, 5° north, from *Heéng-ya Ka-gá**, and on a ravine, with water, a short distance below where Lieutenant Warren camped. *(Winchell)*

Winchell refers to the 1857 expedition under Lt. G.K. Warren that explored the country around the Black Hills. Warren's party stopped southeast of Inyan Kara for a week before turning around—in deference to the demands of a large Lakota hunting party—and circling the Hills to Bear Butte.

Winchell's report of the 1874 Expedition footnotes his exotic spelling of the mountain's name.

*The name "Inyan Kara," given to this mountain by Warren and Raynolds, is a corruption of the Indian word given above, which I carefully obtained from our guide, Cold Hand. *(Winchell)*

Pursuant to circular No. 21, the command did not move today. Gen'l Custer with scientific party and 2 companies of cavalry (L & M) left at 6 A.M. to explore the mountain mentioned yesterday, Inyan Kara. *(Calhoun)*

At the foot of the mountain we leave the cavalry. *(Winchell)*

It resembled a lunar mountain, having a rim in shape of a horseshoe, one and a half miles across. *(Ludlow)*

This central coulée . . . has exactly the contour and opening required for the formation of a local glacier. There can be no doubt but that toward the close of the Glacial Epoch glacier-ice did pass northward from this mountain. The evidence of transportation of drift has already been noted. *(Winchell)*

The mountain, as before noted, is shaped like a tureen cover, with a heavy knob on top. This knob is very steep, being inclined at an angle of 48 degrees. *(New York Tribune)*

As to the geology of this mountain, it comprises a single isolated outburst, which occurred after the deposition of the Carboniferous limestone, and before that of the gypsiferous Red-Beds. The former was greatly tilted and shattered by the disturbance, and the latter are but little displaced. *(Winchell)*

The central peak . . . was gained by means of a narrow spur projecting from it to the southwest. A small spring flowed from the foot of the peak out northward through the opening in the horseshoe rim. The inner space between peak and rim was heavily wooded with pine and clumps of aspen. In the open places were found in abundance strawberries, raspberries, black and red currants, june-berries, and a small red whortleberry. *(Ludlow)*

WHO CARVED CUSTER'S NAME?

Col. Ludlow with much difficulty reached the highest point of the mountain, leading his horse, and high on its flinty side cut the following name and character, viz: "Custer." "74." *(Bismarck Tribune)*

It is still possible to see Custer's name etched in stone at the top of Inyan Kara—if you know exactly where to look. The carving was done on this July day in 1874, and credit is often given to the Expedition's engineer, Capt. William Ludlow—apparently based on the above passage in the Bismarck Tribune. *It is the only original source we have been able to find that names the captain. But take a look at two other sources, and notice not only the discrepancies but also some similarities to the* Tribune *account.*

As difficult and even dangerous as the ascent, Gen. Forsyth led his horse to the very top, and brought him down

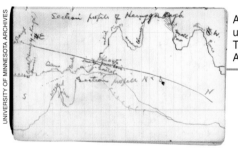

At left is a page from one of the notebooks carried in 1874 by Newton Winchell. He used this sketch to produce the profile of Inyan Kara (below) in the Expedition report. The geologist appears to have crossed out pages after transferring the information. Also, note that he places the camp to the east of Inyan Kara Creek.

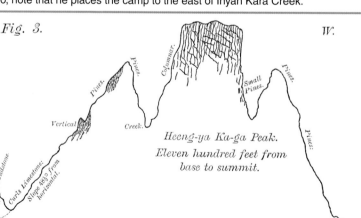

Fig. 3.

W.

Heeng-ya Ka-ga Peak.
Eleven hundred feet from base to summit.

Section Profile from Camp of July 22, through the Peak of Heeng-ya Ka-ga.

again in safety. In the hard, flinty album of the summit, engraven with a cold chisel and hammer, in large and distinct characters, Arabic and Roman, is a date and autograph,

"74

CUSTER"

If the archeologist is puzzled over this inscription, let him consult the commandant of this expedition. *(Pioneer)*

General Forsyth took his horse over the mountain— probably the only horse that has ever been over it. *(Grant)*

The Tribune *reports Ludlow leading his horse to the top, while both the* Pioneer *and Lt. Col. Fred Grant (the President's son) point to Forsyth performing this unique feat. Can we trust the story in the* Tribune*?*

Both newspapers describe the climb as "difficult" or "with difficulty," and both use the word "flinty." Both also mention the horse and the inscription.

The striking similarities continue through the rest of their dispatches. Both mention a reporter being in the party that ascended Inyan Kara, both say the mountain covers 12 square miles, and both say it is 1,500 feet higher than any other point of land in the United States—except that the Pioneer *adds the important modification: ". . . east of the Mississippi," which makes it accurate.*

While the two accounts seem to be working from the same facts, only one of these correspondents had the benefit of first-hand knowledge. Writing for the Pioneer *was Expedition botanist A. B. Donaldson, a known member of the climbing party.*

Passing along this ridge *[of the horseshoe]* toward the south a short distance, one party turns to the right and ascends the mountain from the east or northeast, while I, with Professor Donaldson and Bear's Ears, an Indian guide, cross the gorge separating us from the central mass. *(Winchell)*

The Bismarck Tribune, *meanwhile, was represented by Nathan H. Knappen, who would turn 19 during the summer of 1874. He had briefly run the paper in the owner's absence, but before the Expedition he had been selling life insurance and "White's Portable Fly and Mosquito Net Frames."*

It is hard to escape the assumption that Knappen was cribbing his facts and ideas from Donaldson, managing to get at least three of them wrong in the process—not just the "highest point" but also the leader of the horse and the appearance of the Custer carving, which in reality looks much closer to Donaldson's representation. Finally, the leaden style of Knappen's words only serve to highlight Donaldson's elegant, fluid prose.

This will not be the last time that Knappen of the Bismarck Tribune *leans on Donaldson of the* St. Paul Pioneer. *For now, however, it is enough to*

The view . . . failed to show us a pathway to the interior.

question Ludlow's role, especially since Custer had a closer relationship with Major Forsyth. The general had requested Forsyth be assigned to the Expedition and then made him second in command.

At 5 a.m. Gen. Custer and a party of five, myself included, started for Inyan Kara. *(Forsyth)*

Looking closer at Donaldson's report, notice that he tells of Forsyth leading his horse to the summit and follows immediately with a description of the carving. They seem to be part of the same anecdote. It looks as if Forsyth and not Ludlow wielded the chisel.

Owing to lowering weather and a smoky atmosphere, we did not get as good a view to the east and south as we wished. However, it was a sight well worth seeing, and repaid us for the trouble. *(Forsyth)*

Since Donaldson and Knappen both refer to "one of the reporters" on the climb—and since Fred Power and William Curtis both stayed in camp—it's likely that Samuel Barrows of the New York Tribune *rounded out the "party of five" on Inyan Kara. His account has the feeling of a first-person experience, with plenty of detail, and he is the only reporter to mention this interesting discovery:*

On the top of the ridge, small pieces of white quartz were found. As they had no geological business to be there, they were no doubt left there by the Indians, who are fond of making offerings to their gods from these lofty altars. *(New York Tribune)*

Expedition photographer William Illingworth also rose early to pay his respects to the mountain—but from further away. He went to **Point I** *(see map on page 26) and took* **Photo 805***, "Inyan Kara—altitude 6600 feet," as well as another view (pages 166-169). The photo site is located on private land*

AN END TO THE 'SKIRMISHING'

We found ourselves on the westerly range of the Black Hills, at a point not distant from the center. . . . The view from [Inyan Kara] had failed to show us a pathway to the interior. *(New York Tribune)*

From the summit an extensive view might have been obtained, but the Sioux had fired the prairie to the south and west. After two hours of waiting, the smoke having only grown denser, we returned to camp. *(Ludlow)*

The day was not favorable for obtaining distant views. I decided on the following morning to move due east and attempt the passage of the hills. *(Custer)*

CHAPTER 2

Friday, July 24

Inyan Kara Creek to Cold Springs Creek (Floral Valley) near Moskee

*We didn't have time to hunt a trail, we just went in,
and we had loads of trouble. (Wood)*

From its camp on Inyan Kara Creek, the column moved generally east across three flats and two valleys before reaching what we now call Cold Springs Creek. Here the Expedition was rewarded for a long day of difficult travel, for this was the so-called "Floral Valley" where soldiers picked flowers and made nosegays for their horses. The wagon train descended a steep bluff more than three miles south of Moskee, then moved up the valley toward camp. Distance traveled: 11 miles.

— Taking the trail —

U.S.G.S. MAPS: Inyan Kara, Dry Draw

CAUTIONS: This is a rare situation where the precise location of the trail remains uncertain in several areas. Furthermore, virtually the entire route is on private land. As this book went to press, much of the land was owned by Homestake Mining Company (now a subsidiary of Barrick International) which barred vehicular travel by locking gates near Moskee and Buckhorn. The company was preparing to sell its holdings, however. We will try to post developments on our web site (Custertrail.com) but it is up to you to determine who currently owns the land—if necessary by providing the county tax assessor with township, range and section numbers. If the new owner permits public access, there is enough information in this chapter for you to discover key elements of the trail yourself. Otherwise, you may wish to combine this outing with either the first chapter or the next.

TO START: To view the area of the July 24 camp, go to the state historical sign along Wyoming Highway 585. *From Sundance*, the sign is 14.5 miles south from the Interstate 90 overpass. *From Four Corners* (between Lead and Newcastle), drive 12.3 miles north from the intersection with U.S. Highway 85.

Gen. Custer then determined to bend to the east and enter the very heart of the whole range, with a view of finding the central park which the Indians had reported to exist there. . . . Our Indian guides knew only the general direction, and but little else. They could point out no gap or pass which promised or even broached a way to the interior. The only authentic map of that section is a piece of blank paper. A wall of hills defended by a great army of pines threatened us if we attempted the most direct route. *(New York Tribune)*

The mention of a "central park" suggests the intriguing possibility that Custer had already heard

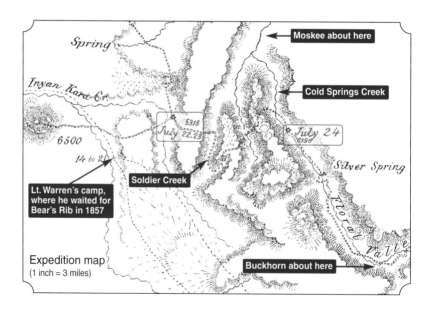

Expedition map
(1 inch = 3 miles)

descriptions of the area along *French Creek* where he would go into *"Permanent Camp"* a week later—near the town that now bears his name. What has never been spelled out is why that particular area of the Black Hills was Custer's ultimate goal.

1 44 13 05.2 This is the location of the historical sign
104 16 13.7 marking the camp for July 22-23 and the soldiers' graves on the hillside (**Point A**; see Chapter 1).

2 44 12 40 These are Capt. Ludlow's latitude and longi-
104 15 57 tude readings for the camp.
  Today, a road cut in the side of the draw behind the sign provides access to Soldier Creek. Without that road the draw would have been too steep for wagons. The Expedition map shows the route turning south briefly (upstream on Inyan Kara Creek), as Ludlow himself described in his journal.

The trail led up the creek a short distance, then turned abruptly east. *(Ludlow)*

The Carboniferous limestone . . . forms the floor of the plain on which we are situated, and is exposed in the bed of the creek half a mile above our camp. *(Winchell)*

Winchell's description helps us confirm the location of this camp, since limestone can indeed be seen in the creek bed less than half a mile above the sign

that marks this historic site (**Point 1** *on the map*). The limestone develops into sharp breaks that the wagon train would have had to avoid.

Set or check your odometer and drive seven-tenths of a mile south on Highway 585, noticing the first appearance of limestone along the edges of Inyan Kara Creek on your right. It is likely that the road crosses the Expedition's route in this vicinity. Continue up the hill and stop just beyond a road cut.

3 44 12 42.5 From here you have a good view (on the
104 16 19.7 right) of the limestone exposure referred to by the geologist. You can also see, on your left, the easiest portion of the day's travel. Note the rolling pasture that ends at the tree line in the distance.

We set out from camp nearly east, and at once ascend the slope underlain by the Carboniferous limestone. This undulates in small knolls, having a changeable dip in all directions, with often smooth, bare surfaces for about a mile, when pieces of a different kind of limestone appear on the surface, demonstrating a change in the underlying rock . . . . coincident with the beginning of timber. *(Winchell)*

The 1st mile was very good, but then a ravine so deep that the wagons had to be let down by ropes, which took considerable time. *(Power)*

Fred Power is referring to Soldier Creek, the first valley to the east of Inyan Kara Creek. Professor Winchell describes this descent in some detail.

The first ridge we pass over has a very steep descent toward the east, and is about one hundred feet high and a fourth of a mile across. It . . . is covered with a considerable soil, that supports the best pines we have yet seen. . . . We pass on east about a fourth of a mile, nearly across the strike of the rocks, when we go down another step, about 100 feet, . . . when we turn southeast down this valley. *(Winchell)*

QUADRANGLES: **Inyan Kara, Dry Draw**

Winchell also describes a distinctive feature he found along Soldier Creek.

I soon discovered a good exposure in the bluff on the right, made up of limestone and white, loosely cemented sandstone, as follows, in descending order:

No. 1. Magnesian limestone . . . . 8-10 feet.

No. 2. White, loosely-cemented sandstone . . . 20 feet. There is also a very steep talus below the sandstone, of about 75 feet, hid by turf, probably made up of the same sandstone. . . .On the opposite side of this valley, which here is not more than 300 yards across, the same sandstone occurs, exposing about 50 feet, but it is here very much stained with iron . . . . It is deeply fractured and parted. *(Winchell)*

> Only one cliff (at **Point B**) has so far been found to fit Winchell's description—the measured layers of rock, the grassy talus slope, and the broken red sandstone visible across the valley. If the command entered above Point B, however, the trail would have had to make a swing to the north that is not shown on the Expedition map.
>
> In fact, Ludlow's map (page 30) is not all that reliable in this area. Soldier Creek is shown running in the wrong direction (Winchell gets it right when he describes traveling "southeast"), and is not shown connecting to Inyan Kara Creek (perhaps because it is generally dry). Until the site of the actual descent can be found—those two "steps" a quarter mile apart—all we know for sure is that the command traveled along Soldier Creek for a mile and a half or so.

blue and gooseberries which abounded plentifully and were really a welcome addition to, or a change from, the coarse army fare. *(Ewert)*

I found Cols Grant, Tilford & Lt Gibson seat[ed] on the remains of a large tree enjoying Straw berries, the 1st of the season. We find berries of all kinds in abundance & could we only get cream would be as well satisfied to remain here as else where. *(Power)*

No landscape architect could design a scene of more perfect enchantment. Rocky points sometimes take the place of trees, and thus give increased beauty and corresponding interest. *(Pioneer)*

We did not remain long in this earthly Eden. Our passage was obstructed by protruding rocks. *(Press.)*

> *If there were protruding rocks in this "Eden," homesteaders removed them long ago. Now there are hayfields in the valley, which becomes wider and turns west at* **Point 4** *on the map. It was here that Custer decided to try a new course.*

The valley we had followed seductively led in another direction as if intentionally to thwart our purpose. The odds of circumstance, therefore, were against us, but the odds of pluck and perseverance were in our favor. Gen. Custer boldly turned his column to the east. *(New York Tribune)*

Our road out of this enchanted valley was equally as rough as the passage down. *(Press)*

Leaving this valley we climbed the pine-clad hills to forest plains. *(Forsyth)*

> The area around **Point 4** corresponds very closely with the departure from Soldier Creek as seen on the Expedition map (page 30). Ludlow shows the valley becoming wider and changing direction, while a smaller branch extends to the east. The trail is shown climbing the north side of this branch.

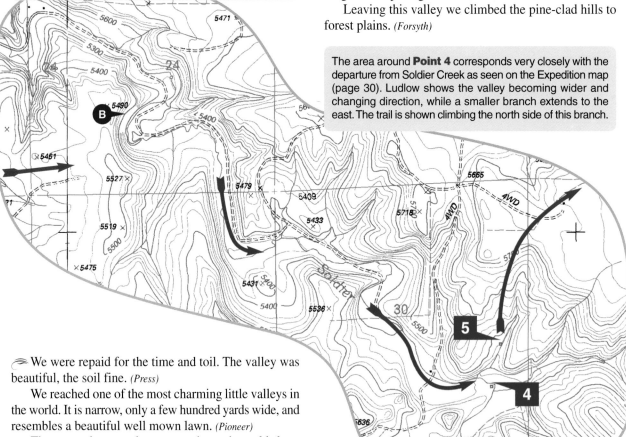

We were repaid for the time and toil. The valley was beautiful, the soil fine. *(Press)*

We reached one of the most charming little valleys in the world. It is narrow, only a few hundred yards wide, and resembles a beautiful well mown lawn. *(Pioneer)*

The men, whenever the command rested, would clamber up among the rocks and hunt and gather straw, rasp,

QUADRANGLES: **Inyan Kara, Dry Draw**

5 44 12 07
104 12 52 The remains of an old trail can be seen here, close to the place where Custer probably left Soldier Creek. This is not public land, although we do not know whether the area above Point 5 belongs to a private rancher or to Homestake's successor.

The elevation lines on the topo map show a climb here of about 300 feet in altitude.

The hill was steep—a hard task for our mules; but they had had a day's rest and plenty of grass, and went at the hill with a good stomach. Their drivers' reputation for profanity and teamstership was staked on the occasion. So they lashed them hard with tongue and whip, and threatened their hearts with never-ending pain if they failed. Encouraged by the gross voice and whip, if not by the dismal theology, the poor "rat tails" pulled as if they were inspired. *(New York Tribune)*

After a time we reached the top of the hill to find it thickly timbered, giving considerable work to the pioneer company, Captain Yates. *(Press)*

Capt. Yates, with his company . . . was ordered to charge on the pine brigade. His men advanced promptly with axes and slew them right and left. *(New York Tribune)*

We travelled through the hills and encountered many bad roads. I never thought it possible that a wagon train could move in such country. *(Calhoun)*

Most of the accounts describe the area between **Points 5** *and* **7** *as one large hill or forested flat be-*

*tween Soldier and Cold Springs Creeks—even though there lies between them a shallow valley watered by Julius Spring (**Point C**, below). Winchell is the only one to mention the middle valley, while two other accounts describe the spring.*

Over this flat we travel several miles, when we descend into a perfectly similar ravine, where we find water. *(Winchell)*

On our march we reached two springs of good cold

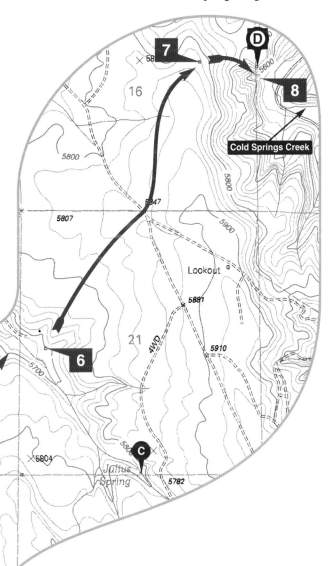

Cold Springs Creek

water. The first one on our right about five miles from our last camp. *(Calhoun)*

We passed several handsome springs; one was christened "Good Templar Spring" and another, "Sumner Spring," at the latter of which we pitched camp. *(Ewert)*

Lt. Calhoun's reference to a spring "on our right" suggests that members of the headquarters staff explored the little valley, which was about halfway along on the day's 11-mile journey—or close to the five miles from the camp mentioned by Calhoun. Private Ewert, meanwhile, has more than likely

QUADRANGLE: **Dry Draw**

passed on to us the temporary name (Good Templar) given to the spring that was later named for the Julius family. The remnants of the Julius homestead still stand near **Point 6** *on the map.*

6 44 13 06 Near the Julius homestead is an old trail in
104 11 23 the side of a draw leading up to the next flat. This is the easiest place to cross the valley, and it lies about seven-tenths of a mile below the Julius Spring. It seems at least possible that the trail up the draw followed a route originally engineered by the Expedition.

Remember that the arrows drawn across the flats are just approximations of the trail based on these accounts and on matching Ludlow's map to the topography. Some of the country is almost as difficult to walk through today as it was in 1874.

☞None of us ever saw so dense or so extended a growth of pine. As far as we could see . . . the forests made an unbroken surface of the darkest green. *(Inter-Ocean)*

The pine timber is good, tall and straight. *(Pioneer)*

We passed over some very rough country where there was splendid water and good timber—some of the trees being as much as 3 feet in diameter. *(Grant)*

These men are talking about trees that Homestake Mining Company would one day harvest for timbers at Lead—trees they tried to protect with fire lookout towers like the one in Section 21 on the map below.

☞The Indian has not been more fortunate than the white man in saving the forests from destruction. Thousands of square miles have been burned over, giving to the burnt districts a sort of desolate and graveyard look. *(Pioneer)*

There seems to have been here . . . very extensive fires, that have burned the former forest and left the charred trunks and limbs scattered on the surface. Among these have sprung up a perfect mesh of shrubs and small deciduous trees, mostly trembling aspen. *(Winchell)*

In some cases it requires great labor to open a road through the fallen timber. *(Pioneer)*

We were nearly fourteen hours in the saddle. "In the saddle," I say, using the words not with their ordinary meaning, for really we were on foot nearly all the time, leading our horses, clearing the brush and logs away, pulling up stumps, pushing the wagons up the hills, and holding them back with long ropes as they went down. *(Inter-Ocean)*

The brush was very heavy and annoying. A festive log in the way tipped over one of Lieut. Chance's Gatling guns by way of amusement, but hurt nothing or nobody. The flanking cavalry had to crash their way through heavy underbrush and young poplar and pine. Hats were impertinently removed and clothes received a good brushing, and those in the advance marched at times more by faith than by sight. . . . We were on a crusade certainly, but like the unlettered enthusiasts of the first crusade, who expected to find Palestine next to Germany, all that we could cer-

QUADRANGLE: **Dry Draw**

tainly say was that we were going east and that the road was a hard one to travel. *(New York Tribune)*

It is interesting to see this reference to the Crusades and remember that the reporter, Samuel J. Barrows, was a student at Harvard Divinity School when he accompanied the Expedition. Each account quoted in these pages is flavored by its author's interests and predilections. William Curtis, for example, clearly picked up a bit of world history at Western Reserve College before joining the Chicago Inter-Ocean.

☞ The same kind Providence that has guided us continually saw us safely through, and in the whole command there was no result more serious than blistered hands and scratched faces. Where is the historian to place our anabasis alongside of Napolean's crossing of the Alps or the famous marches of Artaxerxes? *(Inter-Ocean)*

Many fine elk horns of large size were obtained; several deer killed. *(Calhoun)*

We found . . . elk horns, the largest I ever saw, some measuring over six feet. Gen. Custer, Captains McDougall, French and several others will decorate their parlors with some of the finest. Illingworth, the artist, shot a panther—wounding it—his rifle being too small to kill it. *(Press)*

The wonders of "Floral Valley" were near at hand, but first the wagon train was forced to stop on the flats while headquarters looked for a way down.

☞ Was it by instinct, chance, or good fortune that somewhere about noon Gen. Custer caught a glimpse of the foot—I might almost say the little toe—of a small valley away down at the base of the lofty hills? Louis Egain *[Agard]*, our half-breed guide, thought it was by some sad calamity, for, said he, if we get down into that place we can never get out again. But the nearest problem was how to get down, and whether it would pay to make the descent. Gen. Custer, with a few followers, went on to explore. *(New York Tribune)*

After several hours of waiting, while search was made for a practicable descent, we started again and dropped suddenly into the valley of a small stream flowing northward into the Redwater. *(Ludlow)*

We descend again by steps, caused by the same formations, into the third valley. *(Winchell)*

7 44 13 06 This is the top of an old trail that provides the 104 11 23 easiest descent from the flats to a middle elevation—a kind of bench—before the final drop down a precipitous draw in which there may be remnants of an old rut along the side. The passage from one elevation to another matches the "steps" referred to by Winchell.

Locating at least the second step of this descent is virtually certain thanks to the convergence of several pieces of evidence. First, a map of the trail prepared by C.C. O'Harra in the 1920s contains a notation referring to the draw above **Point 8** as "Custer's Gulch where Custer came down into Floral Valley about one mile below the buildings on McCready Ranch (now Homestake)."

☞ The hill was never intended for a wagon road. . . . The fate of Jack and Jill was written on every feature and lineament of this hill. We had discovered the hitherto unknown site of this great calamity, and mentally took the latitude and longitude. A certain newspaper instinct for "items" impelled me to sit at the brow of the hill and see history repeat itself. But somehow or other—no thanks to the law of gravity—the whole outfit, men, horses, mules, and wagons got down in safety, and neither Jack nor Jill, nor any of the family suffered contusion. But Capt. Smith, our commissary and quartermaster, had to work like a beaver, and the men who held the ropes had to hold hard to secure the desirable result. *(New York Tribune)*

We passed down a steep ravine to FLORAL VALLEY, so named by General Custer, on account of its profusion of wild flowers. *(Pioneer)*

Our horses wade knee-deep among them. *(Forsyth)*

The late Charlotte Reynolds—whose father George Stanton homesteaded on Cold Springs at Stanton Draw—added to the record by telling her daughter Doris Vore Lake that the draw above **Point 8** was Custer's entrance to the valley. Mother and daugher marked the spot by nailing a sign to a tree near the bottom of the draw.

8 44 13 06 This is the *approximate* location of the sign, 104 11 23 which was still posted when this book went to press. If the Moskee Road has been re-opened, you can reach "Custer's Gulch" by driving to the end of Hwy 585 at U.S. 85, turning left (east), and driving another 6.3 miles to the gravel road on your left as you reach Buckhorn. Turn onto the gravel road and drive 8.7 miles, to the draw on your left.

Still another kind of evidence is Dr. Donald Progulske's discovery of an Illingworth photo site directly above the draw at **Point D**. It is hard to imagine the photographer choosing to climb this bluff at random if the Expedition had entered the valley anywhere else. Far more credible is the idea that Illingworth had time to kill while the wagons were being prepared for the final descent.

William Illingworth took **Photo 806**, *"Floral Valley" (page 170), at* **Point D** *on the map at left. Compare the image to this description from Winchell's diary.*

☞ Viewed from the bluff, before descending into it, it forms a long serpentine belt of green among the trees of darker foliage, somewhat suggestive of a slowly-winding river. *(Winchell)*

We had formed many anticipations connected with the Black Hills . . . . But still, for all this, nature took us completely by surprise. We had expected everything but a bounteous floral welcome. We were almost startled by the unlooked-for array which met us as we descended into the valley. Such brilliancy, such beauty, such variety, such profusion! All the glories of color, form and fragrance which Flora could command had been woven into a carpet for our feet. The whole valley was a garden, teeming with the gladness and joy of a new creation. *(New York Tribune)*

The whole valley was a nosegay, and so rich was the soil

The music of the band was weird and fascinating; it seemed to come from genii, concealed in the graves and caves of the mountain's sides.

that everything grew with the greatest luxuriance. Our eyes were opened then to the beauties of the Black Hills. Twenty days in a purgatory of bare plains, saline water, and alkali dust made us appreciate a paradise, and every man in the expedition stood silently to enjoy and admire. *(Inter-Ocean)*

Some said they would give a hundred dollars just to have their wives see the floral richness for even one hour. *(Pioneer)*

"Profusion" is a common term in these accounts, and there was certainly an unparalleled profusion of praise for the valley that can be explained only in part by the contrast with those dry, harsh plains.

No one, from the commanding general down to the humblest private or the most profane teamster, could withstand the effect. . . . Men who had never picked a flower since their childhood days bent and paid the long-neglected homage. Cavalrymen and teamsters decorated their horses and mules; infantrymen plumed their hats; officers gathered nosegays; pocket-books and note-books were brought into requisition to press and preserve the free gift of this valley. *(New York Tribune)*

It is exciting to try and imagine the sight and how it affected the men.

For once grumblers against camps and country were hushed by their own confession. . . . It would be amusing . . . to record the profane encomiums which illiteral enthusiasts bestowed on this new Florida. The same inadmissable adjectives which were used as prefixes to the most blasphemous curses against the barren wastes of Dakota were now transferred to the dialect of praise. But there was no mistaking the difference in sentiment. *(New York Tribune)*

The gaudy sun-flower and the delicate hare-bell, the fair lily and the bright blue daisy, the coarse elecampane and the modest violet, the gay lark-spur and the fragrant peppermint, roses and pinks, asters and phlox, bell-flower and caropsis, geraniums, golden-rod, purple cone-flower . . . *(Pioneer)*

. . . blue bells . . . flowering pea, monk's hood, lupen, flax, primroses, and many flowers that I cannot name, were mingled and repeated in artless and exuberant profusion. *(New York Tribune)*

Our botanist collected fifty-two distinct varieties of flowers in the limits of our camp, and twelve under the walls of his tent. *(Inter-Ocean)*

One of the commonest and most admired in the whole pasture is a beautiful white lily with a beaded throat, first noticed by Dr. Williams, which is not described in the botany books. *(New York Tribune)*

A large number of bulbs were collected, and an attempt will be made to introduce it into the States. *(Inter-Ocean)*

> If you have been able to hike or drive to Point 7, turn around and follow the Expedition south for 1.9 miles.

On reaching this valley, General Custer turned to the right, ascending it toward the center of the main mass of the Black Hills. *(Winchell)*

A finer stream for trout culture could hardly be found on the continent. . . . The water seems perfectly pure and without taste, smell or color. *(Pioneer)*

There was no water where we entered the valley but as we ascended we came upon quite a stream which was very cold and hard water. *(Grant)*

Some of the party followed it down the valley and saw it disappear suddenly in the earth, leaving not one trace to show that its course had ever been above ground. For miles further they sought its reappearance, but it did not come to the surface again, and as the valley rose rapidly, it was concluded that it had found an outlet under the mountains to the world beyond. *(Inter-Ocean)*

Among those who went down the valley was Aris B. Donaldson, who had became a reappearing figure— known as "The Professor"—in the dispatches from William Curtis of the Chicago Inter-Ocean. *In an earlier story, Curtis had described Donaldson with obvious affection.*

[The Professor] is a big-bodied, big-hearted old fellow . . . who is doing the botany. His character is noble, yet funny, for in it are mixed the most generous, manly notions, and a simple childishness it does one good to see. *(Inter-Ocean)*

In this case, Donaldson came back with a "wonderful story."

"A hyperbole," he calls it afterward, without any great scruplousness *[sic]* in regard to the truth. The stream disappeared, he said, in the mouth of a mammoth serpent, twenty-seven feet from "ear to ear," which drank all the water, gulping it down when its mouth filled, three swallows a day. "It will compensate you," he said to me, "to ascend the pinnacle of yonder elevation, and obtain an observation of the reptile." The Professor's imagination is very fertile, and he entertains us frequently. *(Inter-Ocean)*

The Prussian Private Ewert would enthuse over Floral Valley on the following day, but for now he was looking at Soldier and Cold Spring Creeks with a more practical eye.

The grass along these little valleys is so plentiful and nutritious that I could scarce imagine a more fitted spot for a stock raiser. . . . For farming the Black Hills are of no account; the valleys, even of productive soil, are so narrow that it would require a length of ten miles in order to gain sufficient acres to make a farm, and again the seasons are so short in which crops should be raised that a farmer would almost find winter knocking at the door again 'ere his seed would be fairly in the ground. No, no! Farmers have no business in the Black Hills. *(Ewert)*

Today you will indeed find cattle grazing up and down "Floral Valley." The carpet of flowers has had to make way, but you can find them still blooming in places during the late spring and early summer.

9 **44 12 48** At the intersection with Lost Canyon, where **104 09 37** several drainages come into the valley, you may be within the area of the July 24 camp. As the following chapters will show, Col. Ludlow was generally quite accurate with his latitude readings, but the true site of this camp has not been determined with certainty.

E **44 12 40** This location (see the map on page 34) is **104 11 30** Ludlow's actual reading for the camp. You can see that his longitude is too far west by at least 1¾ miles, which may have been due to the effects of travel and altitude on his chronometer (see pages 12-14 for details). One result is that the Expedition map contains distortions created by trying to fit recorded directions and distances between celestial readings that were not always accurate—at least east-to-west.

Our tents were pitched on each side of the valley at the basis of the including hills, embowered in a grove of young aspens. *(New York Tribune)*

Not a fly, gnat or mosquito can be seen. Excepting butterflies there is scarcely an insect. *(Pioneer)*

We found indications of Indians, lodge poles, fresh trail, &c., all bearing evidence that the Indians had spent some time there. *(Press)*

This is the first mention of an Indian trail—or series of trails—that will be followed by the Expedition more or less all the way to the town of Custer.

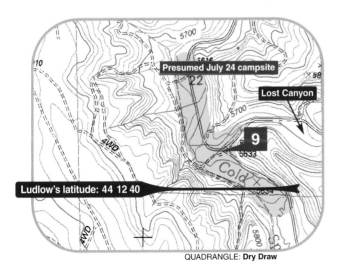

QUADRANGLE: **Dry Draw**

Presumed July 24 campsite

Lost Canyon

9

Ludlow's latitude: 44 12 40

"A. Rider _____, Cohoes, N.Y." on ax found in old Indian Camp. *(Winchell notebook)*

The greed for gold was forgotten. We ceased to look for the nuggets which would make us suddenly rich. Beauty for the time seemed the only wealth. *(New York Tribune)*

"For the time" being the operative words here.

The prospectors accompanying the expedition were busy this evening. *(Calhoun)*

So beautiful was nature outwardly; so rich was mother earth in the resources of vegetable life, that our miners imagined mineral treasures must be lying under our flower bed; and they dug for them—dug all one evening, and found—found a rich loamy soil, four or five feet deep, then a gravel bed on a stratum of limestone rock. *(Inter-Ocean)*

This discovery shaft may have been sunk within sight of the road near the junction of Lost Canyon and Cold Springs Valley—the first mark left by whites where previously there had been only lodge poles, camp fires and millions of flowers.

No one who has not seen Indian Territory in April, or the Florida bottoms in their summer radiance can conceive to any degree of satisfaction how nosegay-like this valley of ours looks; one who has never seen colors mixed as nature mixes them, in her own rare conservatories like these, can realize the artistic effect that is produced; but let the reader imagine if he can such a valley as I have described . . . darkened by the heavy shade to the tinge of twilight, and illuminated—yes, fairly illuminated—by the gold, and the scarlet, and the blue of its flowers. But the picture is not finished. The regimental band is playing on a shelf of one of the walls, and the "Mocking Bird," "Garryowen," "Artist Life," "The Blue Danube," and snatches of "Trovatore," and other strains of music for the first time heard in paradise. *(Inter-Ocean)*

In this valley, every sound is echoed from the timbered borders and the mountain sides. The report of a rifle seems as loud as that of artillery on the plains. The music of the band was weird and fascinating; it seemed to come from genii, concealed in the graves and caves of the mountain's sides, and fancy suggested the haunt of the muses. *(Pioneer)*

One wonders what effect the music will have upon these wonderful flowers; how long the echoes will remain in these cosy hills, and whether some straying savageling has caught the melody afar off, and will wonder for years hence where the sound came from, and whether it was the happy spirits in Paradise; and when the pale face invades this valley, and the savageling talks English, whether he will tell what mysterious noises he heard on the evening of July 24, 1874, or whatever year of our Lord the Indian chronicles call this. *(Inter-Ocean)*

CHAPTER 3

Saturday, July 25
Cold Springs Creek (near Moskee) to Cold Creek

*Game was as plentiful as we could expect,
having a party of Sioux just ahead of us.* (Power)

While the explorers knew they were following a well-used Indian trail, they would find the first signs of recent use by the end of this day. In the meantime they relished their march through a valley filled with flowers from one end to the other. They saw many deer, signs of bear, and even sandhill cranes. Newton H. Winchell also discovered a new geological layer, which he called *Minne-Lusa*—the Indian name of the stream that we now call Cold Springs Creek. Distance traveled: 11.5 miles.

Taking the trail

U.S.G.S. MAPS: Dry Draw, Buckhorn

CAUTIONS: Some of the roads are unimproved dirt, which can be heavily rutted in places and may also be slick if there has been recent moisture. At least a high-clearance vehicle is recommended.

TO START: *From Wyoming*, drive 6.3 miles east of Four Corners on U.S. 85 and turn left onto a gravel road just before you reach the Buckhorn Bar. *From the north, south and east*, drive 9.7 miles west of Cheyenne Crossing on U.S. 85 and turn right onto a gravel road just past the Buckhorn Bar.

From the intersection of the gravel road (**Point 6** on page 41) go one mile north to **Point 4** (page 40).

Here you will find a gate that may be closed and locked. As this book went to press, the land to the north was owned by Homestake Mining Company (now a subsidiary of Barrick International) which prohibited vehicular travel. The company was preparing to sell its holdings, however. We will try to post developments on our web site (Custertrail.com) but it is up to you to determine who currently owns the land—if necessary by providing the county tax assessor with township, range and section numbers. If the new owner permits public access, there is enough information in this chapter for you to discover key elements of the trail yourself. If there is any doubt, you should remain at the gate until the Expedition comes your way.

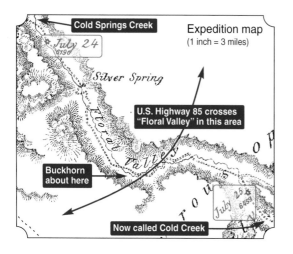

Everybody was sorry to break up camp after our first sweet step in the floral valley. The night was cold, almost frosty, and the morning air was really intoxicating. *(Inter-Ocean)*

The thermometer was nearly down to freezing point when we sat down to breakfast at 3:30 o'clock. Thin ice was actually found on some of our rubber blankets. But still the flowers never seemed to droop or chill. They are better used than we to this mountain air. Huge camp-fires at night, and in the morning before sunrise, are not only comforts but necessities. *(New York Tribune)*

1 44 12 47.8 This is the most likely site for the chilly campfire breakfast among the flowers, where several
104 09 36.8 drainages come into the valley. The band had played the night before to an eerie effect that still lingered the next morning.

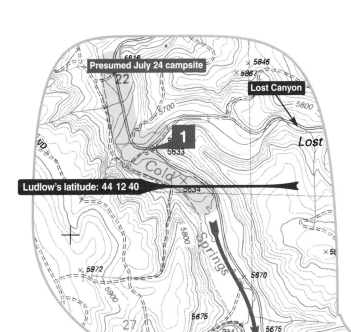

Presumed July 24 campsite

Lost Canyon

1

Lost

Ludlow's latitude: 44 12 40

We went up the river, finding new beauties and fresh gratifications at every step. *(Inter-Ocean)*

Through this beautiful valley meanders a stream of crystal water so cold as to render ice undesirable even at noonday. The temperature of two of the many springs found flowing into it was taken and ascertained to be 44 and 44½ deg. respectively. *(Custer)*

The accounts mention numerous springs in or near the Black Hills, many of which can still be found today. But only three are shown on the Expedition map—as if the futility of trying to mark them all soon became apparent—and only "Silver Spring" was listed by name, along this section of the trail (see Ludlow's map, opposite page). It was probably the first of the two springs mentioned by Custer, but no one recorded a reason for the special consideration it received.

July
25

3 44 11 15.0 This is probably the area of "Silver Spring."
104 08 34.0 Note the valley extending to the south of a hairpin turn in the road, correlating closely (except for direction) with the valley shown southwest of Silver Spring on the Expedition map. Ludlow indicates a jog in the trail at this location similar to the hairpin turn, both of which are shown to be about two miles from camp. We would welcome information about a current or historic spring here.

Being on Orderly Trumpeter, I heard a beautiful echo repeating my "first call" almost entire. *(Ewert)*

As we ascended the valley, our band which favors us every morning with a variety of selections played "How so fair" and "The Mocking Bird." We forgot the mocking bird in listening to the mocking hills which played an echo fuge with the band. . . . Never before had the echoes sung to Hoffmann or Flotow, but they never missed a note in their response. *(New York Tribune)*

2 44 11 29.8 Here the Expedition passed
104 08 28.6 what would later be one of at least four locations for Buckhorn, an address that had a hard time finding a home. A 1903 U.S.G.S. map used by C.C. O'Harra shows the original Buckhorn not far from the mouth of Barnett Draw (**Point A**, next page). Doris Vore Lake tells us that her grandfather, George Stanton, bought the Buckhorn post office from a woman and moved it north to his homestead at Stanton Draw. There it joined his granary, springhouse, creamery, barn, country store, and later a school. Today there is no trace of all this life and activity except for a couple of depressions in the ground. Stanton sold out to Homestake when his children were grown, and Buckhorn moved again, back up the valley as far as the old highway (**Point 5**, next page).

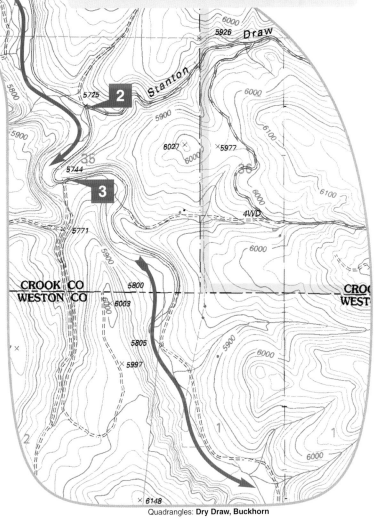

Quadrangles: **Dry Draw, Buckhorn**

Crossed the stream ten times, built bridges of pine poles in seven different places. *(Calhoun)*

The Expedition map splits the difference between Forsyth and Calhoun, showing eight crossings of Cold Springs Creek. It is interesting to imagine what those who followed—Indians and settlers alike—might have thought about those primitive corduroy bridges of timber beams supporting crosspieces of smaller logs that were laid side by side for a road.

From **Point 4**, turn around and drive south half a mile on the old highway.

5 44 08 59.7 To your right is the location of Buckhorn
104 05 42.4 as it is still shown on today's maps, even though U.S. 85 has left it behind. On the 1903 U.S.G.S. map C.C. O'Harra was using in the 1920s, he marked this spot in pen and labeled it "Present Buckhorn." He marked the Stanton homestead (**Point 2**) as "Second Buckhorn," and wrote in "First" above the town's name printed near Barnett Draw (**Point A**). Parker & Lambert's *Black Hills Ghost Towns* refers to a post office there in 1880, "served by a semi-weekly buckboard coming eastward from Raw Hide Buttes."

The whole valley is carpeted with flowers. I have gathered seventeen varieties within 20 square feet. *(Forsyth)*

Every step of the horses would crush ten, fifteen beautiful wild flowers to the earth. *(Ewert)*

About six miles up the stream we found a clear, beautiful spring with a temperature of 44½ degrees. *(New York Tribune)*

4 44 09 09.2 This is the gate to the valley that
104 06 13.0 may or may not be locked, depending on the current ownership of the land. The gate is also very close to six miles south of the July 24th camp, which means that both Custer and the *New York Tribune* reporter (Samuel J. Barrows) may have visited the spring that lies up the draw to your left (south), alongside the partially paved road that was once the main highway.

If this is your starting place for the day, remember that the headquarters staff would have appeared first around the bend ahead of you to the north. It would have been early in the morning, say 8 or 9 o'clock, with the wagon train far behind.

Camp was made by the advance at 11 o'clock. The train, having to bridge the stream many times, did not arrive till some four hours later. *(New York Tribune)*

. . . crossing the creek . . . no less than six times, as it seems to delight in meandering across the valley as often as possible. *(Forsyth)*

Quadrangles: **Dry Draw, Buckhorn**

So luxuriant in growth were they that men plucked them without dismounting from the saddle. . . . It was a strange sight to glance back at the advancing columns of cavalry, and behold the men with beautiful bouquets in their hands, while the head gear of their horses was decorated with wreaths of flowers fit to crown a queen of May. *(Custer)*

A bright pink and a white geranium, the former present in great abundance, seem to be undescribed varieties of the geranium maculatum. A number of other flowers found will have to be reserved until our return for exact classification. *(New York Tribune)*

There was something almost affecting in seeing rough, coarse men softened and refined by the sweetness of the flowers, taking out worn, tobacco-scented pocket-books and putting in a flower or two "just to send to the old woman." *(New York Tribune)*

The sense of having entered a paradise continued to affect the explorers throughout the second day in Floral Valley—even if the reaction was sometimes less than worship.

🖜 Deer abound in this and such valleys as lead into this. At times, when coming around a bend, we would surprise a drove of ten to twenty who would, on seeing us, give a warning whistle, then bound away up the sides of the hill. *(Ewert)*

This must once have been and still may be the favorite grazing ground of the elk. Eight pair of magnificent antlers were picked up. *(Pioneer)*

The woods frequently resounded with the clangorous cry of the crane. *(Ludlow)*

During our march a large male crane was seen on a rocky ledge. Presently it flew down into the valley. The column was halted and Gen. Custer with his rifle advanced under cover of the bushes and read the poor bird his death warrant. His wings measured from tip to tip were nearly seven feet long. Soon after one of our Indians caught a young crane alive, which was added to our Central Park collection. *(New York Tribune)*

Strange to relate, sand-hill cranes visit this valley; some of them were shot, and several of them were captured alive. They will help to increase the menagerie, which already includes hares, prairie dogs, night-hawks, owls, one eagle, and a cage of rattlesnakes. Additions will be made. *(Pioneer)*

Drive half a mile south to U.S. 85 (**Point 6**) and turn left. Go half a mile (passing yet another incarnation of Buckhorn) to a gravel road on your right.

7 44 09 13.7 Turn right onto Forest Service 969 here
104 04 38.3 and drive east eight-tenths of a mile.

B 44 09 13.0 Turn left (north) onto a dirt road that is not
104 03 53.8 shown on the topo map. Go seven-tenths of a mile to Cold Springs Creek.

8 44 09 29.6 Turn right onto FS 268 and follow the
104 03 44.2 Expedition route two-tenths of a mile. (REMINDER: Except for a small corner of the Black Hills National Forest around Point 10, you will be driving through private land the rest of the way. Please stay on the road.)

9 44 09 29.7 An older trail appears on the right from
104 03 31.9 beneath the curve in the present-day road. A deep rut separates itself in turn from the trail and runs along the edge of the creek. A single rut like this is a remnant of a very early trail used by wagons and possibly stage coaches. This trail may follow the wagon road Custer built in this valley in 1874. Continue four-tenths of a mile.

10 44 09 26.8 Just before the cattle guard, you may be
104 03 09.4 able to see a more indistinct rut down the slope about 60 feet.

Welcome to South Dakota, by the way. You crossed the border a couple hundred yards back (at Longitude 104 03 15) and are now in extreme southwestern Lawrence County. Continue a little more than two-tenths of a mile.

🖜 The beautiful stream, from which the Indians call the valley Minne-Lusa, or Running-Water Valley . . . *(Winchell)*

. . . grew larger and more rapid as we neared its source, supplied by cold, deep springs that started out of the mountain side every few rods. This was the only stream any of

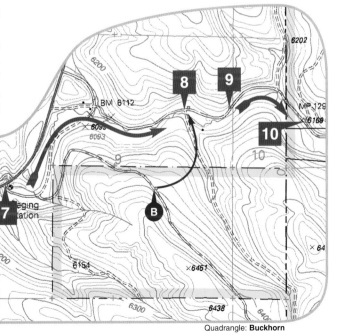

Quadrangle: **Buckhorn**

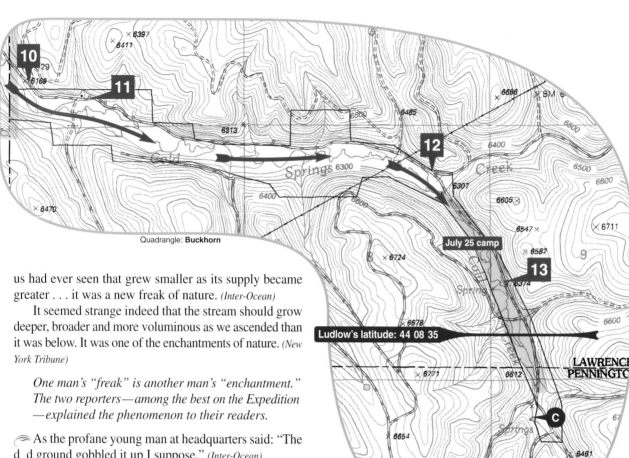

Quadrangle: **Buckhorn**

us had ever seen that grew smaller as its supply became greater . . . it was a new freak of nature. *(Inter-Ocean)*

It seemed strange indeed that the stream should grow deeper, broader and more voluminous as we ascended than it was below. It was one of the enchantments of nature. *(New York Tribune)*

One man's "freak" is another man's "enchantment." The two reporters—among the best on the Expedition—explained the phenomenon to their readers.

As the profane young man at headquarters said: "The d_d ground gobbled it up I suppose." *(Inter-Ocean)*

Prosaic observation broke the spell by noting that the sandy, porous stream bed of the lower valley gave place gradually to a hard, constant, smooth rock bed, over which the water flowed clear, cold and colorless, as perfect as water could be. *(New York Tribune)*

11 44 09 23.7 You should be able to see remnants of a 104 02 51.6 homestead in the draw to the north, which we have been told was once a stage station. The Cheyenne Deadwood Stage did alter its route in 1877, coming up Beaver Creek and crossing Cold Springs Valley on the way to Spearfish Creek and Cheyenne Crossing. Continue 1.4 miles.

If you are a geology buff, you will want to pay attention to the surrounding hills as you continue. Judging by Professor Winchell's description and mileage estimate, it was in this area that he discovered and named a new stratum.

After passing about nine miles from camp up this valley, a change occurs in the contour of the hills . . . . At the same time I see the first of a species of spruce. . . . Very soon a very prominent upheaval of limestone also appears on the left . . . . The stone is nearly white, crystalline, sub-saccharoidal, and coarsely granular when weathered and hard. . . . Twenty-five feet seen. As this is entirely a new development in respect to the geology of the Black Hills . . . I returned and repeated my observations. Noting carefully every indication of dip, and watching the float-pieces on the hillsides, I came to the conclusion that this limestone

underlies the foregoing sandstone. This I shall designate the *Minne-lusa Sandstone*, from the Indian name of the valley in which it was discovered. *(Winchell)*

The last sentence, naming the formation, is not included in the geologist's handwritten journal. The name appears to have been added during the editing process for the published report. Winchell's notebook, with its record of elevation measurements and the description of views from the tops of hills and cliffs, makes it clear that he was one of the more active climbers of the Expedition.

Going on up this valley, which now could more properly be styled a cañon, cut out as it is in a rock so hard, with such high and rocky walls on both sides, this limestone is seen to appear in vast proportions. It reaches a thickness of at least 245 feet, that being the height from the valley to the top of the hills, measured near this point by aneroid *[barometer]*. . . . From the tops of the hills, which are flat-topped and sparsely overgrown with stunted pines, can be seen a wide extent of country, having about the same level, very rough and rocky, cut by a net-work of ravines and cañons into a series of the most forbidding ridges, knolls, and valleys, undulating before the eyes, but shining with the reflected sunlight from the white spots of exposed limestone, and bristling with scattered and stunted pines. *(Winchell)*

As if ice, flowers, cranes and eerie echoes weren't enough, Floral Valley offered the explorers another experience.

Camp was made by the advance at 11 o'clock. . . . Meanwhile, the turgid clouds above came down to visit us and bathed the hills in a heavy mist. We were really camped within the clouds. The barometer marks 23.17. We must now be nearly 7,000 feet above the Tribune counting-room. *(New York Tribune)*

About noon . . . it became cloudy. At first the clouds swept along the mountain tops; but they gradually lowered until they almost touched our heads. *(Pioneer)*

Private Theodore Ewert apparently was not assigned to headquarters on this day. He was back along the trail with the wagon train when the fog came down, and he provides the most sensuous description.

At one time we were passing through a cloud; heavy masses of mist would come down the sides of the mountain and as it passed through the trees it would make a rushing sound as if a heavy wind was blowing, though it was comparatively calm, and our clothing was wet through and through. *(Ewert)*

12 44 09 08.3 This is a fork in the road and the valley.
104 01 09.4 The map shows Cold Springs Creek continuing to the left, but the Expedition felt otherwise. It took the right fork, now called Cold Creek. Follow them half a mile.

The stream suddenly disappeared, but the disappearance was only temporary—a little game of "hide and go seek"—for we found it higher up dividing into several tributary rills, fed by mossy springs. *(New York Tribune)*

About a mile below our present camp, the stream suddenly stopped flowing, and, upon seeking for the cause, we found that we had reached the head. Some six or eight beautiful springs bubbled up within a radius of 300 feet, forming at once a stream sufficient to turn a mill . . . Half a mile farther up we came to another spring, upon which we are now encamped. *(Forsyth)*

13 44 08 45.9 From this point on the road you can see
104 00 48.5 a spring (marked on the map) flowing from the base of the hill on your right—possibly the spring mentioned by Forsyth. In any case this location matches the distance from the fork (Point 12) as shown on the Expedition map. The spring is also about 300 yards north of Ludlow's latitude reading, a margin of error that will be seen a number of times in these pages. (Ludlow's longitude reading for the camp—104 03 34—lies 2.3 miles west of the valley, one of the larger discrepancies.)

Our camp is in the same valley we encamped in yesterday and owing to the want of breadth it is unavoidably scattered. *(Calhoun)*

Wood and water are in abundance, but the vast quantities of flowers crowds out the grasses, and the grazing is only fair. *(Forsyth)*

Finally the creek disappeared, entirely swallowed up in a cluster of springs, which were evidently its source. *(Inter-Ocean)*

Camped at the headsprings of the stream. *(Calhoun)*

C 44 08 17.5 Half a mile above Point 13 (at the inter-
104 00 41.4 section of Forest Service 279 and 268), these may be the "headsprings" mentioned by Calhoun and the *Inter-Ocean*. They were undoubtedly within the "scattered" camp, and Cold Creek is now a dry bed above this point. Forsyth's account, however, seems to place the headsprings below the camp "within a radius of 300 feet."

An old and deeply cut lodge trail ran up the valley, and, halting the command, the valleys leading out of Floral Valley were explored. The trail is said by one of the guides to be the old voyageur pack-trail, and is one of the regular routes between the hostile camp on the Tongue River and the agencies. Near the highest point many old camps and abandoned lodge poles were seen. Pursuing the lodge-trail a spring was reached, the waters of which flowed north and east. *(Ludlow)*

This may refer to the Freel Spring (one of two in the area with the same name) lying along Forest Service 109 almost straight south of the camp. If so, the Indian trail could have divided nearby, because fresh signs of recent travel were discovered to the east.

Gen. Forsyth and Col. Ludlow, after a camp site was chosen, went on ahead for seven or eight miles to learn the prospects for the next day's road. . . . Here *[on Castle Creek]* they noticed a fresh Indian trail and discovered a place on the bank of the little creek where ten or a dozen ponies had drunk the day before. *(New York Tribune)*

The New York Tribune reporter, divinity student Samuel J. Barrows, had apparently stayed in camp, ruminating on philosophical issues.

I am sitting at the door of my tent, looking out upon this lovely vale . . . Two days ago this charm was unknown and untraversed by the white man. Only now and then an Indian trespassed on its quietude. Is Nature a spendthrift that she lavished so abundantly her treasures on this distant solitude? Is there sadness in the thought that so many flowers were "born to blush unseen, and waste their sweetness on the desert air?" No; there is no loss, no wastage, no unrequited beauty here. How sweetly Emerson . . . has anticipated all questioning . . .

*Dear, tell them that if eyes were made for seeing;
Then beauty is its own excuse for being.*

(New York Tribune)

Sunday–Monday, July 26-27

Cold Creek to Castle Creek near Deerfield, with a layover

One of the prisoners endeavored to jerk the gun out of the hands of one of the scouts who resented this by pulling out his pistol. (Ewert)

July
26
27

The command left Floral Valley and crossed a gentle divide to Castle Creek, which was named by Gen. Custer for the limestone bluffs along the valley. A marshy area forced the wagon train to stop for a while, allowing Illingworth to capture one of the Expedition's best-known images. The scouts meanwhile came upon a small Lakota Sioux village where Deerfield Lake is now. Despite efforts at conciliation, there was a struggle and a shooting, and everyone in the village slipped away—except one elderly Sioux whom Custer retained as a hostage and guide. Distance traveled: 14 miles. Some reports said the first signs of gold were seen at the July 26 camp.

Taking the trail

U.S.G.S. MAPS: Buckhorn, Crooks Tower, Crows Nest Peak, Deerfield *(Parmlee Canyon optional)*

CAUTIONS: Most of the roads are smooth gravel, but several miles are unimproved dirt that can be very slick if there has been recent moisture. While a car might be used with extreme caution, a high-clearance vehicle will provide added security.

TO START: *From the north* on U.S. Highway 85, drive 6.8 miles east from Four Corners, Wyoming, or 9.2 miles west from Cheyenne Crossing, and turn south on Forest Service 969 (just east of the Buckhorn bar). Drive eight-tenths of a mile, turn left (north) on a dirt road, continue seven-tenths of a mile, and turn right on FS 268. Go 2.7 miles to the camp of July 25 (**Point 1**). See Points 7-13 in Chapter 3 for more detail. *From the south*, take Highway 17 west from Hill City, around Deerfield Lake and past the town of Deerfield to the intersection with FS 110 (**Point H**, page 50), which is 17.5 miles from Hill City. Follow FS 110 northwest 7.9 miles to the intersection with FS 117 (**Point 8**, page 46). Continue through the intersection another 3.5 miles to FS 109 (**Point B**). Turn right (north) on FS 109 and go 1.5 miles to the intersection with FS 268 (**Point A**). Turn right (north) and go a mile down the hill on FS 268 to Cold Creek (**Point 2**), then turn left and go half a mile to reach the campground of July 25 (**Point 1**).

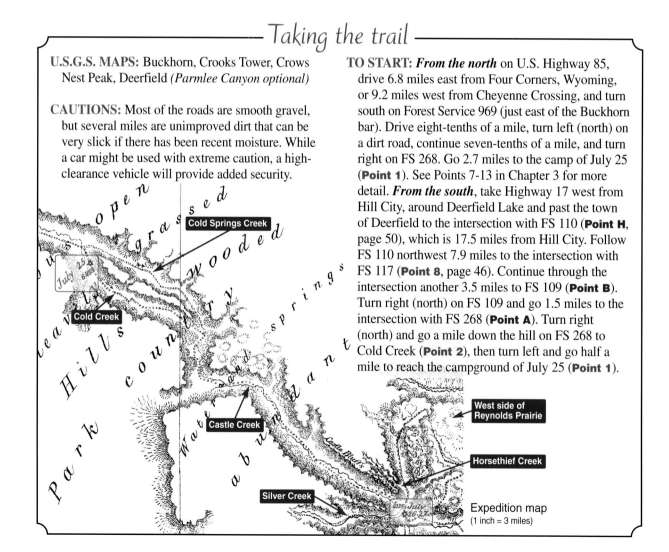

Expedition map
(1 inch = 3 miles)

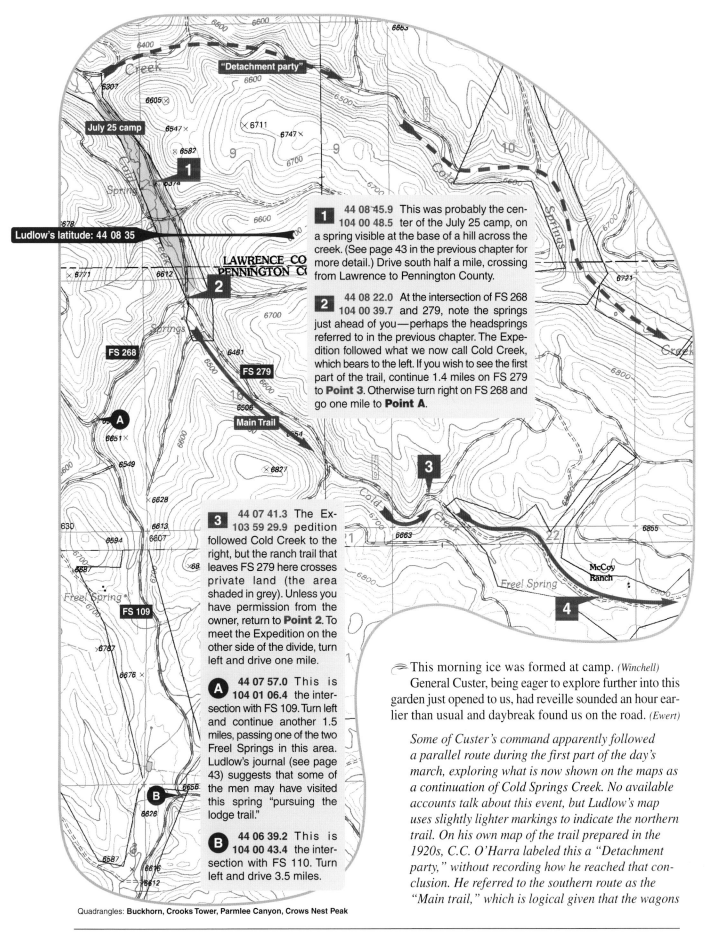

1 44 08 45.9 This was probably the center of the July 25 camp, on
104 00 48.5 ter of the July 25 camp, on
a spring visible at the base of a hill across the
creek. (See page 43 in the previous chapter for
more detail.) Drive south half a mile, crossing
from Lawrence to Pennington County.

2 44 08 22.0 At the intersection of FS 268
104 00 39.7 and 279, note the springs
just ahead of you—perhaps the headsprings
referred to in the previous chapter. The Expedition followed what we now call Cold Creek,
which bears to the left. If you wish to see the first
part of the trail, continue 1.4 miles on FS 279
to **Point 3**. Otherwise turn right on FS 268 and
go one mile to **Point A**.

3 44 07 41.3 The Expedition
103 59 29.9 pedition
followed Cold Creek to the
right, but the ranch trail that
leaves FS 279 here crosses
private land (the area
shaded in grey). Unless you
have permission from the
owner, return to **Point 2**. To
meet the Expedition on the
other side of the divide, turn
left and drive one mile.

A 44 07 57.0 This is
104 01 06.4 the intersection with FS 109. Turn left
and continue another 1.5
miles, passing one of the two
Freel Springs in this area.
Ludlow's journal (see page
43) suggests that some of
the men may have visited
this spring "pursuing the
lodge trail."

B 44 06 39.2 This is
104 00 43.4 the intersection with FS 110. Turn
left and drive 3.5 miles.

Quadrangles: **Buckhorn, Crooks Tower, Parmlee Canyon, Crows Nest Peak**

⌒ This morning ice was formed at camp. *(Winchell)*
General Custer, being eager to explore further into this
garden just opened to us, had reveille sounded an hour earlier than usual and daybreak found us on the road. *(Ewert)*

*Some of Custer's command apparently followed
a parallel route during the first part of the day's
march, exploring what is now shown on the maps as
a continuation of Cold Springs Creek. No available
accounts talk about this event, but Ludlow's map
uses slightly lighter markings to indicate the northern
trail. On his own map of the trail prepared in the
1920s, C.C. O'Harra labeled this a "Detachment
party," without recording how he reached that conclusion. He referred to the southern route as the
"Main trail," which is logical given that the wagons*

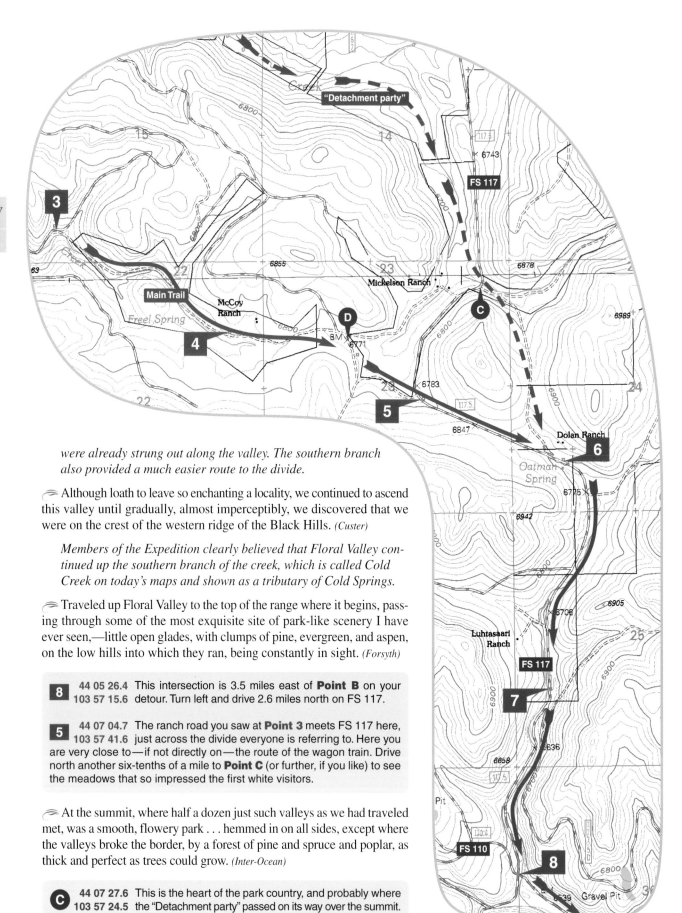

were already strung out along the valley. The southern branch also provided a much easier route to the divide.

⌒ Although loath to leave so enchanting a locality, we continued to ascend this valley until gradually, almost imperceptibly, we discovered that we were on the crest of the western ridge of the Black Hills. *(Custer)*

Members of the Expedition clearly believed that Floral Valley continued up the southern branch of the creek, which is called Cold Creek on today's maps and shown as a tributary of Cold Springs.

⌒ Traveled up Floral Valley to the top of the range where it begins, passing through some of the most exquisite site of park-like scenery I have ever seen,—little open glades, with clumps of pine, evergreen, and aspen, on the low hills into which they ran, being constantly in sight. *(Forsyth)*

8 44 05 26.4 This intersection is 3.5 miles east of **Point B** on your
103 57 15.6 detour. Turn left and drive 2.6 miles north on FS 117.

5 44 07 04.7 The ranch road you saw at **Point 3** meets FS 117 here,
103 57 41.6 just across the divide everyone is referring to. Here you are very close to—if not directly on—the route of the wagon train. Drive north another six-tenths of a mile to **Point C** (or further, if you like) to see the meadows that so impressed the first white visitors.

⌒ At the summit, where half a dozen just such valleys as we had traveled met, was a smooth, flowery park . . . hemmed in on all sides, except where the valleys broke the border, by a forest of pine and spruce and poplar, as thick and perfect as trees could grow. *(Inter-Ocean)*

C 44 07 27.6 This is the heart of the park country, and probably where
103 57 24.5 the "Detachment party" passed on its way over the summit.

Quadrangles: **Crooks Tower, Crows Nest Peak**

Instead of being among barren heaths, as might be supposed, we found ourselves winding our way through a little park whose natural beauty may well bear comparison with the loveliest portion of Central Park. *(Custer)*

Conceive the effect of such a scene upon the senses, at sunrise—the senses of people only half awake, and under that indefinite sort of depression that early rising always creates. *(Inter-Ocean)*

About eight o'clock we came to the head of this floral valley. *(Ewert)*

Did you notice that, speaking of the same place, the Inter-Ocean *refers to sunrise and Ewert to 8:00 A.M.? The reporter William Curtis was evidently riding with headquarters, while Private Ewert was with his company guarding the much-slower wagon train. Also note that Custer refers to "winding" his way through the park, while the wagons only crossed at the southern end. It seems reasonable that the General himself was leading the detachment, which found a kind of crossroads at the summit.*

It is a favorite camping ground of the Indians, and the velvet carpet, with its groundwork of green, and tracery of geranium, lilies, roses, and innumerable other floral designs, was marred in places by the ashes of campfires. Several relics of an ancient and memorable character were found, and immediately seized upon by the curiosity of hunters, and the wagons were soon laden with an old sheet-iron boiler, supposed to have been stolen from Raynolds in 1859, for he reports having lost a greater part of his outfit by Indian thieving; several worthless bows and arrows, and a number of old elk antlers. *(Inter-Ocean)*

The bows and arrows wouldn't be "worthless" today.

There are two springs, very cold, on the summit. *(Grant)*

Today they're called Freel Spring (Point 4, on private land) and Oatman Spring (Point 6), which is about where the "Detachment party" rejoined the main trail.

7 44 06 04.5 103 57 05.5 An old trail is visible on the left (east) side, just beyond the drainage ditch—a deep rut left by some of the earliest wagon traffic. Standing in the depression, you can see that it crosses under the present road and continues beneath a fence on the other side of a cattle guard. This early road may have followed the Expedition's tracks down the valley, just as Custer was following a much older trail. Drive another eight-tenths of a mile, keeping in mind this description by Gen. Forsyth.

Upon leaving the crest of the watershed . . . we found an old Indian trail, which we followed up through a rocky defile, which, after various windings, brought us into another valley, somewhat larger than the one we had just left, with a fine stream of water running in just the direction we wished. *(Forsyth)*

8 44 05 26.4 103 57 15.6 Here begins the "larger" valley referred to by Forsyth, where FS 110 crosses FS 117.

The Expedition was no doubt the largest population ever seen in this corner of the Black Hills, where today you might observe one or two cars passing by in an hour. But it was once a less lonely place. C.C. O'Harra noted on his research map the presence of "Limestone District School No. 7" near the intersection at **Point 8**. *It would have served the ranch families whose names you still see on the topographic maps, even though their home places now lie empty or have vanished altogether. Another note on O'Harra's map reads: "C.C. O'Harra, Chas H. Fulton, Ole A. Soholt, Andrew Mickelson, George Thomson were at this Benchmark (***Point D***) July 25, 1928." These are all echoes of the past, with two of those names now used for draws leading into Castle Creek.*

Expedition accounts suggest there had been a well-used Indian campground near School No. 7.

We followed this "vale of delight" for some few miles, when we found another going to the right at right angles . . . we took the left hand, leading almost directly east. . . . We marched but a few rods when lo! what should we find but an Indian encampment, with all the evidences of having been lately occupied—that

From **Point 5**, drive south eight-tenths of a mile.

6 44 06 51.8 103 57 00.9 Oatman Spring lies south of the road here, steadily filling a tank just as it might have filled canteens and barrels for grateful explorers in 1874.
The "Detachment party" was well ahead of the wagons. Follow it one mile south on FS 117.

Quadrangle: **Crows Nest Peak**

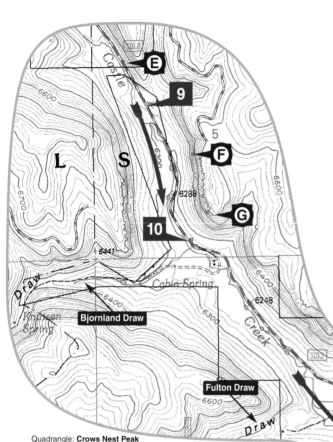

Quadrangle: **Crows Nest Peak**

and finally they were seen only as a rarity. In their place we found a heavy luxuriant growth of grasses, and as the grass had in Floral Valley been crowded out altogether we, and more especially our stock, found it an agreeable change. *(Ewert)*

Mr. Illingworth still continues to photograph the scenery. *(Pioneer)*

*In fact, Expedition photographer William Illingworth had time for three pictures in the upper reaches of the valley, including **Photo 809**, "Wagon train passing through Castle Creek Valley" (page 174; **Point F** on the map at left). Today it is perhaps his best-known view, sometimes called the "String of Pearls."*

E 44 04 44.9 At 2.4 miles from Point 8, look up the em-
103 54 44.4 bankment to your left, where Illingworth exposed **Photo 808**, "Castle Creek Valley, near the divide" (page 172). You can match the photo fairly well from the road, or you can scramble up the bank—to the actual location of these coordinates—for a more exact view.
Continue two-tenths of a mile and stop beside the road.

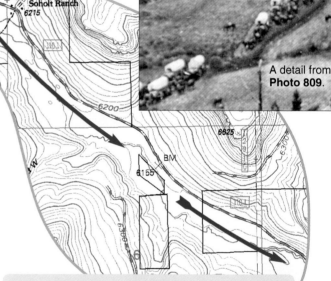

A detail from **Photo 809**.

DEVEREAUX LIBRARY ARCHIVES

is within the past two days. There we found tepee poles, and the remains of antelope and deer. *(Press)*

*This sounds like the intersection at **Point 8**, where FS 117 continues south up a valley "to the right." Since a rod is 5½ yards, the camp area would have been a very short distance east—perhaps within view of the intersection.*

We became aware that we had now, in real earnest, entered the red man's sanctum sanctorum, that this portion of his allotted ground was to have been kept sacred from the prying paleface. We also found that this was his work-shop; large stacks of tepee poles were found along this stream. The chips and bark, as the poles had been reduced to the required size, were still scattered green over the ground. Numbers of small stakes driven in the sod told us that here their hides and furs had been stretched to dry or to undergo their process of tanning; no doubt all trophies of the hunt were here made ready for market. *(Ewert)*

Fresh pony tracks excited a still greater interest. *(New York Tribune)*

Set or check your odometer at **Point 8** and turn left on FS 110, passing through the Indian "workshop" as you begin driving 2.4 miles east along Castle Creek.

The flowers near the summit were as dense as on the other side, but as we descended they gradually thinned out

9 44 04 36.5 From here you should be able to see a
103 54 37.6 pair of limestone towers slightly more than half-way up the hill ahead of you.

F 44 04 25.3 The towers are in **Photo 809**, the "String
103 54 22.7 of Pearls" photo (page 174). Comparing it to the present landscape, you may be able to figure out where your vehicle would have appeared in the picture, and see where the wagons lined up on the other side of the valley.

G 44 04 14.0 Illingworth carried his camera about a
103 54 19.0 quarter mile south to take **Photo 810**, "Castle Creek Valley, looking east" (page 176).

Why did Illingworth have time to ascend a hill and photograph the wagon train stopped in its tracks?

We were made to wait about four hours by a large spring that had made the entire breadth of the valley marsly, and "H" Company, who were pioneers, had a hard job constructing a bridge over it. *(Ewert)*

We came upon large springs of water which made a very large stream. This was dammed up every few hundred feet by Beaver and at one place made quite a large pond. *(Grant)*

10 44 04 08.5   A little more than half a mile from Point 9, 103 54 25.7   pull over at a wide spot on the curve. Note how narrow the valley has become here, where a stream from Bjornland Draw enters Castle Creek among the trees.

The wagon train was stopped just above Bjornland Draw, which suggests that the offending stream came from what is now called Cabin Spring. But it was not the only trouble spot along Castle Creek.

⤳ We entered another of those narrow, graceful avenues . . . having the company of a dashing little trout stream, which opened out, wherever the valley swelled into wider proportions, into tiny little lakes, which were very beautiful to the eye but destructive to a wagon train. Bridges of corduroy were soon supplied, however, from the timber that skirted the edges of the water, and we went on. *(Inter-Ocean)*

"Toots" Soholt, who lived at Soholt Draw for much of the 20th Century, remembered seeing remnants of those corduroy log bridges as a girl. Below Soholt Draw, the valley begins to take on a different appearance.

⤳ The face of nature soon began to change. Our valley descended rapidly and our brook tumbled recklessly over little cataracts; on the tops and sides of the hills great lime-stone rocks began to creep out, which grew in proportions as we went further down, till they seemed like the battlements of some ancient race of giant warriors. The hills were steeper, the valley wider, and the timber thinner and more scattered. *(Inter-Ocean)*

The high limestone ridges surrounding the camp had weathered into castellated forms of considerable grandeur and beauty. *(Ludlow)*

The creek . . . is bordered by high bluffs, on the crest of which are located prominent walls of solid rock, presenting here and there the appearance of castles constructed from masonry. From their marked resemblance I named this stream Castle Creek. *(Custer)*

Continue 4.1 miles on FS 110, noticing the changes and considering the different kinds of traffic the valley has seen.

⤳ This valley seems to have been a thoroughfare for [the Indians] supposed by some to be a trail from Red Cloud's agency to the hunting grounds. . . . One would judge from these trails that the Indian is an admirer of all that is grand and beautiful in nature. They always select the wildest spots for camp ground, surrounded by the most romantic hills and dales, and bounded on one side by the prettiest of rippling streams—a fit place for student or lover. *(Press)*

We found several places where there had been recent encampments. The trail grew more fresh as we went further on, and our scouts began, in their peculiar way, to show impatience. They unbraided their hair, rubbed vermilion on their faces, wrapped towels and white cloths around their heads, putting bunches of feathers in for a crest—all this in the saddle as we marched along—and hummed the dreary monotone of their warsong. *(Inter-Ocean)*

St. Paul Press correspondent Fred Power, who tried riding with the wagons on July 22 and didn't like it (chapter 1), had moved as far forward as possible. Nor was he shy about letting his readers know.

⤳ I was riding with the General, when one of his orderlies called his attention to smoke ahead. From that moment everything was in a state of excitement. . . . On reaching there we found every indication of its having been occupied only a few hours before. *(Press)*

Fires were still burning, deer meat on the ground, pony tracks not one hour old; skeletons of wigwams and lodge poles on which their tepees had recently been hung. *(Calhoun)*

As the site was an excellent one for camp, Gen. Custer concluded to halt here. *(New York Tribune)*

11 44 01 57.6   Park in a turnout (the *second* one you will 103 50 40.4   come to) overlooking the camp of July 26-27. Imagine that Custer has stopped somewhere in the meadow right in front of you. He is hours ahead of the wagon train, accompanied by his scouts and two cavalry companies, and now he has some decisions to make.

⤳ At 10 o'clock A.M. . . . *(Calhoun)*
About noon . . . the advance came upon a camp where the fires were still burning. *(Pioneer)*
After the tents were up, and the preparations for the night made, Bloody Knife and twenty-five Ree

Prickett Ranch

Miller Ranch

Castle

Camp of July 26-27

Silver

Deer Lodge

Historic Site

Quadrangle: **Deerfield**

scouts were sent out to see where the trail led, with orders to attack no one but simply to reconnoiter and report. It was the work of only a moment for the Rees to put themselves in war dress, and they were off. *(Inter-Ocean)*

Consider the managerial challenge Custer faced in a possible confrontation with the Sioux. His intentions seem to have been genuinely peaceful—you will be able to judge for yourself in a moment—but his Arikara (Ree) scouts were still suffering from recent losses at the hands of their bitter enemies.

☞A few days before we left Fort Lincoln, the Sioux attacked a Ree village near Fort Berthold; and a battle ensued, in which a son of Bloody Knife and a brother of Bear's Eye were killed, with several other warriors of the band we have with us. These deaths they were anxious to revenge. *(Inter-Ocean)*

Custer clearly trusted his head scout, or felt in control of him, in a situation where Bloody Knife (seen in the "bear photo," pages 254 and 256) could easily have provoked a fight.

☞We had just dismounted and unsaddled our horses, and thrown our weary bodies down to rest inside of the pines that surrounded us, when our advance scouts returned. *(Press)*

Black Medicine and Bare Arm soon returned, reporting that there were five lodges . . . encamped about two miles below us, and just around a point in the valley. *(Pioneer)*

"Bloody Knife," as directed, had concealed his party in a woody ravine, where they awaited further orders. *(Custer)*

Boots and saddles was sounded, and Gen. Custer, with one company of cavalry, went dashing down the valley to where the scouts were secreted, and your correspondent, armed with a lead pencil, followed. *(Bismarck Tribune)*

After a run of about two miles along the valley we halted just under the crest of a hill which rose between us and the Indian village about three-quarters of a mile further on. *(New York Tribune)*

If you care to follow this series of events, leave the parking area at **Point 11** and drive south six-tenths of a mile.

H 44 01 30.5 At the intersection with FS 17, turn right
103 50 21.5 and continue 1.5 miles. On the way (near the intersection with FS 291 at **Point I**) you will come around a "point in the valley."

J 44 01 30.5 Here is a good place to pull off the road,
103 50 21.5 at 2.1 miles from the camp, where several ridges come down into Deerfield Lake. Any one of them could be the "crest of a hill"—now underwater—behind which Bloody Knife was waiting for Custer. The Sioux lodges were another three-quarters of a mile down the lake.

☞Gen. Custer . . . leaving the command in the valley, climbed to the crest of the hill overlooking the Indian village. *(Bismarck Tribune)*

The opposite side of the valley was flanked with a hill covered with a dense wood. What an opportunity this offered to conceal a foe. Gen. Custer sent an orderly back to camp telling Col. Hart to come up immediately with his whole company. The Sioux are wily enough. It was possible that the five teepees might only be a decoy. The precaution was well taken, but proved to be unnecessary. *(New York Tribune)*

It is hard to miss the irony of Custer's precautions against five lodges in light of his precipitous actions at Little Big Horn two years later. But there was no declared war in 1874, and the village—lying in the valley now covered by Deerfield Lake—was just what it appeared to be.

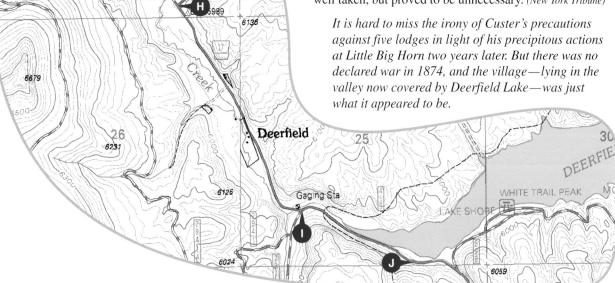

Quadrangle: **Deerfield**

How pretty the little village of clean, white new-covered teepees looked in the nestling valley below. *(New York Tribune)*

How pretty the little village of clean white tepees nestling in the valley below appeared. *(Bismarck Tribune)*

Do you detect an odd echo from the New York Tribune *to the* Bismarck Tribune *in these descriptions? A great many more echoes—with a similar deterioration in the grace of language—can be found if you compare the accounts of this day as printed in the book* Prelude to Glory. *The same subjects are discussed in the same manner, often word for word, including the following:*

I amused myself by taking a phonographic report of the conversation *[soon to take place within the village]*, being the first phonographic report ever made in the Black Hills; and I am sure on looking it over that, in point of intelligence and interest, it is painfully superior to the senseless twaddle which so often distinguishes social entertainment in civilized circles. *(New York Tribune)*

. . . your correspondent amusing himself reporting the conversation infinitely superior to the senseless gossip which is too apt to prevail in civilized society. *(Bismarck Tribune)*

You may recall from chapter 1 that the Bismarck reporter was Nathan H. Knappen, the erstwhile mosquito netting salesman who apparently cribbed his facts on Inyan Kara from the St. Paul Pioneer— *getting several of them wrong in the process. In this case he at least did not try to claim an ability to take "phonographic" reports, which refers to an early system of shorthand.*

The real mystery is whether Samuel J. Barrows of the New York Tribune *was aware of Knappen's plagiarism and, if so, why he permitted it. Perhaps Barrows—preparing for the life of a Unitarian minister—was simply a kind man. To be fair, there are also some marked similarities in the* St. Paul Press *dispatch as well. Although all three reporters claim to have been present at the village, it is possible that Barrows—with his "phonographic" abilities—acted as an early pool reporter, sharing information with the other correspondents.*

But we left the General and a few observers on a hill overlooking the village.

As soon as the Rees had heard of the proximity of this Sioux camp they were wild with delight. . . . They were only restrained from an immediate onslaught on the village with the greatest difficulty. . . . "Do not dare to fire a shot unless the Sioux attack you," was the General's only reply to this murderous breathing, said, however, in a tone which implied a penalty not expressed, and which the Rees did not dare to incur. *(New York Tribune)*

The Rees . . . gave every indication of being in a bad humor with the General because he would not let them go forward and slake their thirst for blood. *(Press)*

DEVEREAUX LIBRARY ARCHIVES

This enlarged, enhanced detail of the headquarters area from the distant right side of Illingworth's **Photo 814** (page 186) shows abandoned lodge poles to the left of the Sibley tent that belonged to Custer—one of several photographs in which it appears.

Our scouts . . . remember the vengeful and merciless cruelties of the Sioux, and . . . themselves are not distinguished, any more than white people, by a practical love for the Christian law of forgiveness. *(New York Tribune)*

The scene in the valley now flooded by Deerfield Lake remained tranquil a while longer, the occupants unaware that they were being observed.

I must confess that the encampment looks beautiful, as we saw it through our glasses. The white buckskins newly tanned, that covered the lodge poles, were as white as an officer's tent before it comes on contact with storm or sunshine. The squaws seated on the ground cutting up deer meat, others eating and some beading moccasins, the young Indians lying around in every attitude enjoying their freedom and the sunshine, and the dogs, lying in the shade of a teepee, were happy. *(Press)*

They were all alone in this beautiful valley with their wives and children. No harm could come to them for the white man was far away and so was the hostile Ree. Neither of them ever came to this lovely hunting-ground. So the village rested in fancied security. *(New York Tribune)*

But Indian dreams of security, like those of the white man, are often only dreams. *(Press)*

Custer sent his men in three waves, the second and third of which seem to have defeated the purpose of the ones just before them.

I then dispatched Agard, the interpreter, with a flag of truce, accompanied by two of our Sioux scouts, to acquaint

Slow Bull soon after went into the woods and did not return again.

the occupants of the lodges that we were friendly disposed and desired to communicate with them. *(Custer)*

Again cautioning the Rees against shedding blood, and sending the Sioux guides with them, Gen. Custer ordered both to advance to the village, presuming that the sight of a body of Indians coming down the valley would create less alarm than the approach of a body of cavalry. *(New York Tribune)*

To prevent either treachery or flight . . . I galloped the remaining portion of my advance and surrounded the lodges. This was accomplished almost before they were aware of our presence. *(Custer)*

Fearful that the Rees might not be able to control themselves, we were coming down the valley at what a cavalryman calls "a rattling pace." Our gait and appearance were not calculated to allay alarm. *(New York Tribune)*

Imagine the surprise and fright of the unsuspecting women and children when a man, half Indian and half white, mounted on an Indian pony, with a white flag in his hand, came riding into the village, and close behind him, almost reaching the village before he had time to assure them of his friendly mission, a band of 25 Ree Indians dressed in war garb and looking murderously cruel. The children were struck with consternation and fled to the bushes. The squaws were almost dumb with fright. [Agard's] words did little to reassure them. Slow Bull, one of their warriors, was near by and bravely came forward. But what was he against so many? [Agard] pointed up the valley: "Here comes the White Chief himself," he said in Sioux, "the one in the blue shirt galloping at the head of the gray horses; he will protect you." *(New York Tribune)*

Gen. Custer was the first to alight from his horse and greeting Slow Bull with the customary Indian salutation, "How," grasped Slow Bull by the hand. *(Bismarck Tribune)*

He invited us to be seated, when an interpreter told him we were not come to fight, but to make peace with them, and ask them about the country, to which the warrior nodded significantly, and, filling a pipe, passed it around, each member of the circle taking a whiff and blowing the smoke — if he could, and with killikinick tobacco it is not a very agreeable experiment — through his nose. *(Inter-Ocean)*

Guards were immediately stationed at the entrance of each tent with strict orders to allow none of our scouts to enter. *(Ewert)*

Soon the children began to peep out of the bushes, and then timidly to come forward and look at the new comers. Slow Bull was hospitable, and . . . invited us inside. Meanwhile some of the older children were sent to call One Stab,

the chief of the band, and three other bucks who were in the woods hunting near a neighboring deer-lick. *(New York Tribune)*

Which band did the hunters belong to? Take your pick.

They belonged to the Brule tribe of Sioux. *(Inter-Ocean)*
They were a hunting party of the Ogilalah tribe. *(Pioneer)*
The party were mostly Unkpapas from the Red Cloud Agency. *(New York Tribune)*

Red Cloud was Oglala, in any case, and it turned out that one of his daughters was about to act as Custer's hostess. Waiting for One Stab, Samuel Barrows had time to examine his surroundings in the lodge.

Slow Bull went out to watch for the other Indians. Slow Bull's squaw we found was a daughter of Red Cloud. . . . with a broad full face and a straight nose, a little hooked at the end, long black hair braided into a pair of "tails," dark, bright eyes, and a fine set of teeth, which just then were composedly chewing the gum of the pine tree. . . . The family effects, such as were not needed for immediate use, were packed up in clean skins tied with thongs and disposed around the tent. Other skins were spread on the ground to lie upon. In one corner was a long dress or gown of buckskin, completely covered with beads. . . . Mrs. R.C. Slow Bull had given a pony for it. *(New York Tribune)*

Mrs. Slow Bull . . . informed Gen. Custer that she had not a bit of coffee or sugar and the children had been crying for some days for both. The General informed her that he would make the little ones happy by supplying this deficiency, when she chatted more sweetly, Agard acting as interpreter. *(Bismarck Tribune)*

This was the conversation recorded "phonographically" by Barrows as they waited for the head man.

One Stab, the chief, an old man with a dilapitated (sic) felt hat which would have branded him as a pauper anywhere, a breech-clout and colored cotton agency shirt, came in, and we smoked the pipe of peace again. He told us all he knew about the country, the course of the streams, the bend of the hills, and gave us some suggestions about the road. He told us that there were twelve men and women and fifteen children in his village. *(New York Tribune)*

General Custer told them . . . that the Great Father at Washington had sent him into the Black Hills to find out what sort of a country it was, and whether the Sioux had a good reservation. They had not come to fight, but only to see, and to make a map of the country. *(Inter-Ocean)*

"Tell him," said the General to the interpreter, "that . . . we are making short marches, not longer than they make

I was of the opinion that they were not acting in good faith.

with their lodges, and if they will go with us until we get out of the Black Hills, I will give rations every day to all of the party." *(New York Tribune)*

One Stab apparently did not think much of the idea, and Custer's response—as recorded by Barrows—shows that the general himself was capable of irony.

One Stab replied: "We have only five Indians here but if you want today I can do it. I can show you the way clear up this creek here; and then you can go yourselves. I do not want to have any trouble with the white man; I have always been with the white man; I never stayed with the hostiles." "I have seen a great many Indians," said the General, "but I have never seen any that have been with the hostiles." *(New York Tribune)*

In a later dispatch (which was actually published first), Barrows adds another side of the story:

One Stab has recently returned from the hostile camp on Powder River, and says that the Indians lost 10 killed in the fight with the Bozeman Exploring Party. *(New York Tribune)*

They did not know that there were any white people in the Black Hills, and had not heard of the expedition. . . . Some of them seemed reserved and timid and showed some fear of the Rees, their bitter enemies; others seemed social and anxious for further acquaintance. The timid ones said they had been in the Hills about two months, and that their time was up, and that they must return at once to the agency to draw their annuities; the others thought there was no need of so hasty a return. *(Pioneer)*

The General again asked if [One Stab] could not give them a man for a few days, and if they could not stay over in camp for two or three days. One Stab at first hesitated, but Red Cloud's daughter said, "Yes, they could stay over a couple of nights as well as not," and One Stab assented. It was then arranged that the male Indians should come to our camp that afternoon and get some rations. *(New York Tribune)*

This passage raises some interesting questions about a woman's—or at least this woman's—role in the making of decisions. Did the daughter of Red Cloud have more influence with the head of the village than was usual? Or was she in fact the wife of the elderly One Stab—as both Ludlow and the Inter-Ocean reported—and not of Slow Bull? Given the events that were about to take place, we also wonder whether she had already devised a strategy.

I entered into an agreement with the leading men that they should encamp with us a few days, and give us such information concerning the country as we might desire. *(Custer)*

We took our departure for camp, there to await the wagons, which were some distance in the rear; but in the course of time they made their appearance in good order. *(Press)*

July
26
27

If you are stopped at Deerfield Lake, you may wish to return to the site of the remaining events. Turn around and drive back to FS 110 (**Point H**) and continue just two-tenths of a mile to the lower parking area, on the left.

12 44 01 41.9 This turnout is near the southern end of
103 50 26.4 the camp, which can be said with certainty thanks to the photographs of William Illingworth. His first image in this area, of the wagons coming into camp, was recorded from a spot directly across the valley, about 375 yards away.

K 44 01 42.2 This is roughly where Illingworth set up
103 50 41.7 his camera for **Photo 811**, "Lime Stone Peak and Castle Creek Valley" (page 178). The wagon train appears to be traveling along the foot of the slopes on the far side of the valley, where the road is today.

Later in the afternoon . . . *(Custer)*

Two or three hours after . . . *(New York Tribune)*

Four of the men came up, and were received at headquarters with every mark of attention, respect and kindness including much hand-shaking. *(Pioneer)*

Perhaps we should have had no difficulty in retaining their confidence, if it had not been for the close proximity of the Rees, who still looked upon them with an evil eye. . . . Slow Bull soon after went into the woods and did not return again. *(New York Tribune)*

Pretty soon another did the same thing. *(Grant)*

The other two seemed uneasy and did not want to wait for the presents, but proposed to come up in the morning and get them. The general then borrowed the rations from one of the companies, the supply train still not having come. *(Pioneer)*

*If the supply train had not arrived, it would seem that all of this took place before Illingworth photographed (from **Point K**) the arrival of the wagons, which came in at 5:00 P.M. according to a table in Ludlow's report.*

"One Stab" expressed a fear of the Rees. *(Inter-Ocean)*

I ordered presents of sugar, coffee, and bacon to be given them; and, to relieve their pretended anxiety for the

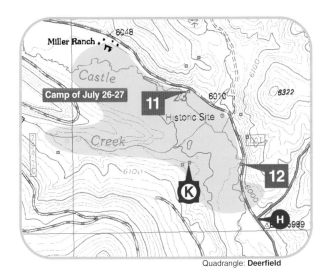

Quadrangle: **Deerfield**

safety of their village during the night, I ordered a party of fifteen of my command to return with them. *(Custer)*

The General sent word to Lieut. Wallace to select fifteen of his most reliable Santees [*Sioux*] and send them down with the two men carrying the rations, with orders to stay on guard at their encampment all night, to prevent molestation, and to come up with them in the morning to our camp to receive more rations. Wallace requested the ration bearers One Stab and Long Bear to wait a few minutes until he could select the friendly escort. *(Pioneer)*

While they were saddling up, One Stab and the other Indian, who did not know of this intention, mounted their ponies and rode off. *(New York Tribune)*

There is a small discrepancy here, the Tribune *perhaps giving One Stab the benefit of a doubt.*

They took their departure without much ceremony. *(Press)*

I was of the opinion that they were not acting in good faith. In this I was confirmed when the two remaining ones set off at a gallop in the direction of the village. *(Custer)*

The General sent a Sioux scout to request their return. But to return, they refused. The General, not wishing his guard of fifteen to go down alone, but in company with the men carrying the rations, lest going down alone might cause alarm in the Ogilalah camp, directed the ration bearers to be brought back, and ordered several Santees to follow them. *(Pioneer)*

I sent a second party with orders to repeat the request, and if not complied with, then to take hold of the bridles of their ponies and lead them back, but to offer no violence. *(Custer)*

This order was obeyed to the letter; but Long Bear, refusing to return, one of the Santee sergeants took hold of the pony's bridle. *(Pioneer)*

The Indian at the same time grasped the Santee's gun and saying, "I may as well be killed today as tomorrow," tried to wrest it from him. *(New York Tribune)*

The sergeant only saved it by throwing himself from his horse; and, regarding Long Bear's act as the beginning of hostilities, he fired at him as he retreated up the hill from the valley. One or two other shots were fired at him. *(Pioneer)*

Eight or ten shots were fired after him. *(Ewert)*

Custer's own account makes the whole thing sound accidental, as if there was no overt act or intent in violating his order to "offer no violence."

One of the two Indians seized the musket of one of the scouts and endeavored to wrest it from him. Failing in this he released his hold after the scout became dismounted in the struggle, and set off as fast as his pony could carry him, but not before the musket of the scout was discharged. From blood discovered afterward it was evident that either the Indian or his pony was wounded. I hoped that neither was seriously hurt. *(Custer)*

The Indian and the pony made good their escape . . . . Poor old One Stab was not so fortunate, and was captured and brought back to camp. *(Press)*

The chief was brought to headquarters and scouts sent after the fugitives. When they reached the village the lodges were all gone, and the trail led down to the valley toward the east. It seems that immediately upon our departure the whole outfit pulled up stakes and departed. *(Inter-Ocean)*

Hours before the squaws had folded their tents like the Arabs and silently stolen away. *(New York Tribune)*

The visit of the four Indians to our camp was not only to obtain the rations promised them in return for future services but to cover the flight of their lodges. *(Custer)*

Had the daughter of Red Cloud already thought of this when she encouraged One Stab to accept Custer's invitation? Remember, it was her father's campaign that forced the U.S. government to close the Bozeman Trail and abandon three forts in 1867. That set the stage for the Fort Laramie Treaty of 1868, which would soon be violated as a result of the Expedition's discoveries.

The fear felt by the people in the village would prove costly to them.

They had destroyed all their camp equipage, chopped up their tent poles, cut holes in their kettles, and thrown away their dried meat. Their trail was followed for a long distance; but they had been many hours on the way. *(Pioneer)*

Bloody Knife and his men were out five hours or more, but returned scalpless, having been unable to follow the trail in the dark, and there were howls of disappointment, and anger around the Indian camp. *(Inter-Ocean)*

The Scout remained out until after 10 P.M. . . . . Genl Custer was very uneasy until they did return. . . . After they returned he made Eagard [*Agard*] tell The Man Who Stabs [*One Stab*] that his party had all escaped . . . which news seemed to relieve the old fellow very much. *(Power)*

"One Stab" is 63 years of age and has many a wrinkle in his face, and other marks indicative of the imbecility of old age. He is guarded by soldiers, and the Commdg. Officer

DEVEREAUX LIBRARY ARCHIVES

One Stab was probably in custody when Illingworth photographed the wagon train in **No. 811** (page 178), from which this detail is taken. The wagons may be waiting while camp areas are designated for each of the companies.

has so fixed it that during his incarceration the Indian scouts will have no chance of gobbling him up. *(Calhoun)*

In an interview with the General he claimed to know nothing of the flight of his village, and explained it by saying the squaws must have been frightened. *(Inter-Ocean)*

He had nothing to do with it. It was all the work of the young bucks. He did not know himself that the village was going to move. *(New York Tribune)*

He received a lecture on truthfulness, and was told that he would be kept a hostage until we were out of the Hills, and must show us a good road. He was evidently quite relieved to know that he wasn't to be tortured and shot, but the expression on his lean, wrinkled face showed "there was trouble in the old man's mind," and he wrapped himself in his blanket, and silence for the remainder of the night. *(Inter-Ocean)*

He . . . says he would be happy if his people only knew that he was alive and well cared for. *(New York Tribune)*

This may have been a legitimate concern. The Aug. 5

Chicago Inter-Ocean *quoted a report by a "large number of Indians . . . who say that Stabber [One Stab], a prominent Indian in the disturbances last spring at the agencies, and several others, were killed by Custer's men. There seems to be much feeling in consequence among the Indians." Eight days later the newspaper reported that Spotted Tail's band was refusing to move to a new reservation. "The Indians at both reservations are in a high state of excitement over the killing of Stabber and party, reported a few days ago."*

The fate of Long Bear is involved in mystery. But the next day, his saddle and blankets were found in the woods. *(Pioneer)*

He had evidently thrown them off to lighten his pony. The saddle and blanket were covered with blood, and one thickness of the blanket had been perforated by the bullet. The ball had probably entered the man's thigh and passed out in front of the saddle, inflicting probably only a flash wound. *(New York Tribune)*

Monday, July 27
Layover on Castle Creek

Monday broke clear & brig[ht] and having had orders to remain over, the most of us did not arise quite as early as usual but rather refreshed our selves with a long nap. *(Power)*

The soldiers were exceedingly pleased with the expedition, and think it a pleasure excursion. *(Calhoun)*

A good many fish in the stream. *(Grant)*

During at least part of the day, Illingworth added to his detailed photographic record of the camp (pages 178-191), which allows us to indicate its true outlines on the map below.

L 44 02 02.2 Illingworth pointed his camera south from 103 50 42.3 this hill for **Photo 812**, "Sioux Camp in Castle Creek Valley" (page 180). Had you been parked at Point 12 at the time, you would have been to the left of the double row of wagons. Also note the tents strung along a far ridge behind the wagons. Forest Service Road 17 now runs on the other side of that ridge, toward Reynolds Prairie.

M 44 02 03.9 This is the site for one of two attempts at 103 50 38.5 photographing a rocky peak to the north of camp (page 182).

N 44 01 47.4 **Photo 813**, "Camp in Castle Creek Valley" 103 50 24.4 (page 184), shows part of the camp extending up Silver Creek to the west of the photo site. Illingworth turned his camera for another view from roughly the same location, **Photo 814**, "Headquarters in Castle Creek Valley" (page 186). Here Custer's tent appears to be on the right side in the distance, to the right of lodge poles left standing by recent Indian occupants. On the map at right, headquarters would have been roughly to the right of the circle with the "K."

O 44 01 52.1 This is the site for the other view of a promi-103 50 26.1 nent outcrop to the north, "Limestone Peak in Castle Creek Valley" (page 188).

P 44 01 41.7 **Photo 816**, "Lime Stone Peak and Castle 103 50 43.8 Creek Valley" (page 190), is very similar to No. 811, except that the wagons have been unloaded and camp apparently established. A study of the lighting suggests that the picture was taken close to sunset—but on which evening? Illingworth may have waited a while for better light or a different view after exposing No. 811, or he may have come back at the end of the second day for another try. We have no way of knowing for sure.

13 44 01 45 The photographs establish the remarkable 103 51 20 accuracy of the camp's latitude and longitude recorded by Capt. William Ludlow. Point 13 is still west of the headquarters area, where he presumably made his observations, but only by half a mile or so.

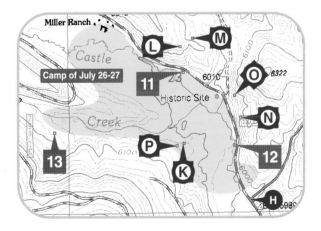

≈The men have been washing & cleaning up generally. I tried to wash for the 1st time & only managed tolerably well. *(Power)*

*Keep in mind that the Expedition had now been in the field 25 days. (Perhaps Fred Power had brought plenty of extra clothes.) You can see clothes laid out to dry in Illingworth's **Photo 813** (page 184). For others in the command, it was yet another day of labor.*

≈Four exploring parties out surveying and mapping the country. *(Forsyth)*

Each tributary valley had its springs and little streams; was heavily grassed and often filled with flowers. The grass in places was as high as a horse's shoulder. *(Ludlow)*

"F" and "H" went on detached service for the purpose of exploring the neighboring valleys. The party that I was with was under command of Colonel Benteen and was accompanied by civil engineer Wood and the two miners. We went through some very narrow ravines, Mr. Wood taking directions . . . . We returned to camp at 5 o'clock p.m., having ridden twenty-four miles. *(Ewert)*

We are at present in the heart of the unexplored country. The Col will give the world a map of it in a few weeks after getting in. *(Power)*

It took longer than a few weeks, but the map Ludlow published with a report of the Expedition in 1875 reflected the efforts of this day. In the enlarged section below, note the trails of detachments up Silver Creek

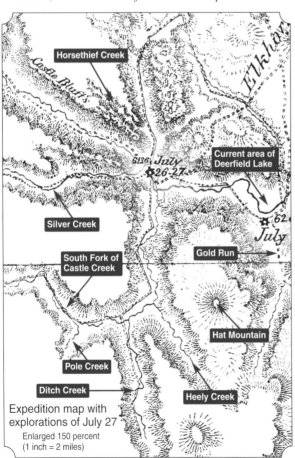

Expedition map with explorations of July 27
Enlarged 150 percent
(1 inch = 2 miles)

to the west; down the south fork of Castle Creek to Pole and Ditch Creeks; and over to Reynolds Prairie. After only one day of working with compass and odometer, while William Wood wrote notes and quickly sketched the landscape, the mapped area bears a striking resemblance to the topography as it appears on today's maps.

THE FIRST GOLD?

≈The gold-hunters were very busy all day with shovel and pan exploring the streams. *(Ludlow)*

There have been reports over the years that Castle Creek should be considered the site of the first gold discovery, based on a series of hints and uncertain sources. "Antelope Fred" Snow, for example—who drove Custer's private ambulance—placed himself on the scene in a reminiscence written 20 years later.

≈On July 27 the command laid over. Ross and myself had passed the forenoon in prospecting a small stream . . . but without success and were on our return when in crossing a divide Ross picked up a small piece of Float or Blossom Quartz. Before leaving the divide we found several fine specimens and followed the croppings for more than a mile. *(Snow)*

Miners with the party report indications of silver in quartz rock along the banks of the creek. *(Forsyth)*

The specimens Snow refers to are only of quartz. While it is often associated with gold deposits, finding quartz—even if there are "indications" of something—is not the same as saying it contains gold.

≈Half a mile below camp this mica-schist becomes more a talcose slate, holding isolated beds and pockets of quartz. *(Winchell)*

There are actually two sources—which contradict each other—concerning the miner William T. McKay, who gets little attention in the Expedition literature. The first is a diary of McKay's quoted in an article by Dr. William M. Blackburn in the 1902 South Dakota Historical Collections:

≈One of the scientific miners, W.T. McKay, wrote in his journal: "Monday, July 21—Entered the Black Hills through the west pass. Our course was now directed to the south and for two days and a half the country traversed was literally one vast bed of gypsum. . . . No sign or trace of mineral ore was discovered until the end of the three days' march, when we struck slate and quartz, and found some indications of silver. The next day's travel was through a slate country . . . . The following day brought us into a country of granite and slate formation (Custer's Park). In the evening I took a pan, pick and shovel, and went out prospecting. The first panful was taken from the gravel and sand obtained in the bed of the creek; and on washing was found to contain from one and a half to two cents, which was the first gold found in the Black Hills.

The succession of days is problematic in the alleged journal, of which we have been able to find no other record or mention. It does agree with the emphasis on quartz at what appears to be Castle Creek, and specifically places Discovery on French Creek—even if McKay gives himself the credit.

On the other hand, the quoted journal disagrees with Brown & Willard's The Black Hills Trails, *which says William T. McKay "asserted that gold was first discovered upon the tributary of Castle Creek which he called Gold Run Creek." This is the only reference we've seen to finding actual gold in this area in 1874, although there is one more hint in* South Dakota Geographic Names, *which says Gold Run "was mentioned by Custer in his report by this name, which he presumably gave it." So far we have not seen such a report.*

Gold Run is now the name of the creek Custer followed on July 29 (Chapter 6), and traces of gold would be found the next year in that area by an expedition under Colonel Richard Dodge and geologist Newton Jenney (Chapter 17). "It is only a little 'show'," wrote Dodge on June 12, 1875, "but it is gold." Margaret Hobart of Gillette Prairie told us there was dredging on the upper part of the creek in the 1930s. According to her father, Don Hobart, a lot of gold was taken out, including many nuggets.

The miners would explore wherever they thought gold *might* be, but they found nothing this day to reward them for their trouble. *(Ewert)*

Is there any chance that Ewert was wrong, that gold really was found on or near Castle Creek in 1874? We can't rule it out, but it seems extremely unlikely. The Brown & Willard quote was at least second- or third-hand, and Snow himself makes the distinction that the "first colors or Free Gold" were found in "Custer Valley." It is also hard to believe that any discovery of gold could have been kept a secret. Certainly the news circulated quickly at French Creek a few days later. Finally, keep in mind that when Horatio Ross returned to the Black Hills in 1875, he went straight to French Creek and remained there the rest of his life. In fact, over the years he took many visitors and tourists to the site of his original discovery—within the city limits of Custer.

Here, on the 26th of July . . . we found also the first good evidence of quartz rock. Our miners . . . began to prospect here, but did not find the glittering encouragement they sought. The discovery further on of large quantities of feldspathic and granitic rock, and ledges of gold-bearing quartz . . . set our miners to work still more diligently. *(New York Tribune)*

Note that the Tribune *says gold-bearing quartz was found "further on." It is certainly safe to say quartz*

was first seen near Castle Creek, and perhaps that was reason enough for excitement—whether or not it contained gold. Dodge mentioned the quartz, too, when he followed Custer down Castle Creek Valley.

We are now encamped at Custer's camp of 26 July.. . . . We have benefited somewhat by Custer's work, finding our bridge in tolerable repair, & several side cuttings which saved us work. . . . Quartz has been found today in considerable quantities – some of it seems gold bearing. Jenney is going to stop & work part of tomorrow. *(Dodge, June 11)*

Dodge mentions nothing more about Castle Creek, so perhaps Jenney also failed to find any gold in the quartz. Custer's Expedition was getting closer, however. The true discovery site was still waiting south of Harney Peak.

From a high hill near camp, the first well-defined view was gained of Harney's Peak, twenty miles to the southeast. The position of this peak . . . was known from Warren's map. We were nearly in the heart of the unexplored portion of the hills, and the results of energy and good management had been shown in the entire success of the expedition. *(Ludlow)*

In the foreground of this detail from **Photo 814** (page 186) is what appears to be a two-wheeled vehicle that could be the odometer cart ridden by Sergeant Becker. We do know that a solid housing protected the odometer. In the background is an awning that covers an interesting-looking object.

DEVEREAUX LIBRARY ARCHIVES

CHAPTER 5

Tuesday, July 28

A tour of Reynolds Prairie

Our eyes were made glad by beholding a rolling prairie with a prospect of a good days march. (Power)

July 28

Here we have a day of puzzles that will probably never be solved with certainty. After traveling generally south since entering the Black Hills, and having had a full day to explore the area, Custer suddenly turned the command north. The route took them to yet another mystery—an old pile of elk horns unlike anything they had seen before. Eventually the wagons had to turn around, and camp was made where Deerfield Lake is now, four miles below the previous camp. Distance traveled: 10 miles.

Taking the trail

U.S.G.S. MAP: Deerfield

CAUTIONS: The roads are all smooth gravel, but much of the actual trail is on private land.

TO START: *From Hill City*, check your odometer and drive west on Deerfield Road (Forest Service 17). As you pass the head of Deerfield Lake, notice how nar-row the valley becomes (near **Point A** on the map at right). While you may have taken this road for granted before, it is built up in a way that was not available in 1874. The gap will play a role in the day's events, and be described by the head of another expedition that tried to use it a year later. At 17.5 miles from Hill City, turn left on FS 110 (**Point 3**) and drive two-tenths of a mile to a turnout on the left (**Point 1**).

Last night we had frost. The night air is very very cold and the days pleasant, some times rather warmer than we care for. *(Power)*

This will sound familiar to anyone who has the impression that Deerfield is often the coldest spot on the local weather maps. The exact location of this camp (July 26 and 27) is revealed in full in a series of photographs taken by William Illingworth (see pages 53 and 55 in the previous chapter; the photos are found on pages 178-191).

1 44 01 41.9   The parking area here is a convenient
103 50 26.4   starting point. It would have been visible in Illingworth's **Photo 812** (page 180), at the base of the hill near the double row of parked wagons. Headquarters would have been almost directly across the valley, along with abandoned lodge poles from a previous Lakota camp. Two of the peaks photographed by Illingworth are also visible from the pullout.

2 44 01 45   This is Capt. Ludlow's recorded latitude and
103 51 20   longitude for the camp, one of his more accurate readings within the Black Hills.

The command moved at 5 o'clock. Left the valley and ascended the bluffs. *(Calhoun)*

The valley below us was rather too marshy for the wagons, and the easterly course lay up the hills to the left out upon a high rolling prairie. *(Ludlow)*

. . . thus escaping a very narrow and deep cañon, through which the creek passes, in this mica schist. *(Winchell)*

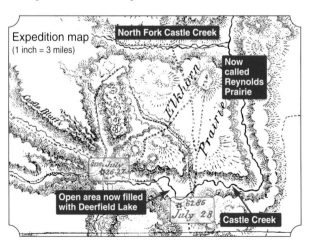

Expedition map
(1 inch = 3 miles)

North Fork Castle Creek

Now called Reynolds Prairie

Elkhorn Prairie

Castle Bluffs

Site July 26-27

Open area now filled with Deerfield Lake

62.86 July 28

Castle Creek

The *"deep cañon" Winchell refers to is the area at the head of Deerfield Lake (near* **Point A**). *Camped in the same place a year later (on June 11, 1875), Col. Richard Irving Dodge believed he could cut a better trail than Custer had. He tried going down Castle Creek, creating misery for every living thing he commanded.*

Custer's trail here led off from the Creek to make an aimless journey around a park . . . . In spite of the bog I determined to make a route down the creek, & started at once. Finding it practicable I sent back an orderly, & brought the train through its most frightful and fatiguing day. Bog bog, all the time—16 mules on a team, & as many men as could get hold prying & lifting the bed out of the mud. *(Dodge)*

There isn't much question, then, that the canyon was a good place to avoid. The real question is why—once he was on the prairie—Custer kept going north. Exploring parties had already looked the area over, as described in the previous chapter. In fact, on the enlarged section of Ludlow's map at right you can see that one of the parties had gone up on the prairie and even passed through the area that would be tonight's camp.

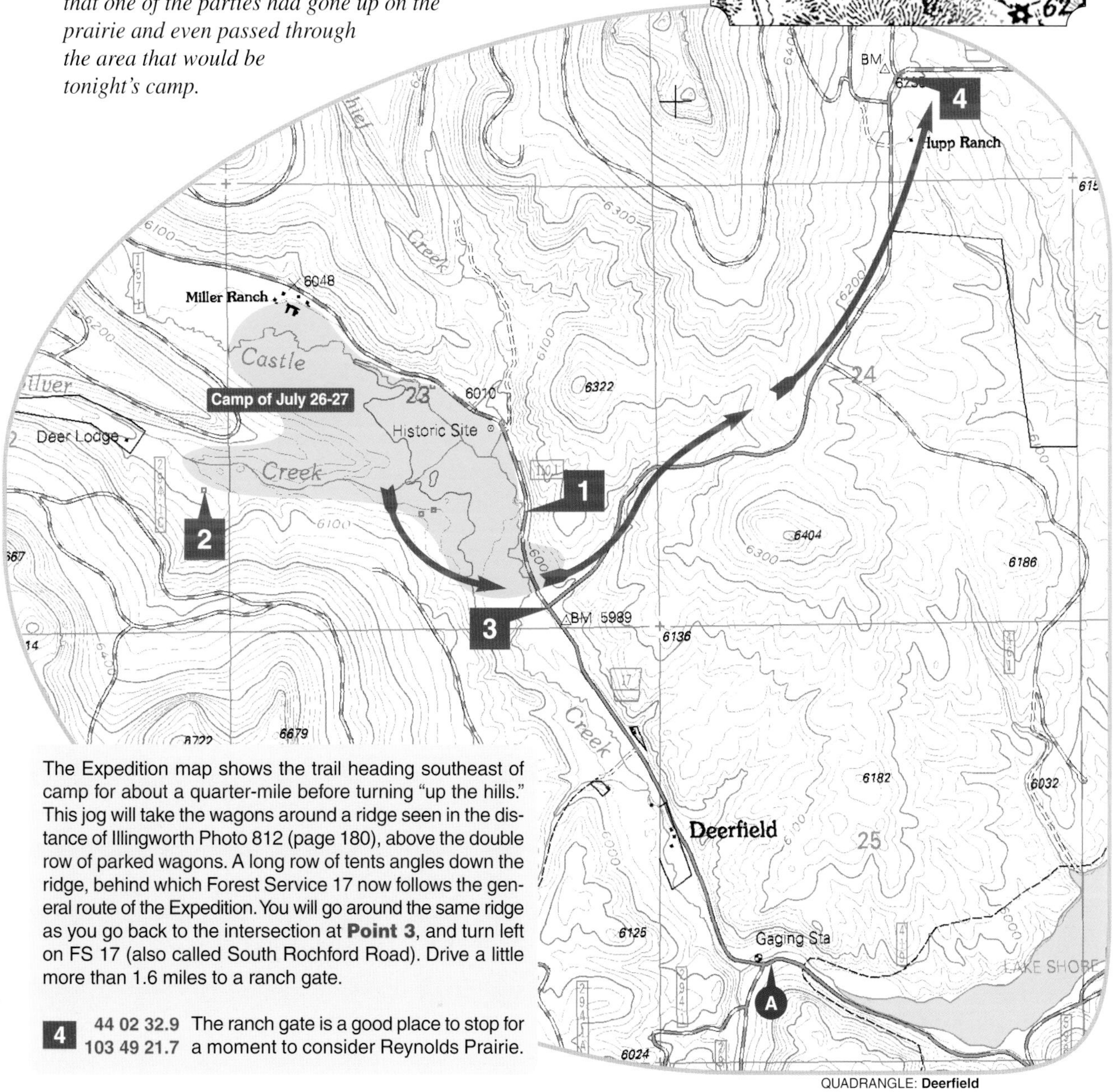

July 28 reconnaissance

July 26-27

July 28

The Expedition map shows the trail heading southeast of camp for about a quarter-mile before turning "up the hills." This jog will take the wagons around a ridge seen in the distance of Illingworth Photo 812 (page 180), above the double row of parked wagons. A long row of tents angles down the ridge, behind which Forest Service 17 now follows the general route of the Expedition. You will go around the same ridge as you go back to the intersection at **Point 3**, and turn left on FS 17 (also called South Rochford Road). Drive a little more than 1.6 miles to a ranch gate.

4   44 02 32.9   The ranch gate is a good place to stop for
103 49 21.7   a moment to consider Reynolds Prairie.

QUADRANGLE: **Deerfield**

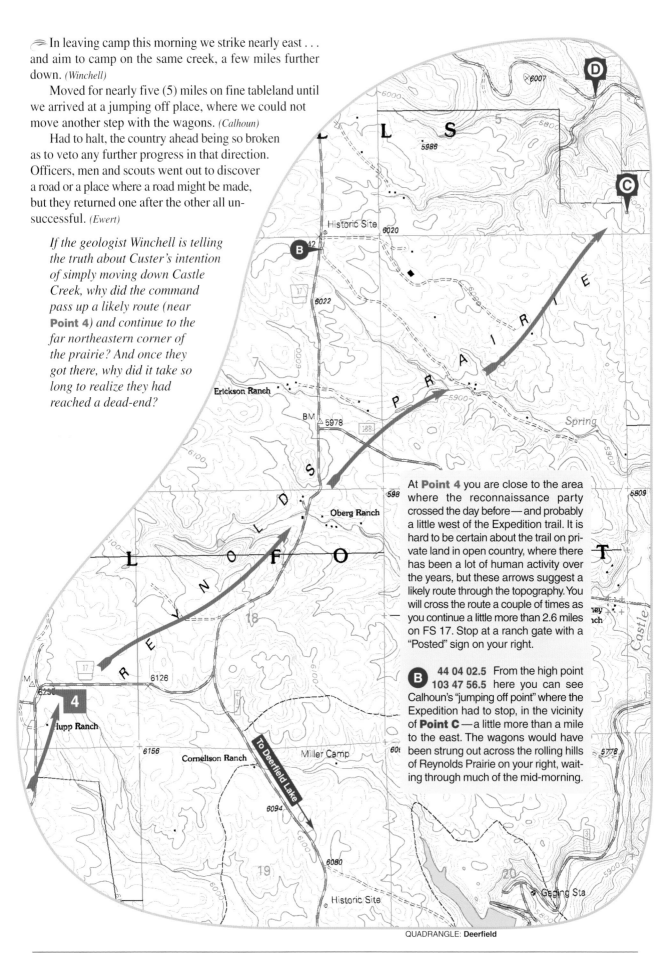

〰 In leaving camp this morning we strike nearly east . . . and aim to camp on the same creek, a few miles further down. *(Winchell)*

Moved for nearly five (5) miles on fine tableland until we arrived at a jumping off place, where we could not move another step with the wagons. *(Calhoun)*

Had to halt, the country ahead being so broken as to veto any further progress in that direction. Officers, men and scouts went out to discover a road or a place where a road might be made, but they returned one after the other all un-successful. *(Ewert)*

If the geologist Winchell is telling the truth about Custer's intention of simply moving down Castle Creek, why did the command pass up a likely route (near **Point 4**) *and continue to the far northeastern corner of the prairie? And once they got there, why did it take so long to realize they had reached a dead-end?*

At **Point 4** you are close to the area where the reconnaissance party crossed the day before — and probably a little west of the Expedition trail. It is hard to be certain about the trail on private land in open country, where there has been a lot of human activity over the years, but these arrows suggest a likely route through the topography. You will cross the route a couple of times as you continue a little more than 2.6 miles on FS 17. Stop at a ranch gate with a "Posted" sign on your right.

B 44 04 02.5 From the high point 103 47 56.5 here you can see Calhoun's "jumping off point" where the Expedition had to stop, in the vicinity of **Point C** — a little more than a mile to the east. The wagons would have been strung out across the rolling hills of Reynolds Prairie on your right, waiting through much of the mid-morning.

QUADRANGLE: **Deerfield**

⬧ We remained on this hill some two or three hours awaiting the return of the Scouts who were sent out to find the best route down. *(Power, journal for the 29th)*

We were unable to find an available pass. *(Forsyth)*

The Expedition was able to find a pass further west when it came back this way on August 7. It seems inescapable that Custer and his scouts had a reason for coming to this particular corner of the prairie—something more than just a way down to Castle Creek, which had already turned north here. Perhaps they had been promised a good route beyond it to the south. It's not likely we will ever know, however. In all of the journals and newspaper reports available, there are only two remarks that relate to the mystery.

⬧ Genl Custers prisoner led the party this AM north of our former line of march across the hill. *(Power)*

Our interpreter having misunderstood the guide, we marched from our first camp on Castle Creek, about 5 miles eastward over the rolling prairie of Elk Horn Park, and there found that deep ravines and rocky canors (sic) prevented our further advance. *(Pioneer)*

The prisoner mentioned by Fred Power was One Stab, the 63-year-old Lakota headman who was being held against his will and who was expected to guide the Expedition. (See previous chapter.) It is just possible that on this day he got the best of Custer.

Researcher Joe Sanders has suggested that One Stab deliberately misled the Expedition to give his band more time for their escape. The Indian trail went south (as you will see in the next chapter), and he took Custer north. Whatever happened, Custer was not happy with the result. Here is his official report.

⬧ The direction of Castle Creek having commenced to lead us more to the northeast than we were prepared to go, and the valley having become narrow and broken, I left this water course and ascended the valley of a small tributary, which again gave us a southeasterly course. *(Custer)*

What we now call Reynolds Prairie has been made to disappear completely within this sentence, which takes us from the camp above Deerfield to the trip down Gold Run—the "small tributary"—on July 29. The General who did his own scouting and road-building apparently preferred to ignore his mistakes.

Custer's reaction may have been even stronger on the day in question. A typescript in the Cartwright archive contains this story about Charley Reynolds, a well-known frontiersman, and Bloody Knife, Custer's favorite Indian scout.

⬧ Owing to a misunderstanding between Reynolds and Bloody Knife the command marched northeast away from the river and then back again. Custer, infuriated, asked who was to blame. Reynolds blamed Bloody Knife. Custer drew his pistol and emptied it at the fleeing Rees who managed to escape into the brush without harm. A few hours later Bloody Knife rode up to Custer and remarked: "My brother's blood was hot today. Had mine been as hot, blood would have been spilt." Custer explained that his anger was but that of a moment, the two men shook hands and seemingly the affair was forgotten. *(Cartwright)*

Unfortunately, the account in the typescript is not attributed. Cartwright talked with Charles Windolph, a Lead neighbor who in 1874 had been a soldier in H Company. We cannot be certain this story came from Windolph, however, or, if it did, how much it had been distorted by memory. Perhaps a reader will know more, but in the meantime it is just one more story. How you feel about it may depend in part on how you feel about Custer.

⬧ We found, at the place where we halted . . . *(Ewert)*

. . . a stack of several hundred Elk horns. It is doubtless, the Indians votive offering to some deity. It has been standing many years, and the horns are bleached perfectly white. It was probably twelve or fifteen feet high when first built, but has settled down until it is now only five or six. It was photographed by our artist. *(Pioneer)*

DEVEREAUX LIBRARY ARCHIVES

A detail from the Illingworth **Photo 817** (page 192).

Point C is the knoll on which Illingworth took **Photo 817**, "Elk Horn Prairie" (page 192). Please note that the location is on private land, and heed the "Posted" sign you found at **Point B**. You can see the site from here, however, if you look to the right—just slightly north of east. It is the highest knoll just before the timber line, a mile and a quarter away.

Imagine the careful stacking of elk horns on that knoll, and the ceremonies that may have taken place there long ago.

⬧ A huge pile of elk-horns of ancient date, and of which the Indians disclaimed any share in the construction, was found on the northeast part of this prairie. *(Ludlow)*

The Indians call it Elk Horn Valley, a name which is appropriately changed to *Elk-Horn Prairie*. *(Winchell)*

The Indians' professed ignorance is not surprising, since Custer's Arikara and Santee Sioux scouts were all from the Missouri River or farther east. Brian Bade of Rapid City, South Dakota, called our attention to the fact that Swiss artist Karl Bodmer found a similar pile of elk horns along the upper Missouri in 1833. His drawing "Elk Antler Pyramid" appeared in the book Karl Bodmer's America, *with an annotation that the pile was a charm to insure a successful hunt. Piegan Blackfeet hunting parties added to the pile each time they passed, picking up horns that had*

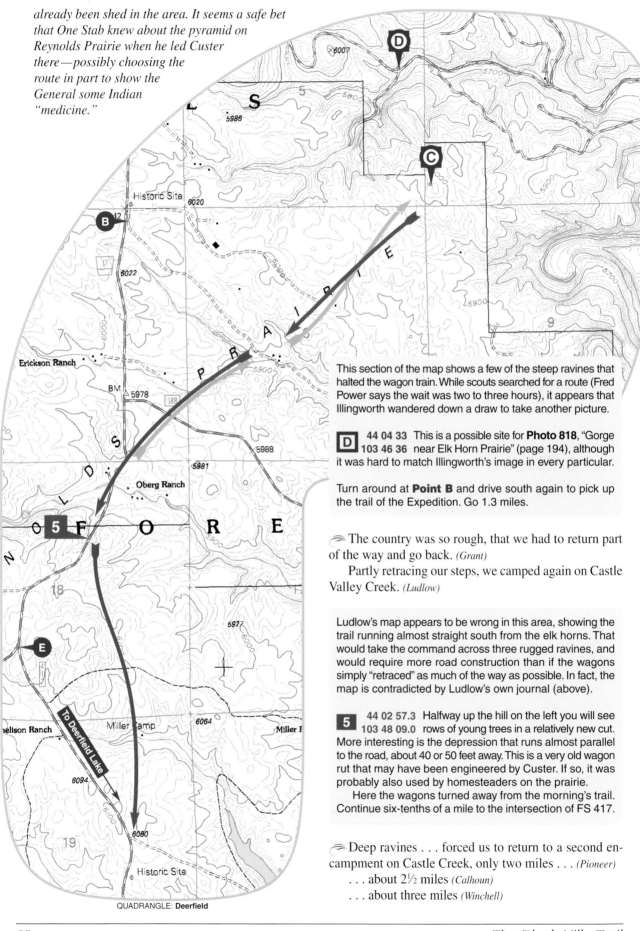

already been shed in the area. It seems a safe bet that One Stab knew about the pyramid on Reynolds Prairie when he led Custer there—possibly choosing the route in part to show the General some Indian "medicine."

This section of the map shows a few of the steep ravines that halted the wagon train. While scouts searched for a route (Fred Power says the wait was two to three hours), it appears that Illingworth wandered down a draw to take another picture.

D 44 04 33   This is a possible site for **Photo 818**, "Gorge 103 46 36   near Elk Horn Prairie" (page 194), although it was hard to match Illingworth's image in every particular.

Turn around at **Point B** and drive south again to pick up the trail of the Expedition. Go 1.3 miles.

☞ The country was so rough, that we had to return part of the way and go back. *(Grant)*

Partly retracing our steps, we camped again on Castle Valley Creek. *(Ludlow)*

Ludlow's map appears to be wrong in this area, showing the trail running almost straight south from the elk horns. That would take the command across three rugged ravines, and would require more road construction than if the wagons simply "retraced" as much of the way as possible. In fact, the map is contradicted by Ludlow's own journal (above).

5 44 02 57.3   Halfway up the hill on the left you will see 103 48 09.0   rows of young trees in a relatively new cut. More interesting is the depression that runs almost parallel to the road, about 40 or 50 feet away. This is a very old wagon rut that may have been engineered by Custer. If so, it was probably also used by homesteaders on the prairie.

Here the wagons turned away from the morning's trail. Continue six-tenths of a mile to the intersection of FS 417.

☞ Deep ravines . . . forced us to return to a second encampment on Castle Creek, only two miles . . . *(Pioneer)*

. . . about 2½ miles *(Calhoun)*

. . . about three miles *(Winchell)*

QUADRANGLE: **Deerfield**

. . . about 3½ miles *(Grant)*

. . . five miles *(Ewert)*

. . . about 4 miles lower down than our last camp was located, encamping a little below where the Indian village had been, and upon a little stream emptying into Castle Creek. *(Forsyth)*

Forsyth may be pretty close to the true distance, but more important is his location of the camp on Gold Run—the "little stream" that Ludlow also mentions coming in from the south. The junction of Castle Creek and Gold Run (now underwater) helps us place the general area of the camp as well as the Indian village, which would have been a little to the west. The mouth of Gold Run was also the site of the original town of Deerfield, which grew out of a stage stop called Mountain *or* Mountain City.

E 44 02 35.3 Where FS 17 veers right, keeping going
103 48 30.5 straight on FS 417. Continue 1.4 miles.

6 44 01 26.3 This will take you right down to the water's
103 47 48.9 edge on the boat ramp, not far from where the Expedition entered Castle Creek Valley once again. The arrows provide only a general idea of the trail in this area, but the campsite is well-documented.

7 44 00 52 These are Capt. Ludlow's latitude and longi-
103 48 27 tude readings for the camp, little more than half a mile west of the Gold Run inlet. The original Deerfield was located within the camp area shown on the map.

☞General Custer, Forsyth and other officers were busy the remainder of this day finding a place where we could pass with the wagon train. *(Ewert)*

After dinner made a reconnaissance with General Custer up the creek below camp. A good road was found up the valley, which is heavily grassed and flowered for two and one-half miles. Then ascended a hill on the left and reached, through some timber, the open prairie I was on in the afternoon. *(Ludlow)*

This description suggests that Ludlow had traveled earlier in the day as far as the area now known as Gillette Prairie, and returned later with Custer. They continued further south for a view of the landscape, climbing a peak that could only be Copper Mountain. What they saw inspired the engineer to one of his most lyrical passages.

☞Harney's Peak was visible from the top of a high, bare hill, and the sun having just set, we were in a few minutes rewarded for the ride of five miles. The moon was rising just over the southern shoulder of Harney, and masked by heavy clouds. A patch of bright blood-red flame was first seen, looking like a brilliant fire, and soon after another so far from the first that it was difficult to connect the two. A portion of the moon's disk became presently visible, and the origin of the flame was apparent. While

it lasted the sight was superb. The moon's mass looked enormous and blood-red, with only portions of its surface visible, while the clouds just above and to the left, colored by the flame, resembled smoke drifting from an immense conflagration. The moon soon buried herself completely in the clouds, and under a rapidly darkening sky we returned to camp. *(Ludlow)*

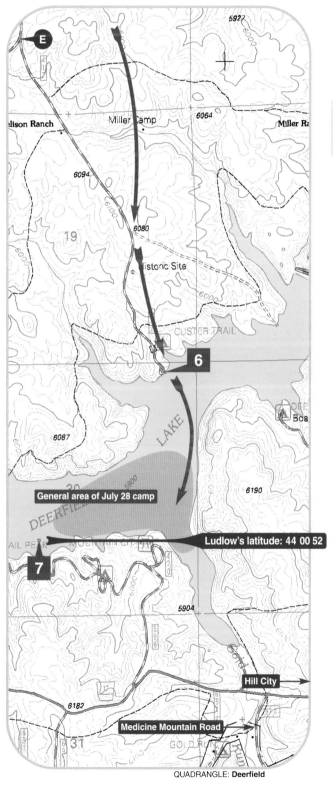

QUADRANGLE: **Deerfield**

CHAPTER 6

Wednesday, July 29

Deerfield Lake to Vanderlehr Creek

"I guess they can come this far." (General Custer, quoted by Wood)
The train does not reach the place selected till daylight next morning. (Winchell)

Going back to the Indian trail it had followed since Floral Valley, the Expedition traveled up Gold Run toward Gillette Prairie—probably the same trail taken by the Lakota who fled their village on July 26. The route crossed a divide to Negro Creek, which proved to be the most difficult stretch encountered by the pioneer crew and the wagons. Most of today's route would later be used for a short time by the Cheyenne-Deadwood Stage. Distance traveled: 15 miles.

July 28

— Taking the trail —

U.S.G.S. MAPS: Deerfield, Ditch Creek, Medicine Mountain, Berne

CAUTIONS: The roads are all smooth gravel except for a short (and optional) side trip on a rougher trail.

TO START: *From Hill City*, check or set your odometer and drive 14.3 miles west on Forest Service 17, the Deerfield Road, until you reach FS 465 (**Point A**). Turn right and stop at the trail head (**Point 2**).

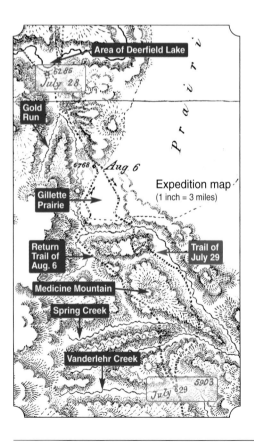

Area of Deerfield Lake

July 28

Gold Run

Aug 6

Gillette Prairie

Return Trail of Aug. 6

Medicine Mountain

Spring Creek

Vanderlehr Creek

July 29

Trail of July 29

Expedition map
(1 inch = 3 miles)

The river—if I may so call a stream some 10 feet wide—supplied us with fresh fish, the surrounding woods with deer, so there was no lack of good eating. Straw berries were also plentiful. Our table besides being supplied with the necessaries of life have some of its luxuries—a beautiful boquet adorned it. A gift of the valley—which abound in flowers of all kinds. But, like all things will, our encampment came to an end & we took departure on the 29th not at all willingly—though I must confess with some curiosity as we were to follow the Indian trail, that being the only way to get out and that even taking [us] over a rough road. *(Power)*

This idyllic description refers to the stopping place of July 28, now covered by Deerfield Lake. The camp centered on the confluence of Gold Run and Castle Creek, where a stage station was established in the spring of 1877 that grew into Mountain City, later called Deerfield. The town moved to its present location when Castle Creek was dammed to create the reservoir.

1 44 00 52 This is the last latitude and longitude reading recorded
103 48 27 before the Expedition reached permanent camp, three miles east of present-day Custer. Ludlow's map of the area in between is based entirely on distance measurements, compass bearings and sketches of the topography.

2 44 00 27.6 Your starting point for the day is a trailhead just south
103 47 28.4 of Deerfield Lake, directly on the route.

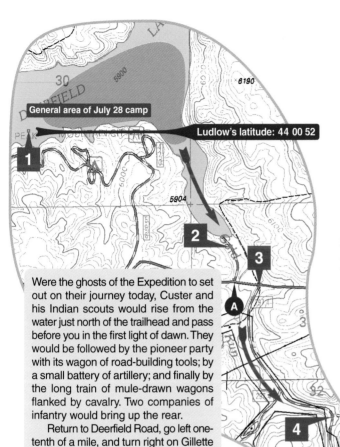

General area of July 28 camp

Ludlow's latitude: 44 00 52

Researchers Joe Sanders and Jack McCulloh made one of their more exciting discoveries on this portion of the trail: a rut that almost certainly was made by the Custer Expedition (and probably used by the Cheyenne stage in 1877). The antiquity of the trail was demonstrated in 2001 when the authors took core samples from mature pines growing within the rut, and found the trees to be about 120 years old.

This is a case where physical evidence coincides with both the Expedition map and the written record. Ludlow described this part of the trail in his journal entry of the day before.

◿ A good road was found up the valley, which is heavily grassed and flowered for two and one-half miles. Then ascended a hill on the left and reached, through some timber, the open prairie. *(Ludlow, July 28)*

Two-and-a-half miles from camp is where the wide valley of Gold Run turns to the right and FS 297 continues straight—precisely where the stream and trail separate on Ludlow's map. The Expedition went up a draw "through some timber" at **Point 5.** *It used the same trail on the way back (August 7), leaving a mark like the one they, in turn, had been following.*

◿ An old, deeply-worn Indian trail led up the creek, following which took us across a high prairie exhibiting bowlders of quartz. *(Ludlow)*

July 29

Were the ghosts of the Expedition to set out on their journey today, Custer and his Indian scouts would rise from the water just north of the trailhead and pass before you in the first light of dawn. They would be followed by the pioneer party with its wagon of road-building tools; by a small battery of artillery; and finally by the long train of mule-drawn wagons flanked by cavalry. Two companies of infantry would bring up the rear.

Return to Deerfield Road, go left one-tenth of a mile, and turn right on Gillette Prairie Road (FS 297) at **Point 3.** Continue seven-tenths of a mile to the intersection of a side trail on your left.

◿ Broke camp at 4:45 a.m. Moving on an old Indian trail up the valley through which ran the little tributary to Castle Creek, upon which we encamped last night. *(Forsyth)*

. . . finding heavy grass with wild oats and barley and many flowers. *(Ludlow)*

On our left are seen, on the tops of the hills, occasional columns, formed by jointing planes, from which the surrounding rock has been denuded, left standing 10 or 20 feet high among the pines. *(Winchell)*

4 **43 59 52.2** One of the "columns" Winchell talks about **103 46 59.1** stands on the hillside to your left. Imagine the time it took to wear away the layers of rock it was once part of, rising high above your head. You will see more of these surviving oddities as you continue. Also note that Gold Run turns off within the next mile, where FS 297 continues up a drainage on the left. It was this upper part of Gold Run that was being dredged in the 1930s, according to Margaret Hobart of Gillette Prairie. Her father Don Hobart said a lot of gold was found there, including many nuggets.

Continue 1.6 miles (2.3 miles from Deerfield Road) and stop at a pair of green junction boxes on your left, near a maintenance trail for the utility lines.

5 **43 58 41.0** Beyond the maintenance road, about 75 **103 46 04.4** feet from FS 297, is a deep and well-defined rut that you can follow a good distance up the draw.

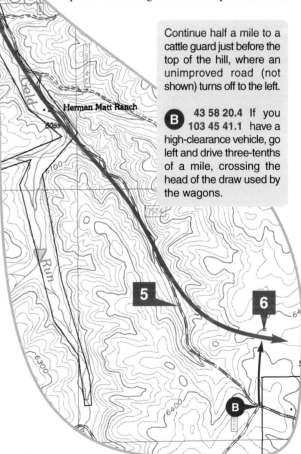

Herman Matt Ranch

Continue half a mile to a cattle guard just before the top of the hill, where an unimproved road (not shown) turns off to the left.

B **43 58 20.4** If you **103 45 41.1** have a high-clearance vehicle, go left and drive three-tenths of a mile, crossing the head of the draw used by the wagons.

QUADRANGLES: **Deerfield, Ditch Creek**

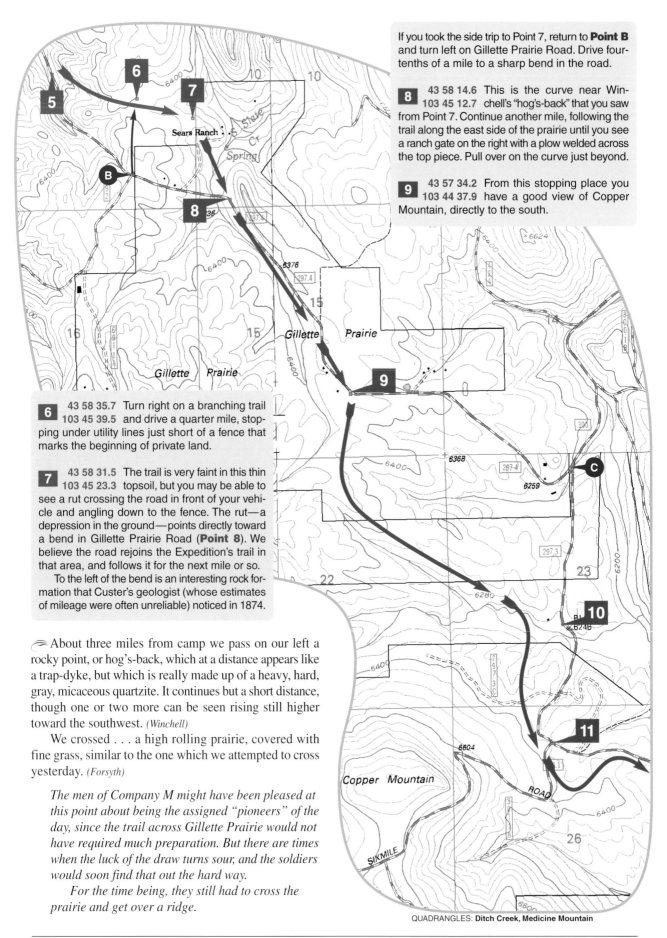

If you took the side trip to Point 7, return to **Point B** and turn left on Gillette Prairie Road. Drive four-tenths of a mile to a sharp bend in the road.

8 43 58 14.6   This is the curve near Winchell's "hog's-back" that you saw from Point 7. Continue another mile, following the trail along the east side of the prairie until you see a ranch gate on the right with a plow welded across the top piece. Pull over on the curve just beyond.
103 45 12.7

9 43 57 34.2   From this stopping place you have a good view of Copper Mountain, directly to the south.
103 44 37.9

6 43 58 35.7   Turn right on a branching trail and drive a quarter mile, stopping under utility lines just short of a fence that marks the beginning of private land.
103 45 39.5

7 43 58 31.5   The trail is very faint in this thin topsoil, but you may be able to see a rut crossing the road in front of your vehicle and angling down to the fence. The rut—a depression in the ground—points directly toward a bend in Gillette Prairie Road (**Point 8**). We believe the road rejoins the Expedition's trail in that area, and follows it for the next mile or so.
103 45 23.3

To the left of the bend is an interesting rock formation that Custer's geologist (whose estimates of mileage were often unreliable) noticed in 1874.

About three miles from camp we pass on our left a rocky point, or hog's-back, which at a distance appears like a trap-dyke, but which is really made up of a heavy, hard, gray, micaceous quartzite. It continues but a short distance, though one or two more can be seen rising still higher toward the southwest. *(Winchell)*

We crossed . . . a high rolling prairie, covered with fine grass, similar to the one which we attempted to cross yesterday. *(Forsyth)*

The men of Company M might have been pleased at this point about being the assigned "pioneers" of the day, since the trail across Gillette Prairie would not have required much preparation. But there are times when the luck of the draw turns sour, and the soldiers would soon find that out the hard way.

For the time being, they still had to cross the prairie and get over a ridge.

QUADRANGLES: **Ditch Creek, Medicine Mountain**

☞ At six miles from camp the view of these hills is also cut off on the west by the intervention of a high conical hill of the kind of rock last noted. *(Winchell)*

This was likely Copper Mountain, which dominates the southern end of Gillette Prairie—the "high, bare hill" climbed by Captain Ludlow the previous night (page 63). Copper Mountain also drew the attention of Colonel Dodge a year later (June 12, 1875), when he stopped to camp on Castle Creek.

☞ About 6 miles from camp we were attracted by a high bare hill, & going to the top were amply repaid for our trouble—The view is more than fine or grand or magnificent. We seemed to be fixed in the center of a circle formed of huge hills & mountains. *(Dodge)*

The view caused Dodge, writing in his journal, to admit grudging admiration for Custer.

☞ The interior of this basin was filled with a mass of hill and canon mixed together in the most indiscriminate manner & apparently without system or order. Generally such a view would give some idea of the water shed, the course of the streams &c — but very little can be gained from any study of this most disorderly mass of material. The more I see of the Black Hills & its travel, the more credit I am disposed to give to Custer for his exploration of last year—I find his map remarkably correct, & it is of the greatest use to me. Even with it, I find it no easy matter to go where I want—& to him who had nothing but his compass & the capacity of his wagons for ups & downs to direct him, the finding of any route was a success. *(Dodge)*

What is it about some people that causes others to grit their teeth when forced to compliment them? Private Ewert had the same problem (Chapter 1), and a number of Custer's fellow officers disliked him as well. To this day the General's name can spark passionate arguments.

The "remarkably correct" map Dodge refers to is of course the Ludlow map that has been useful to us in locating the trail within the Hills. It suggests that the wagons briefly turned south from where you are parked at **Point 9**, then followed a drainage to the far end of Gillette Prairie. Note the shape of the trail on the enlarged section at right, and how well it correlates to the arrows on the opposite page (though they could not be verified on private land).

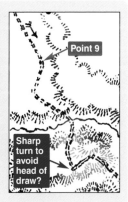

Point 9

Sharp turn to avoid head of draw?

The old stage stop on Gillette Prairie, as it appeared in 2001. (Compare to the photo on page 100 in Parker and Lambert's *Black Hills Ghost Towns*.)

Drive one mile to **Point C**, the intersection of FS 297 and FS 300 (East Slate Road). Turn right on FS 297, now called Medicine Mountain Road. Drive six-tenths of a mile to a fence gate on a curve, the first safe place to pull off the road.

10 43 56 46.0 Just behind you on the right, if it is still
103 43 37.0 standing, is the ruin of a stage station.

At the far southeastern corner of Gillette Prairie (near **Point 10***) are the remains of a stop on the Cheyenne-Deadwood stage line that is generally believed to have been operated by a man named Gillette.* South Dakota Geographic Names *says the Prairie's first occupant, Uriah Gilette (with one "l"), became a "successful rancher and famous hunter." A man named Uri Gilette is described as "an old-time frontiersman" in Casey's* The Black Hills and Their Incredible Characters. *The book reported that Gilette assisted stage-line superintendent William Ward after the famous Canyon Springs robbery of 1878. It would be interesting to know more about the man whose main legacy now seems to be a name on the map.*

The Expedition came down the drainage to the left in the photograph above, probably the "small valley" mentioned by Forsyth:

☞ The Indian trail . . . led us along over the prairie, through a small valley, across a wooded crest. *(Forsyth)*

It appears that Custer reached the "wooded crest" through a draw to the west of FS 297. Continue a quarter of a mile.

11 43 56 21.5 This is the intersection with Six Mile Road
103 43 40.3 (FS 301), which climbs the shoulder of Copper Mountain. The Expedition's route passed near here, going around the head of a drainage just beyond the intersection. This would account for a sharp jog in the trail shown at left on the enlarged, enhanced section of Ludlow's map.

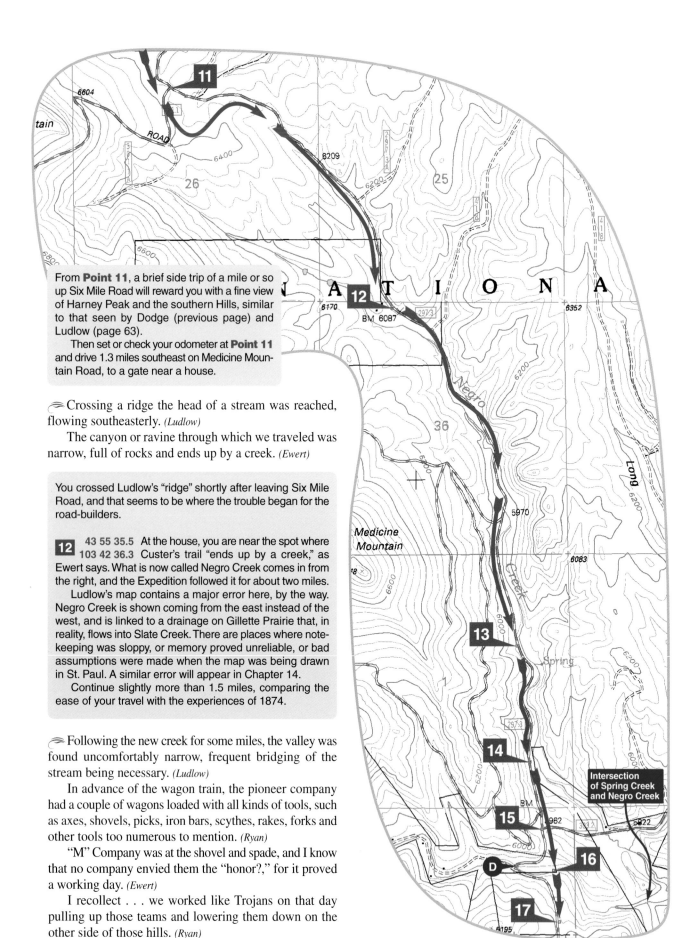

From **Point 11**, a brief side trip of a mile or so up Six Mile Road will reward you with a fine view of Harney Peak and the southern Hills, similar to that seen by Dodge (previous page) and Ludlow (page 63).

Then set or check your odometer at **Point 11** and drive 1.3 miles southeast on Medicine Mountain Road, to a gate near a house.

⌒ Crossing a ridge the head of a stream was reached, flowing southeasterly. *(Ludlow)*

The canyon or ravine through which we traveled was narrow, full of rocks and ends up by a creek. *(Ewert)*

You crossed Ludlow's "ridge" shortly after leaving Six Mile Road, and that seems to be where the trouble began for the road-builders.

12 43 55 35.5 At the house, you are near the spot where 103 42 36.3 Custer's trail "ends up by a creek," as Ewert says. What is now called Negro Creek comes in from the right, and the Expedition followed it for about two miles.

Ludlow's map contains a major error here, by the way. Negro Creek is shown coming from the east instead of the west, and is linked to a drainage on Gillette Prairie that, in reality, flows into Slate Creek. There are places where note-keeping was sloppy, or memory proved unreliable, or bad assumptions were made when the map was being drawn in St. Paul. A similar error will appear in Chapter 14.

Continue slightly more than 1.5 miles, comparing the ease of your travel with the experiences of 1874.

⌒ Following the new creek for some miles, the valley was found uncomfortably narrow, frequent bridging of the stream being necessary. *(Ludlow)*

In advance of the wagon train, the pioneer company had a couple of wagons loaded with all kinds of tools, such as axes, shovels, picks, iron bars, scythes, rakes, forks and other tools too numerous to mention. *(Ryan)*

"M" Company was at the shovel and spade, and I know that no company envied them the "honor?," for it proved a working day. *(Ewert)*

I recollect . . . we worked like Trojans on that day pulling up those teams and lowering them down on the other side of those hills. *(Ryan)*

QUADRANGLE: **Medicine Mountain**

The country . . . becomes more completely wooded and more mountainous, rendering it almost impassable for the train. *(Winchell)*

This is a hard day's march for the wagon train—Very bad roads. Hard work for the pioneer party. Travelled thro' narrow ravines, timbered hills, steep and stony places. *(Calhoun)*

13 43 54 25.6 There is nothing to see here now but an 103 42 01.4 overgrown knoll, where you can find a small spring back against the hill. According to local tradition, however, this was the location of another stage station.

Despite the difficulties of the Expedition, its trail in this area was followed briefly by the Cheyenne and Deadwood stage after the route was shifted west from Hill City and Pactola in the spring of 1877. One of the stations on the line was called Twelve Mile Ranch, and said to be located on Spring Creek.

*The actual site of Twelve Mile may have been a little to the north, according to Tom Kilian, a long-time summer resident on Spring Creek who has been a director and a chairman of the board of the South Dakota State Historical Society. A Norwegian pole-cutter named Freddy Martinson showed him remnants of a structure on Negro Creek (***Point 13***) in the 1950s. Foundation rocks and a threshold were still visible at the time. Martinson, who by then had lived for many years in the area, said the structure was an early stage station. Kilian believes that the statement was based on things Martinson had heard from old-timers along Spring Creek.*

In any case, the owners of the stage line benefitted greatly from the work of Expedition soldiers.

Rocks had to be removed, the creek had to be bridged every half a mile and once the point of a mountain had to be dug down 'ere the wagons could pass. *(Ewert)*

The country is a hard one to pass over with a wagon-train and we were 24½ hours making it. *(Grant)*

Recourse was had to the hills on the right. *(Ludlow)*

The place where the wagons climbed a hill to get away from Negro Creek is half a mile further on.

14 43 54 01.7 Medicine Mountain Road just begins its 103 41 58.2 ascent here. On your left, Negro Creek swings east toward its confluence with Spring Creek—where Colonel Dodge would again try to ignore Custer's lead.

Most of the road construction nightmares occurred on Negro Creek, where Colonel Dodge—trying to follow the road a year later (June 13, 1875)—read the story of this day in physical scars on the landscape.

Had a D—l of a time working Custers trail out of a morass in which almost every wagon seems to have been stuck and to have each got out on its own hook. The first

seven miles *[taking him over the ridge past Six Mile Road]* were easily made, & in good time. We crossed a divide & struck a stream *[Negro Creek]* which Joe *[Merivale, a guide]* says is the head of Spring Ck & which is the origin of the Morass spoken of. *(Dodge)*

When Dodge came to the area of **Point 14***, not far from the end of Reno Gulch Road, he had his heart set on following Spring Creek to the east. He did not give up on the idea very easily.*

Custer's trail . . . turned off from the creek, & I wishing to make my permanent camp on it, followed it down. It got worse & worse, & after several bad crossings, & a lot of bad road, I sent Spaulding down to look at the prospect. He returned after an hour & & told me it was impossible to go down the Creek. Still hoping I left him to put the Comd in camp, and went down myself for about 4 miles. I can go down with wagons, though it will take a deal of work but could do nothing after I got there, the sides of the immense gorge being impassable even for pack mules. After a hard search for a better fate, I had to yield to imperative necessity & decide to go back tomorw to Custer's trail. *(Dodge)*

The Colonel apparently never realized that Custer was following a route developed over time by Native Americans. How must Dodge have felt, having to write almost the same words twice within two days:

The more I see of the Country the more disposed I am to give credit to Custer for his march through here. He must have had a corps of guides more reliable than usual —for they certainly have struck almost the only route at all practicable for wagons. *(Dodge)*

Follow the Expedition wagons up the hill almost three-tenths of a mile, to the junction with Reno Gulch Road.

15 43 53 47.7 This is a safe place to pull over for any 103 41 55.0 reading you may wish to do, or exploring on foot. Where Medicine Mountain Road turns sharply to the right just ahead, you should be able to see ruts going straight down the hill.

Drive another two-tenths of a mile, to a pullout on the right (**Point D**) just before the stone bridge over Spring Creek.

16 43 53 39.2 This reading is at the far end of the 103 41 51.8 meadow to your left, where there is a ford on the creek. You will find ruts on the hill to the north, and you should be able to see an old trail across the creek.

*The Expedition crossed Spring Creek at **Point 16**, where the impressions of old trails are still found on either side. Tom Kilian remembers being able to see the remains of bridge abutments on each bank in this area, presumably for a reinforced or rebuilt version of the bridge first engineered by Custer.*

A ravine had to be bridged, and up one steep grade the teams had to be doubled. *(Pioneer)*

Rifle shot could be heard on all side, which told the

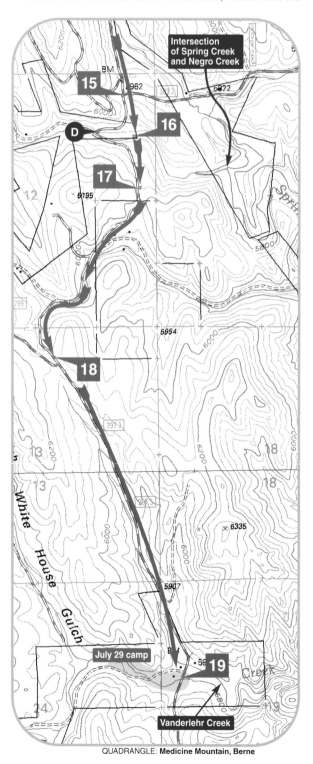

QUADRANGLE: **Medicine Mountain, Berne**

death tale of some passing deer. Lt. Chance brought his gun, a Gatlin, to bear on one, a fine buck, who seem[ed] to be admiring the passing troops, & with one bound fell dead. *(Power)*

Lieut. Chance . . . received a kick from a horse ridden by Capt'n French and was badly hurt. *(Calhoun)*

. . . which gave him a ride in the ambulance. . . . His wound is just below the knee & while it is quite painful is still not dangerous, being only a flesh wound. The Lt was also unfortunate enough to dismount one of his guns & render it unfit for action—one wheel being broking in coming down a hill. *(Power)*

Let's consider these events for a moment: after killing a deer with a piece of artillery (the Gatling gun), Lt. Chance is not only kicked in the leg by a horse but also has a piece of his artillery damaged. The spirit of the deer must have been powerful that day.

Sergt. Clair of the Hd Qts detachment, not satisfied with killing two fine deer, shot one of the men. *(Power)*

A private of Company C . . . accidentally wounded in the right arm from a carbine shot. *(Calhoun)*

Check your odometer at the Spring Creek bridge (**Point D**) and drive three-tenths of a mile up the hill. Stop before you reach a set of buffalo corrals on the left.

17 43 53 28.6 About 30 feet to the left of the road are 103 41 50.4 a pair of ruts that angle up the hill from the ford on Spring Creek. Stage coaches and other early traffic would have used this grade as well. Medicine Mountain Road rejoins Custer's trail at the top of the hill.

Continue another nine-tenths of a mile. You will pass through a valley on the way, where there may be an electric fence on the left and grazing buffalo in a pasture beyond. Take note of this valley; it may be where the wagons stopped briefly during the night.

18 43 52 53.9 This stop is near the crest of a hill just be- 103 42 16.5 fore the junction of FS 299. Large pines mark an early trail about 20 feet to the left of the road.

Drive the last leg of your journey on FS 297, continuing 1.3 miles over the crest and down a long slope to Vanderlehr Creek. Stop before you get there, just this side of a house on the right.

Look down the valley to your left (east) and notice the jumble of rock outcrops that seems to block the way. Compare the scene to Winchell's description.

Camp was chosen . . . on a little ravine running east. We are surrounded by high mica-schist hills, and the little stream passes into a narrow cañon in this rock, about half a mile below our camp. *(Winchell)*

Genl & Hd Qts guard found at last a romantic spot over the hills & far away from our old camp—supplied with all the necessaries of life (Indian life): deer, Straw bers, Water, Wood & grass, & determined there to pitch our tents, providence permitting, but it did not. *(Power)*

There was no letup with Custer. He went ahead and

picked out a camping place. One afternoon especially I remember, he picked out a camping place and said, "I guess they can come this far." *(Wood)*

Continue one-tenth of a mile to a large culvert that carries Vanderlehr Creek beneath the road.

19 43 51 47.8 It was in the valley to your right that Custer
103 41 39.6 stopped and waited for the wagons.

⌒The advancing night found us still at work. General Custer, who had gone no one knew where, was as good as lost to us 'till about ten o'clock p.m., when an orderly came back with orders for all the companies, except "M" (pioneers) and "E" (rear guard) to come ahead to camp. Accordingly, we got our camp kettles, coffee, sugar and crackers and started up hill, down hill, over a mountain, through the rocky bed of a mountain brook, now breaking our way through a dense growth of young cottonwood trees, then again riding along on a bare, narrow ridge 'till nearly twelve o'clock when we came into a very pretty little park and there found General Custer encamped. *(Ewert)*

The result was night came, and the train rested in a little valley three miles from headquarters. The command was divided, the greater portion being with the train. *(Pioneer)*

Private Ewert and the Pioneer *differ on where the majority of the cavalry companies spent the night. The newspaper is also the only source to suggest that the wagons stopped along the way, although it seems reasonable that the teamsters and pioneer crew would need some kind of a break. The valley of the buffalo pasture, about two miles north of Vanderlehr Creek, was a likely resting place.*

Exactly what happened and where will probably remain unclear, since there was no one to speak for those who stayed with the wagons. The men who recorded their observations for posterity were all up ahead. Custer himself ignored the difficulty of the train in his official report.

⌒We camped on a small creek, furnishing us an abundance of good water and grass. The direction of this creek was nearly east. *(Custer)*

The advance prepared for a bivouac. Several deer had been brought in, and over the camp fires slices of the tender venison were roasted on the ends of forked sticks. This, with "hard tack" and the icy-cold water made our evening meal. The meat was delicious; but to an appetite sharpened by the day's ride through the cool, mountain air, almost anything is good. *(Pioneer)*

Could you hear the profane language which emanated from the lips of some soldiers and civilian employees because they could not reach camp in time to get something to eat you would verily believe that the heathen deity "Hecate, goddess of the lower regions," was let loose. *(Calhoun)*

Poor "M" and "E" with the wagon train came into camp just as the first light came into the eastern sky.

The men riding with headquarters were not too terribly inconvenienced.

⌒Beneath the deep foliage of the pines bright fires were built, and with no other mantle than the starlit heavens, we passed away the hours of night in telling stories, or in sleeping on the ground. After a while the moon rose, and its soft lambent light chased the darkness from the valley, and the paler stars faded from the sky. *(Pioneer)*

Rank-and-file soldiers had dinner after midnight, but Private Ewert paints an upbeat picture.

⌒The moon was at a full, and in its hazy dimness we saw some real splendid pieces of wild landscape. Having unsaddled, watered and picketed our horses, we built fires and cooked our cup of coffee, and during this meal we enjoyed many a hearty laugh over tales and stories that were told; toil, trouble and hardship of the day were forgotten and everyone contributed something to make the present moment enjoyable and pregnant with fun. After our midnight repast we again watered and then groomed our poor, tired horses, after which we spread down our single, solitary horse blanket and, with the sky for our ceiling and the moon for our lamp, we had scarcely more than touched our bed 'till sleep took possession. *(Ewert)*

While some slept, others were still on the trail. It is hard to fully imagine what it was like to build roads or drive wagons through the night—even with a full moon.

⌒At length, at about half past three the lumbering train came in, and by sunrise breakfast was ready. *(Pioneer)*

When we got through our work and arrived at camp, it was four o'clock the next morning before we got the last wagon into camp, and the command was about ready to move out on another day's march. *(Ryan)*

All the train was not in at 4 a.m., when reveille sounded. *(Forsyth)*

Poor "M" and "E" with the wagon train came into camp just as the first light came into the eastern sky and, when the sun made its appearance we were again leaving camp for another day's toil. *(Ewert)*

General Custer allowed us two days fatigue duty for that day. *(Ryan)*

CHAPTER 7

Thursday-Friday, July 30-31

Vanderlehr Creek to the City of Custer, with a layover

*One of our miners . . . washed out a pan or two of earth
right from the grass roots. There was gold there.* (New York Tribune)

Starting late, the command kept to an Indian trail that is still followed today in places by Medicine Mountain Road. Some of the men got excited over a mountain of "silver," while others remarked on their first good view of granite. Custer was forced to abandon the Indian trail and find his own way into the area that would soon bear his name. It was there that gold was first panned in the Black Hills, or at least first reported. Distance traveled: 10.2 miles. While Custer climbed Harney Peak the next day, some soldiers played baseball and several officers enjoyed a "champagne supper."

— Taking the trail —

U.S.G.S. MAPS: Berne, Custer

CAUTIONS: The roads are smooth gravel or paved, but part of the trail is on private land.

TO START: *From Custer*, drive 3.2 miles north on U.S. 16/385 from the center of town. Turn left and make sure you stay on Medicine Mountain Road (FS 297), driving 5.9 miles to a culvert that carries Vanderlehr Creek beneath the road. Turn around.

From Hill City, drive 8.5 miles west on Deerfield Road (FS 17) to E. Slate Road (FS 300) and turn left. After 4.2 miles, keep left at the "Y" onto Medicine Mountain Road (FS 297). Go another 7.7 miles to a culvert that carries Vanderlehr Creek beneath the road. (If you don't mind narrow Forrest Service roads, you can save about six miles and five minutes by using the Reno Gulch Road, starting a mile and a half south of Hill City and ending at Medicine Mountain Road. Turn left there and go 2.8 miles to the culvert.)

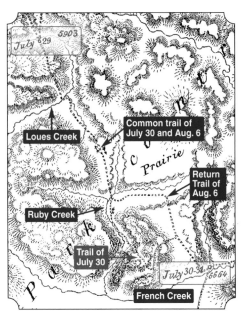

Expedition map
(1 inch = 3 miles)

Map labels: July 29 5903; Loues Creek; Common trail of July 30 and Aug. 6; Prairie; Return Trail of Aug. 6; Ruby Creek; Trail of July 30; July 30-31 6664; French Creek

The wagon train arrived a short time before daylight. Reveille 3:45. *(Calhoun)*

The wagons got into camp at 4:30 A.M. this morning—after marching all night. *(Grant)*

The headquarters staff, along with the soldiers who had come in sometime after midnight, were already awake again when the wagons appeared carrying their tents and food supplies.

After spending a night in the open air & having our appetites sharpened by a fast of 24 hours, we were well prepared to enjoy a good breakfast. So after arranging our toilett we made our way to the mess tent, but alas for our stomach's hope. We were scarcely seated when Genl was sounded & then boots & Saddle, the aforesaid calls scarcely giving us time to drink a cup of coffee. *(Power)*

Fred Power may not have been invited to the venison-and-hardtack dinner that Expedition botanist Aris

Donaldson described in his Pioneer *story (page 71). But both men had it better than the new arrivals.*

⤶About ten minutes before, Capt McDougall might have been seen coming in to camp, having spent the night on the road with the wagons. Col Wheaton & Maj Sanger of the Infy also were on the go all night. *(Power)*

The recently discovered Power diary confirms Private Ewert's account (page 71) that E Company—led by 1st Lieutenant Thomas W. McDougall—stayed behind when the other companies were called in the night before. The two infantry companies (G and I) were also guarding the wagons and teamsters. Imagine the feelings of these men as they struggled along a tortuous road in the dark while those who chose the route were resting up ahead in relative comfort. When the teamsters and the rear guard finally arrived, they had only a couple of hours in which they could either sleep or eat.

⤶Leaving camp at 7 a.m. we travel southeast, and soon strike a smooth valley running in the same direction. *(Winchell)*
. . . still following the Indian trail, which led us through the valley by a fine road, out into an open, park-like country, very beautiful, with vales and natural avenues in every directions, running between low hills covered with a fine growth of good pine, and with numbers of good springs in all directions. *(Forsyth)*

1 43 51 47.8 This is your starting place on Medicine
103 41 39.6 Mountain Road at Vanderlehr Creek, in or near the July 29 camp. Follow the command over the divide, crossing Loues Creek at 1.4 miles (**Point 2**). Go another two-tenths of a mile and stop on a curve.

3 43 50 32.7 Note that the present-day road passes
103 41 14.3 through a cut dug out from the point of a hill. About 40 feet to the left, between you and the drainage, is a wagon rut that represents the earliest version of the road—and was likely following the Expedition's tracks.
Continue nine-tenths of a mile through a landscape that clearly enchanted the explorers.

⤶We traveled all day through a beautiful pastoral and agricultural country, half wood, half glade, full of deer and abundantly grassed. *(Ludlow)*
. . . through handsome groves, along valleys green, and over prairies, rich for tillage and grazing. On our left was a high, stony, granite ridge. *(Pioneer)*

The soldiers of the 7th Cavalry got their first good look at the granite range as they crossed the head of Graveyard Gulch (near **Point 4***). Within that view was the peak that would one day be carved as a memorial to Crazy Horse, who helped annihilate some of these same cavalry companies less than two years later.*

4 43 49 51.8 Shortly after passing FS 285 on the right,
103 40 50.7 start trying (carefully) to catch glimpses of the Crazy Horse carving and other granite peaks through the trees on your left. You may want to park and walk along the road for a better view from the route of the Expedition.

⤶We pass Harney Peak early this AM. *(Power)*
. . . eight or nine miles on the left. *(Ludlow)*

William Illingworth was apparently drawn by the view to follow the rim of Graveyard Gulch to the area of **Point A**, where he took a photo that included Harney Peak. (See the next two pages for more detail; Photo on page 196.) You may have trouble seeing Harney Peak from the road, but you should be able to see the huge triangular slab of granite that figures prominently in the picture.
Continue 1.1 miles from Point 4 (3.6 miles from the camp) and pull over on a curve.

5 43 49 04.8 There is a very
103 40 13.4 well-defined rut going up the hill to the south here, continuing in line with the road from the north. Mature trees in the rut suggest that it was part of the early trail engineered by Custer.

QUADRANGLE: **Berne**

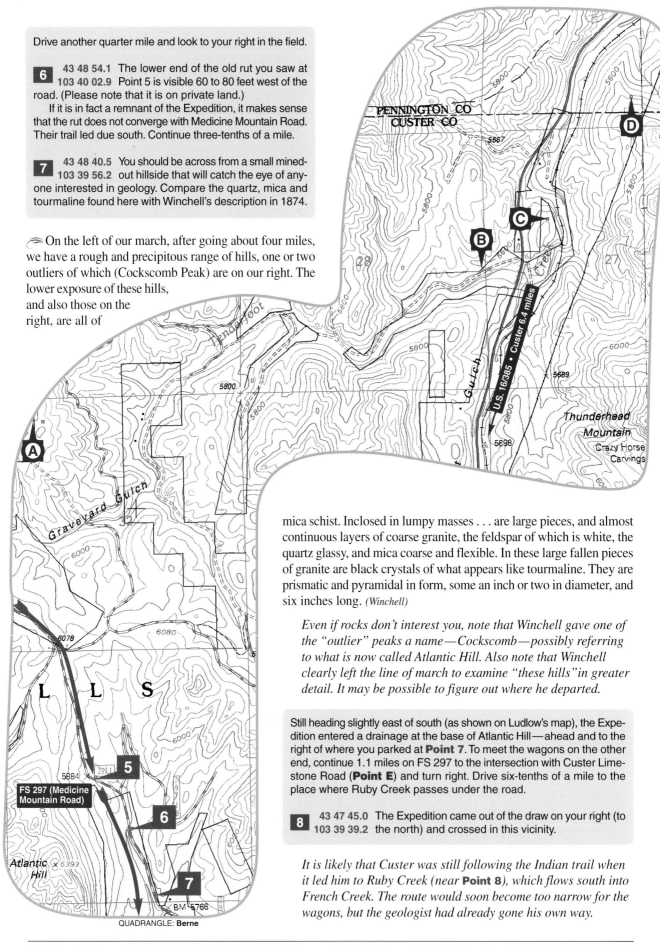

Drive another quarter mile and look to your right in the field.

6 43 48 54.1 The lower end of the old rut you saw at
103 40 02.9 Point 5 is visible 60 to 80 feet west of the
road. (Please note that it is on private land.)

If it is in fact a remnant of the Expedition, it makes sense that the rut does not converge with Medicine Mountain Road. Their trail led due south. Continue three-tenths of a mile.

7 43 48 40.5 You should be across from a small mined-
103 39 56.2 out hillside that will catch the eye of any-
one interested in geology. Compare the quartz, mica and tourmaline found here with Winchell's description in 1874.

On the left of our march, after going about four miles, we have a rough and precipitous range of hills, one or two outliers of which (Cockscomb Peak) are on our right. The lower exposure of these hills, and also those on the right, are all of

PENNINGTON CO
CUSTER CO

U.S. 16/385 • Custer 6.4 miles

Thunderhead
Mountain
Crazy Horse
Carvings

mica schist. Inclosed in lumpy masses . . . are large pieces, and almost continuous layers of coarse granite, the feldspar of which is white, the quartz glassy, and mica coarse and flexible. In these large fallen pieces of granite are black crystals of what appears like tourmaline. They are prismatic and pyramidal in form, some an inch or two in diameter, and six inches long. *(Winchell)*

Even if rocks don't interest you, note that Winchell gave one of the "outlier" peaks a name—Cockscomb—possibly referring to what is now called Atlantic Hill. Also note that Winchell clearly left the line of march to examine "these hills" in greater detail. It may be possible to figure out where he departed.

Still heading slightly east of south (as shown on Ludlow's map), the Expedition entered a drainage at the base of Atlantic Hill—ahead and to the right of where you parked at **Point 7**. To meet the wagons on the other end, continue 1.1 miles on FS 297 to the intersection with Custer Limestone Road (**Point E**) and turn right. Drive six-tenths of a mile to the place where Ruby Creek passes under the road.

8 43 47 45.0 The Expedition came out of the draw on your right (to
103 39 39.2 the north) and crossed in this vicinity.

*It is likely that Custer was still following the Indian trail when it led him to Ruby Creek (near **Point 8**), which flows south into French Creek. The route would soon become too narrow for the wagons, but the geologist had already gone his own way.*

FS 297 (Medicine
Mountain Road)

Atlantic
Hill

QUADRANGLE: **Berne**

≈ Passing on about three miles farther, and a little to the east, we come in full view of a range of granite hills running nearly north and south. *(Winchell)*

Consider the geologist's distance estimates. From the camp to Graveyard Gulch and the first sighting of the granite range is less than three miles—not the four he says on the previous page. But it is indeed about three miles from there to Ruby Creek.

*The problem is that no peaks are visible from Ruby Creek (**Point 8**), which runs through a valley. When we examined Winchell's field notes, however, we saw that the phrase "and a little to the east" was added later between the lines, as if to clarify that he had to travel east before he could see the peaks. He also added the note, "They are sketched on the next page," and the sketch itself—not included in the 1875 report—is so accurate in its detail that part of it was recreated in a photograph taken due east of Ruby Creek (**Point F**). The photo and sketch are on page 3.*

≈ Approaching the foot of these hills I pass over one or two low parallel granite ridges that seem to lie in the mica-schist, and are now thrust 10 or 20 feet above it. *(Winchell)*

It seems inescapable that when headquarters staff came to Ruby Creek, Winchell took advantage of the open prairie to the east—where these ridges can be found—and went to examine the granite formations.

≈ Prof Winchell spends his time in finding out their hidden wealth. *(Power)*

Having left camp at 7 a.m. and ridden horseback about six miles as part of the headquarters staff, the geologist would have started his exploration in the middle or late morning. The place and time are interesting by themselves as we try to build a picture of daily life in a western expedition. But they may also shed light on a

series of photographs taken in the area by William Illingworth, numbered 819 through 824.

A 43 50 18.2 After taking no pictures that we know of 103 40 27.2 the day before, Illingworth seems to have been inspired to a flurry of activity by the granite range. This is the approximate site of **Photo 819**, "Harney's Peak at 10 miles distance, altitude 9200 feet" (page 196).

B 43 50 47.8 Going by numbers, the next picture was 103 38 16.3 taken less than two miles away: **Photo 820**, "Pulpit Knob, altitude 8700 feet" (page 198).

C Illingworth then moved a little farther east, onto a small hill that is now private land. Here he took three views from almost exactly the same location:
821, "Pulpit Knob, altitude 8700 feet" (page 200)
822, "Gold Quartz Mountain, altitude 3600 feet" (page 202)
823, "Turkey Rock" (page 204).

D 43 51 23.2 Finally, Illingworth climbed a nearby hill 103 37 33.3 for **Photo 824**, "Illingworth Valley, near Harney's Peak." (page 206).

*Looking at the relationship of **Point A** to **Point B** on the opposite page, it is hard not to assume that Illingworth followed Graveyard Gulch down to Tenderfoot Gulch, where his next photo site was located. It is equally hard to imagine, however, that he would have been allowed to wander off on his own, or that he would try to take his wagon down those draws and find his own way to camp later on.*

It is far more plausible that Winchell was given an escort for his explorations, that Illingworth took advantage of the detachment to work under its protection, and that they returned north in the area of today's Highway 16/385 to see the formations first noticed from the head of Graveyard Gulch. They might even have been accompanied by other members of the scientific corps, like botanist Aris Donaldson, who wrote for the St. Paul Pioneer.

≈ On our left was a high, stony, granite ridge. . . . there is no regularity or symmetry in their forms, and they constantly change in profile as viewed from different points. This was a busy day for the landscape photographer. *(Pioneer)*

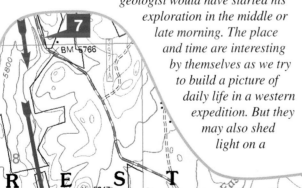
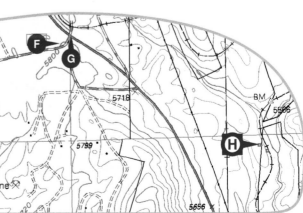

QUADRANGLES: **Berne, Custer**

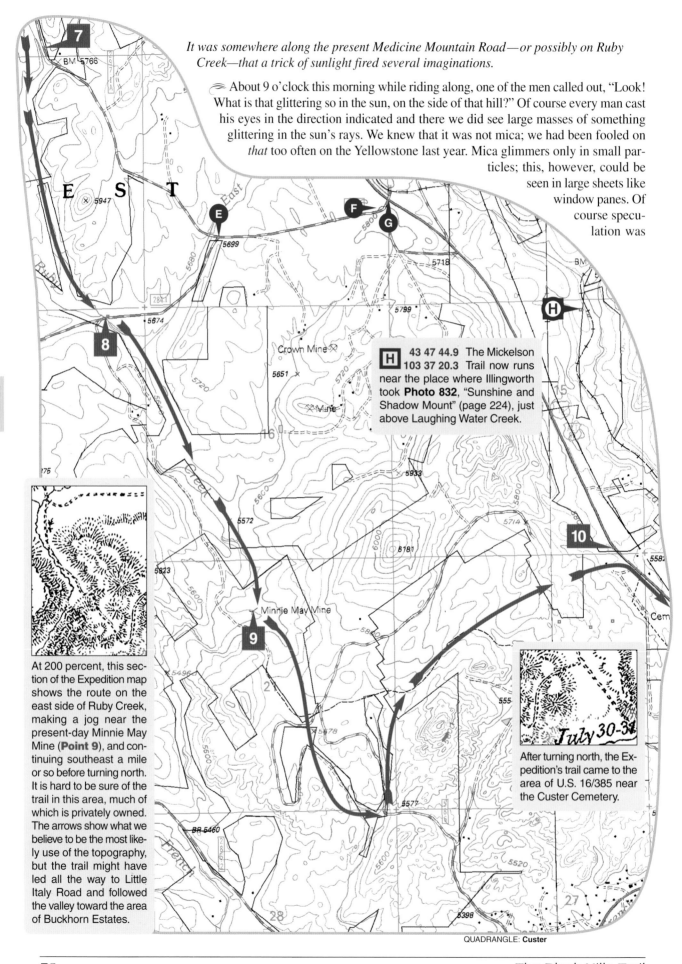

It was somewhere along the present Medicine Mountain Road—or possibly on Ruby Creek—that a trick of sunlight fired several imaginations.

☞ About 9 o'clock this morning while riding along, one of the men called out, "Look! What is that glittering so in the sun, on the side of that hill?" Of course every man cast his eyes in the direction indicated and there we did see large masses of something glittering in the sun's rays. We knew that it was not mica; we had been fooled on *that* too often on the Yellowstone last year. Mica glimmers only in small particles; this, however, could be seen in large sheets like window panes. Of course speculation was

H 43 47 44.9 The Mickelson
103 37 20.3 Trail now runs
near the place where Illingworth took **Photo 832**, "Sunshine and Shadow Mount" (page 224), just above Laughing Water Creek.

At 200 percent, this section of the Expedition map shows the route on the east side of Ruby Creek, making a jog near the present-day Minnie May Mine (**Point 9**), and continuing southeast a mile or so before turning north. It is hard to be sure of the trail in this area, much of which is privately owned. The arrows show what we believe to be the most likely use of the topography, but the trail might have led all the way to Little Italy Road and followed the valley toward the area of Buckhorn Estates.

After turning north, the Expedition's trail came to the area of U.S. 16/385 near the Custer Cemetery.

QUADRANGLE: **Custer**

rife; everyone knew it was *something*, only they couldn't tell exactly what. Finally one suggested that it looked mightily like silver, and another immediately *knew* it to be silver. He remembered having heard that the Black Hills could show mountains of solid silver and this was one of those mountains. Another said that his claim of 160 acres should be staked off immediately after dismounting on that very identical mountain. Another thought that both saddle pockets full would be sufficient load for his horse to carry, but then he was a pretty good friend of the company teamsters, and he would, no doubt, let them carry a hundred pounds or so in the wagons. *(Ewert)*

Private Theodore Ewert—Prussian-born and a lieutenant during the U.S. Civil War—proved himself quite a stylist in making his sly observations about human nature. To reflect the mid-morning sun rising behind the granite peaks to the east, this mountain of alleged silver would most likely have been to the southeast, which was along the line of march.

☞ When we came near the hill we were told that all that glittering stuff was only Eisenglass [sic]. *(Ewert)*

*Mica—sometimes called isinglass—is plentiful in the area, so it is hard to know which hill inspired these silver dreams. If Ewert's company was with the wagons at 9 A.M., they might have been coming down to **Point 7**, where a hillside has been mined out. If it happened farther on, the dreamers might have seen the Crown Mine hill or one of the smaller mica mines near it. (The Minnie May was an underground gold and silver mine.)*

QUADRANGLE: **Custer**

Ewert had more fun with the reaction of his companions to this dose of reality.

☞ A half dozen or more of the men immediately knew—and had known all this time—that it was only Eisenglass [sic]. The man that wanted to put a hundred pounds or so in a wagon was one of these. On closer inspection this hill did not suit the one that had wanted to locate his claim here immediately on dismounting, and he thought he'd wait 'till prospects for silver, or gold—he wouldn't be particular—were better. *(Ewert)*

The Expedition map is our only source for the route from Ruby Creek to the next camp, since none of the accounts talks about what happened. It appears from the map (see boxes, opposite page) that the wagons were already committed to Ruby Creek before Custer found out he couldn't take them all the way through.

Much of the trail between Ruby Creek and Custer is on private land. To connect with it again, turn around at **Point 8** and go back to Medicine Mountain Road (**Point E**). Turn right and drive seven-tenths of a mile to U.S. 16/385 (**Point G**) and turn right again. Go 1.5 miles to a bend in the highway and pull off the pavement, in front of a house on the right.

10 43 46 55.8 Buckhorn Estates Drive is just ahead. The
103 37 11.7 Expedition came down the slope on your right and turned south in front of you, probably crossing the northern corner of the Custer Cemetery.

☞ Passed near the base of a range of mountains, which hid Harney's Peak from our view. *(Forsyth)*

Preparing this book has brought home to us just how often the roads we use were first laid out by Custer or other early explorers, and in some cases by Native Americans before that. An old survey map proves as much in the Piedmont area (page 151). Here, a section of U.S. 16/385 lies on top of or very close to the Expedition route in and out of Custer, as described on page 98. It is therefore possible that on a hot day near the end of July, the man credited with discovering gold in the Black Hills rode over his own grave. Horatio Nelson Ross was buried in the Custer Cemetery 30 years later, in 1904.

Continue six-tenths of a mile and turn right on 3rd Street, a gravel road just past the Black Hills National Forest office.

11 43 46 31.4 Follow the road down an easy grade,
103 36 36.5 approximating the route to French Creek.

We descended into a beautiful valley. The fruits of the bramble gathered in large quantities. Wild raspberries and gooseberries, currants & cherries seen everywhere on our line of march. *(Calhoun)*

Blueberries were found in great numbers today and the men are having quite a feast of them. *(Ewert)*

Encamped about 3 p.m. in a fine open country, among a lot of low, wooded hills, with vales opening in all directions, on the bank of a still creek. *(Forsyth)*

The official report lists the arrival of the wagon train at 1 p.m., and the New York Tribune *said noon. But there was little disagreement over the qualities of the valley.*

Evening found us encamped in one of the most charming and lovely natural parks in the world. *(Pioneer)*

A perfect fairy land in summer. *(Power)*

Travelers tell me that nothing known compares with it. The scenery is more interesting than that of the Yosemite, of the Yellowstone or Central Park. *(Bismarck Tribune)*

From **Point 11** continue all the way down 3rd Street to U.S. 16 (Mt. Rushmore Road). Note the steady, gentle grade that would have been easy on the wagons. In fact, part of 3rd Street may have been the original road into town (following the Expedition) until a cut was made in a hillside to accommodate the present Highway 16/385.

Turn left on Mt. Rushmore Road and drive east to 8th Street. Turn right and go one block to the far end of the grocery store parking lot on your left.

12 43 46 00.1 This puts you very close to the heart of 103 35 40.0 the camp, which the map locates on the intersection of French and Laughing Water Creeks. You can find French Creek on the other side of the Mickelson Trail, just south of the parking lot. If you follow the trail east a short distance, you'll come to a bridge that spans Laughing Water Creek. If the bridge had been here in 1874, it would have given you a very interesting vantage point.

Gen. Custer is probably the first civilized man whose eyes beheld this scene of beauty. After much entreaty, his modesty so far gave way as reluctantly to consent to the request of the topographical engineer that the name be Custer Park. *(Pioneer)*

Capt. Ludlow may have been the one to overcome Custer's deep, deep reserves of modesty, but he did not describe Custer Park in the same idyllic terms the others had used.

Our proximity to the outer plains in the east was evident as camp was neared. The air was milder, the grass drier, and the streams contained less water. Grasshoppers appeared, and a rattlesnake was captured in camp. All strong indications of the vicinity of the prairie. *(Ludlow)*

I am informed that "One Stab" the Indian prisoner guided us to this place. I had nearly forgot this poor captive. The Interpreter tells me that "One Stab" is exceedingly pleased with the treatment received from the Commanding Officer, that he never lived better, and the only thing troubling him is that his relatives suppose he is dead, and are lamenting over his demise. He sincerely hopes when he is restored to freedom that the Ree Scouts may be ignorant of the fact and be prevented from doing him harm. He is not afraid of the whites, for he has always found them friendly and charitable. "One Stab" has a son-in-law, a white man who has five children. *(Calhoun)*

This was a fateful day for One Stab's people, the Lakota Sioux, who had held onto the Black Hills for several decades and managed to keep the whites at bay. The presence of the Expedition would probably have been the beginning of the end in any case, but this was the day on which it became certain that everything was about to change.

On the 30th of July we halted about noon in a pleasant valley, within 10 miles of Harney's Peak. One of our miners took his pan, went to the stream and washed out a pan or two of earth taken right from the grass roots. There was gold there, but it was merely a color, requiring careful manipulation and an experienced eye to find it. *(New York Tribune)*

The gold-seekers who accompany the expedition report the finding of gold in the gravel and sand along this valley. *(Winchell)*

Some gold said to have been found. *(Grant)*

The discovery announced created a good deal of interest but little commotion, not half the excitement, indeed, that the blooming exuberance of Floral Valley produced. Perhaps many were still incredulous. *(New York Tribune)*

This is one part of the answer to that perennial debate over the first discovery of gold in the Black Hills. There are tantalizing

QUADRANGLE: **Custer**

hints that it was first seen in the area of Castle Creek (pages 56-57), and it would soon be found in greater quantities—enough to justify the staking of claims further down the valley (page 87). But here we have solid testimony that the first real color—the first grains of actual gold—were found not long after noon on July 30, 1874, on French Creek in the southeast corner of Custer.

The few glittering grains, with a slight residue of earth, were carefully wrapped up in a small piece of paper and put in the miner's pocketbook. It was simply an earnest of what was to come. *(New York Tribune)*

Reporter Samuel Barrows is foreshadowing events that were more momentous than he probably could have known. Horatio Nelson Ross's simple act of panning on French Creek was about to unleash a tide of gold-seekers that would sweep into the Black Hills in violation of the 1868 Treaty of Fort Laramie, helping to set the stage for Little Big Horn two years later and—14 years after that—the massacre at Wounded Knee. The course of history in the West was literally being altered on this afternoon.

But the biggest concern among the soldiers was a chance to do their laundry.

Orders were issued in the evening that the command would remain in camp tomorrow to enable the men to wash clothes and allow the exploring of the surrounding country, and Harney's Peak in particular. The men are rejoiced as the clothing from riding through bushes and briars has become worn and torn and needs mending. *(Ewert)*

This is part of a tree preserved in the 1881 Custer County Courthouse Museum. The Expedition roster included John McDonnell, a private in G Company. (The "h" in "John" would have been above the "1" of "1874" on a missing piece of wood.)

Friday, July 31
Climbing Harney Peak · The first baseball game

Companies A & G, 7th Cavalry, divided into four detachments. *(Calhoun)*

Four engineering parties went out in various directions to map the country. *(Forsyth)*

Company G included Private John McDonnell, who carved his name into a tree at some point during his stay in this valley. The carving (pictured above) was preserved when the tree was cut down, and is now in the 1881 Courthouse Museum on Mt. Rushmore Road in Custer—along with many other items of interest on the Expedition and Black Hills history in general.

The expedition delays here a day or two to allow the animals to recuperate. *(Winchell)*

The miners had a chance to renew their search. The result was the discovery of a good bar, yielding from five to seven cents per pan, which could easily be made to pay if water were more plentiful there. *(New York Tribune)*

General Custer and myself, with Professors Winchell and Donaldson and Mr. Wood, escorted by a company of cavalry, set out to ascend Harney. *(Ludlow)*

The climbing party started north along Laughing Water Creek, then managed to cross the granite range above Buckhorn Mountain. This improbable

route is not only shown on Ludlow's map (next page) but described in Winchell's field notebook.

Gen. Custer accompanied us, the whole party shaping its movements according to the desire of Col. Ludlow *[his breveted rank]* for topographical purposes. We set out N. and passed to the south east the peaks which I sketched the day before in coming to camp. *(Winchell notebook)*

The climbing party passed among bald knobs and through grassy valleys, then went up a granite ridge.

On ascending this ridge a most magnificent prospect burst suddenly upon us, which caused us each, on reaching the summit, to utter an exclamation of surprise and wonder. . . . To the northeast, however, was the grandest sight I ever beheld. This was a truly Alpine view. Here was Pelion on Ossa. . . . Very near us, and cutting off our view north, was a series of spindled peaks which, though massive and imposing, proved to be mere pygmies to the giants of the same shape and character that rose in the distance. . . . In the valley before us stood up scattered, conical, granitic "sugar-loaves," in the background of which, rising nearly as high as old Harney himself, was a perfect nest of organ-pipe peaks whose sharp spindling tops immediately suggested the name Organ Peaks, which name they

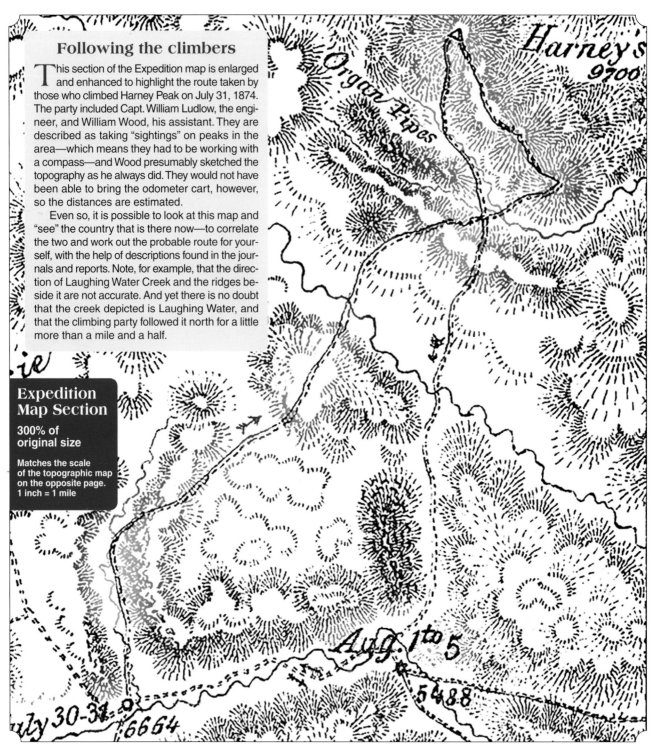

Following the climbers

This section of the Expedition map is enlarged and enhanced to highlight the route taken by those who climbed Harney Peak on July 31, 1874. The party included Capt. William Ludlow, the engineer, and William Wood, his assistant. They are described as taking "sightings" on peaks in the area—which means they had to be working with a compass—and Wood presumably sketched the topography as he always did. They would not have been able to bring the odometer cart, however, so the distances are estimated.

Even so, it is possible to look at this map and "see" the country that is there now—to correlate the two and work out the probable route for yourself, with the help of descriptions found in the journals and reports. Note, for example, that the direction of Laughing Water Creek and the ridges beside it are not accurate. And yet there is no doubt that the creek depicted is Laughing Water, and that the climbing party followed it north for a little more than a mile and a half.

Expedition Map Section

300% of original size

Matches the scale of the topographic map on the opposite page.
1 inch = 1 mile

retain. There are two such nests, and they were both in view, separated not more than three-quarters of a mile. *(Winchell)*

Here is the first recorded description of the Needles and Cathedral Spires. As spectacular as they were, they hid Harney Peak from the climbing party, which would cause serious delays. Instead of "Organ Peaks" Winchell probably meant to say "Organ Pipes," the name on Ludlow's map (above) and in the titles of two Illingworth photographs (pages 212-215).

The reconnaissance party, meanwhile, moved on to a familiar-looking peak.

We commenced a winding course toward the peak which we took for Harney's. Its crest presented a sharp ridge, with perpendicular sides . . . and had been seen by Colonel Ludlow and myself from a limestone bluff in Castle Valley a few days before. *(Winchell)*

Then came the climbing of stony ridges, picking our way through burned and fallen timber, boring through the

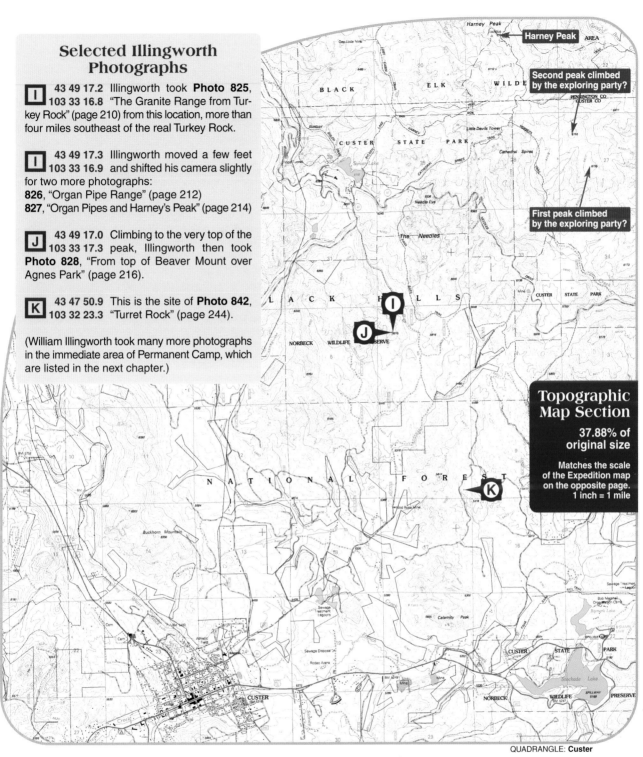

Selected Illingworth Photographs

I 43 49 17.2 Illingworth took **Photo 825**,
103 33 16.8 "The Granite Range from Turkey Rock" (page 210) from this location, more than four miles southeast of the real Turkey Rock.

I 43 49 17.3 Illingworth moved a few feet
103 33 16.9 and shifted his camera slightly for two more photographs:
826, "Organ Pipe Range" (page 212)
827, "Organ Pipes and Harney's Peak" (page 214)

J 43 49 17.0 Climbing to the very top of the
103 33 17.3 peak, Illingworth then took **Photo 828**, "From top of Beaver Mount over Agnes Park" (page 216).

K 43 47 50.9 This is the site of **Photo 842**,
103 32 23.3 "Turret Rock" (page 244).

(William Illingworth took many more photographs in the immediate area of Permanent Camp, which are listed in the next chapter.)

Harney Peak

Harney Peak AREA

Second peak climbed by the exploring party?

First peak climbed by the exploring party?

Topographic Map Section

37.88% of original size

Matches the scale of the Expedition map on the opposite page.
1 inch = 1 mile

QUADRANGLE: **Custer**

tanglewood of the gorges, and occasional flounderings through treacherous morasses. *(Pioneer)*

The trees had been thrown down by fire or tempest, often half consumed and left charred, and a thousand shrubs and small aspens . . .had made a perfect netted mesh, through which no horse could pass. *(Winchell)*

But all the way there was cool water and abundance of berries. *(Pioneer)*

Remember that there was no ice on the Expedition,

no corner store for soda, candy, chips or pastries. Keeping that in mind, the purple raptures over cold water and berries have a lot more meaning.

In the dark wet bottoms the june-berry bushes grew to a height of 10 or 12 feet, and hung full of fruit. *(Ludlow)*

Large and luscious service berries hung in such thick clusters that beneath their weight branches were bending down and almost breaking. There were a few trailing blackberries or dewberries. But of raspberries there was

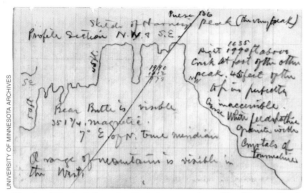

Newton Winchell drew the first close-up view of the Harney Peak summit in his notebook on July 31, 1874.

no end. . . . They grow best where the forests had been burned, and were found all the way up to the top of Harney's Peak. *(Pioneer)*

A rough ride of eight or nine miles . . . brought us to the foot of a granite elevation. *(Ludlow)*

Leaving the horses we had to scale the almost verticle wall for about 200 feet. Wedging ourselves into the clefts, and pushing ourselves up after the fashion of chimney sweeps, clinging to projecting points and straddling over ridges, we at last reached the top. *(Pioneer)*

I emerged upon the top, and sat down, or dropped down, to rest, almost exhausted. The rest of the scaling-party soon came up. *(Winchell)*

The geologist's account puts him at the top first, ahead of Custer, who had tried another route. The only problem was . . .

We climbed the highest peak in site only to discover one still higher. *(Forsyth)*

General Custer fired a salute of three shots from his rifle, we drank from our canteens to General Harney, and, after a lunch, decided to visit another peak lying toward the northwest, which rises some feet higher than that we had ascended. . . . General Forsyth and the writer descended as we came up, for the purpose of taking our horses, while the rest advance northwest toward that peak. *(Winchell)*

In due time we reach the top, and after a hurried glance start down again, calling to those below, "Stop! there is a higher peak beyond!" A council is held, and it is unanimously and enthusiastically resolved to visit No. 3 the true Harney's Peak . . . not visible from No. 1, on account of the intervention of No. 2. *(Pioneer)*

I with difficulty led my horse, and took him over the very summit just as the foot party were starting on the descent again. *(Winchell)*

Away we go! There is no time to lose. It is already late in the afternoon. Among trees, bushes and rocks we must go down an angle of nearly 45 degrees to the bottom of a ravine a thousand feet deep and a good deal more than a thousand up on the other side. *(Pioneer)*

They were soon out of sight. Here I found myself, with my horse, on the summit of a mountain alone, with no certainty of being able to follow the foot party, for General Forsyth had been delayed by taking charge of the escort. *(Winchell)*

TAKE ME OUT TO THE BALL GAME

A picked nine of the band and right wing consisting of Ryan and Rudolph of the band, Gilbert and Williams of "E" and McCarthy, Atzler, Logue, Warren and Krinkle of "L" company, calling themselves the Actives Base Ball Club of Fort Lincoln, D.T., played the Athlete Base Ball Club of Fort Rice, D.T., consisting of Long and Weston of "C," Rafter, Chesterwood and Gordon of "K," and Wine, Davis, McCort, and McCurry of "H" companies in the first of a series of match games today. Score: Actives – 11, Athletes – 6. *(Ewert)*

While Custer and his scientists were still working their way toward the true Harney Peak, some of the soldiers were playing a fairly new American game on a field that may well have been laid out within the city limits of present-day Custer. Three of the players would later die at the Little Big Horn. Two more would be wounded—one of whom, George "Fatty" Williams, reportedly signed papers in 1877 to play baseball professionally.

Time of the game: 2 hours and 25 minutes. The umpire, being from Fort Lincoln, favored the home club to such an extent that it was evident to every spectator on the ground, though the Athletes finished the game without a murmur. This club lost a prominent member and good player in Cunningham, who died at Inyan Kara. . . . Nearly the entire command was on the improvised field to witness the first game of baseball ever played in the Black Hills. *(Ewert)*

MEANWHILE, NEAR HARNEY PEAK . . .

The foot party, by a detour to the left . . . reached the foot of the difficulties of the real Harney's Peak some time later than I with my horse. *(Winchell)*

The geologist, left alone on Harney Peak number two, had managed to pass the climbing party by. Then he let himself be distracted.

Dismounting to fire at a doe that was startled by my approach, and following it up unsuccessfully, General Custer encountered my horse and rode it up to the same place. The ascent of this peak was very similar to that of the first. We made it together, the rest of the party being delayed. *(Winchell)*

Winchell made an entry in his notebook—apparently that night—that was not included in the elaborate account he wrote for the official report. But it gives us a feeling for the man.

Custer, Winchell, Wood, Ludlow, Forsyth, Donaldson, in the order of ascending. I should have been first up, as I was on the peak we visited first . . . except that I loaned my horse to Gen. Custer, who had walked several miles, just before reaching the summit. Hence we went up along-

July
30
31

side. He found my horse where I left him to hunt deer, for I was half a mile ahead, and on coming up I let him go on ahead. *(Winchell notebook)*

Pushing forward we completed the ascents about 4:30 p.m. *(Forsyth)*

We stood on the most elevated portion of the hills . . . except that alongside us rose a mass of granite 40 feet in height, with perpendicular sides that forbade an attempt to scale them without the aid of ropes and ladders. *(Ludlow)*

Prof. Winchell made the attempt and partially succeeded, but a loose rock just above him made it dangerous to climb higher. He stood above us all. *(Pioneer)*

Technically speaking, the first man on the summit of Harney Peak was Valentine McGillycuddy, who climbed that last block of granite in 1875 and whose ashes are now buried in the lookout tower there.

~ Bear Butte, forty-odd miles to the north, was again seen over the wooded ranges; and all but Inyan Kara of the principal peaks were in view. Two of the prominent ones I have named for General Terry and General Custer. *(Ludlow)*

The following memoranda was written and closely folded and put inside an empty copper cartridge shell. The point of the shell was beaten into a wedge shape and then driven into a seam in the rock: "Gen. G. A. Custer, Gen. G. A. Forsyth, Col. Wm. Ludlow, W. H. Wood, A. D. Donaldson, N. H. Winchell, Script. July 31, 1874." *(Pioneer)*

This cartridge case was found in the 1930s by Troy L. Parker of Hill City, who said the piece of paper had vanished. His son, the well-known historian Watson Parker, tells us the shell has now also been lost.

~ It was nearly sundown. The dark shadows nearly filled the ravines and sunlight only gilded the highest peaks. *(Pioneer)*

Picking up our escort about half-way down, we started for camp. *(Forsyth)*

The return to camp was a struggle against almost every possible obstacle—rocks, creeks, marshes, willow and aspen thickets, pine timber, dead and fallen trees, steep hillsides and precipitous ravines. Every difficulty multiplied by the darkness, and only the stars for a guide. *(Ludlow)*

On we go again! . . . The rocks strike fire from the horses' shoes. . . . The clatter and clang of iron hoofs, the words "Halt," "Dismount," and "Mount," and the crackling of branches, are about the only sounds. *(Pioneer)*

"Whiskey was not slighted"

~ Champaign supper in the Black Hills given by Capt Hale, Col Tilford, Benteen & Lt Hodgson. *(Power)*

Colonels Joseph Tilford and Frederick Benteen, well-known for their strong distaste for Custer, probably enjoyed this opportunity to relax without the General nearby. Power says in his diary that the absence of the climbers caused "considerable uneasiness," and the New York Tribune *reported that signal fires were built for their guidance. But that all came later.*

~ In the evening Major Tilford, who had a large tarpaulin stretched under the pine trees, gave a champagne supper to a number of officers. As the entire party became rather "boozy" before ten o'clock p.m., I had better omit all names, only assuring you that Lieut' Col' Fred Grant was one of the party and not the most sober one either. *(Ewert)*

*Grant can indeed be seen in the photograph Illingworth recorded of this event, the so-called "drinking party" photo (page 208). We now know the tarpaulin was stretched very close to what is now the corner of 8th and Montgomery Streets (***Point L***).*

~ Capt McDougall, Col Grant, Lt Gibson & others distinguished themselves by making very appropriate addresses. Benteen had a quartette from his Co come up & sing. *(Power)*

"H" Company's Glee Club serenaded this party, after which Lieutenant McDougall took them to the tent of Mr. Barrows, the New York Tribune correspondent. They disturbed his peaceful slumbers with "Come Where My Love Lies Dreaming," "Dinah's Wedding," "Vacant Chair," and "Under the Willows." Mr. Barrows called the serenaders into his tent, thanked them in his gentlemanly way for the honor, etc., and made an impressive finale by producing from some hiding place a couple of long-necked bottles not filled with water and not retained after this evening's use. *(Ewert)*

To visit the site of the "Drinking Party" photo (page 208), cross Mt. Rushmore Road and continue to the end of 8th Street.

L 43 46 15.3 Note the rock outcropping to the north, 103 35 49.8 partially cut away to make room for Montgomery Street—possibly in the very area of the party. A similar kind of rock is seen to the left in Illingworth's photo.

~ Champagne flowed plentiful, and also whiskey was not slighted. The whole party were pretty well hobbled. Hodgson found some difficulty crossing the creek—but finally made it all "O.K." On reaching camp I found him dreaming sweetly. *(Power)*

The climbers' return

~ Soon we struck the open avenues, followed them down to the broader meadows, and looking away of the park four or five miles ahead, we saw a beacon burning on a mountain peak near the camp, to light us home. . . . We rode up the valley through the chill and damp of midnight and entered camp about one o'clock. O how glad they all were to see us back in safety and in such fine spirits. Col. Grant said that he had never before in his life felt so glad to see anybody! They had feared that we were lost or captured and had sat up watching for us. Such cordial and hearty greetings it is a pleasure to receive. *(Pioneer)*

QUADRANGLE: **Custer**

CHAPTER 8

Saturday-Wednesday, August 1-5

Reconnaissance parties explore from Permanent Camp

*During our absence the soldiers were busy
diging for precious treasures.* (Calhoun)

General Custer slept late after his arduous climb of Harney Peak, but then the camp moved down French Creek to a better location. (Distance traveled: 3.5 miles.) It was here that gold was found in larger quantities, and that the first mining claims were staked out. It was also from here that one detachment was sent east on French Creek, while another went south to the Edgemont area. "Lonesome Charley" Reynolds left from there for Fort Laramie, carrying the news of gold to the rest of the world.

— Taking the trail —

U.S.G.S. MAP: Custer

CAUTIONS: The roads are paved or smooth gravel, with one short side trip on a slightly rougher trail.

TO START: *In Custer*, go to the far side of the parking lot at 8th and Washington (behind a grocery store) close to the heart of the camp that stretched out from the junction of French and Laughing Water Creeks.

The Genl not getting in until late did not feel very much like trying so early so remained in his little bed until after 7. McD [*Capt. McDougall*], H [*Lt. Hodgson*], Barrows & myself discussed womans right over ½ gal of Smith best. I took one drink, they several. Genl was finally sounded, then Boots & S & the command started. *(Power)*

Between the "hair of the dog" and the aftereffects of a grueling climb, the morning of August 1 must have been a tough one for some members of the command. They lingered a while (by military standards) in their first camp on French Creek, which covered part of the area now occupied by downtown Custer.

Moved 3½ miles down stream for fresh grass. *(Forsyth)*
Moved our camp down the creek where we could get more water and grass. *(Grant)*

Grass is the reason most often given in the accounts for this short move, although the valley seems plenty wide in the Custer area. Grant may have been closer to the truth in placing a higher priority on water, given Forsyth's description of the first site.

Encamped . . . on the bank of a still creek, with plenty of good water in holes, but it is not running water at this season of the year. *(Forsyth, July 30)*

Along with these official reasons, a few lines in Winchell's notebook suggest an added possibility.

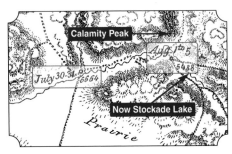

Expedition map
(1 inch = 3 miles)

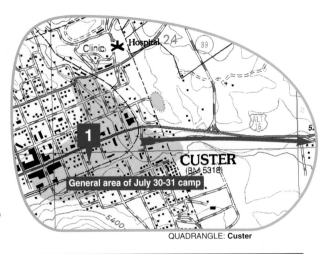

QUADRANGLE: **Custer**

The Black Hills Trail

◿We make a short march, as the miners report the discovery of gold & silver, to give time for exploration. We shall stay here also tomorrow, when we shall send home the second lot of dispatches by Mr. Reynolds (Charley) to Ft. Laramie. *(Winchell notebook)*

This passage, not included in the final report, at least raises a question about whether Custer wanted to delay the dispatches until he could announce a gold strike. Was it a coincidence that miners would be able to sink a discovery shaft in safety at the edge of the new camp? Or had they found something the previous day (while Custer climbed Harney Peak) to influence the location of what came to be called Permanent Camp? In any case, Custer did wait one more day before leaving for the Cheyenne River.

◿We moved three miles and pitched our tents in "Agnes" Park, named after Miss Agnes Bates, a friend of Mrs. General Custer's. The park is as near faultless as nature, unassisted by human hands, could make it. A beautiful creek nearly encircled the open-center. *(Ewert)*

1 43 46 00.1 This is your first stop, in the parking lot 103 35 40.0 behind the grocery store, very near the heart of the camp that was centered on French and Laughing Water Creeks.

The command started out on the north side of French Creek, generally following today's U.S. 16A to the east. Return to Mt. Rushmore Road, set or check your odometer, and drive 2.8 miles east to Forest Service Road 346 on the right. Headquarters will be your next stop.

A 43 46 14.5 Turn right at this point onto FS 346 and 103 32 22.7 continue one-tenth of a mile to a kind of bowl against the hillside on your right.

2 43 46 10.2 Standing here in 1874, you might have 103 32 25.3 been able to reach out and touch Custer's tent. It appears in William Illingworth's **Photo 845**, which he exposed from a prominent granite outcrop to the southeast.

B 43 45 58.1 Illingworth recorded a total of four views 103 32 16.3 from this outcrop, including a panoramic photograph (pages 160-161, the beginning of Part 2) published as an engraving in *Harper's Weekly* the following September (page 277). Three other images were stereoviews:
844, "Granite Knob and Harney's Peak" (page 248)
845, "Gold Mountain Range and Headquarters" (page 250)
846, "Permanent Camp in Agnes Park" (page 252)

*Headquarters was on the west side of this camp (at **Point 2**), labeled as such in Illingworth's* **Photo 845** *(page 250; **Point B**). At the center of the front line is a Sibley tent we assume to be Custer's, shown in the enlarged detail at right. Compare its unique profile to the tent directly behind Custer in his poses with the bear (pages 254, 256). Lt. James Calhoun, who was Custer's brother-in-law and also his Acting Assistant Adjutant General, would have made his home in one of the other tents. Agnes Park was his front yard, and he saw it this way:*

◿In our front extends one of the most beautiful parks the human eye ever beheld. I have travelled extensively both in Europe and America and I have never seen a more elegant park. Here nature in all her glory has performed a system of created things perfect and wonderful. The ornamental parks and graceful enclosures which I have seen in London, Liverpool, Paris, New York and Philadelphia cannot present such a natural appearance for beauty as this park. *(Calhoun)*

Remained in camp writing letters. Engineer mapping parties out in all directions. Rained very hard from 4 to 7 p.m. *(Forsyth)*

In the evening a heavy rain storm passed over our camp but, as we could almost feel the velocity of the clouds, it did not last long. *(Ewert)*

Some more gold and silver said to have been found— but to me they looked like the same pieces that were shown to me yesterday and the day before yesterday. *(Grant)*

Perhaps it was due to a hangover, but the President's son sounds grumpy even in his journal. He is the only one, however, to mention the prospectors on this date. Ross and McKay certainly had most of the day to work, but everything else written about gold would refer to the following day.

◿Fish were caught in this stream by hundreds, cat, blue and silver. On all sides of our camp, high rocky and pine-covered peaks and hills arose, some of them 8400 feet in

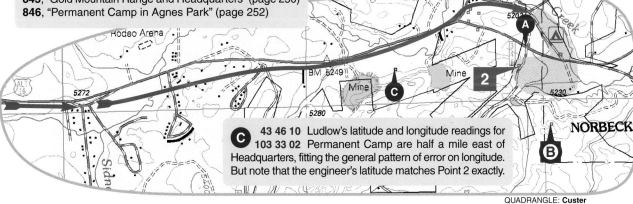

C 43 46 10 Ludlow's latitude and longitude readings for 103 33 02 Permanent Camp are half a mile east of Headquarters, fitting the general pattern of error on longitude. But note that the engineer's latitude matches Point 2 exactly.

QUADRANGLE: **Custer**

height. These were named after the several officers with the expedition, and when one looks over the list of stereoscopic views now finished, we find, Custer's Gulch, Forsyth's Glenn, Custer's Valley, Grant's Peak, Custer's Canyon, Godfrey's Peak, Custer Park, etc., etc., ad lib., this showing that [the] Custer Brothers believe too that "Charity begins at home," and if no one else will preserve their name to posterity, they will do so themselves "via Black Hills." *(Ewert)*

Ewert's snide tone aside, this is an intriguing passage for a number of reasons. First, there is haunting irony in the phrase, "If no one else will preserve their name to posterity." The General took care of his posterity on a June morning in 1876.

Ewert's passage makes it clear, by the way, that he edited and filled out his journal later on, since most or all of the stereoviews he refers to as "now finished" had not been photographed on August 1.

Finally, the passage is tantalizing because it names two of the three Illingworth photographs that the authors had not been able to find at the time of publication: Godfrey's Peak *(page 226), thought to be in the Custer area, and* Forsyth's Glenn *(page 262), possibly in the Nemo area. Our assumptions are based on Illingworth's numbering of the pictures, but we have shown that the photographer got his sequence out of order on at least one other occasion (page 19.)*

☞ The Genl informed us that the mail would leave some time in the next 36 hours, to have our letters in readiness. From that time until after "Taps" I had my hands full writing two long letters to the Press, one home and a still longer one to my darling . . . . Every body spent their time pretty much as I did, writing. *(Power)*

We can indicate the area of Permanent Camp with certainty on the map thanks to a series of Illingworth photographs. The images taken from **Point B** *(previous page) offer a comprehensive view of the northern part of the camp. Two of the stereoviews—* **844** *and*

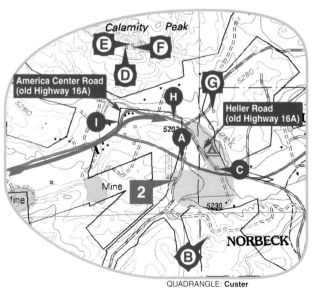

QUADRANGLE: **Custer**

846—*include a line of tents that are seen from a reverse angle in* **Photo 839**, *taken from* **Point E** *on Calamity Peak.*

Another instance of new roads following old is revealed in the detail of **Photo 839** *on the opposite page. Note the trail curving into camp close to French Creek, at the bottom left of the frame. The middle of this bend is almost exactly where present-day Heller and America Center Roads intersect. The two roads are indicated on the topo map below: the beginning of America Center Road on the left and Heller Road on the right. They were both part of U.S. Highway 16A at one time, and you'll notice that together they form a loop that is strikingly similar to the loop in the Expedition map detail at right. Both the road and the trail are also shown crossing a bend in French Creek.*

It seems clear that, once again, part of Custer's trail became a convenient route for the pioneers and ultimately the road-builders who followed. The trail you see in the 1874 photograph (**No. 839** *) through the simple act of continued use, became a United States highway that wasn't bypassed until a straighter road was constructed in 1963.*

Return to U.S. 16A (**Point A**) and turn right. Drive less than two-tenths of a mile and turn left on Heller Road.

C 43 46 12.4 Find a safe place to park beside the road, 103 32 12.9 as close to the highway as possible. From here you have a good view of two Illingworth photo sites. The first is Point B, a granite outcrop to the south and above the meadow, where he took Photos 844-846 (previous page). If you turn around and look straight up Heller Road to the north, you'll see the top of Calamity Peak—the location of three more stereoviews.

D 43 46 37.5 This may have been Illingworth's first 103 32 39.5 exposure from Calamity peak, **Photo 838**, "Looking west from Granite Knob" (page 236).

E 43 46 38.1 Part of the camp appears in **Photo 839**, 103 32 37.6 "Looking east from Granite Knob" (page 238). In the photo detail on the opposite page, you would have been parked at the other end of the nearest tent line, where a fire is producing a long plume of smoke.

F 43 46 37.4 This was the location of Illingworth's 103 32 37.1 **Photo 840**, "Spectre Canyon" (page 240).

For yet another view of the camp, continue on Heller Road. (You might see a sign about the camp, with erroneous dates, and a stone monument to a Fifth Cavalry soldier who came into the Black Hills in 1876 with Gen. George Crook.) Turn right on America Center Road and go one tenth of a mile.

G 43 46 24.2 If you wish, leave the car and climb a 103 32 14.0 slope on your right for a good view of the camp area. This is the site of **Photo 843**, "Permanent Camp in Agnes Park" (page 246). This was the best overall view of the camp, showing its full extent except for a small area that can be seen in **Photo 839**.

Sunday, August 2

Gold discovery; French Creek Reconnaissance

☞Lieutenant Gibson of Company "H," with nine men, were sent out with the photographic artist. They take two day's rations. Mr. Illingworth carries his lenses and apparatus with him on horseback; he expects to add fifteen or twenty views to the number already taken. *(Ewert)*

*It would be fun to deduce Illingworth's route from the order of his photographs, but either some of the stereoviews were misnumbered or it was an idiosyncratic route. At least thirteen views were made in the rugged country north of French Creek (**825-35** and **841-42**). The missing "Godfrey Peak" (**833**) is part of this group, while "Sunshine and Shadow Mountain" (**832**) appears to be out of sequence—a long ride from the area of the photos numbered immediately before and after it. Nine more stereoviews (**836-840** and **843-846**) and two panoramic photos were taken in the area of the camp itself—presumably after Illingworth returned from his trip.*

"THEY SAY THEY HAVE FOUND GOLD . . ."

☞The discovery was made on the 2d of August . . . and the yield was about thirty-five cents in dust to three pans—a pretty good yield if one could keep it up for a year or so, and enough to assure our miners they have struck a lead. *(Inter-Ocean)*

There is much talk of gold, and industrious search for it is making. I saw in General Custer's tent what the miner said he had obtained during the day. Under a strong reading-glass it resembled small pin-heads, and fine scales of irregular shape, perhaps 30 in number. *(Ludlow)*

This could be called "Discovery Part Two." While a few particles of gold had been washed out two days earlier, in what is now downtown Custer, here it was found in enough quantity to justify a miner's labor.

☞The prospectors accompanying the Expedition discovered gold this morning. *(Calhoun)*

They scraped a little along the bed of a brook till they got the color, then with spade and pick began to dig beside it a hole about as long and wide and deep as a human grave. From the grass roots down it was "pay dirt." *(Inter-Ocean)*

This hole was not far from the Illingworth photo site at Point G. Turn around and drive west, staying on America Center Road. A short distance past the intersection with Heller Road will be a sign on your right marking Discovery. (You may find it awkward to stop here. If so, drive another two-tenths of a mile to a pullout on the right just short of the highway—**Point I**—and continue reading there.)

H 43 46 23.3 It was near this point that the practical
103 32 25.1 miners dug a shaft beside French Creek, with results that began to excite the other explorers.

*The true beginning of the Black Hills gold rush was the grave-sized hole dug by Horatio Nelson Ross and William T. McKay on the fringe of Permanent Camp (**Point H**). Custer included the news in his report, and newspaper stories fanned the flames.*

☞After a dozen pans or more had been washed out, the two persevering men who will be the pioneers of a new golden State came into camp with a little yellow dust wrapped carefully up in the leaf of an old account book. It was examined with the microscope; was tried with all the tests that the imaginations of fifteen hundred excited campaigners could suggest, and it stood every one. It was washed with acid, mixed with mercury, cut, chewed and tasted, till everybody was convinced and went to bed dreaming of the wealth of Croesus. *(Inter-Ocean)*

In this enlarged detail from Illingworth's **Photo 839**, "Looking east from Granite Knob" (page 238) Ross and McKay's gold discovery shaft would have been just off the bottom center of the photo—behind the granite outcrop and next to the well-used trail where America Center Road is now. Heller Road is in the general area of the tracks in front of the tent line. The unloaded wagons are parked down the valley, and another part of the camp is seen at upper right.

DEVEREAUX LIBRARY ARCHIVES

RECONNAISSANCE ON FRENCH CREEK

↪ Col. Hart's and Major Hale's companies of 7th Cavalry, with Lieut. Godfrey . . . as engineer, took three days rations and explored the country from our camp to the Bad Lands on the south-east of the Black Hills. *(New York Tribune)*

The members of this reconnaissance—including the geologist—were already far away when gold fever started to spread at Permanent Camp.

↪ Having been assigned to . . . trace out to the plains the creek on which we are camped, and to visit the Bad Lands toward the southeast, we set out from camp early, hoping to obtain before our return a collection of mammalian fossils from the Tertiary. This party is also accompanied by topographical observers and by Mr. G. B. Grinnell, of Yale College, and his assistant, Mr. North. *(Winchell)*

George Bird Grinnell, who was 25 at the time, would one day influence President Theodore Roosevelt's conservation policies. Grinnell had already developed a friendship with Luther North, 28, who would be known as one of the great scouts in the West. This was not one of their better experiences, however.

↪ We . . . for some reason or other struck most of the ravines and water courses at right angles, climbing down one very steep side and then up the other. *(Grinnell)*

My horse actually did overbalance backward and plunged headlong down the hill over a man, who was only saved by a log that was above him. The man was somewhat hurt, but the horse was not. . . . We seemed to have reached the small end of a funnel-like valley, through which we could not take our horses, so we had to retreat to some place where we could ascend the bluffs. Having found such a place, by returning about two miles, here we formed camp in the valley. The aggravation of this defeat is not diminished by the fact that we had seen the prairie beyond from some of the hill-tops. *(Winchell)*

Anyone who has hiked French Creek in Custer State Park will recognize the "funnel-like valley." The explorers camped within the canyon and climbed the south side on the morning of August 3.

↪ Getting on the bluffs we see the open prairie immediately before us. We slept within three-quarters of a mile of open, smooth traveling last night. *(Winchell)*

The new route may have taken them across Jolly Flats in Custer State Park. The party didn't return to French Creek until several miles beyond the present town of Fairburn, but the difficult travel had robbed them of a chance to reach the Badlands.

↪ Before we reached the river, the provisions of the outfit were exhausted, and the horses, already weak and worn-out, began to fail. A number of them were killed, and their saddles and equipment burned. The men took from their saddle pockets their rations—a little bacon and hard bread—put the food in their shirts and walked after the command. *(Grinnell)*

Colonel Hart, finding it impracticable to proceed farther, we reluctantly abandon the idea of seeing the Bad-Lands on the other side of the Cheyenne, and make a camp. *(Winchell)*

This restrained expression of the geologist's disappointment was for official consumption. Writing in his notebook on August 6, Winchell would point out that Custer's reconnaissance to the Cheyenne River (page 90) covered a greater distance even though the General left a day later. Winchell laid the blame squarely on Colonel Verling K. Hart.

↪ We had a whiskey drinker for commanding officer and he defeated the chief objects of this trip, though I succeeded in making incidentally some valuable observations by taking a detail of men and leaving the main party. *(Winchell notebook)*

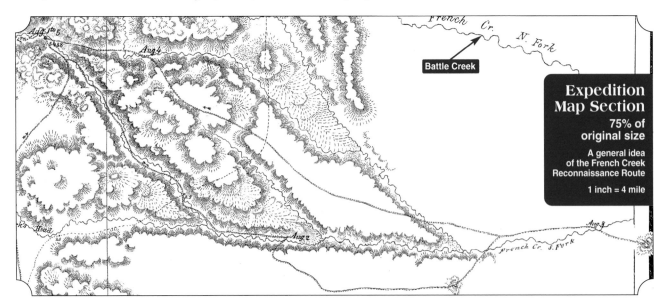

Expedition
Map Section
75% of
original size

A general idea
of the French Creek
Reconnaissance Route

1 inch = 4 mile

Battle Creek

The map on page 88 is based only on estimates by the party's engineer, Lt. E.S. Godfrey. "On the evening of the second day," Grinnell said in his official report, "we found ourselves . . . still twelve or fifteen miles from the point where the river was supposed to run." The party turned around on August 4 and headed back through northern Custer State Park.

We follow the valley of the creek to the hills, and then turn off to the right, passing to the north, more directly toward camp, and camp early on a stream that has very little current, thickly beset with beaver-dams. . . . We are about six miles from the general camp, in the midst of large pines, on a small creek, which is shut in by high hills of schist. *(Winchell)*

Monday, August 3
Gold fever; Custer's reconnaissance

At daybreak there was a crowd around the "diggins," with every conceivable accoutrement. Shovels and spades, picks, axes, tent-pins, pot hooks, bowie knives, mess pans, kettles, plates, platters, tin cups, and everything within reach that could either lift dirt or hold it was put in service by the worshippers of that god, gold. And those were few who didn't get a "showing"—a few yellow particles clinging to a globule of mercury that rolled indifferently in and out of the sand. Officers and privates, mule-whackers and scientists, all met on a common level, and the great equalizer was that insignificant yellow dust. *(Inter-Ocean)*

When it came to the gold discovery, it was William Curtis of the Chicago Inter-Ocean *who wrote most descriptively and most passionately. He was also the only reporter—throughout the journey—who took the time to introduce us to some of the personalities.*

The most excited contestant in this chase after fortune was "Aunt Sally," the sutler's colored cook, a huge mountain of dusky flesh, and "the only white woman that ever saw the Black Hills," as she frequently says. She is an old frontiersman, as it were, having been up and down the Missouri ever since its muddy water was broken by a paddle wheel, and having accumulated quite a little property, had settled down in Bismarck to ease and luxury. *(Inter-Ocean)*

"Aunt Sally" was Sarah Campbell, who told Curtis it wasn't money that brought her to the Black Hills.

"I'se got done workin fur money, I have . . . an ye wouldn't cotch dis gal totin' chuck out hyar now, I tells ye, if it hadn't bin for seein' dese hyar Black Hills dat Custer fetched us to. I'se here'd 'bout dese 'ere hills long 'fore Custer did. . . . But I wanted to see dese Black Hills—an' dey ain't no blacker dan I am." *(Inter-Ocean)*

The very name of the Black Hills had apparently given Sarah Campbell the wrong idea.

Aunt Sally expected to find the Black Hills in some indefinite way or other adapted to the colored race, and was

terribly disappointed; but the gold discoveries compensated for the lack of any distinctive mark of her race, and she joined in the developments with religious fervor. She talked incessantly about them from morning to night, and when she packed her mammoth body into a little wagon that was provided for her and her "traps," her dreams were of gold mines, and "'ery thing dats good on dis hyar earth, now I 'low." She went to the stream when the strike was made, "scratched grabble," and staked out her claim, and she says she's coming here as soon as anybody, "now you hyar me." *(Inter-Ocean)*

Also planning to return was the man who actually drew what we call "Ludlow's map."

Becker, a solemn old spectacled sergeant, of the engineer corps, who rides in the awkward, two-wheeled "go-devil" that carries the odometers, and who is platting [sic] the map that gold-hunters will go by when they come here to defile this holy silence with their oaths, and call these beautiful valleys their characteristic names, has taken a wonderful fancy to this spot, has surveyed it, and staked out 160 acres which he says he will pre-empt. On a little shaded knoll, back of the line of the left wing, true to his nationality, he said he laid out the limits of a lager-beer garden. *(Inter-Ocean)*

It would be fun to imagine what Sgt. Charles Becker might have built here—and which knoll he had his eye on—but there is no record that he ever returned. Two years later he went to the Little Big Horn as part of the Army's investigation, riding his "go-devil" to chart the final hours of Custer's command. Had he forgotten about his beer garden by then? Or did French Creek remain an unfulfilled dream?

DEVEREAUX LIBRARY ARCHIVES

An interesting arrangement of wagons appears in at least three Illingworth photographs. The top detail is from his panoramic view of Permanent Camp (see the title page), while the bottom view is from **Photo 812** (page 180) on Castle Creek. The formation is also visible in **Photo 801** (page 23 and back pages) on the far left corner of the camp. In each case the wagons are bunched one against the other, and three of the wagons appear to be covered by a large tarpaulin. Canadian researcher George Kush believes this was the Ordnance Park, where wagons loaded with ammunition and explosives were segregated from the parked supply wagons as well as the rest of the camp. He said the pioneer company would dig a trench around the wagons and clear away combustibles.

CUSTER'S RECONNAISSANCE

 We mailed our letters, that is, took them to Hd Qts for Reynolds, who was going to start to Laramie. *(Power)*

Gen. Custer . . . started at 5 a.m. for the South Fork of the Cheyenne River. His object was the exploration of the country in that direction, and to give the scout, Reynolds, who was to carry dispatches to Fort Laramie, a good send-off, by putting him 50 miles nearer his destination and outside of the Black Hills. *(Forsyth)*

The headquarters, with five companies of cavalry and a few pack-mules, leaving the train and the balance of the command in camp, started on the reconnaissance. *(Ludlow)*

The Expedition map of this reconnaissance—made without benefit of an odometer cart—was apparently distorted by overestimating the distance traveled between Permanent Camp and the Cheyenne River. When we matched its scale to the Black Hills National Forest map, a distinctive loop in the river was between five and six miles too far south. We then matched that point on the two maps (opposite page) for a general idea of the route and for the use of those who are familiar with the area.

Ludlow's map and the descriptions recorded by the explorers suggest they traveled southwest from the first French Creek camp, cut over to Pleasant Valley, and continued south through Red Canyon.

 The headquarters trail led . . . through the park country, until the head of a creek flowing southwardly was reached. This was pursued all day, leading us at first into a narrow valley, hemmed in by high wooded hills. The valley grew broader, the hills lower, grass dryer, and timber more and more scarce. *(Ludlow)*

We finally struck an old Indian trail, which we followed for 14 or 15 miles, until it finally led us through a pass out into the outlying hills beyond the main range of the Black Hills country. *(Forsyth)*

At 2 o'clock we found ourselves marching through an undesirable country barren and destitute of grazing. *(Calhoun)*

We halted for a couple of hours to rest, and enjoy a thunderstorm, mixed with hail,—for the day was very warm, and the storm cooled the air perfectly. *(Forsyth)*

Crossing the red-clay belt which encircles the hills, the creek increased in size and plunged into a cañon 500 or 600 feet in depth . . . . Emerging from this into smoother country, we halted for the night a few miles from the South Fork. *(Ludlow)*

We were in the saddle for fourteen long hours. *(Calhoun)*

It is generally accepted that this camp was near the mouth of Red Canyon, confirmed by Forsyth:

 Entering a deep ravine . . . . we finally encamped near its mouth at 10½ p.m., having made 47 miles. *(Forsyth)*
. . . a march of forty-five miles. *(Ludlow)*

The distance was only guessed at, and it is the opinion of many that we travelled fifty-five miles. *(Calhoun)*

The scout Charley Reynolds still faced more riding, but the General wanted to write a few more words.

 Postscript—10:30 p.m., Aug. 3—I left our main camp near Harney's Peak, at 6 o'clock this morning . . . . From this point Reynolds, the scout, sets out in one hour with this dispatch for Fort Laramie. *(Custer)*

He had about seventy-five miles in an air-line to make to Laramie alone *[Reynolds later said it was 90 miles]*, through a country infested with Indians, with the additional disadvantage of crossing their probable routes at right angles, and coming upon them suddenly. *(Ludlow)*

Ambulance driver Fred Snow said Reynolds wrapped the hooves of his horse in "leather boots" to "blind his trail." Another tale was told by two Expedition veterans who came back to the Hills. In a typed manuscript, R.G. Cartwright described a drive with Charles Windolph (formerly of Company H and then living in Lead) to talk with Daniel Newell of Sturgis.

 Newell stated that as farrier of M Troop he had been the one who shod Charley Reynolds' horse with the prongs of the shoes pointing forward in order to mislead the Indians. During our return Windolph was questioned . . . and he replied that it was current gossip in the regiment that Reynolds' horse had been shod in that manner. *(Cartwright)*

The last dispatches were written by the light of our campfires, and Reynolds started on his way, with our best wishes, a little after midnight. *(Forsyth)*

"Lonesome Charley" spent four nights getting to Fort Laramie with dispatches and Custer's report.

 Gold has been found at several places . . . . I have upon my table forty or fifty small particles of pure gold. *(Custer)*

They found it just before Reynolds left, and he carried the news to the world. The INTER-OCEAN, I think had the privilege of telling it first, for Reynolds was to telegraph you the golden tidings from Laramie. *(Inter-Ocean)*

The reconnaissance party, meanwhile, dipped down to the Cheyenne River early the next morning.

 A ride of three miles down the creek brought us to the South Fork. . . . The water was alkaline with a metallic gypsum flavor. . . . Going down stream two or three miles the course turned abruptly to the left and struck due north. *(Ludlow)*

Took the backward track by a different route. *(Calhoun)*

Water was very scarce, and the day exceedingly hot. Had to abandon two horses. *(Forsyth)*

We entered and crossed at right angles the Red Clay Valley . . . . Having crossed another valley tending southeast, deeply cut out of the red clay, we entered pine timber again on the north side, and finally halted near some big pools and springs. The ride of thirty miles succeeding another of forty-five was very fatiguing . . . . We enjoyed, however, a fine camp . . . and rolling ourselves on the ground in our blankets slept without dreaming. *(Ludlow)*

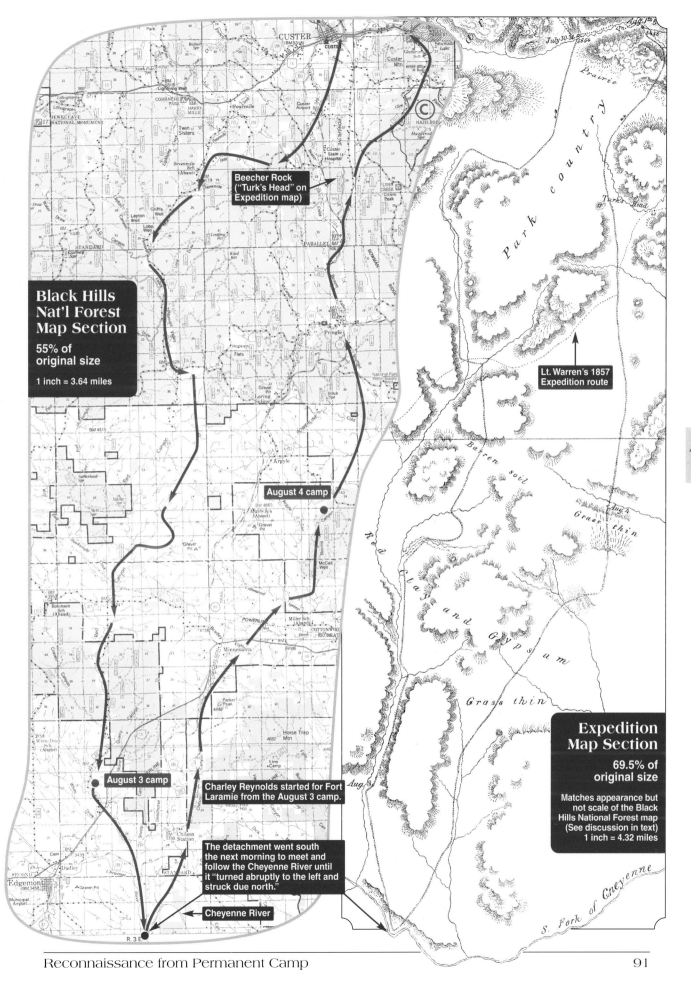

Black Hills Nat'l Forest Map Section

55% of original size

1 inch = 3.64 miles

Beecher Rock ("Turk's Head" on Expedition map)

August 4 camp

August 3 camp

Charley Reynolds started for Fort Laramie from the August 3 camp.

The detachment went south the next morning to meet and follow the Cheyenne River until it "turned abruptly to the left and struck due north."

Cheyenne River

Lt. Warren's 1857 Expedition route

Expedition Map Section

69.5% of original size

Matches appearance but not scale of the Black Hills National Forest map (See discussion in text)
1 inch = 4.32 miles

Aug 1-5

Tuesday, August 4
Exploring and naming the territory

☞ Major Tilford remained in command of the camp. He issued an order changing reveille from 2 o'clock to 4 o'clock a.m. I scarcely believe that he did this for the benefit of the men, but simply because he wanted to change existing orders, for General Custer and himself were not on the most friendly terms at no time since he had to leave his comfortable quarters at Fort Rice . . . and had to share of the hardships and dangers of this summer's campaign. *(Ewert)*

Private Ewert simply should have been grateful for the extra sleep, but it's not likely that anyone ever accused him of looking on the bright side.

☞ The last pans taken out of Custer Gulch—for so the miners call it—averaged ten cents a pan, but this was from the rich bars. *(New York Tribune)*

"Custer Gulch," where the gold was found in the largest quantities, will appear as Golden Valley. Shadow Park will be hereafter known as "Libbie Park," in honor of Mrs. Custer, and Elk Creek Valley was christened "Genevieve Park" because Colonel Ludlow's wife bears the name of Wordsworth's lady love. *(Inter-Ocean)*

These place names don't appear on the Expedition map, but it might be useful to try and deduce them. The last sentence actually refers to an area near Nemo, we believe. (See pages 140-141). For the others we can look to Illingworth for help.

I 43 46 22.1 / 103 32 39.8 You should be stopped beside the road here, a few yards away from U.S. 16A. To your left (east) is a distinctive pillar of rock that appears in two Expedition photographs.

J 43 46 21.2 / 103 32 37.3 Illingworth set up beyond the pillar and aimed his camera in your direction for **Photo 836**, "Golden Valley Gulch" (page 232).

K 43 46 17.8 / 103 32 37.7 He then moved a little south and turned his camera north for **Photo 837**, "Golden Park, where Gold was first found" (page 234).

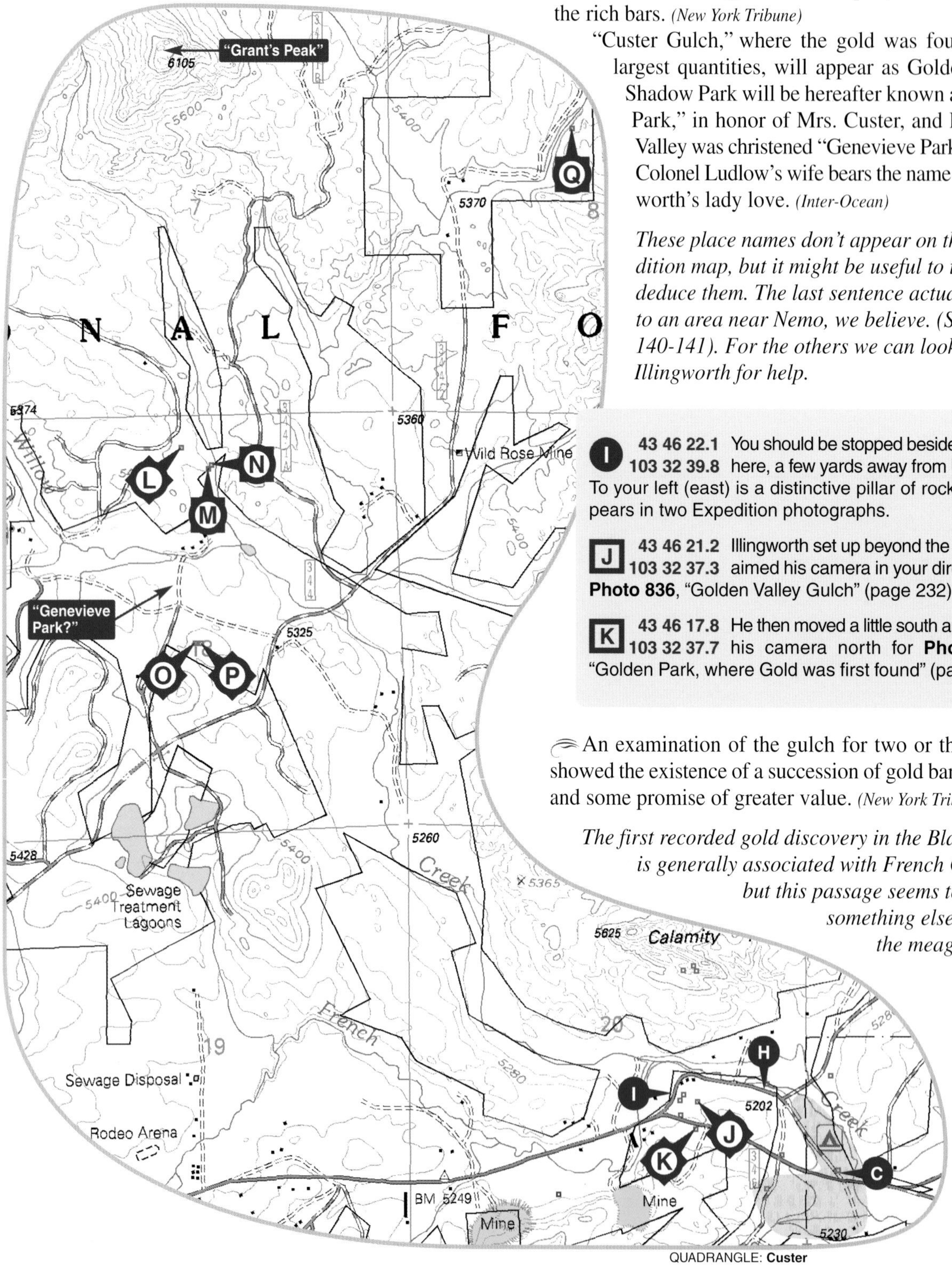

☞ An examination of the gulch for two or three miles showed the existence of a succession of gold bars of equal and some promise of greater value. *(New York Tribune)*

The first recorded gold discovery in the Black Hills is generally associated with French Creek, but this passage seems to refer to something else — not the meager results

QUADRANGLE: **Custer**

The Black Hills Trail

found at the first camp, where the city of Custer is now. Note that the Discovery shaft (**Point H**) was just below the mouth of what is now known as Willow Creek. This may have been the true source of the rich deposits that generated all the excitement. Illingworth confirms that idea with **Photo 836** (*page 232;* **Point J**), a view looking up Willow Creek that is called "Golden Valley Gulch."

    Photo 837 (*page 234;* **Point K**) shows part of French Creek just below the entrance of Willow Creek, and is titled "Golden Park, where gold was first found." Four men are visible in the photo—perhaps including Ross and McKay—and the Discovery shaft was probably just to the right of the picture.

☞The gold section had an extent of fifteen miles, running some eight or nine miles below camp, and about five miles above. *(New York Tribune)*

    The miners traced up the creek some distance finding color at every step, till the lead ran under a huge quartz mountain. *(Inter-Ocean)*

It seems very likely that "up the creek" refers here to Willow instead of French. The titles of two more Illingworth views, while they contradict each other, add further evidence that Willow Creek was the "Golden Valley" of Expedition reports.

    The first of these two views, **Photo 830**, *"Head of Golden Valley" (page 220) looks north from* **Point N**. *The second is* **Photo 841**, *"The Organ Pipes & Golden Valley" (page 242), a view of the Cathedral Spires to the northeast of* **Point Q** *(on private land). Illingworth, who mis-titled several of his views, has here given the same name to two different drainages. But each of them is a tributary of what is now called Willow Creek.*

L   43 47 43.3   This is only an approximate location for
    103 34 07.0   two Illingworth views of a mountain, one of which he published as **Photo 831**, "Grant's Peak" (page 222).

M   43 47 40.6   **Photo 829**, "Flora Park" (page 218), is a
    103 34 02.2   view to the southeast from this point. The name of the park appears nowhere else in the reports.

N   43 47 41.1   Grant's Peak appears again in **Photo 830**,
    103 34 01.6   "Head of Golden Valley" (page 220), a view slightly west of north along a tributary of Willow Creek.

Finishing up with place names, "Shadow Park" and "Libbie Park" were not mentioned by anyone except Curtis writing for the Inter-Ocean. *Illingworth erred with* **Photo 835**, *"Agnes Park" (page 230;* **Point O**, *on private land), which is in fact a view of "Golden Valley" more than a mile from what we already know to be the true Agnes Park at Permanent Camp.*

    As for the park named after Capt. Ludlow's wife, Illingworth gave the title "Genevieve Park" to his

Photo 834 (*page 228;* **Point P**, *on private land*). *This is also a view of the Willow Creek valley, but the name may have been another mistake—either that, or two separate areas were named "Genevieve." (See pages 140-141.)*

    While everything else is difficult to pin down, then, it seems a good bet that the prospectors were following Willow Creek when, according to the Inter-Ocean, *they ran into "a huge quartz mountain."*

☞The miners in the meantime had not been idle; they had been out at the first glimmer of light each morning and worked 'till late each evening. *(Ewert)*

    I went over early to Knap [Nathan Knappen] tent, thinking to while away an hour or so. McKay said something about hunting. So after an early dinner McKay, Knappen . . . and I went out. Saw two deer & one bear. My horse as usual went off. McKay got two shots into it—I wanted to charge him with pistol & Rifle but McK was very much afraid that I would get hurt. *(Power)*

Wednesday, August 5
Reconnaissance parties return; gold claims filed

☞Gen. Custer and party (escort) returned to camp . . . . A full account of the trip I am unable to give, as I remained in camp; my horse feeling rather too feeble to undertake an extra one hundred miles. We spent the time in camp very agreeably, hunting and fishing. I saw the first bear, but did not get it. Ross and McKay busied themselves prospecting. *(Press)*

    We encamped in Custer Park about seven days. There is but one sentiment in regard to it: In natural beauty it cannot be surpassed. *(Pioneer)*

EXPEDITION REUNION, PART ONE
The French Creek reconnaissance party (pages 88-89) had spent the night six miles from Permanent Camp.

☞Reached camp after traveling about two hours, at 9:30 a.m. *(Winchell)*

    Mr. Grinnell . . . hoped to find some tertiary fossils on the Bad Lands. Time proved insufficient for even a casual exploration of this section, and they were obliged to come home without bringing back any bones more ancient than those they took with them. *(New York Tribune)*

    We got back to the command . . . extraordinarily hungry and bring with us no fossils except a part of the lower jaw of a rhinoceros. *(Grinnell)*

    The reconnaissance toward the south, accompanied by Colonel Ludlow, took one day less time, and arrived back to-day two hours later than we. *(Winchell)*

EXPEDITION REUNION, PART TWO
☞Our march early this morning was over some high hills; rough travelling for man and beast. *(Calhoun)*

    At half past 9 we passed a huge knob, resembling a

turbaned head, some 200 feet in height, which we had seen off to the eastward on the first day. *(Ludlow)*

. . . its lofty head far above the tallest tree tops, so as to be seen for miles. We named it Turk's Head, from its top-heavy turban-like summit. *(New York Tribune)*

These are references to the landmark now known as Beecher Rock, about five miles south of Custer.

About noon the permanent camp was reached, after a march of twenty-five miles that day, and one hundred miles in three days. *(Ludlow)*

Nothing was written about the afternoon's activities, as the command presumably prepared for departure.

"Glad to be free again"

On our return to the permanent camp, One Stab, the old Sioux chief . . . was released from duty and sent on his way rejoicing. *(New York Tribune)*

Gen. Custer returned . . . his pony, rifle, and all his other things, gave him five days rations, bid him good bye, and had him quietly passed beyond our lines about nine or ten o'clock, so that he might put at least a night's travel between himself and danger from our bloodthirsty Rees. *(Pioneer)*

The night was fearfully dark and rainy. *(Press)*

He was glad to be free again, and ere daylight came was doubtless many miles on his way to the agency; nor long would he delay till the smoke of his own tepee should gladden his eyes and his arrival make happy the hearts of his squaw and papooses, and the wonderful story of his captivity and deliverance he related to his astonished countrymen. *(Pioneer)*

I would like to learn the tale which this Indian tells when he reaches the Indian village. *(Calhoun)*

One Stab's return may have soothed some of the bad feelings at Spotted Tail's Agency, where people had been in "a high state of excitement." (See page 55.)

The Gold Rush begins

The restless spirits from all localities will flock to the frontier towns, and they will break for the Black Hills, and will reach them, too, and to prevent it would require a larger army than it would take to guard the Rio Grande, were every Mexican determined to supply himself with American stock. *(Bismarck Tribune)*

Nathan Knappen was a prophet, although he was

effectively comparing prospectors to cattle rustlers. The Lakota Sioux would have agreed that the gold rush amounted to theft, but popular beliefs of the time were reflected in Knappen's justifications.

Why not occupy the Black Hills? It is now well-known that though the Black Hills country belongs to the Indians, it is not occupied by them, and is seldom visited by them. Because of their superstition it has been held as a sacred spot to them . . . . I dare say that none . . . will for a moment agree with those who think that this country should still be left in the hands of the Indians, who like the dog in the manger, will neither occupy it themselves or allow others to occupy it. *(Bismarck Tribune)*

While One Stab headed south, Charley Reynolds rode through the third of four nights it would take him to reach Fort Laramie. Libbie Custer wrote in Boots and Saddles *that the scout, on foot and leading an exhausted horse, arrived with his tongue so swollen from thirst that he could not close his mouth.*

On French Creek that night, many knew or suspected that the reports carried by Reynolds would soon bring trouble to the Black Hills. Their own dreams had already been aroused by the color of gold found on land they didn't own—that the United States itself didn't own.

An attempt to solve the Indian question was made around a camp fire . . . and a conclave shook hands together to look fate in the face. It was a company of rough men; men—the most of them—who enjoy life on $13 a month and rations, but they feel that this expedition had in some dim wise opened a future for them, and they saw reflected in the gloss of that little gold dust great possibilities, and great hopes grew out of them for better things. Some who saw that meeting may laugh at me for this moralizing—but they saw nothing but the brown and hard faces of adventurers, and I thought I saw something more—ambition; not mercenary alone, but an ambition throbbing with pulsations of hope. *(Inter-Ocean)*

Curtis offered a nicely written description of the hunger for financial gain that is tied up with desires for "a better life"—something that seems nobler, with a higher purpose. His heading for this section was "The First Miners' Meeting in the Black Hills," which probably took place somewhere in view of U.S. 16A.

The result of this meeting around a camp-fire among

This enlarged detail from the panoramic view of Permanent camp **(Point G**, page 86) shows laundry hanging on a picket line be-

tween two wagons, propped up in the middle by a pole or stick. The ghostly figure of a man appears near a fire left of center.

a cluster of wagons was the formation of the Custer Park Mining Company, to be a working organization from that day forward, dividends to be paid annually until further notice. The company was duly formed according to the laws of the United States and the Territory of Dacotah, with authorized officers and Board of Directors. *(Inter-Ocean)*

Though the announcement of the discovery of gold created less excitement than might have been expected, a score of teamsters and wagon-masters were provident enough to locate claims in Custer Gulch. *(New York Tribune)*

The following notice was posted on the inside of a hard-tack box cover, out of the rain, and placed on the claim. . . .

DISTRICT NO. 1, CUSTER PARK MINING COMPANY, CUSTER'S GULCH, BLACK HILLS, D.T. AUG. 5, 1874

Notice is hereby given that we the undersigned claimants do claim four thousand (4,000) feet, commencing at number eight (8) above, and running down to number twelve (12) below discovery for mining purposes, and intend to work the same as soon as peaceable possession can be had of this portion of Dakota Territory by the General Government. *(Inter-Ocean)*

The discovery claim belonged to Horatio Nelson Ross, who had been trying to find a place for himself in the brand new town of Bismarck before the Expedition. According to the William A. Falconer papers in the State Historical Society of North Dakota, Ross failed in his effort to become one of the first commissioners of Burleigh County when it was formed the year before. He was appointed the first sheriff on July 16, 1873, but he quit less than a month later saying, "I think law is a farce in this territory."

Ross came back to the Hills in 1875, leading a party from Bismarck, and lived out his life in Custer. Annie Tallent mentioned him as one of the locators of the Old Bill mine near there in 1879, "having charge of the mine." Later he worked as a jailer and deputy sheriff.

He also enjoyed a certain amount of attention. There is a popular story that the gold discovery site at Permanent Camp was nearly lost because Ross tired of paying the livery bill for horses and buggy to take people there. He is said to have told Eric Heidepriem that "in the dark of night he removed the original site sign and placed it on French Creek at 8th Street." If the story is accurate, Ross didn't have to engage in fiction. He just found it easier to show the place where he found the first color on July 30.

☞Perhaps if this announcement were translated into Sioux, and copies sent to Red Cloud and Two Bears, this announcement would create more of a sensation than it is likely to make in Wall-st. *(New York Tribune)*

Much less is known about William T. McKay, the other practical miner, who held claim No. 4 below Discovery. A footnote to an article by Dr. William M. Blackburn in the 1902 South Dakota Historical Collections *reported that he was "known on the frontier as Billy McKay," had been elected to the Dakota Territorial legislature in 1874, and was accused of involvement in the lynching of two stock thieves. The article referred also to a journal, and McKay was quoted in the book* Black Hills Trails *(pages 56-57), but after the Expedition he seems to have faded from view.*

The names of all 21 claim-holders were published in the Chicago Inter-Ocean *(page 97), and there at No. 7 below is Sarah Campbell. She made good on her promise to return to the Black Hills, and was buried in 1887 at Galena.*

The mining company's claim notice was also published in the Bismarck Tribune, *by the way, with a major difference: No. 7 below discovery is shown to be held not by Sarah Campbell but by the* Tribune's *Nathan Knappen—the same reporter who was caught plagiarizing another writer (Chapters 1 and 4). Here he has removed the name of the black cook and inserted his own—apparently in an effort to gain status in his home town.*

☞Somehow there is a fascination in digging gold directly from the earth instead of getting its equivalent by other forms of labor. The effect of the reports from the Black Hills, therefore, may be to create, especially in the West, a new gold fever, which, like all such diseases, must have its run. Reason and wholesome advice have little power to check the malady when once it has begun. *(New York Tribune)*

It is in the very heart of Sioux territory—in their choicest hunting ground . . . . No one can come here with any safety, or with any legal right as long as the treaties that now exist hold good, and the wealth that we have found must be for several years yet under the ban. *(Inter-Ocean)*

The ban was broken within five months. The Gordon Party arrived two days before Christmas and built a stockade east of Agnes Park. (You may wish to visit the replica that now stands on the site near Stockade Lake.) Annie Tallent and her party were evicted by soldiers the following April, but thousands of adventurers came to take their place—just as members of the Expedition had expected. It would be interesting to know what became of their claim notice posted on the inside of a hard-tack box cover.

☞Thus were made, insignificantly, and illegally, perhaps, the incipient efforts toward the development of one of the most rich and beautiful pieces of Nature's embroidery on God's foot-stool. *(Inter-Ocean)*

CHAPTER 9

Thursday, August 6

Permanent Camp to Gillette Prairie

*The thunder . . . is here composed of a succession of sharp, abrupt peals.
The lightning is very brilliant.* (Ewert)

Starting for home, the explorers were able to cover a great deal of ground using parts of the trail they had carved out on the way to French Creek. Even though they avoided the miseries of Negro Gulch (Chapter 6), it was still a long and tiring day that did not inspire a great deal of writing by the diarists, newspaper correspondents and scientists. That leaves room for entertaining or illuminating stories and new perspectives we haven't been able to include elsewhere. Distance traveled: 23.5 miles.

Taking the trail

U.S.G.S. MAPS: Custer, Berne, Medicine Mountain, Ditch Creek

CAUTIONS: The roads are all smooth gravel or paved, except for a short (and optional) side trip on a Forest Service trail that would be safer for a high-centered vehicle.

TO START: *From downtown Custer*, drive 3.1 miles east on U.S. 16A and turn left on Heller Road (**Point 1**). Pull over as soon as you can.

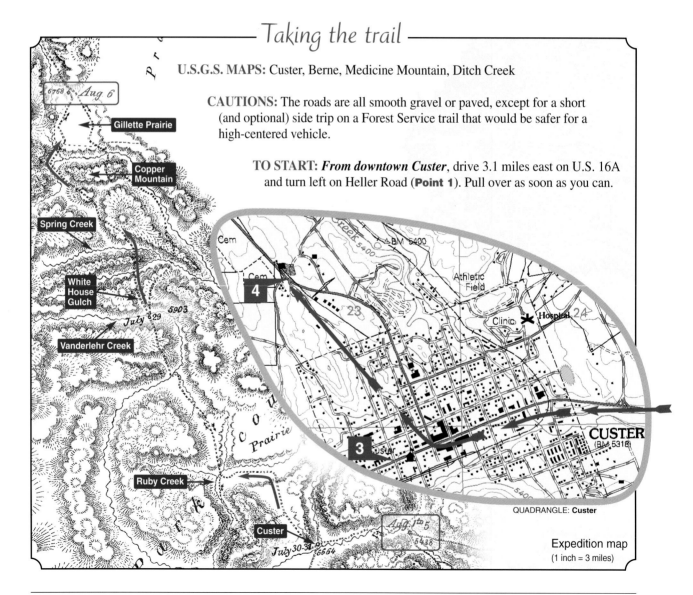

QUADRANGLE: **Custer**

Expedition map
(1 inch = 3 miles)

Aug
6

~ We leave camp this morning after a light thundershower in the night . . . . It is a bright, cool, pleasant morning and we return on our trail. *(Winchell notebook)*

On the morning of leaving Custer Park, in what will hereafter be known as Custer's Gulch, the following notice might have been seen posted by the side of a shaft sunk by Mssrs. Ross and McKay:

District No. 1, Custer's Gulch,
Black Hills, August 5th, 1874

Notice is hereby given, that the undersigned claimants do claim (4,000) four thousand feet, commencing at No. 8 above discovery, and running down to No. 12 below and do intend to work the same as soon as peaceable possession can be had of this portion of the territory. *(Bismarck Tribune)*

The condition of "peaceable possession" had been worked out during a campfire meeting the night before (see previous chapter), in recognition of the fact that no one had a right to file these claims.

~ The country is the recognized home of powerful bands of hostile Indians who have sworn to repel any intrusion of the white man. . . . Until it is purchased from them by the Government they have a prior claim and a perfect right to protect it. *(New York Tribune)*

It could be argued that their "perfect right" had been violated by the Expedition itself. There is no question that the newspaper reports of gold—on the heels of a financial panic the year before—sparked a series of events that overwhelmed the Lakota Sioux. After Little Big Horn they were compelled to cede the Black Hills, a transaction that some tribes still refuse to recognize.

~ It was a wise forethought which induced Gen. Custer to secure, in addition to the scientific corps appointed by the Department, the service of two skilled and experienced miners . . . . The result of their labors has justified this foresight, and converted a glittering fable into a glittering fact. *(New York Tribune)*

The names of the miners appeared on Discovery and claim No. 4, respectively. It isn't

~ H. N. Ross, 400 feet, discovery.
M. Smith, No. 1 below discovery.

M. Conner, No. 2 below discovery.
W. J. Kennelly, No. 3 below discovery.
W. T. McKay, No. 4 below discovery.
Dan Manning, No. 5 below discovery.
Henry Harvey, No. 6 below discovery.
Sarah Campbell, No. 7 below discovery.
D. Mathieson, No. 8 below discovery.
Harry Roberts, No. 9 below discovery.
J. Roach, No. 10 below discovery.
Tim Hayes, No. 11 below discovery.
G. Bosworth, No. 12 below discovery.
James McGee, No. 1 above discovery.
George McCabe, No. 2 above discovery.
Samuel O'Connell, No. 3 above discovery.
C. Bassett, No. 4 above discovery.
A. McBeth, No. 5 above discovery.
F. Weddell, No. 6 above discovery.
C. W. Freede, No. 7 above discovery.
Pat. Smith, No. 8 above discovery. *(Inter-Ocean)*

Did the 21 claim-holders leave camp on this morning with dreams of wealth? With plans to return and make their mark? Horatio Ross and Sarah Campbell did come back, but we don't know about the others. Perhaps they were drawn into the patterns of their old lives, and faded from history.

1 43 46 12.5 At the intersection of Heller Road and 103 32 12.9 U.S. 16A, you are in the August 1-5 camp area. To follow the trail out, drive two-tenths of a mile north on Heller Road and turn left on America Center Road. Almost immediately you will see a wooden sign on the right, marking the discovery site.

2 43 46 23.3 Practical miner Horatio N. Ross said it was 103 32 25.1 here that he dug a hole on French Creek and found enough color to justify a claim—presumably the center of mining claims "filed" inside the cover of a hardtack box, perhaps a few feet from where you are parked.

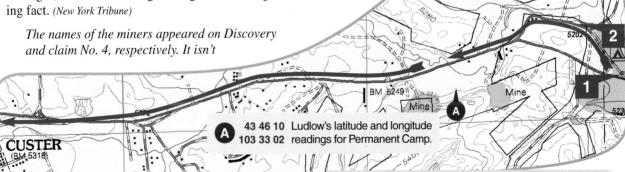

A 43 46 10 Ludlow's latitude and longitude
103 33 02 readings for Permanent Camp.

QUADRANGLE: **Custer**

likely that any other gold strike in the history of the West received such complete or immediate news coverage, including a list of all the first filers.

Continue west to the end of America Center Road and turn right on U.S. 16A. Drive back to Custer, turn right at 3rd Street (**Point 3**), and go as far as U.S. 16/385 (**Point 4**). This approximates the Expedition's climb out of the valley on a steady, gradual slope. (The older topographic map at the bottom of the following page shows diagonal streets in the area, parts of which may have followed Custer's route.)

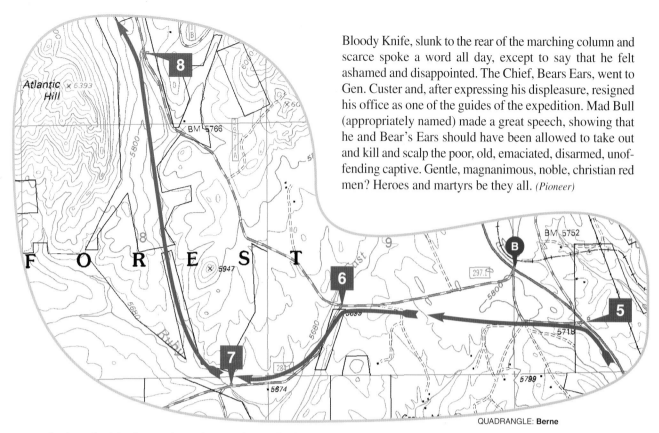

QUADRANGLE: **Berne**

Bloody Knife, slunk to the rear of the marching column and scarce spoke a word all day, except to say that he felt ashamed and disappointed. The Chief, Bears Ears, went to Gen. Custer and, after expressing his displeasure, resigned his office as one of the guides of the expedition. Mad Bull (appropriately named) made a great speech, showing that he and Bear's Ears should have been allowed to take out and kill and scalp the poor, old, emaciated, disarmed, unoffending captive. Gentle, magnanimous, noble, christian red men? Heroes and martyrs be they all. *(Pioneer)*

Aug
6

As described in the previous chapter, Custer had released his hostage the night before, sneaking One Stab out of camp in the middle of the night. The Arikara guides learned of his absence this morning.

☞ When our Rees found that he was indeed gone and out of their reach, they were moody and silent. The Chief,

To be fair, sons and brothers of some of the Arikara had been killed by Sioux warriors a few weeks earlier.

☞ The country grows wilder and more rugged as we go on, and doubts are expressed as to the possibility of passing it with a wagon train. *(Inter-Ocean)*

General Custer determined, instead of going eastward

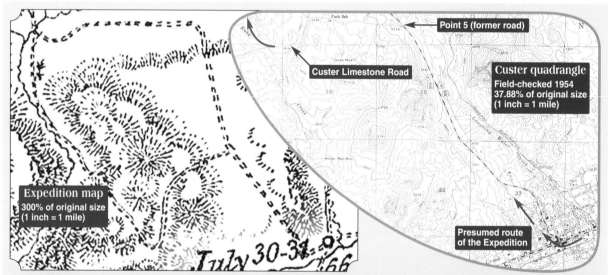

Placing a section of the Expedition map next to an older topographic map (representing roads as they appeared in 1954) strongly suggests that Custer's exit route from French Creek was used by the miners, stage drivers and homesteaders who followed—a road that eventually became U.S. Highway 16/385. Note the similar bend at virtually the same distance from town. Also, precisely where the Expedition is shown turning west is

a draw that was still used by a road in 1954, later replaced by the Medicine Mountain Road (Forest Service 297). To the west, Custer Limestone Road (FS 284) forms the beginning of a semicircle around the end of a ridge that forced the wagon train to take a similar path to reach its trail of July 30. These roads we use today are at least close to Custer's trail, and some sections may cover the original wagon tracks to this day.

upon the prairie, to partly retrace his steps, and examine into the practicability of a route northward through the hills, emerging somewhere near Bear Butte, and so complete the examination of them. The old trail was accordingly run back with some slight divergence. *(Ludlow)*

Set or check your odometer at **Point 4** and drive 1.9 miles north on U.S. 16/385. You will soon pass the Custer Cemetery on the way, about where the trail came in from the west on July 30 (Chapter 7). Here, in the first "slight divergence," the Expedition's trail continues to the north.

5 43 47 57.7 At 1.9 miles north
103 37 54.5 of 3rd Street, stop across the highway from a private home. Note the driveway that leads toward the draw behind it, toward the west. This was once where Forest Service Road 297 left the highway, following the Expedition wagons on their way home.

Continue three-tenths of a mile and turn left on today's Medicine Mountain Road (**Point B**). Drive west seven-tenths of a mile to the intersection with Custer Limestone Road (**Point 6**).

⊰ In no portion of the United States, not excepting the famous Blue Grass region of Kentucky, have I ever seen grazing superior to that found growing wild in this hitherto unknown region. I know of no portion of our country where nature has done so much to prepare homes for husbandmen, and left so little for the latter to do as here. In the open and timbered spaces a partly prepared farm of almost any dimensions, of an acre and upward, can be found here. Not only is the land cleared and timbered for both fuel and building, conveniently located with streams of pure water flowing through its length and breadth, but nature oftimes seems to have gone further, and placed beautiful shrubbery and evergreens in the most desirable locations. . . . The soil is that of a rich garden, and composed of a dark mould of exceedingly fine grain. . . . Nowhere in the States have I tasted cultivated

raspberries of equal flavor to those found growing wild here . . . . Wild strawberries, wild currants, gooseberries, and wild cherries are also found in great profusion and of exceedingly pure quality. Cattle would winter in these valleys without other food or shelter than that that can be obtained from running at large. *(Custer)*

The General's somewhat overheated paean to the Black Hills was included in the August 2 report that went out with Lonesome Charley Reynolds. It was after painting this picture of an earthly paradise that Custer added, almost as an afterthought—because it would "appear in any event in the public prints"— that there was also gold here.

6 43 48 01.2 The wagons turned southwest near this
103 39 06.3 intersection, or perhaps a little farther to the south. Turn left on Custer Limestone Road (FS 284), closely following the Expedition's route. Go another six-tenths of a mile.

7 43 47 45.0 Ruby Creek passes beneath the Custer
103 39 39.2 Limestone Road here, not far from the place where the Expedition took up its old trail of the week before. The wagons would have rolled into the drainage on your right (to the north), and the pioneer party of the day might have breathed a sigh of relief. Teamsters would simply be able to follow their old tracks for a few miles.

Return to the intersection at **Point 6** and turn left on Medicine Mountain Road. Drive just short of 1.4 miles, and pull to the side of the road.

8 43 48 53.5 From here you should be able to see a
103 40 02.6 rut about 50 yards to your left, west of the fence. The Expedition came up through the draw you see to the south, and the rut can be traced up this drainage. Mature trees are growing here and there in the middle of the trail, but it is on private land. To get a better look, drive another three-tenths of a mile.

QUADRANGLES: **Custer, Berne**

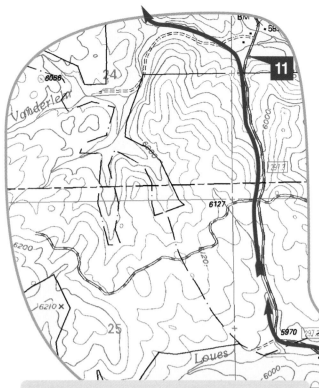

Creek, since Custer had already passed through the French Creek camp on his way to the Cheyenne River. His threat of pioneer duty would not have been taken lightly among the soldiers, as you can imagine from what you already know about the work it entailed. In the Black Hills it sometimes meant cutting down hundreds of trees and clearing thick undergrowth. It always meant building roads.

When we reach a gulch that cannot be spanned, a grade is made to its bottom and up again . . . . General Custer is a famous road maker, and to him, as to the great Napoleon, nothing is impassable. In our regular marching order following the scouts and the color guard comes the pioneer company, with a wagon full of spades, shovels, picks, axes, scythes and other tools. Reaching a place that has to be bridged, the General selects the most available point and with a shovel in his hand he directs and assists at the work himself. The modus operands (sic) of bridging is somewhat novel. If cobble stones and sod or willow branches and rushes will not make a roadbed the train master cries "poles," and every teamster brings the extra wagon tongue he always carries with him and lays it devotedly down at Custer's feet. These

Aug 6

9 **43 49 04.6** On the bank across the road you should **103 40 13.8** be able to see a well-defined rut going up the hill to the south, continuing the direction of FS 297 before the bend. Mature trees in the rut suggest that it was part of the early trail engineered by Custer—used in both directions—and bypassed not long after.

From this point until you turn off further north, Medicine Mountain Road is either on or close to the Expedition trail. You will also be following the Cheyenne-Deadwood Stage road for part of 1877, before the route was moved further west. Continue 1.9 miles, stopping beside a pasture on the right.

10 **43 50 31.0** Note that the present-day road passes **103 41 13.6** through a cut dug out from the point of a hill. About 40 feet to the right, between you and the drainage, is a wagon rut that you can see for several hundred feet. Again, it is a likely artifact of the Expedition, although it may have been used by later traffic.

Drive 1.6 miles and stop short of Vanderlehr Creek, across from a fence gate on your left.

11 **43 51 44.8** Part of the Expedition camped along this **103 41 40.9** creek on July 29, while the wagon train struggled all night to get here. About half a mile up the valley to your left you can see the mouth of White House Gulch (see map on page 102), which was the second "divergence" of the command from the old trail.

On the morning of the 6th, we took our back trail, passed two of our old camps, Nos. 25 and 26. *(Ewert)*

We found that much of the grass had been burnt off through the carelessness of soldiers and teamsters in leaving fires burning when starting out on the march. A renewed order by Gen. Custer requires every camp-fire to be put out before starting, any company failing in this to be permanently detailed to pioneer duty. *(New York Tribune)*

The burned grass would have been along Vanderlehr

QUADRANGLE: **Berne**

poles are then placed crosswise—two or three layers of them, cobhouse fashion, and the crevices are filled with brush, sod, mown rushes, and every available substance three or four hundred bridge-builders can lay their hands on. *(Inter-Ocean)*

This description was written on the prairie, and suggests that pioneers might have received assistance in the worst places—since a cavalry company was made up of 40 to 60 men. In the Black Hills, logs could be cut and laid across the streams, with smaller logs placed across them to create a corduroy bridge.

The bridge done, the artillery and ambulances are sent across, being of the lightest tonnage, and when they cut through, repairs are made; then the mule teams are sent across; and did you ever see a lot of six-mule teams cross one of these bridges? It is an event of a lifetime. The animals are driven by a single line and a long snake-whip, especially the whip. The line is attached to the left-hand bit of the "nigh leader," and he may be considered the rudder of the "outfit." The helmsman sits astride of the "nigh wheeler," and if he wants the team to "gee," he jerks at the line savagely, and it is a moral certainty that the mule will turn his head away from it and go "gee." If he wants to "haw" he pulls steadily on the line, drawing the mule's head around, and he goes "haw." . . . His chief requirements are to crack a black snake whip and swear—and such swearing, it would make the hair of a Chicago hackman stand on end. *(Inter-Ocean)*

We are lucky to have had the presence of a journalist who could paint such vivid pictures punctuated by sound. In this case it is not a pleasant image.

With a dart, a few jumps, and final tug, under a frightful torrent of oaths and whip-lashes over the poor animals' heads, the other side is reached. The mules hop around a moment under the smarting of the cuts they have just received, and with a bray of relief tug on patiently just as good, meek people do when they have met one of the trials of life, passed through it, and come out purified. A wagon train crossing a creek or a gully is as good as a Fourth of July celebration, and reminds me strangely of one when I stand at a distance—the cracking, and shouting, and hurrahing that is always done, and I suppose is absolutely necessary." *(Inter-Ocean)*

Fewer words were written about this day than any other. Familiarity with the landscape must have been a factor, but it's also true that the explorers were on their way home. They may have felt that the trip was already over, in a way. William Curtis wrote this on August 2, the day of the gold discovery.

In the field thirty days or so, one begins to think of something else besides Indians, gold nuggets, or game. When he has gone through his "outfit," put on his last clean shirt, and used his last pocket handkerchief, and attempts a change to campaign haberdashery and soldier laundry work, he begins to think of the loved ones at home, and to count the number of days out and the date of the prob-

able return. Without a calendar, and even with one, it is a somewhat difficult matter to determine the day of the week, and I heard an animated dispute this morning between two members of the West Point Alumni Association resulting in a wager, as to whether it is Saturday or Sunday. Some fellow who kept a diary said it was Sunday, and the Saturday party paid the drinks. *(Inter-Ocean)*

The second divergence

Passed through two of our old camps; then turned to our left. *(Grant)*

It was at Vanderlehr Creek—the place of the burned grass—that Custer turned away from the difficulties of the July 29 march (Chapter 6). He undoubtedly had noticed White House Gulch that day as he waited for the wagons, and now he used it.

We marched northward, recovering our old trail some 10 or 15 miles, and then boldly struck into the woods and made a new trail, which, though calling for some extra pioneer work, was a shorter and more direct route. *(New York Tribune)*

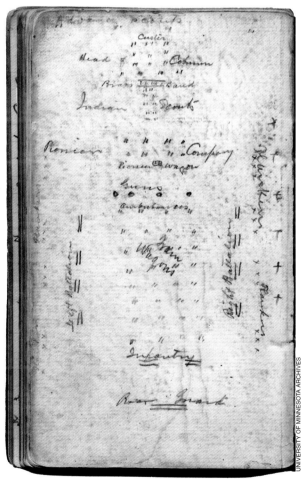

Geologist Newton Winchell sketched the order of march in his notebook. Note that the "Brass Band" is out in front of the Indian Scouts, followed by the pioneer company and its wagon. The "guns" are the Rodman (a rifled cannon) and three Gatling guns. In the Black Hills, the wagons generally formed a single file.

Aug
6

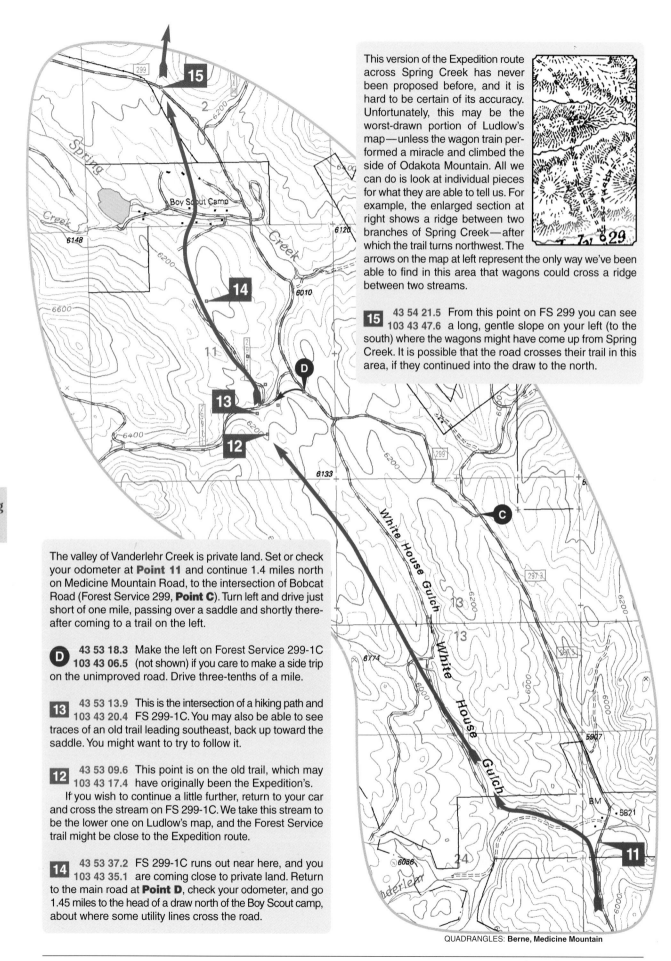

This version of the Expedition route across Spring Creek has never been proposed before, and it is hard to be certain of its accuracy. Unfortunately, this may be the worst-drawn portion of Ludlow's map—unless the wagon train performed a miracle and climbed the side of Odakota Mountain. All we can do is look at individual pieces for what they are able to tell us. For example, the enlarged section at right shows a ridge between two branches of Spring Creek—after which the trail turns northwest. The arrows on the map at left represent the only way we've been able to find in this area that wagons could cross a ridge between two streams.

15 **43 54 21.5** From this point on FS 299 you can see **103 43 47.6** a long, gentle slope on your left (to the south) where the wagons might have come up from Spring Creek. It is possible that the road crosses their trail in this area, if they continued into the draw to the north.

Aug 6

The valley of Vanderlehr Creek is private land. Set or check your odometer at **Point 11** and continue 1.4 miles north on Medicine Mountain Road, to the intersection of Bobcat Road (Forest Service 299, **Point C**). Turn left and drive just short of one mile, passing over a saddle and shortly thereafter coming to a trail on the left.

D **43 53 18.3** Make the left on Forest Service 299-1C **103 43 06.5** (not shown) if you care to make a side trip on the unimproved road. Drive three-tenths of a mile.

13 **43 53 13.9** This is the intersection of a hiking path and **103 43 20.4** FS 299-1C. You may also be able to see traces of an old trail leading southeast, back up toward the saddle. You might want to try to follow it.

12 **43 53 09.6** This point is on the old trail, which may **103 43 17.4** have originally been the Expedition's.
If you wish to continue a little further, return to your car and cross the stream on FS 299-1C. We take this stream to be the lower one on Ludlow's map, and the Forest Service trail might be close to the Expedition route.

14 **43 53 37.2** FS 299-1C runs out near here, and you **103 43 35.1** are coming close to private land. Return to the main road at **Point D**, check your odometer, and go 1.45 miles to the head of a draw north of the Boy Scout camp, about where some utility lines cross the road.

QUADRANGLES: **Berne, Medicine Mountain**

The Black Hills Trail

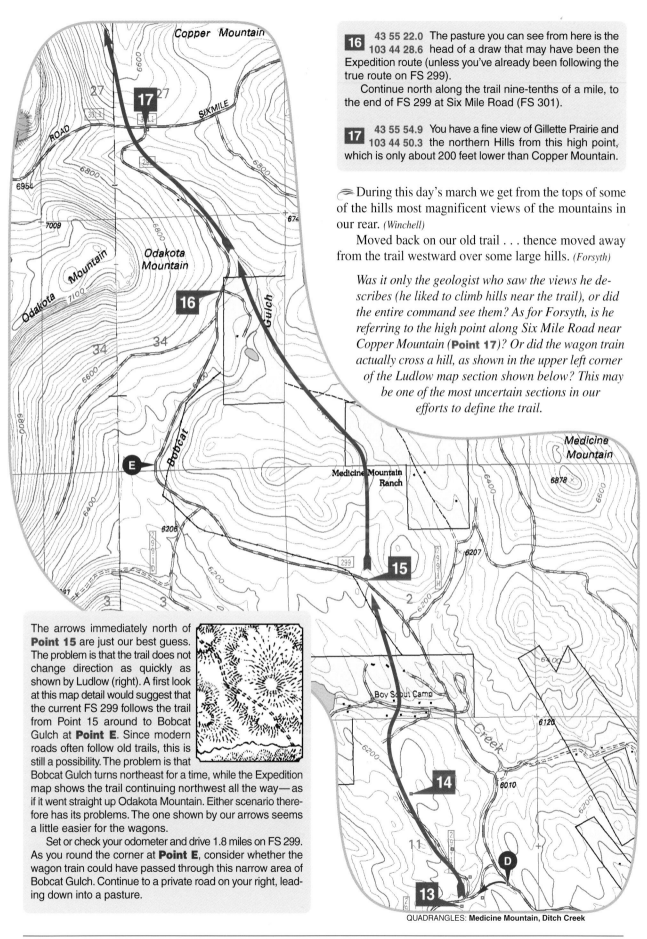

16 43 55 22.0 The pasture you can see from here is the
103 44 28.6 head of a draw that may have been the
Expedition route (unless you've already been following the
true route on FS 299).

Continue north along the trail nine-tenths of a mile, to
the end of FS 299 at Six Mile Road (FS 301).

17 43 55 54.9 You have a fine view of Gillette Prairie and
103 44 50.3 the northern Hills from this high point,
which is only about 200 feet lower than Copper Mountain.

⌐ During this day's march we get from the tops of some
of the hills most magnificent views of the mountains in
our rear. *(Winchell)*

Moved back on our old trail . . . thence moved away
from the trail westward over some large hills. *(Forsyth)*

*Was it only the geologist who saw the views he de-
scribes (he liked to climb hills near the trail), or did
the entire command see them? As for Forsyth, is he
referring to the high point along Six Mile Road near
Copper Mountain (**Point 17**)? Or did the wagon train
actually cross a hill, as shown in the upper left corner
of the Ludlow map section shown below? This may
be one of the most uncertain sections in our
efforts to define the trail.*

Aug
6

The arrows immediately north of
Point 15 are just our best guess.
The problem is that the trail does not
change direction as quickly as
shown by Ludlow (right). A first look
at this map detail would suggest that
the current FS 299 follows the trail
from Point 15 around to Bobcat
Gulch at **Point E**. Since modern
roads often follow old trails, this is
still a possibility. The problem is that
Bobcat Gulch turns northeast for a time, while the Expedition
map shows the trail continuing northwest all the way—as
if it went straight up Odakota Mountain. Either scenario therefore has its problems. The one shown by our arrows seems
a little easier for the wagons.

Set or check your odometer and drive 1.8 miles on FS 299.
As you round the corner at **Point E**, consider whether the
wagon train could have passed through this narrow area of
Bobcat Gulch. Continue to a private road on your right, leading down into a pasture.

QUADRANGLES: **Medicine Mountain, Ditch Creek**

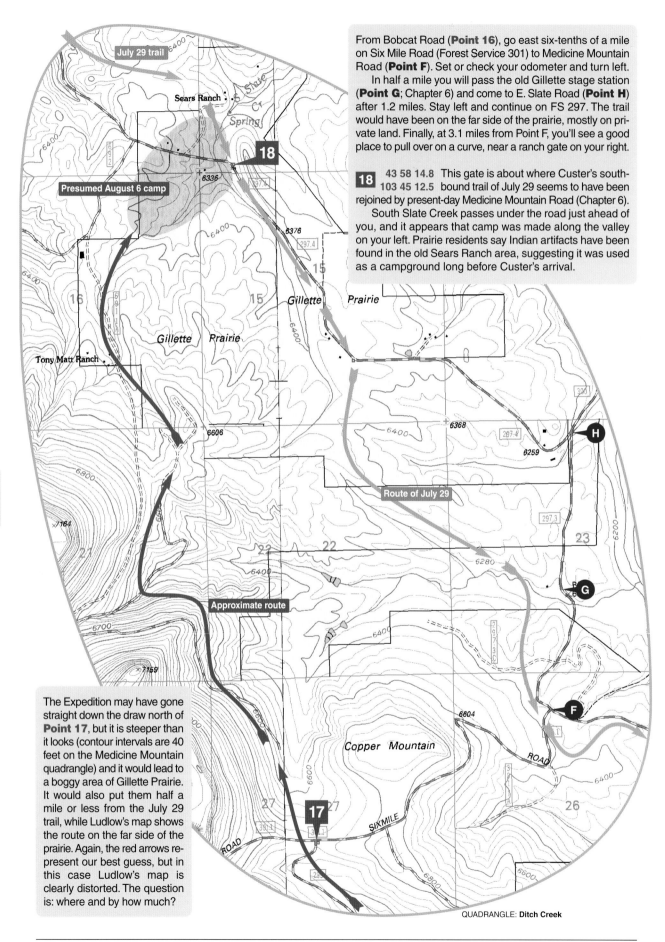

Sears Ranch

Presumed August 6 camp

6336

Spring

18

16

15

Gillette Prairie

Tony Matt Ranch

Gillette Prairie

6606

×7164

21

22

22

6400

Approximate route

6700

×7159

Copper Mountain

27

27

17

ROAD

SIXMILE

6606

8376

15

Gillette Prairie

6368

6259

Route of July 29

297.3

23

H

G

F

6604

ROAD

26

From Bobcat Road (**Point 16**), go east six-tenths of a mile on Six Mile Road (Forest Service 301) to Medicine Mountain Road (**Point F**). Set or check your odometer and turn left.

In half a mile you will pass the old Gillette stage station (**Point G**; Chapter 6) and come to E. Slate Road (**Point H**) after 1.2 miles. Stay left and continue on FS 297. The trail would have been on the far side of the prairie, mostly on private land. Finally, at 3.1 miles from Point F, you'll see a good place to pull over on a curve, near a ranch gate on your right.

18 43 58 14.8 This gate is about where Custer's south-
103 45 12.5 bound trail of July 29 seems to have been rejoined by present-day Medicine Mountain Road (Chapter 6).

South Slate Creek passes under the road just ahead of you, and it appears that camp was made along the valley on your left. Prairie residents say Indian artifacts have been found in the old Sears Ranch area, suggesting it was used as a campground long before Custer's arrival.

The Expedition may have gone straight down the draw north of **Point 17**, but it is steeper than it looks (contour intervals are 40 feet on the Medicine Mountain quadrangle) and it would lead to a boggy area of Gillette Prairie. It would also put them half a mile or less from the July 29 trail, while Ludlow's map shows the route on the far side of the prairie. Again, the red arrows represent our best guess, but in this case Ludlow's map is clearly distorted. The question is: where and by how much?

QUADRANGLE: **Ditch Creek**

☞Travelled through timber for about five miles. General C. killed one dear. *(Calhoun)*

It would seem that this unlucky deer met his fate between White House Gulch and descending to the park country near Copper Mountain. While the General succeeded this time, he wasn't quite the marksman he fancied himself— at least according to the young George Bird Grinnell, who had come along to collect fossils for Yale University.

☞General Custer was friendly, sociable and agreeable. He was very fond of hunting and a great believer in his skill as a rifle shot. . . . On the plains General Custer did no shooting that was notable. It was observed that, though he enjoyed telling of the remarkable shots that he himself commonly made, he did not seem greatly interested in the shooting done by other people.

This is from Two Great Scouts, *Grinnell's book about Luther North and his brother Frank. In it, Grinnell talks about an event on the Plains, in the Missouri badlands.*

☞While riding with General Custer ahead of the command we came to a small pond, near which a duck had nested. Seven or eight half grown young ones were swimming about and General Custer got off his horse and said, "I will knock the heads off a few of them." I looked at Luther North and made a sign to him and he dismounted and sat down on the ground behind the General. General Custer fired at a bird and missed it and North shot and cut the head off one of the birds. Custer shot again and missed and North cut the head off another bird. Custer looked around at him and then shot again and again missed and North cut the head off a third duck.

It would have been interesting to see the look Custer gave North, who apparently had no interest in a career with the Army. Fortunately for the rest of those innocent ducklings, the General had not been thinking about the effects of his target practice.

☞Just then an officer rode up over a hill near the pond and said that the bullets after skipping off the water were singing over the heads of his troops. The General said "We had better stop shooting"; and mounted the horse and rode on without saying a word.

Imagine being the officer who had to tell the General that his carelessness was endangering the troops.
It was during the Expedition that Custer made a rather famous remark, or at least repeated it. This, too, is from Grinnell's Two Great Scouts.

☞On the return trip, soon after crossing the Little

Missouri river, the abandoned camp was found of a great body of Indians. In conversation that evening in front of General Custer's tent, Luther North remarked that perhaps it was just as well the Indians had gone before the expedition got there, as there were a great many of them. Custer commented, "I could whip all the Indians in the northwest with the Seventh Cavalry."

This was all still in Custer's future during the long march of August 6. When the wagons came down to Gillette Prairie, they had already traveled more than 20 miles that day. They wouldn't reach camp until 7:30 in the evening, according to Ludlow's report. It may have been even later.

☞Went into camp at 9:30 p.m. *(Grant)*
. . . on a tributary of Castle Creek, where we found good wood and grass. *(Forsyth)*
Rich pasturage. Abundant supply of water from a running stream of pure water. *(Calhoun)*
. . . just beyond the high prairie. *(Ludlow)*

Capt. Ludlow didn't have a chance to measure latitude and longitude here, but his map shows the camp tucked up against the July 29 trail. The only location that seems to match all the requirements—a stream "beyond" the prairie next to the old trail—is where today's Medicine Mountain Road crosses South Slate Creek, between the prairie and the current tree line.

☞Had a heavy rainstorm accompanied by thunder and lightning. The thunder here has no long-rolling sound as it has in the east; it is here composed of a succession of sharp, abrupt peals. The lightning is very brilliant. *(Ewert)*
A heavy thunder-storm came up during the night, and the echoes among the hills were exceedingly grand. *(Ludlow)*
We did not get into camp 'till after dark, and, being wet through, we passed a very unpleasant night. *(Ewert)*

Out on the plains, far to the south, Charley Reynolds was in the fourth and final night of his ride to Fort Laramie. Newton Winchell, catching up on items in his personal notebook, thought about the scout on this night and entered a story he must have heard from one of the men on the southern reconnaissance.

☞Reynolds took dispatches and mail to Ft. Laramie. . . . When Bloody Knife shook hands with him on parting, he said he did not think he would get through. *(Winchell notebook)*

CHAPTER 10

Friday, August 7

Gillette Prairie to the north fork of Rapid Creek

Now I reassert that no grizzly bear was seen or killed in the Black Hills, but only one bear and that was a cinnamon. (Ewert)

The Expedition followed its old trail through the July 28 camp and up onto Reynolds Prairie, passing the mysterious pile of elk horns there (Chapter 5). Then the pioneer party really had to go to work, and it was not an easy day. Above the North Fork of Castle Creek the command crossed a hilly and forested area. As the wagons came into camp, William Illingworth was photographing a bear (it really was a grizzly) that Custer had dragged to a knoll for prominent display. Distance traveled: 16.2 miles.

— Taking the trail —

U.S.G.S. MAPS: Ditch Creek, Deerfield, Nahant
(Optional: Minnesota Ridge)

CAUTIONS: The roads are all smooth gravel or fairly well-maintained Forest Service roads—except for

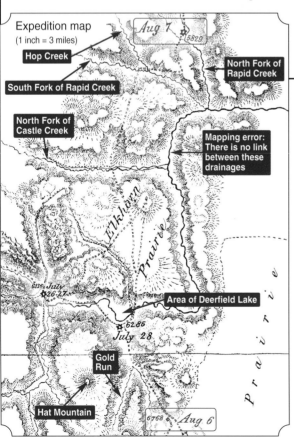

Expedition map
(1 inch = 3 miles)

Aug 7
5829

Hop Creek

North Fork of Rapid Creek

South Fork of Rapid Creek

North Fork of Castle Creek

Mapping error: There is no link between these drainages

Elkhorn Prairie

5136 July 26-27

Area of Deerfield Lake

6286 July 28

Gold Run

Hat Mountain

6768 Aug 6

Prairie

one optional side trip. The only way to see the camp of August 7, however, is a round-trip hike or bicycle ride of nearly six miles.

TO START: *From Hill City*, drive 8.5 miles west on Deerfield Road (Forest Service Road 17) and turn left on E. Slate Road (FS 300). After 4.2 miles, turn right onto Gillette Prairie Road (FS 297) and go 2 miles to a gate on the right at a bend in the road.

Heavy thunder shower this morning early. We also had one or two yesterday in different parts of the Black Hills, none striking us. *(Winchell notebook)*

The storm of the night before had swelled the brooks, but the old trail furnished a good road. *(Ludlow)*

1 **43 58 14.8** At the starting point beside the gate, you
103 45 12.5 probably would have been in the way of the wagons on July 29 as they came down the slope ahead of you, making their way south toward French Creek. (See Chapter 6.) The present Gillette Prairie Road generally follows the route for about a mile south of this bend.

This is the "old trail" Ludlow referred to, used by the command after spending the night along South Slate Creek. If you haven't already worked with Chapter 6 to follow the trail in this area—or wish to see it now from a different perspective—drive four-tenths of a mile on FS 297 to an unimproved road (not shown) on your right.

A **43 58 20.4** If you have a reasonably high-clearance
103 45 41.1 vehicle, turn right here and drive three-tenths of a mile to a road that branches to the right.

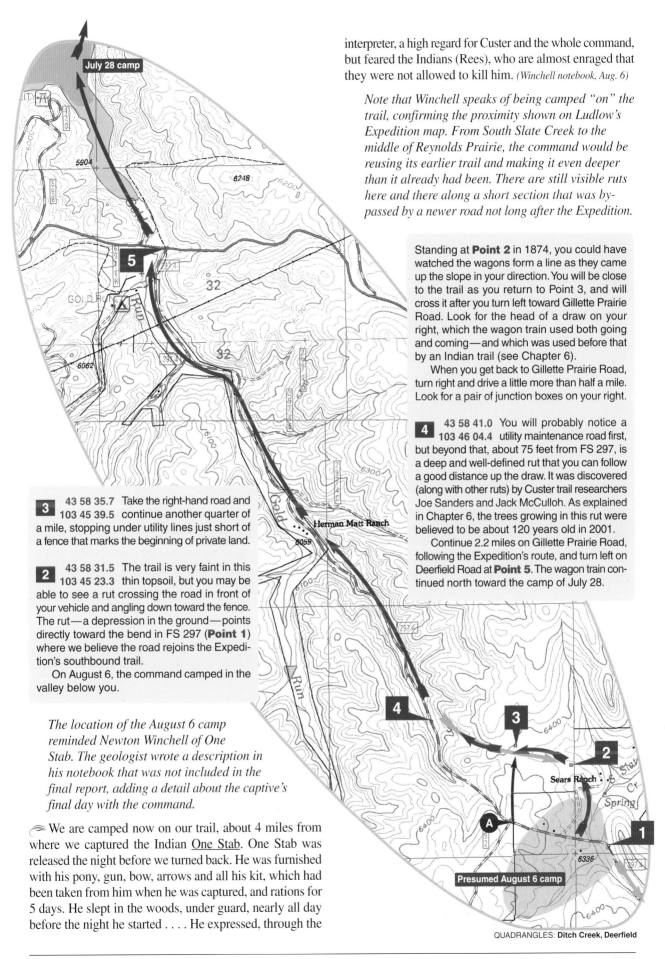

interpreter, a high regard for Custer and the whole command, but feared the Indians (Rees), who are almost enraged that they were not allowed to kill him. *(Winchell notebook, Aug. 6)*

Note that Winchell speaks of being camped "on" the trail, confirming the proximity shown on Ludlow's Expedition map. From South Slate Creek to the middle of Reynolds Prairie, the command would be reusing its earlier trail and making it even deeper than it already had been. There are still visible ruts here and there along a short section that was by-passed by a newer road not long after the Expedition.

Standing at **Point 2** in 1874, you could have watched the wagons form a line as they came up the slope in your direction. You will be close to the trail as you return to Point 3, and will cross it after you turn left toward Gillette Prairie Road. Look for the head of a draw on your right, which the wagon train used both going and coming—and which was used before that by an Indian trail (see Chapter 6).

When you get back to Gillette Prairie Road, turn right and drive a little more than half a mile. Look for a pair of junction boxes on your right.

4 43 58 41.0 You will probably notice a 103 46 04.4 utility maintenance road first, but beyond that, about 75 feet from FS 297, is a deep and well-defined rut that you can follow a good distance up the draw. It was discovered (along with other ruts) by Custer trail researchers Joe Sanders and Jack McCulloh. As explained in Chapter 6, the trees growing in this rut were believed to be about 120 years old in 2001.

Continue 2.2 miles on Gillette Prairie Road, following the Expedition's route, and turn left on Deerfield Road at **Point 5**. The wagon train continued north toward the camp of July 28.

Aug 7

3 43 58 35.7 Take the right-hand road and 103 45 39.5 continue another quarter of a mile, stopping under utility lines just short of a fence that marks the beginning of private land.

2 43 58 31.5 The trail is very faint in this 103 45 23.3 thin topsoil, but you may be able to see a rut crossing the road in front of your vehicle and angling down toward the fence. The rut—a depression in the ground—points directly toward the bend in FS 297 (**Point 1**) where we believe the road rejoins the Expedition's southbound trail.

On August 6, the command camped in the valley below you.

The location of the August 6 camp reminded Newton Winchell of One Stab. The geologist wrote a description in his notebook that was not included in the final report, adding a detail about the captive's final day with the command.

☞ We are camped now on our trail, about 4 miles from where we captured the Indian <u>One Stab</u>. One Stab was released the night before we turned back. He was furnished with his pony, gun, bow, arrows and all his kit, which had been taken from him when he was captured, and rations for 5 days. He slept in the woods, under guard, nearly all day before the night he started . . . . He expressed, through the

QUADRANGLES: **Ditch Creek, Deerfield**

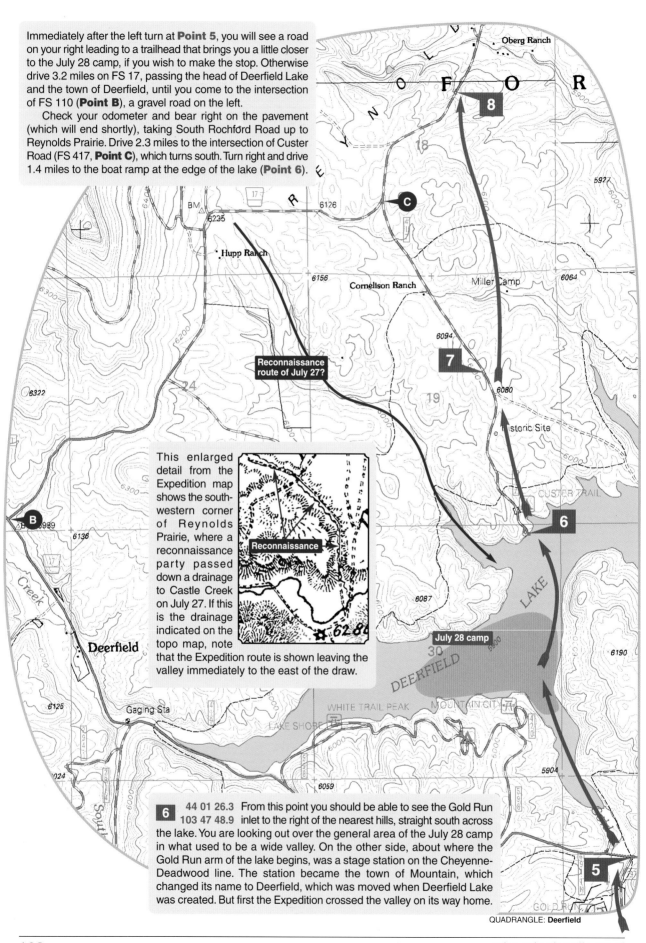

Immediately after the left turn at **Point 5**, you will see a road on your right leading to a trailhead that brings you a little closer to the July 28 camp, if you wish to make the stop. Otherwise drive 3.2 miles on FS 17, passing the head of Deerfield Lake and the town of Deerfield, until you come to the intersection of FS 110 (**Point B**), a gravel road on the left.

Check your odometer and bear right on the pavement (which will end shortly), taking South Rochford Road up to Reynolds Prairie. Drive 2.3 miles to the intersection of Custer Road (FS 417, **Point C**), which turns south. Turn right and drive 1.4 miles to the boat ramp at the edge of the lake (**Point 6**).

Oberg Ranch

Hupp Ranch

Cornelison Ranch

Miller Camp

Reconnaissance route of July 27?

This enlarged detail from the Expedition map shows the southwestern corner of Reynolds Prairie, where a reconnaissance party passed down a drainage to Castle Creek on July 27. If this is the drainage indicated on the topo map, note that the Expedition route is shown leaving the valley immediately to the east of the draw.

Reconnaissance

Historic Site

CUSTER TRAIL

Deerfield

Gaging Sta

July 28 camp

DEERFIELD

WHITE TRAIL PEAK

MOUNTAIN CITY

LAKE SHORE

6 44 01 26.3 / 103 47 48.9 From this point you should be able to see the Gold Run inlet to the right of the nearest hills, straight south across the lake. You are looking out over the general area of the July 28 camp in what used to be a wide valley. On the other side, about where the Gold Run arm of the lake begins, was a stage station on the Cheyenne-Deadwood line. The station became the town of Mountain, which changed its name to Deerfield, which was moved when Deerfield Lake was created. But first the Expedition crossed the valley on its way home.

GOLD RUN

QUADRANGLE: **Deerfield**

☙ We got on our old trail very soon and passed our last camp on Castle Creek. Followed the trail so as to get upon Elk-horn prairie. *(Grant)*

The next morning we left camp at daybreak, passed Camp No. 24 during the forenoon and soon after we left our old trail going to the right. *(Ewert)*

In passing again over Elk-Horn Park, we travel about a mile east of the interrupted line of limestone bluffs. *(Winchell)*

In fact, the limestone bluffs of Flag Mountain, Nipple Butte and Castle Rock are a mile and a half or less from the trail shown on the topo map (scale: 1 mile = 2.64 inches). The Expedition continued north somewhere near you at **Point 6**, based on the interpretation of Ludlow's map in the middle box of the opposite page. Unfortunately, the same section of the map suggests that the new trail left the old trail east of **Point C**, near Miller Camp. If that were true, the wagons would have had to return from the elk horns on July 28 across the eastern side of the prairie, which is fairly rough and hilly.

While it is possible that the Ludlow map is correct (if only there were a way to prove it) the arrows at right represent what seems the most likely route over the topography. They are also influenced by the number of times that roads seem to have followed the Expedition trail.

Turn around and drive north seven-tenths of a mile.

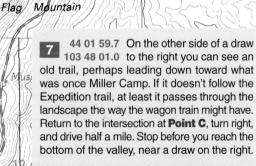

7 44 01 59.7 On the other side of a draw 103 48 01.0 to the right you can see an old trail, perhaps leading down toward what was once Miller Camp. If it doesn't follow the Expedition trail, at least it passes through the landscape the way the wagon train might have. Return to the intersection at **Point C**, turn right, and drive half a mile. Stop before you reach the bottom of the valley, near a draw on the right.

8 44 02 57.3 You may notice young trees 103 48 09.0 in a relatively new road cut, but closer to the road—about 40 or 50 feet away—is an early wagon rut that angles up the hill. This is a possible remnant of the Expedition, traveling both ways, as well as the stage coaches and other traffic that came later.
Continue 2.3 miles on S. Rochford Road.

9 44 04 54.5 About 25 feet to the right of 103 48 06.0 the road, on private land just beyond the fence, is an old rut descending from the prairie. Continue four-tenths of a mile, just past the buildings of the early Reynolds stage stop, and park carefully on the curve at **Point 10**, before you cross the creek.

Presumed return route of July 28

Aug 7

QUADRANGLE: **Deerfield**

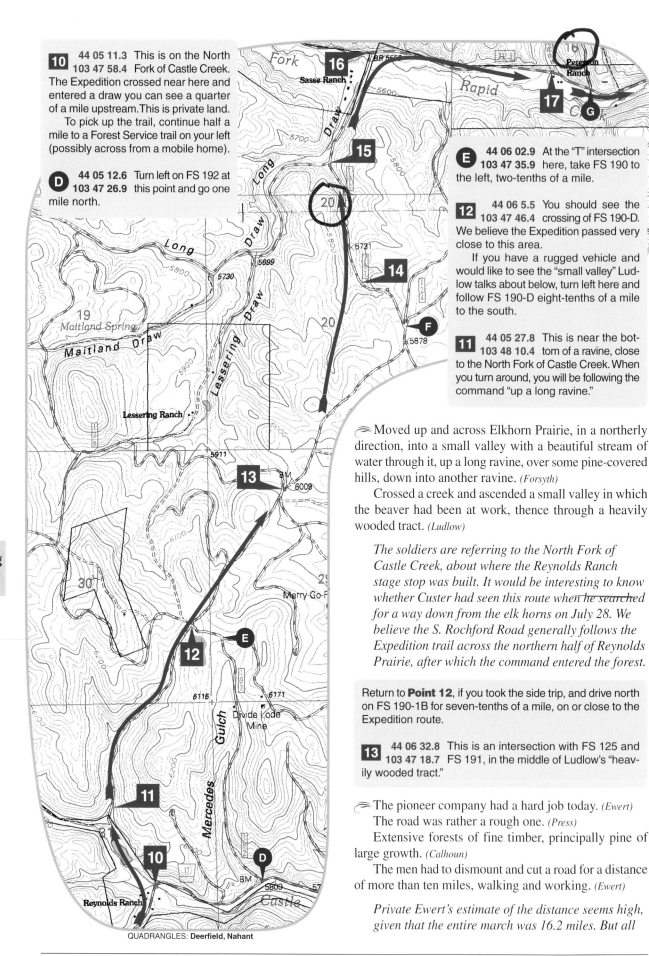

10 44 05 11.3 / 103 47 58.4 This is on the North Fork of Castle Creek. The Expedition crossed near here and entered a draw you can see a quarter of a mile upstream. This is private land.

To pick up the trail, continue half a mile to a Forest Service trail on your left (possibly across from a mobile home).

D 44 05 12.6 / 103 47 26.9 Turn left on FS 192 at this point and go one mile north.

16

Fork

BR 5550

Sasse Ranch

Rapid

Peterson Ranch

17

G

C r.

15

E 44 06 02.9 / 103 47 35.9 At the "T" intersection here, take FS 190 to the left, two-tenths of a mile.

12 44 06 5.5 / 103 47 46.4 You should see the crossing of FS 190-D. We believe the Expedition passed very close to this area.

If you have a rugged vehicle and would like to see the "small valley" Ludlow talks about below, turn left here and follow FS 190-D eight-tenths of a mile to the south.

11 44 05 27.8 / 103 48 10.4 This is near the bottom of a ravine, close to the North Fork of Castle Creek. When you turn around, you will be following the command "up a long ravine."

20

5731

14

124

20

F 5878

Long

Draw

5699

5730

Long Draw

5800

Lessering Draw

19
Maitland Spring

Maitland Draw

Lessering Ranch

5911

13 BM 6009

6100

30°

29
Merry Go-F

E

192

6116 6171

Divide Lode Mine

Mercedes Gulch

12

11

10

D BM 5809 57

Reynolds Ranch

Castle

QUADRANGLES: **Deerfield, Nahant**

Aug 7

Moved up and across Elkhorn Prairie, in a northerly direction, into a small valley with a beautiful stream of water through it, up a long ravine, over some pine-covered hills, down into another ravine. *(Forsyth)*

Crossed a creek and ascended a small valley in which the beaver had been at work, thence through a heavily wooded tract. *(Ludlow)*

The soldiers are referring to the North Fork of Castle Creek, about where the Reynolds Ranch stage stop was built. It would be interesting to know whether Custer had seen this route when he searched for a way down from the elk horns on July 28. We believe the S. Rochford Road generally follows the Expedition trail across the northern half of Reynolds Prairie, after which the command entered the forest.

Return to **Point 12**, if you took the side trip, and drive north on FS 190-1B for seven-tenths of a mile, on or close to the Expedition route.

13 44 06 32.8 / 103 47 18.7 This is an intersection with FS 125 and FS 191, in the middle of Ludlow's "heavily wooded tract."

The pioneer company had a hard job today. *(Ewert)*

The road was rather a rough one. *(Press)*

Extensive forests of fine timber, principally pine of large growth. *(Calhoun)*

The men had to dismount and cut a road for a distance of more than ten miles, walking and working. *(Ewert)*

Private Ewert's estimate of the distance seems high, given that the entire march was 16.2 miles. But all the accounts together give us a sense of traveling some distance through the woods between the North Fork of Castle Creek and South Fork of Rapid Creek.

Continue to follow FS 191 by going straight and slightly to the right. After eight-tenths of a mile you will come to a complicated intersection in the forest.

F **44 07 06.5** The Expedition appears to have traveled **103 46 42.0** down the draw to your left, although it is hard to say exactly where they entered it. Stay on FS 191 by bearing left at this intersection. You may start to notice an old trail on the other side of the drainage.
Continue about a quarter of a mile.

14 **44 07 15.5** At this point, just before the draw opens **103 46 53.2** out, you can see an old rut or trail about 40 feet to the left. This might be a remnant of the Expedition and/or the stage trail that followed during part of 1877.
Continue half a mile to an intersection.

15 **44 07 39.7** This is where you enter Long Draw, which **103 47 04.0** comes in from the left. Continue north in the draw—as did the Expedition—nearly half a mile to the next intersection.

16 **44 08 02.7** FS 191 meets FS 203 (County Road L305) **103 46 50.8** here at the South Fork of Rapid Creek.

Custer and his scouts might have been amused to know they were cutting a trail that would be used for many miles in 1877 by the Cheyenne-Deadwood Stage. Where the Expedition came to the South Fork of Rapid Creek is the site of yet another stop on the line, according to Parker and Lambert's Black Hills Ghost Towns. *The Rapid Creek Stage Station was located where the Sasse Ranch is shown on the topographic map today. An old barn building still stood on the site in 2002.*

This is the third station along today's route alone, in addition to Gillette's and Spring Creek to the south as well as Rapid Creek and the Bulldog Ranch to the north, on either side of Nahant. It is surprising that so many stations were operating along a route that was used for only a few months in 1877.

The Expedition map shows the trail crossing the creek and continuing to the east at **Point 16**, which suggests that the present county road follows closely on the old trail. Drive three-quarters of a mile east on the county road, to a creek.

17 **44 07 58.3** Hop Creek, which is drawn on Ludlow's **103 45 58.2** map, passes beneath the road here.
You will soon pass Telegraph Gulch on the left (**Point G**). For many years it was believed that the command turned up this gulch on its way to the area now known as Nahant.

⌒ Turning sharply to the left over a slight ridge . . . *(Ludlow)*
After crossing a mountain ridge, a camp was located in a green meadow beside a cool mountain stream. *(Pioneer)*

You will see where the camp area was on the next page. "Headquarters," meanwhile, was traveling far out in front to choose the trail and give the pioneer party a chance to open a road.

⌒ Gen. Custer and the party who accompanied him . . . got to the camping ground early in the afternoon. They found the valley filled with game. *(Press)*

The train was still several hours behind and Gen. Custer and Col. Ludlow, Bloody Knife and private Noonan, went up the valley a short distance, looking for a road out the next morning and also having an eye for any game that might be near. Presently Col. Ludlow saw a herd of deer and commenced counting them, one, two, three, four, five—when Bloody Knife exclaims motto! motto! (bear! bear!). Immediately the deer were forgotten and all parties paid their compliments to the bear in rifle shots. *(Pioneer)*

His bearship was discovered on the side of a hill about 75 yards away. A shot in the thigh from Gen. Custer's Remington caused him to halt. *(New York Tribune)*

On receiving the first shot he cocked himself up on his hind legs, and showing his huge teeth, he grinned in defiance; but like all who fight Custer, he was compelled to surrender. *(Bismarck Tribune)*

Well, almost everyone. Here's another version, which makes it hard to tell whether the bear reared up right away (as described above) or first tried to run.

⌒ Bruin ran off some distance through the brush and among the trees. Finding himself wounded and hotly pursued, he came to bay and prepared for fight at close quarters. He reared his huge form up [on] his hind legs, with his back against a pine tree and his face to the foe, and with his fore paws very politely gestured to his lately made acquaintances to to come forward to a friendly pow-wow and hand-shaking, and a still more friendly hugging. His courteous invitations were only answered by cold lead, soon to be followed by a keen bloody knife in the hands of Bloody Knife, searching for the great jugular through which flowed the tide of life. *(Pioneer)*

Another shot from Gen. Custer and three more contributed by the General's companions, put an end to his career, and he consented to be photographed 15 minutes afterward. *(New York Tribune)*

The Tribune's language is colorful, but the timing seems wrong. The accounts point to the bear being killed early or mid-afternoon, while the wagon train is seen arriving in the background of one of Illingworth's pictures. Ludlow's table for the Expedition puts that arrival at 5:30.

Besides, it must have taken a while to drag the bear to a place where all the camp could admire Custer's prize.

⌒ Bruin died. He was an old dark-brown grizzly. He was taken into camp that all might see the first grizzly bear ever

Aug 7

shot by a white man in the Black Hills. He was placed on a big rock, his four captors just in the rear, and the group was photographed. *(Pioneer)*

I should judge his weight to be about 600 lbs. The following named persons shot him:

General Custer, USA

Capt. W. Ludlow, Engineer Corps, USA

Private Jno. Noonan, Co. L, 7th Cavalry

Bloody Knife, Indian Scout

Mr. Illingworth, a photographer from St. Paul, Minn., . . . took a photograph of the hunters on a high knoll behind the tent of the Commanding Officer. *(Calhoun)*

This is a fortuitous remark by Calhoun, because it removes any doubt about the distinctive-looking tent in the background of **Photo 847**, *"Our First Grizzly, killed by General Custer" (pages 254-257 and back cover). The knoll on which the bear was displayed— identified here for the first time—was on the north side of camp at* **Point H**. *Please note that it is on private land.*

For more about the story of Custer's tent, which is visible in several other photographs, see page xii *(facing the first page of the Prologue).*

Illingworth, meanwhile, got marketing and promotional support from three of the correspondents.

Gen. Custer and Col. Ludlow had a picture (photograph) taken of the bear and themselves, by Prof. Illingworth . . . . The picture is indeed a fine one. *(Press)*

You will want this picture. *(Pioneer)*

A PICTURE WORTH HAVING. *(Bismarck Tribune)*

New York Tribune *reporter Samuel Barrows did mention the photograph, but the* Inter-Ocean's *Curtis seems to have ignored the event altogether.*

Luther North offers an interesting sidelight on the bear in Man of the Plains *(University of Nebraska Press, 1961, p. 187).*

The General sent liberal pieces of the meat to the different messes, and we got our share, but a very little of it went a long way with most of us, for it was tough and very strong. Bear meat from a young animal is good, but from an old one is hardly fit to eat.

The same book quotes North later in life (p. 192) describing how he and his friend George Bird Grinnell missed the excitement.

Grinnell and I were eating red raspberries on the side of a nearby hill, and could hear the bombardment, but the bear was dead before we reached the spot—so I didn't have a chance to get in a shot and claim that I killed it!

Custer ignored the bear in his official report, but not in a letter to his wife Elizabeth (quoted in Marguerite

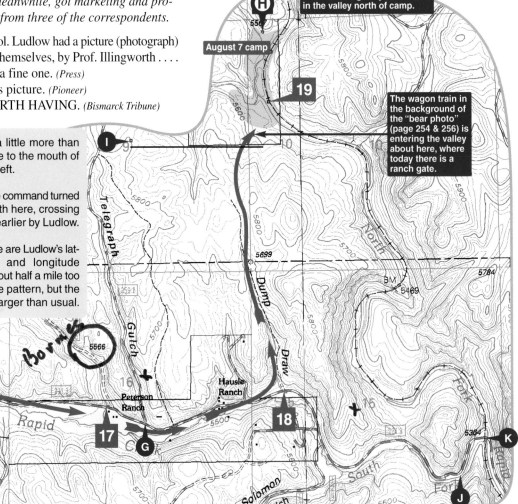

The doomed grizzly was found in the valley north of camp.

August 7 camp

The wagon train in the background of the "bear photo" (page 254 & 256) is entering the valley about here, where today there is a ranch gate.

From **Point 17**, go a little more than seven-tenths of a mile to the mouth of Dump Draw on your left.

18 44 08 00.8   The command turned 103 45 05.7   north here, crossing the ridge referred to earlier by Ludlow.

I 44 08 53   These are Ludlow's lat- 103 45 50   itude and longitude readings. They are about half a mile too far west, which fits the pattern, but the error to the south is larger than usual.

QUADRANGLES: **Nahant, Minnesota Ridge**

Merington's The Custer Story, *p. 275) that was sent, coincidentally, from Bear Butte on August 15.*

I have reached the hunter's highest round of fame . . . I have killed my Grizzly.

General Custer claimed that it was a grizzly and nearly everyone chimed in with him simply because he was the commanding officer, but as I knew it was no grizzly but a genuine cinnamon, I expressed myself to that effect, but when I noticed the sour looks and angry frown this assertion brought me, I did not insist. *(Ewert)*

Such a wonderful display of naivete—or something. As if the men would appreciate the private's truthful candor. "I did not insist," indeed.

As it turns out, Ewert was wrong. We showed Illingworth's photo to Kevin Casey, co-owner of a Black Hills tourist attraction called Bear Country USA, who said the hump between the shoulder blades and the long snout are both common to grizzly bears, as are the long, straight claws visible in the photo. Black bears are smaller than Custer's specimen, and their claws are more curled, like a cat's. (Casey cited an old joke: "How do you tell what kind of bear is chasing you? Climb a tree. A black bear will climb up after you but a grizzly will shake you down.") The "cinnamon" referred to by Ewert, according to Casey, is actually one coloration of a black bear, which can be many different shades.

General Custer, of course, wishes to magnify his discoveries to the fullest extent, but I cannot comprehend in what manner the species of a single bear is to add to, or detract from the importance of his work. Surely no man would wish to go to the Black Hills for the sole and lone purpose of hunting bear, be these cinnamon, black or grizzly. *(Ewert)*

The collision with the grizzly as well as the route of the next few days were an accident of geology. Custer had tried to follow the South Fork of Rapid Creek.

Further progress was barred by a cañon, and turning sharply to the left over a slight ridge we camped on the bank of another creek. *(Ludlow)*

Camp known as Fruiting Brooke. The supplies of raspberries was certainly equal to any thing I ever saw. *(Power)*

The first grasshoppers seen in the hills in any numbers were swarming in both creek valleys. *(Ludlow)*

As you continue east on the county road from **Point 18**, notice how narrow the canyon becomes. After about a mile, for example (**Point J**), you'll see where a point of land had to be cut away to make room for the road—perhaps the very area where Custer gave up and decided to turn north. The Mickelson Trail crosses the road after another two-tenths of a mile (1.2 miles from Point 18).

K   44 07 50.0   A hike or ride of 2.3 miles north from here
103 44 07.6   will take you to Point 19 in the camp.

19   44 09 10.8   This is on the old railroad bed that is now
103 45 08.3   the Mickelson Trail, with a view of the camp
shown in the photo below.
  When you are done for the day, Rochford is 1.3 miles east.

"Red Bird," a Santee scout, succeeded in killing the mate to the [bear] already killed. *(Press)*

The one killed by Custer and Ludlow had claws fully five inches long, and teeth or tusks as long as a man's finger, which were set outside the lips, making an animal somewhat ferocious in appearance. I have rode (sic) inside the columns since I saw those jaws—would rather see old Sitting Bull than such a bear. *(Bismarck Tribune)*

There has been considerable hunting since by the officers, and others who were at liberty to go. *(Press)*

The killing of two grizzly bears in one afternoon would, of course, create intense excitement. . . . Around the evening campfires, hunting stories were told and hunting parties were organized for the next day. Some were so excited that they hardly closed their eyes in sleep that night. *(Pioneer)*

Aug 7

The Mickelson Trail is seen at right in this view of the August 7 camp area from Point 19, looking north.

CHAPTER 11

Saturday, August 8

North fork of Rapid Creek to Reausaw Lake on Nemo Road

We . . . drew the revolver from its holster, placed a finger on the trigger, and thumb on the hammer, thought of home and its loved ones. (Pioneer)

It was a generally dismal day for the explorers, who woke up in a cold fog that got so bad the wagons had to stop for a while. Then they traveled through a burned-over wasteland of fallen timber that Forsyth called an "extent of deadening," which made hard work for the pioneer crew. The botanist got seriously lost, meanwhile, and there was a troublesome creek crossing that kept most of the wagon train away from camp until after midnight. Distance traveled: 14.7 miles.

— Taking the trail —

U.S.G.S. MAPS: Nahant, Minnesota Ridge, Deadwood South, Deadman Mountain *(Optional: Nemo)*

CAUTIONS: You will have the option of staying on paved and gravel roads, but a high-clearance vehicle will give you access to several interesting portions of the trail. Also, visiting the previous night's campsite will require a round-trip hike or bicycle ride of four miles from one of the stops along the way.

TO START: *From downtown Rochford*, check your odometer and drive north toward Nahant on Forest Service 17. Look carefully for an unimproved trail on the left at 2.8 miles (**Point 6**) and make the turn. (If the gate is closed, please be sure to close it again behind you, in each direction.) Continue almost six-tenths of a mile (to **Point 4**) or as far as you feel comfortable with the condition of the road.

Aug 8

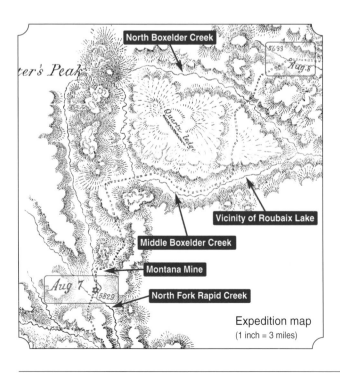

North Boxelder Creek

Vicinity of Roubaix Lake

Middle Boxelder Creek

Montana Mine

North Fork Rapid Creek

Expedition map
(1 inch = 3 miles)

Reveille sounded at 3 o'clock in the morning, and soon the whole camp was active. The fires were rekindled and blazed up brightly, warming and drying the chill, damp, foggy air. Breakfast was soon prepared and over, tents were struck and loaded, and before it was fairly light the camp ground was deserted. *(Pioneer)*

The killing of the grizzly bear the night before inspired at least two hunting parties to go their own way as the wagons departed. One was joined by Professor Aris Donaldson, the St. Paul Pioneer *correspondent, who wrote this description from the perspective of those being left behind.*

A fog had settled down over mountain and valley, and nothing could be seen beyond fifty yards distance . . . . For some time the advance of the train and its direction could be known by the playing of the band. At length the playing ceased or the sound was lost in the distance. *(Pioneer)*

This haunting image of band music fading into

the mist confirms Luther North's story in Man of the Plains *that the band was not just for special occasions.*

☞ We left the fort with the band of sixteen men mounted on white horses playing Garry Owen . . . . This was the first and last expedition that I was ever on in an Indian country that had a band along. Every morning upon leaving camp the band would play for two or three miles, and nearly every evening after supper the general would have them come over in front of his tent and play for an hour or so.

Contrary to long-accepted belief, the August 7 camp was about two miles south of Nahant. The band and the wagons were disappearing up the North Fork of Rapid Creek—in the general area where Custer and his men had come across the doomed grizzly (Chapter 10) while looking for a good route out of the valley.

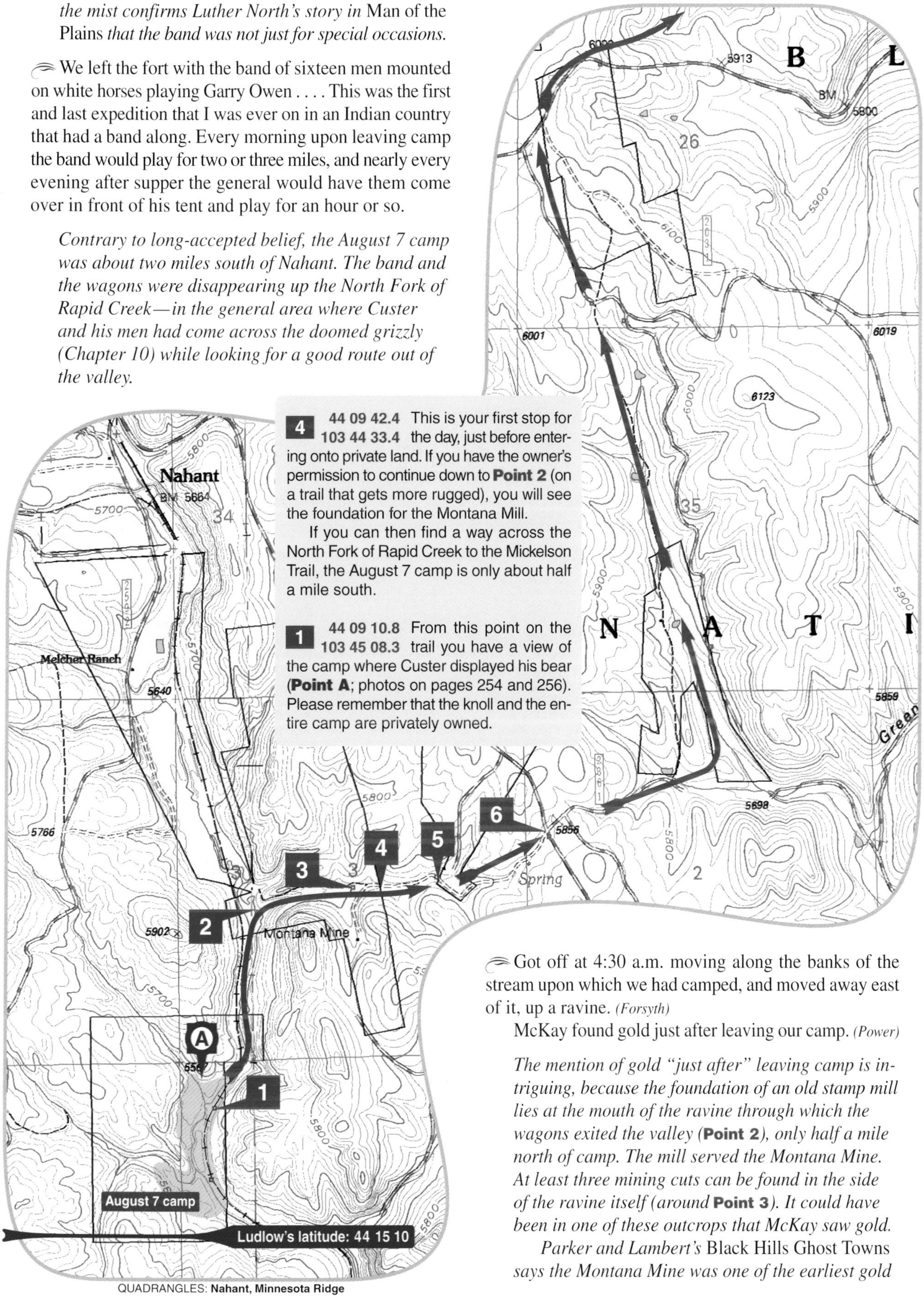

4 44 09 42.4 This is your first stop for 103 44 33.4 the day, just before entering onto private land. If you have the owner's permission to continue down to **Point 2** (on a trail that gets more rugged), you will see the foundation for the Montana Mill.

If you can then find a way across the North Fork of Rapid Creek to the Mickelson Trail, the August 7 camp is only about half a mile south.

1 44 09 10.8 From this point on the 103 45 08.3 trail you have a view of the camp where Custer displayed his bear (**Point A**; photos on pages 254 and 256). Please remember that the knoll and the entire camp are privately owned.

☞ Got off at 4:30 a.m. moving along the banks of the stream upon which we had camped, and moved away east of it, up a ravine. *(Forsyth)*

McKay found gold just after leaving our camp. *(Power)*

*The mention of gold "just after" leaving camp is intriguing, because the foundation of an old stamp mill lies at the mouth of the ravine through which the wagons exited the valley (**Point 2**), only half a mile north of camp. The mill served the Montana Mine. At least three mining cuts can be found in the side of the ravine itself (around **Point 3**). It could have been in one of these outcrops that McKay saw gold.*

Parker and Lambert's Black Hills Ghost Towns *says the Montana Mine was one of the earliest gold*

August 7 camp

Ludlow's latitude: 44 15 10

QUADRANGLES: **Nahant, Minnesota Ridge**

discoveries in the Rochford area. The mill cost $160,000 to build, but amalgamation couldn't extract gold from this ore, and the mill was used for only a couple of months. Nevertheless, the town of Gregory grew nearby (complete with post office) built directly on the route of the Expedition.

Turn around at **Point 4** and drive back less than two-tenths of a mile, stopping near a stock dam.

5 44 09 43.6 On the left (if it is still there) is an old out-
103 44 22.1 building that is covered with lids from cyanide cans—about the only thing that remains of the once-thriving town of Gregory. It's the same structure seen in the photo on page 105 of *Black Hills Ghost Towns*, next to a home that survived into the 1970s.
Follow Custer up the draw, back to the highway.

6 44 09 49.1 The Expedition crossed on or close to this
103 43 58.8 point in 1874. (There was of course no built-up roadbed in the way.) As a matter of fact, the end of the wagon train might have stopped here for a time.

☞ After having made scarcely two miles we were compelled to come to a halt, a dense fog having settled over the earth and being unable to see a hundred yards in any direction. *(Ewert)*

We halted a couple of hours until the sun dissipated it and enabled us to look out our course. *(Forsyth)*

As it was cold and damp, we built large fires around which both men and horses huddled. *(Ewert)*

Imagine a line of wagons across the road at **Point 6**, looming out of the early-morning fog. Teamsters and soldiers would be gathered around crackling fires, not long after dawn, perhaps talking in somber, muted tones.

The road on the other side of FS 17 continues along this leg of Custer's trail. You may want to explore it for a short distance, but there is a gate that is sometimes closed and the road itself dead-ends at private land.

The Expedition cut back to the northwest in the area of **Point 7** (as shown on Ludlow's map) to take advantage of a long, straight valley. You can see most of this valley by approaching from the north. Begin by checking your odometer at Point 6 and driving two miles to an intersection.

B 44 10 53.6 This puts you above the former town of
103 45 26.6 Nahant, where it had been assumed until now that Custer camped on Swede Gulch.

This is your opportunity to visit the true August 7 camp by foot or bicycle, if you haven't already done so. The Mickelson Trail is just below the highway on your left, and the distance is a little more than two miles to **Point 1** (see previous page). The camp is south of Milepost 87.

Otherwise continue three-tenths of a mile to **Point C** and turn right on Custer Crossing Road (Forest Service 256). Then drive 1.4 miles to a Forest Service trail on your right.

10 44 11 27.9 Take FS 203 to the right if you have a high-
103 44 03.0 clearance vehicle. Drive six-tenths of a mile and look for a trail on the right that may sneak up on you.

D 44 11 03.1 Bear to the right on FS 203-1B and con-
103 43 41.7 tinue 1.1 miles. Look for a small knoll near the bottom of the valley, with a place to pull off the road.

8 44 10 16.1 The road is about to enter private land be-
103 43 24.9 low this location, and here you have a convenient place to turn around. You can also see, straight south, the place where Custer entered the valley. The head of the wagon train may have gotten this far before it was stopped by the heavy fog.

☞ About 9 o'clock the sun broke the misty veil. *(Ewert)*
. . . and we went on our way rejoicing. *(Press)*
. . . through an Immense extent of deadening—a place where the trees have been probably burned, and have then fallen or been blown down, crossing one another in every direction, with corpses of young populars here and there, sparsely covering the slate or sandstone which crops out in vertical ledges at the crest of the hills. *(Forsyth)*

It is difficult to fully imagine the extent of the devastation being described, unlike anything most of us have seen. The affected area apparently started somewhere along the Lead-Rochford Road (FS 17), or to the east of it, and extended to the Middle fork of the Boxelder.

☞ The whole country was once covered with heavy pine forest. At least twenty years and probably thirty years ago it was nearly all destroyed by fire. A young forest sprung up, in some places of pine, but generally popple; but it, too, has been destroyed by fire within three or four years. This doubly scourged region is the most drear of any part of the Black Hills. The very richness and unbrokenness of the forest caused its more utter destruction. *(Pioneer)*

Lieut. Hodgson, commanding Company B, was pioneer, and had a hard day's work of it. *(Press)*

Trees covered the ground, they lying sometimes six, seven and eight on top of each other, their branches interlocked, and to remove these so that the wagon train could pass was the work of the pioneer company. *(Ewert)*

Turn around at **Point 8** and check your odometer. Retrace your path, traveling parallel to the command down in the valley. Continue past **Point D**, for a total of almost 1.2 miles.

9 44 11 05.7 You should find yourself in the head of the
103 43 48.4 valley used by the command. Continue the return trip to Custer Crossing Road, in what was probably the heart of the burned-over area.
One advantage of the destruction was a clear view.

☞ The line of limestone bluffs is plainly visible about five miles away toward the west, but northwest there is a single bluff or peak, capped with limestone, not more than four miles away. *(Winchell)*

Winchell probably saw Custer's Peak, already named by Ludlow near Harney Peak on July 31 (Chapter 7).

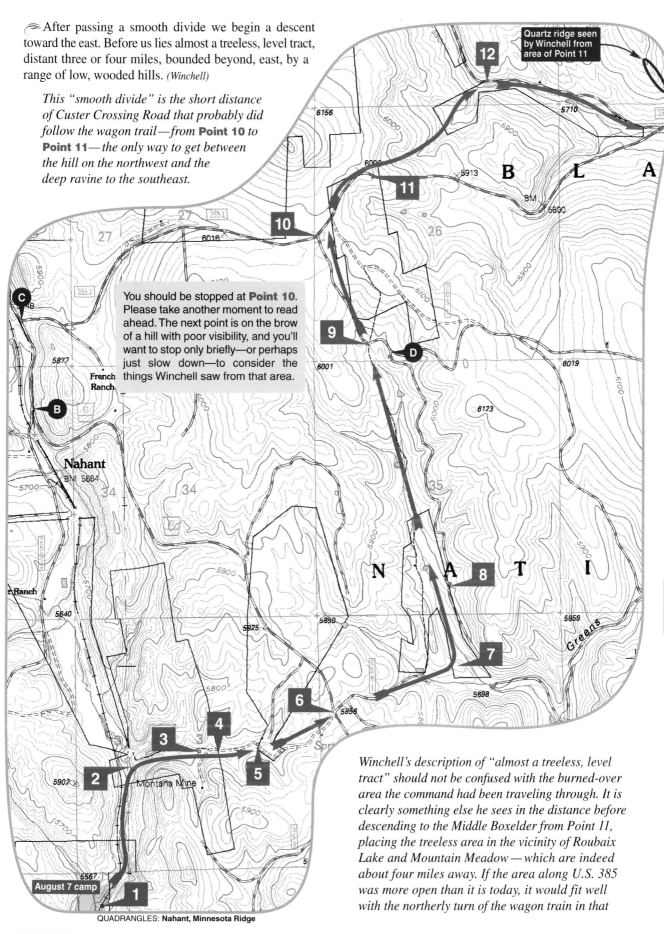

⌐After passing a smooth divide we begin a descent toward the east. Before us lies almost a treeless, level tract, distant three or four miles, bounded beyond, east, by a range of low, wooded hills. *(Winchell)*

*This "smooth divide" is the short distance of Custer Crossing Road that probably did follow the wagon trail—from **Point 10** to **Point 11**—the only way to get between the hill on the northwest and the deep ravine to the southeast.*

Quartz ridge seen by Winchell from area of Point 11

You should be stopped at **Point 10**. Please take another moment to read ahead. The next point is on the brow of a hill with poor visibility, and you'll want to stop only briefly—or perhaps just slow down—to consider the things Winchell saw from that area.

Winchell's description of "almost a treeless, level tract" should not be confused with the burned-over area the command had been traveling through. It is clearly something else he sees in the distance before descending to the Middle Boxelder from Point 11, placing the treeless area in the vicinity of Roubaix Lake and Mountain Meadow—which are indeed about four miles away. If the area along U.S. 385 was more open than it is today, it would fit well with the northerly turn of the wagon train in that

QUADRANGLES: **Nahant, Minnesota Ridge**

vicinity. But first there was something nearby that excited even greater interest.

In the distance before us, but on this side of the open ground, can be seen a ridge of white rock, rising some distance above the general surface and crowning an elevation of about 100 feet. This ridge seems to run north and south. On visiting it, I find an immense quartz "vein" that runs north 50° west by compass. It rises about 15 feet above the talus, and for that distance consists of bare quartz rock... . . . Fragments from the quartz are strewn over the surface toward the west as far as to the creek about one-half mile. . . . Very industrious "prospecting" is carried on in the neighborhood of these "veins" by gold-seekers, who accompany the expedition. *(Winchell)*

The view from the divide also revealed the Middle Boxelder Creek.

Moved east into a small valley in which was a running stream, which we skirted for some miles. *(Forsyth)*

Now you are ready to follow Winchell, although your view will be hampered by all those inconvenient trees. It was somewhere in this area that he caught a glimpse of the prairie, according to a footnote in his report, and you may feel you can almost see it yourself. As you move toward Point 11, be aware that you are crossing the "smooth divide" on the rim of the deep ravine to your right.

Set or check your odometer at **Point 10** and turn right (east) on Custer Crossing road. Drive a quarter mile.

11 | 44 11 40.1 This is the tricky stopping place, just before
103 43 46.0 you go downhill. It was after this point that Winchell saw the open area to the east as well as the white ridge of quartz. The wagon train descended in a draw you will see on the left as you continue.

Drive 1.3 miles to an intersection.

13 | 44 11 49.3 Make a sharp left turn onto FS 256-1L and
103 42 20.4 drive three-quarters of a mile.

12 | 44 11 59.5 You should be stopped just before a bend
103 43 11.6 in the road, with glimpses of a meadow (which is private land) through the draw on your left. If you look carefully, you may also be able to see the grade of an old trail coming up from the creek.

It appears that the Expedition came through the draw and crossed near here. Notice that Ludlow's map depicts the trail joining the creek about where the creek changes direction from almost north and south to east and west—just as the Middle Boxelder does near Point 12. The trail also stays on the north side of the creek, as does the present-day road.

Continue north one-tenth of a mile to take advantage of a convenient turn-around in front of a closed gate. If you would like to see what may be the quartz ridge explored by Winchell, stop half a mile from the turn-around and climb northeast. You should start to notice fragments of quartz almost immediately, just as the geologist reported.

E | 44 12 03.0 This is one reading along a quartz ridge
103 42 24.6 that could be Winchell's, although it is farther south than the notation on Ludlow's map. There is another possible spot to the north, where very white quartz is being removed from a private mining claim.

Return to **Point 13** and turn left. Drive a little more than three-tenths of a mile to a pull-out on the right.

14 | 44 11 55.9 This should give you a good view down
103 41 59.8 the valley of the Middle Boxelder, which the command continued to follow for a time.

We marched by the side of a copious stream of water. We are now travelling in the worst part of the Black Hills, in fact this is the most undesirable portion of country yet moved over. Dead trees and fallen timber lie across our path. Nothing but huge rocks and concretion of earth welcome our onward march. *(Calhoun)*

The open country mentioned is rolling, and has formerly been covered with pines, as shown by an occasional dead trunk. . . . Just before entering this open tract, we encounter a little creek *[the Middle Boxelder]* and follow it toward the east; but not far, before striking more to the north. *(Winchell)*

This further confirms the location of the "open tract" as near U.S. 385. From Calhoun we learn that the command was still encountering dead trees on what is now called the Middle Boxelder, but Winchell tells us there was only the occasional memory of a tree— a "dead trunk"—in the open tract, which is said to come after encountering the creek.

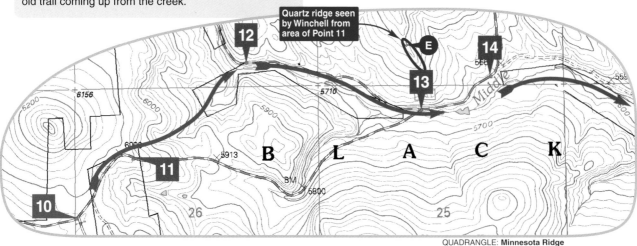

QUADRANGLE: **Minnesota Ridge**

The road that turns off near **Point 14** to follow the creek is shown on old maps as a continuation of the main road all the way through to Mountain Meadow. Unfortunately it now comes to a dead end after entering private land.

Continue north 3.8 miles on Custer Crossing Road to U.S. 385 at **Point F**. Turn right and go 1.2 miles to the entrance to Roubaix Lake (**Point G**). Go through the picnic and camp areas, traveling 1.1 miles to "Loop D" (**Point H**). The road goes a little further, but soon ends at a locked gate with no place to turn around. Nor do we know exactly where the wagon train turned north in this area.

The main point here is to see the kind of country in which it did so. The geologist called it "rolling," and it is not hard to imagine the command picking its way across such a landscape as you see here—particularly if it were denuded of trees. The command didn't have much choice, in any case. Note the line of hills at right, between Highway 385 and the North Boxelder. Then remember that Winchell said the open tract was "bounded beyond, east, by a range of low, wooded hills."

⌒ Moved east into a small valley . . . thence directly north up the hill into another deadening. *(Forsyth)*

This continues a passage already quoted, for the purpose of connecting elements of the landscape. Driving north on Highway 385 from the Mountain Meadow area, you get a definite sense of going "up the hill," as Forsyth puts it. The Expedition left the Middle Boxelder somewhere near today's Roubaix Lake and apparently crossed the North Boxelder a little east of where Highway 385 crosses it now.

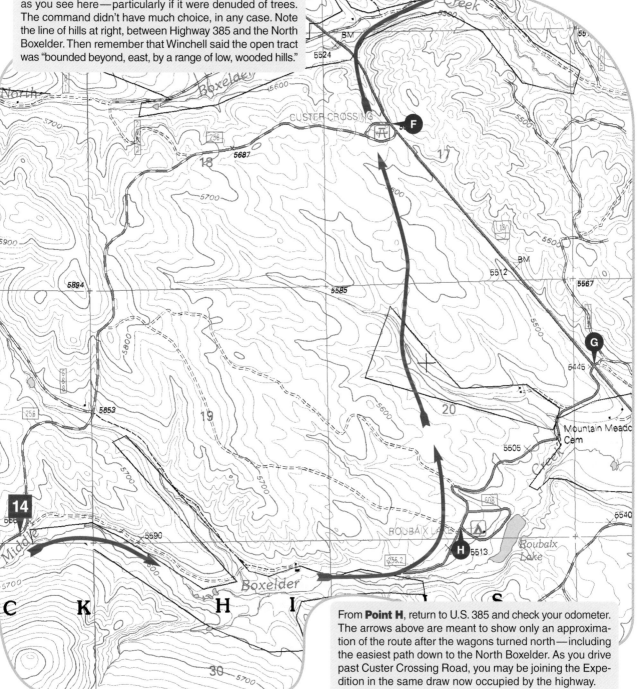

Aug
8

From **Point H**, return to U.S. 385 and check your odometer. The arrows above are meant to show only an approximation of the route after the wagons turned north—including the easiest path down to the North Boxelder. As you drive past Custer Crossing Road, you may be joining the Expedition in the same draw now occupied by the highway.

QUADRANGLE: **Minnesota Ridge**

☞ Moved east . . . thence directly north up the hill into another deadening, across some stony, pine-covered hills, over another creek. *(Forsyth)*

We return to Forsyth's account a third time because he is the only one to describe the route between the North Boxelder and what is now called Corral Creek. This was the creek that would cause the most trouble on this day, where Ewert will later describe huge bon fires providing light for repair work on a bridge.

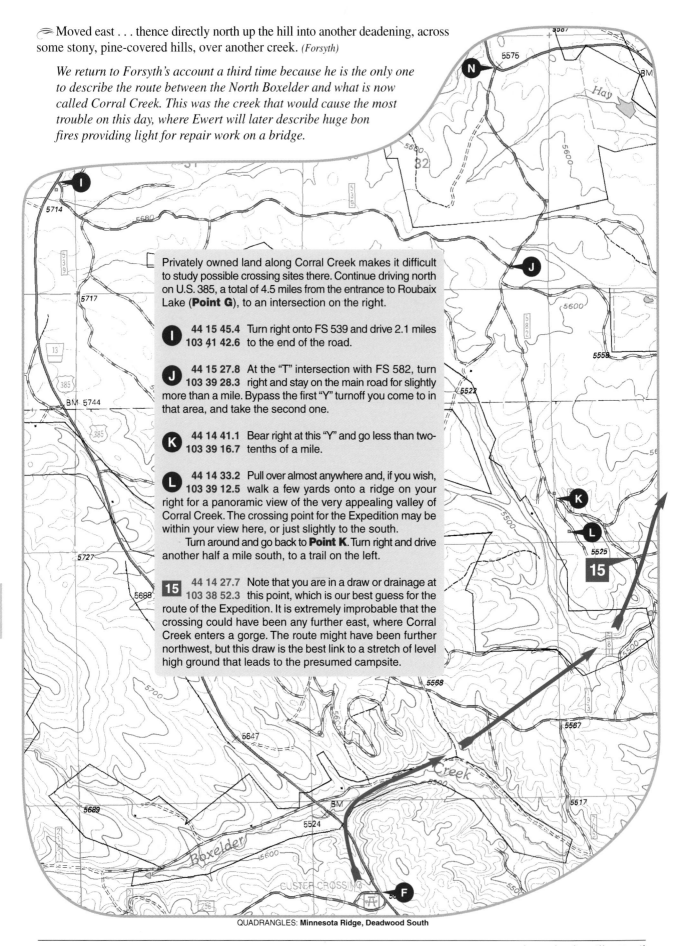

Privately owned land along Corral Creek makes it difficult to study possible crossing sites there. Continue driving north on U.S. 385, a total of 4.5 miles from the entrance to Roubaix Lake (**Point G**), to an intersection on the right.

I 44 15 45.4 Turn right onto FS 539 and drive 2.1 miles
103 41 42.6 to the end of the road.

J 44 15 27.8 At the "T" intersection with FS 582, turn
103 39 28.3 right and stay on the main road for slightly more than a mile. Bypass the first "Y" turnoff you come to in that area, and take the second one.

K 44 14 41.1 Bear right at this "Y" and go less than two-
103 39 16.7 tenths of a mile.

L 44 14 33.2 Pull over almost anywhere and, if you wish,
103 39 12.5 walk a few yards onto a ridge on your right for a panoramic view of the very appealing valley of Corral Creek. The crossing point for the Expedition may be within your view here, or just slightly to the south.
　　Turn around and go back to **Point K**. Turn right and drive another half a mile south, to a trail on the left.

15 44 14 27.7 Note that you are in a draw or drainage at
103 38 52.3 this point, which is our best guess for the route of the Expedition. It is extremely improbable that the crossing could have been any further east, where Corral Creek enters a gorge. The route might have been further northwest, but this draw is the best link to a stretch of level high ground that leads to the presumed campsite.

QUADRANGLES: **Minnesota Ridge, Deadwood South**

Aug 8

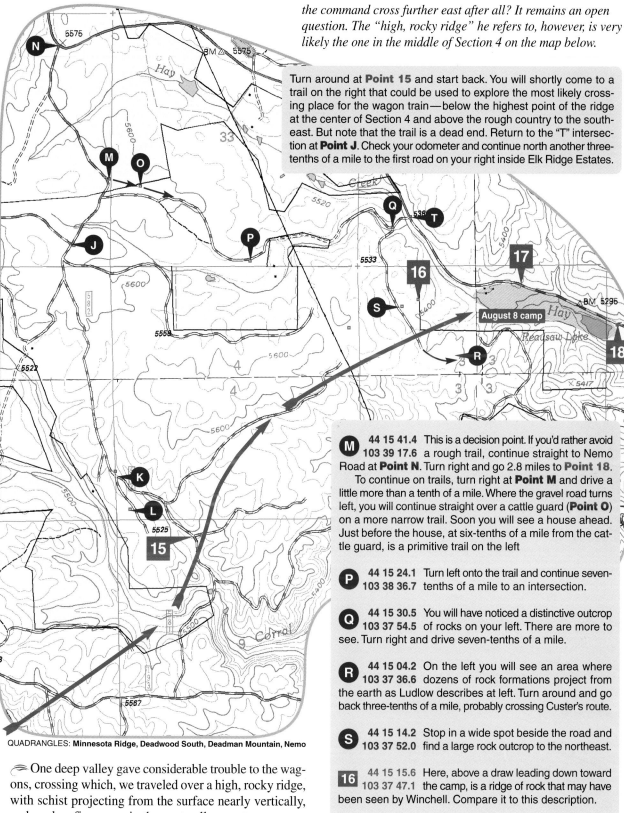

the command cross further east after all? It remains an open question. The "high, rocky ridge" he refers to, however, is very likely the one in the middle of Section 4 on the map below.

Turn around at **Point 15** and start back. You will shortly come to a trail on the right that could be used to explore the most likely crossing place for the wagon train—below the highest point of the ridge at the center of Section 4 and above the rough country to the southeast. But note that the trail is a dead end. Return to the "T" intersection at **Point J**. Check your odometer and continue north another three-tenths of a mile to the first road on your right inside Elk Ridge Estates.

M 44 15 41.4 This is a decision point. If you'd rather avoid 103 39 17.6 a rough trail, continue straight to Nemo Road at **Point N**. Turn right and go 2.8 miles to **Point 18**.
To continue on trails, turn right at **Point M** and drive a little more than a tenth of a mile. Where the gravel road turns left, you will continue straight over a cattle guard (**Point O**) on a more narrow trail. Soon you will see a house ahead. Just before the house, at six-tenths of a mile from the cattle guard, is a primitive trail on the left

P 44 15 24.1 Turn left onto the trail and continue seven-103 38 36.7 tenths of a mile to an intersection.

Q 44 15 30.5 You will have noticed a distinctive outcrop 103 37 54.5 of rocks on your left. There are more to see. Turn right and drive seven-tenths of a mile.

R 44 15 04.2 On the left you will see an area where 103 37 36.6 dozens of rock formations project from the earth as Ludlow describes at left. Turn around and go back three-tenths of a mile, probably crossing Custer's route.

S 44 15 14.2 Stop in a wide spot beside the road and 103 37 52.0 find a large rock outcrop to the northeast.

16 44 15 15.6 Here, above a draw leading down toward 103 37 47.1 the camp, is a ridge of rock that may have been seen by Winchell. Compare it to this description.

QUADRANGLES: **Minnesota Ridge, Deadwood South, Deadman Mountain, Nemo**

⌒ One deep valley gave considerable trouble to the wagons, crossing which, we traveled over a high, rocky ridge, with schist projecting from the surface nearly vertically, and made a fine camp in the next valley. *(Ludlow)*

*The engineer is definitely referring to Corral Creek (since camp is in the "next valley"), but raises doubt about the suggested crossing site south of **Point 15**. Would the valley be considered "deep" there, or did*

⌒ We passed one very prominent ridge, apparently formed thus by protruding quartz, standing erect, similar to that already described, but black on the exterior and not so long. It was a very striking object, the jointing-planes having

Aug 8

caused the dislodgement of some of the separated blocks, giving the crest a serrated edge. Another is about a mile below our camp, in the valley of the creek. *(Winchell)*

We have so far not been able to find such a rock outcrop along Hay Creek ("in the valley") that would either confirm or disprove our location for the camp.

From **Point S**, continue north on the trail and bear right at Point Q to reach Nemo Road in another tenth of a mile. (Please make sure to close the fence gate on the way.)

T **44 15 32.7** Turn right on Nemo Road (pavement at **103 37 49.2** last!) and drive six-tenths of a mile to a pullout on the right near a fence gate.

17 **44 15 17.8** If you look back over your shoulder across **103 37 16.9** the pasture, you can see the shallow draw where we believe the command entered the valley.
Continue four-tenths of a mile along the edge of camp and pull over at the dam below Reausaw Lake.

18 **44 15 10.0** This will give you a final view of the pre- **103 36 48.1** sumed camp of August 8. Note that the latitude here is exactly the same as the engineer's.

U **44 15 10** Ludlow's longitude was only half to three- **103 38 08** quarters of a mile too far west. The camp on Hay Creek proved to be a welcome but too-brief respite.

☞We are in a beautifully grassed valley, through which runs a creek. *(Winchell)*
Our camp was beautifully situated in a valley, in which we found deer and beaver. *(Press)*
The edges of the valley are clothed with good Norway pine. *(Winchell)*

Remember Aris Donaldson, the St. Paul Pioneer *correspondent who joined a hunting party before dawn? He spent much of this day lost and alone. At first he was with a group that included Newton Winchell, "groping" through the fog until . . .*

☞Coming towards us, uprose, like apparitions out of the mist, three armed horsemen. They were a sergeant and two men out hunting. They thought the train was to the left hand and going westward; we thought to the right hand and going eastward. One or both parties must be wrong. *(Pioneer)*

The rest of Donaldson's party decided to play it safe and return immediately to the wagons. Donaldson joined the sergeant, an experienced woodsman.

☞I thought it safe to follow him. My object was to find a pair of elk horns attached to the skull—detached horns could be found by the wagon load. I had declined the offer of a rifle, and did not expect to kill any game. *(Pioneer)*

The new group traveled far from the "burned-over" country seen by everyone else. The mossy regions Donaldson described for his readers are like

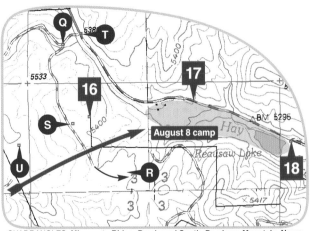

QUADRANGLES: **Minnesota Ridge, Deadwood South, Deadman Mountain, Nemo**

another world altogether, even eerie, and it would be fascinating to know just where he went.

☞In some places the timber came quite down to the brook's edges, and the tall pines and spruces were festooned with long, pendant mosses, and the shade beneath was never broken by the entrance of a single sunbeam. Everything was cool and damp, and covered with the softest carpeting of moss. The cold water lay like purest crystal in the pebbly, rocky pools, fit mirror and fit boudoir for the innocent does and spotted fawns to make their toilet in. We passed slowly through these fairy dells. . . . We were so interested and so charmed that hours and miles passed by uncounted. At length awakened as from some reverie or vision of delight, we saw that the sergeant was still leading us westward. He said he was right. We thought he was certainly wrong. *(Pioneer)*

Donaldson faced a tough decision between the safety of numbers and following his own instinct.

☞The morning hours were all gone, our horses were already tired and hungry, and to follow [the sergeant] was only to go further astray. With his men, he started west, up the mountain side, and in a moment was lost to view. We were alone. *(Pioneer)*

Donaldson's "we" is clearly a formality of the newspaper article. He is completely by himself now, and seriously lost. It is hard to imagine how alone he must have felt in the middle of the Black Hills, with no rifle and a tired horse, simply hoping that he could find his way back to the wagons.

☞The silence which had before been simply impressive, now became terrible. We had miles and miles to ride alone, and must be careful not to overtask an already jaded horse. We might need all his wind and speed for some emergency. Down the creek for miles, at length we saw the trail made by the train, leading eastward from the valley through a narrow, rocky defile. *(Pioneer)*

If the Professor was not exaggerating distance or direction, it is possible that he saw the upper reaches of East Spearfish Creek or Whitewood Creek. And if the sergeant kept going west, he and his men may have gotten close to the Cheyenne Crossing area—an intriguing prospect. But Donaldson was at least no longer lost now that he could follow the trail. "Narrow, rocky defile" is a good description of the area above the mill site at **Point 2.** *It meant something much different to Donaldson.*

These rock formations on the hills above Hay Creek recall Ludlow's description: "We traveled over a high, rocky ridge, with schist projecting from the surface nearly vertically."

© ERNEST GRAFE

⌘ We were near the camp of last night. It is said that hostile Indians watch us every hour of the day and night, and that we are scarcely more than out of our camps till the Indians are in them hunting with the greediness of scavengers for what we throw away. What a place for an almost unarmed man to meet them! . . . If such a meeting must occur, must we offer up ourselves an unresisting sacrifice or resist to the utter end? We chose the latter. We ungloved our hands, the better to use them, drew the revolver from its holster, placed a finger on the trigger, and thumb on the hammer, thought of home and its loved ones, besought a higher power to defend us, and rode down to the defile, the only place near in the steep mountains side through which it was possible to go eastward. We enter the defile, the trail is all dry and has been for hours, we watch every turn, every recess, every tree and bush, every place where a wiley savage might be lurking. Thus we go for miles and miles. . . . At last we catch a glimpse of the long line of white-tented wagons. But it is still miles ahead and before overtaking it we go down into a valley out of sight. Finally, making a turn around a point, we overtake the rear guard. My thankfulness was not unexpressed, though not to human ears. That I escaped is no proof that there was not danger. That the sergeant and his men at last turned about and reached camp in the dusk of the evening, does not prove that he and his whole party were not liable to be cut off. . . . Don't get lost in the Black Hills. It is bad enough to be scared, but worse to be scalped. *(Pioneer)*

Donaldson and the men with the wagons still had a long and difficult time ahead of them.

⌘ The road during the day has been very rough, some of the creek-crossings having delayed the train so that it does not arrive in camp till about 10:30 p.m. . . . the hills about are generally very barren and desolate. Indeed, we have passed through to-day the poorest and most repulsive part of the Black Hills we have yet seen. *(Winchell)*

I was Orderly Trumpeter with General Custer. He reached our camping place about 2 o'clock p.m. At dark the first wagons were seen to come over the hills two miles away. At 7 o'clock p.m., I took a circular to all the company commanders ordering them to bring their companies into camp at once, except "B" (pioneer) and "M" (rear guard) companies. These were to bring the trains in. After having shown this circular to such captains as were up the front part of the train, I rode back along the old trail, meeting one wagon here, another a half a mile further; then I would find six or seven together. One of the wagons stuck against two trees, all trying in the darkness to get it free. Three miles back I found "B" company busy with axe, shovel and spade repairing the bridge which the last wagon that had crossed had broke. *(Ewert)*

Private Ewert's attention to detail adds greatly to the images we have of day-to-day life on the trail.

⌘ A huge pine fire on each side of the creek gave the necessary light. Waiting to cross this bridge I found about thirty wagons, the mules braying and the teamsters swearing. I inquired of the last teamster (who was munching hardtack and swearing in intervals between each mouthful) if his was the last wagon of the train? "Last be d—d! No, there's twenty of them four miles back from here!" This was pleasant, riding in Indian country alone and in the dark. Notwithstanding, I turned my horse's head in that direction and started. As the teamster had told me I found the last part of the train at a creek about seven miles from camp with "M" company and the two of infantry. *(Ewert)*

It sounds as if the wagon train was strung out all the way back to the Middle Boxelder.

⌘ I gave the circular to Captain Saenger who read it then gave it back to me. One of the wagons was broken down, the mules worn out and the teamsters sullen and careless, and Captain French sent word to General Custer that he could not tell what time he should be in with the last of the train. I left and reached headquarters about eleven o'clock p.m. The rear guard came in about 2½ o'clock a.m., the next morning. *(Ewert)*

The time of arrival varies widely among the accounts, probably according to which part of the wagon train they were associated with. There was talk that the prairie was close at hand.

⌘ Train did not get in until 12 & I dinned at mid night—Hodgson came in—was too sleepy to eat much—was soon in the arms of Merphius with my boots on. . . . Bloody Knife reported Bears butte about 5 miles N.E. of our camp. *(Power)*

We . . . sought our tents and were soon dreaming of "Bear Butte." *(Press)*

CHAPTER 12

Sunday, August 9

Hay Creek (near Reausaw Lake) to Little Elk Creek

*Climbing, crawling, jumping, wading, sliding, rolling, tumbling,
and falling 'till the sun went down in the west.* (Ewert)

Bear Butte was almost in sight this day, a symbol of the homeward journey. Several men even caught tantalizing glimpses of the prairie from a hilltop beside the trail. But scouting parties never found a way to get there, defeated by the steep canyons in the Elk Creek area. Custer was forced to turn south instead, and it would be another five days before the Expedition reached Bear Butte. Distance traveled: 7.5 miles.

— Taking the trail —

U.S.G.S. MAPS: Deadman Mountain, Nemo

CAUTIONS: The roads are paved or smooth gravel.

TO START: *From Nemo*, drive 8 miles northwest on

Nemo Road to a turnout on the left at the Reausaw Lake dam. *From Highway 385 near Brownsville*, drive 5 miles east on Nemo Road to a turnout on the right at the Reausaw Lake dam. (Bring fishing gear if you are so inclined.)

Our camp was beautifully situated in a valley, in which we found deer and beaver. The stream that watered this sloping plain was well filled with fish, but as time was wanting we did not partake of them, but sought our tents and were soon dreaming of "Bear Butte," which was just over the hill, as Bloody Knife informed us. *(Press)*

The rear guard came in about 2½ o'clock a.m., the next morning. *(Ewert)*

Sunrise found [us] as usual on the go. *(Power)*

1 44 15 10.0 The first stop is the pullout near the dam
103 36 48.1 that forms Reausaw Lake, on the same latitude as Ludlow's reading for August 8. We believe the camp extended up the valley beyond the lake.

It is clear that much of the command never saw Hay Creek by daylight. In fact, the rear guard and last-arriving teamsters didn't even have time to sleep.

Flagstaff Mountain

Hay Creek   Little Elk Creek

Expedition map
(1 inch = 3 miles)

Before you leave Reausaw Lake, consider that it also plays a role in Black Hills history. The dam is part of an old railroad bed that you can still see running down the valley. Homestake Mining Company operated the Black Hills & Fort Pierre narrow gauge line, building this southern branch in 1889—only 15 years after the Expedition—to carry wood from a lumber camp at Este, which was about two miles south of present-day Nemo. A western spur later reached a lumber camp at Merritt, where Trout Haven is now on Highway 385.

Reausaw was a station on the BH&FP Railroad (after 1901 the Chicago, Burlington & Quincy) where the tracks swung north along the curve of the dam and went up the draw across the road from you, toward stations at Apex and Bucks.

Moved at 4:45 due east along the bank of the creek upon which we had been encamped, passing three of the largest beaver dams I have ever seen; thence north, and again east. *(Forsyth)*

The route of August 9 has remained something of a mystery in the past, but one course appears to fit everything we know. A close reading of Forsyth's journal suggests a short jog to the north before continuing a generally eastern course—which is borne out by Ludlow's map at left. One problem has been Ludlow's own report, which seems to contradict the map on how far down the valley they marched.

The course lay down the valley, which was in possession of the beaver, for several miles, then turned to the left over a ridge. *(Ludlow)*

If the Expedition traveled "several miles" down the valley, why does the map indicate a turn after just a mile and a half? A handwritten copy of Ludlow's journal in the National Archives solves the problem. Either he or a transcriptionist used dashes of different lengths as punctuation, which had to be translated into commas and periods. In this case there are two long dashes on either side of a short one, which should have been rendered this way:

The course lay down the valley—which was in possession of the beaver, for several miles—then turned to the left over a ridge. *(Ludlow)*

The power of punctuation is revealed. The beaver dams went several miles down the valley, not the command. Custer left it much sooner.

The arrows below represent only our best guess about the route over the ridge, but there is little doubt that it was crossed in this vicinity. The command is then shown traveling a little more than two miles virtually straight east, and on the next page you will see the only place in this area where that would have been possible for the wagon train.

From **Point 2**, continue 1.5 miles on Nemo Road to the intersection of Forest Service 151 (**Point A**) and turn left. Drive one mile to the intersection at **Point B** and bear left to stay on FS 151. Go one more mile to a trail on your right.

5 44 15 35.6   The trail ends after a few yards at a fence
103 35 14.0   gate on private land. But you can walk up to the gate, if you wish, to see where the long eastward leg of the Expedition route begins. Note where the land slopes off on the far side of the pasture, slightly south of east, which you will see from another angle in a moment.

Check your odometer and drive east along Hay Creek, where once you might have seen three large beaver dams. They apparently caused the command to travel over the gently rolling country on your left. Pull over across the road from a draw exactly one mile from the dam.

2 44 14 47.2   Note that Nemo Road curves around a
103 35 44.3   point of land ahead, which is the end of a ridge visible on the topo map below. Ludlow's map actually shows this ridge, where he says the command "turned left."

If you would like to walk one possible version of the route over the ridge, enter the following "Go To" points in your GPS.

3 44 14 59.0   This is just over the ridge in a fairly steady,
103 35 28.9   easy climb.

4 44 15 05.1   Here you join a more recent trail, which
103 35 23.7   might follow part of the Expedition route.

5 44 15 35.6   This appears to be a little above where the
103 35 14.0   command turned east again, but it is the best place to see the meadow they crossed. This will be your next stopping place after you return to your car.

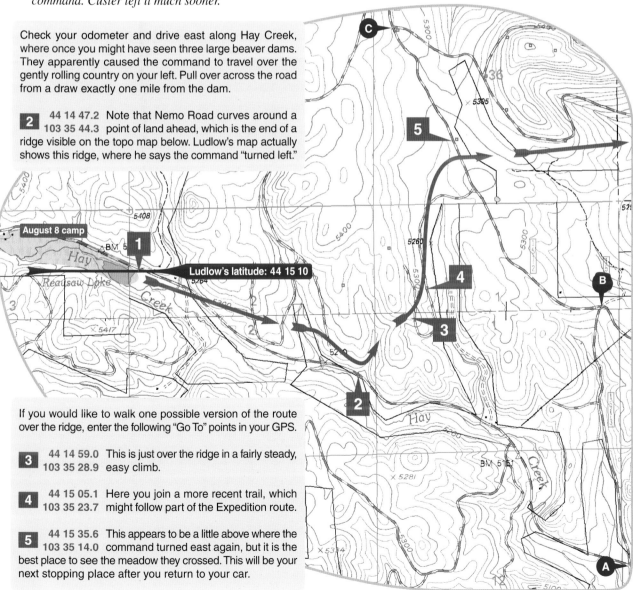

QUADRANGLES: **Deadman Mountain, Nemo**

From **Point 5**, continue half a mile to the next intersection.

C 44 15 58.3 Turn right on FS 136 and set or check your
103 35 31.1 odometer. The next stop will depend on
whether you would like to explore a hill possibly climbed by
Winchell during the morning. If not, skip to Point 6, nine-
tenths of a mile down the road. To stop for the climb, drive
four-tenths of a mile to a rough trail that cuts back to the left.

About three miles from camp, we ascend a grassy
knoll, from which can be seen ahead, a mile distant, a few
hills capped with stratified limestone. This is toward the
northeast. . . . We are very near the edge of the belt of schist
and slate, some of the ferruginous sandstone of the Lower
Silurian appearing on the tops of the little knolls. These
knolls are at first weathered down smooth and turfed over,
but the sandstone can still be detected by the occurrence
of small fragments among the grass. *(Winchell)*

On reaching the top of a hill some 3 or 4 miles from
camp, Bears Butte could not be seen. *(Power)*

From an occasional open spot glimpses of the open
prairie a few miles away were caught. *(Ludlow)*

*Point F on the map below is a knoll that does indeed
lie about three miles from camp, within half a mile
of the march. It is still covered primarily by grass,
in which pieces of reddish sandstone ("ferruginous,"
or iron-bearing) can be found. Although the view is
obscured by a few more trees than the headquarters
staff probably had to deal with, it is still possible to*

*see the limestone outcrops above Meadow Creek
about a mile to the northeast. It is also possible to
catch glimpses of the prairie through the trees. At
5,500 feet, the knoll is the highest point in this area.*

D 44 15 48.5 If you prefer to walk from here, park off
103 35 04.8 the road and enter **Point F** as a "Go To"
in your GPS receiver. If your vehicle can negotiate the trail
on the left, drive three-tenths of a mile to a cut in the side
of a hill.

E 44 15 48.5 The cut in the hillside on your right makes
103 35 04.8 a good place to turn around and park off
the trail while you make the short hike up to Point F.

F 44 15 54.7 This is the center of the knoll. You might
103 34 51.7 have to wander around a bit to find the
best views of the limestone, east of north at about 30 degrees.
You can also see more distant limestone outcrops a little south
of east, at 115 degrees. On hazy days, the prairie may be
hard to distinguish from the sky. A pair of binoculars will be
helpful.

G 44 15 53.6 This is at least one place with a view of
103 34 44.4 the prairie through a gap in the trees.

To continue from **Point D**, drive east a little more than four-
tenths of a mile (or almost nine-tenths of a mile from the
turnoff onto FS 136).

6 44 15 34.9 Pull over just before the road starts down
103 34 41.8 the hill. As you can see from the map, you
are very close to the trail. Note the shallow slope to your
right (southeast) down to Little Elk Creek.
Continue another six-tenths of a mile.

7 44 15 39.0 Looking behind you to the right, you can
103 34 13.8 see the likely route down from the pasture.

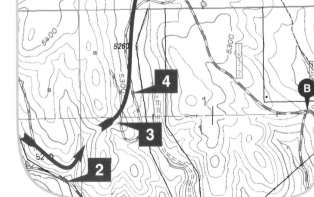

At 8 o'clock William Davis and I received permission
to go hunting. Accordingly we left the trail and proceeded
to beat along the valleys. About twelve o'clock we stopped
at a deep creek bottom, and when we came to look for our
trail we found that we were lost, neither knowing in what
direction the train should be. *(Ewert)*

*Sound familiar? We don't know whether Private
Ewert had heard about Aris Donaldson's difficulties
after getting lost the day before (Chapter 11), but if
he did, he hadn't learned any lessons.*

QUADRANGLES: **Deadman Mountain, Nemo**

⌒ We descended the bed of this creek 'till we came to an abrupt fall of over a hundred feet. . . . Nothing remained but to climb up, and such a climb! Almost like a wall, steep, with scarcely any foothold! Horses [had] to be led, coaxed and petted into following and we, sweating, puffing, fuming, fretting, half mad and half scared, and to crown it all, the sun fairly burning. *(Ewert)*

During the forenoon, while Ewert and Davis were getting lost, the wagons would have been working their way along the upper reaches of Little Elk Creek.

After you leave **Point 7**, FS 136 will swing across Little Elk Creek (as well as the Expedition's trail) which then becomes lost to view behind a heavy screen of trees. After 1.8 miles you should see a gated driveway on the left, leading to a home beyond the creek.

H **44 15 26.9** This is your only chance to glimpse the **103 32 08.3** part of the valley where Custer's wagons veered north toward a hoped-for exit from Hills.
To see where the wagons stopped and turned around, go almost a mile to the end of FS 136.

I **44 15 03.1** Note that the current highway in this area **103 31 38.0** is slightly east of the road as depicted on the old topo map. Turn left on the paved road and go just short of one mile to a ranch trail on the left.

8 **44 15 48.1** Pull over at the intersection of the ranch **103 31 53.1** trail, which may not be too far from where the wagons came out of the valley along the foot of Flagstaff Mountain.

⌒ We attempted to effect a passage through some one of the many valleys whose water courses ran directly through the hills in the desired direction. *(Custer)*

The creeks flowed eastward, and in piercing through the outward range of hills had cut deep cañons, which were often blocked by bowlders and fallen trees. *(Ludlow)*

If our interpretation of the trail is correct, the wagons were heading toward the area of today's Wonderland Cave and Elk Creek before they turned around. It is virtually certain that the scouts explored Elk Creek Canyon, and Little Elk Creek also seems likely. But how many others did they try, and which ones?

⌒ After looking in almost every direction for some outlet by which we could go to the Butte, the General concluded to travel eastward. *(Press)*

In every instance we were led into deep, broken canyons, impassable even to horsemen. Through one of these I made my way on foot and from a high point near its mouth obtained a view of the plains outside. *(Custer)*

Could Custer have been in Tilford Gulch? Breakneck? Forbes? Beaver? Wherever it was, he would not get

QUADRANGLES: **Deadman Mountain, Nemo**

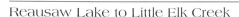

any closer to the plains on this day. The wagons turned back less than 16 miles from Bear Butte.

⤸Retracing my steps I placed the command in camp in a fine valley in which it had halted, and devoted the remainder of the day to a further search for a practicable route through the hills. *(Custer)*

According to the scale of the Expedition map, the wagons traveled about three-quarters of a mile after turning back. Turn your car around at **Point 8** and drive eight-tenths of a mile south, stopping at a pond on the right.

9 44 15 11.7   The pond here is fed by a large spring, and
103 31 38.1   appears to have been within the camp.

Private Ewert and his friend Davis had managed to reach the top of the ridge they were climbing. They went down the other side of it, but only Davis's horse was willing to climb the next ridge. An embarrassed and exasperated Ewert had to climb back up the first ridge and circle around to find Davis.

⤸After two hours riding and climbing I rejoined Davis, hot, mad, hungry, dry and nearly worn out. . . . We followed the ridge on which we were 'till it terminated abruptly over a creek. We could see the glistening of the water far below us through the green pines, and being very much in want of a drink we determined to go down and then follow the creek southeast as far as it would lead us that way. The descent was steep and our progress rapid tho' not very dignified and 'ere we were aware of it, we rolled plump into a beautiful large spring which we found to be the headwaters of this creek. The water was cold and both our horses and selves felt refreshed after cooling ourselves and satisfying our thirst. The rocks around us formed a beautiful glen and to leave this we followed the bed of the creek for a quarter of a mile, then emerged into a pretty valley. Here we found an abundance of wild cherries, and these, with the hardtack we carried in our haversacks, furnished us a very excellent lunch. Here, too, we saw the only game of the entire day; one single, solitary deer saw us and bounded away as if afraid of us. Davis and I did not dream of hunting now. Our only and all thought was to find the wagon train. The frightened deer was scarcely more harmless than we. To our surprise we found, as we turned a sharp curve of the valley, that the prairie lay before us, [and] that we were virtually out of the Black Hills. *(Ewert)*

Ewert might have been gratified to know that in leaving the Hills with his horse he accomplished what General Custer had not. But by this time the camp was already being set up for the night.

⤸Went into camp at 1 P.M. to-day in a very pretty valley. *(Grant)*

. . . upon a beautiful stream fed by an immense spring of the coldest water, save ice-water, I ever drank. Distance 7½ miles east. *(Forsyth)*

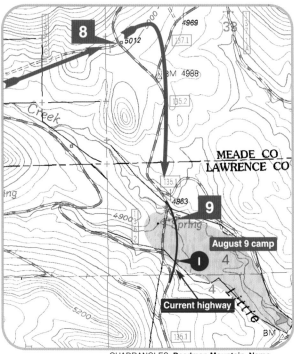

QUADRANGLES: **Deadman Mountain, Nemo**

At the headspring of this stream there are two little fountains of cold water rising out of the ground; spurting the icy fluid with great force. *(Calhoun)*

*Forsyth and Calhoun may be referring to the spring beside the Vanocker Canyon Road, where Little Elk Creek passes beneath the pavement (**Point 9**). You might have noticed the pond formed by the spring if you have ever driven between Nemo and Sturgis.*

If the explorers really did think of the heavy spring at **Point 9** as the headspring of Little Elk Creek, it would explain at least one of the anomalies on Ludlow's map that made it hard to work out this portion of the trail. Little Elk traces a distinctive "S" shape in the area, also seen on the Expedition map—except that in real-

ity the top of the "S" runs up next to Flagstaff Mountain, which Ludlow fails to show. How could the engineer have followed what we call Little Elk Creek until just before turning around, yet fail to show the camp on the same creek? Everything else pointed to our interpretation of the route except this detail.

One possible explanation is that the engineers didn't link the drainages the way we do today. The long narrow valley you see extending northwest from Point 9 may not have been considered part of Little Elk Creek, as we do today. Ludlow could instead have linked it to the short drainage extending directly west from the spring. If so, the "S" shape takes on a new meaning and the location of headquarters within the top curve is consistent with a camp in the wide valley below the spring.

Aug
9

Got in camp early, about 12 or ½ past 12. Hodgson & I went to sleep and slept until dinner. Nearly sunset. *(Power)*

As we camped at an early hour, after attending to a few little matters, I stepped out of the office tent for the purpose of eliciting information. I had the satisfaction of listening to Mr. Ross inform the Veterinary Surgeon of the regiment that he was perfectly satisfied with the general appearance of this country, and that it was his candid opinion that the many valleys were rich with gold. . . . Mr. Barrows, the N.Y. *Tribune* correspondent, informs me that this is the only land in this latitude worthy of publicity, and where the industrious classes can be honestly invited or encouraged to emigrate. Speaking to several others I find that they look upon these hesperian hills, as vast possessions of intrinsic wealth, capable of insuring enjoyment and rapid prosperity. *(Calhoun)*

Springs were abundant, of clear, cold water, with a temperature of 46°. The heavy pine forests on the hill-sides were full of deer. *(Ludlow)*

A great many deer killed now by men of the comd, killing or participating in killing one [hundred] or more. *(Power)*

General C killed a deer. *(Calhoun)*

As it turned out, the safest deer in the neighborhood was the one scared up by the hunters Ewert and Davis, who had lost their heart for killing. While Fred Power (and probably many others) were catching up on their sleep, the lost Ewert and Davis had stumbled out of the Black Hills and onto the prairie. They decided to skirt the Hills for a while, hoping to run into scouting parties. Suddenly they heard a hoarse "HOW" behind them.

 I wheeled with my carbine cocked and aimed at the Indian who had just given us the worst kind of a scare. My heart was in my throat and I would have surely pulled the trigger had not our red friend thrown up his hands and shouted, "Me Ree big scout Cusser. Good me! Good me!" and looking at him I knew that I had seen him in our camp. Our surprise (and scare) over, we informed the scout by signs, motions and broken English mixed with Dutch, French, Spanish and Indian (of each of these languages Davis and I would speak about five words) that we were lost, could not find camp (teepee), that we would be inseparable friends to his entire tribe, himself and family in particular if he would help us out of our dilemma and guide us to camp. To this he replied, also by motions, signs, etc., that the teepee was lost from him, he was here, could not lose himself, but would like first class if the teepee would come and find him. Seeing that no assistance could be derived from the scout we determined to continue our search. The "red brother" followed us, verifying the adage that "Misery loves company." We now

ascended a ridge and entered the hills. The Indian rode his pony up while we led our horses and when we gained the top, Mr. Lo had disappeared, our progress being, no doubt, too slow for him. *(Ewert)*

"Mr. Lo" or "Poor Lo" had become a popular term for American Indians in the West, sometimes spoken in a joking or even sneering way—although that doesn't seem to have been Ewert's intent. The term was derived from Epistle I of Essay on Man *by the British poet Alexander Pope:*

> Lo, the poor Indian! whose untutor'd mind
> Sees God in clouds, or hears him in the wind;
> His soul proud Science never taught to stray
> Far as the solar walk or milky way.

Ewert would certainly have accepted any help at all from the "untutor'd" Arikara scout.

 Up hill and down hill, now away up near the clouds, then down into ravines where it was twilight even at midday, climbing, crawling, jumping, wading, sliding, rolling, tumbling and falling 'till the sun went down in the west. *(Ewert)*

This account has the quality of a terrible nightmare, the kind you wake from huffing and sweating, and it is probably something Ewert and Davis never forgot.

 We were crawling up a very high hill and Davis had just remarked that if we did not see camp or signs of it from this point we would descend into the next valley and encamp 'till the next morning, and to which I had assented. When we did get up to the top I discovered a sheet of smoke floating over a valley about three miles away. Davis contended that it was not smoke but mist. Finally he assented to come along and—well, a little while after dark we entered camp tired, hungry and angry, our horses ready to drop, and Davis and I enemies to any man that said "hunting" in our hearing. The scout whom we met on the prairie had come to camp about five o'clock p.m. That night Davis and I pledged ourselves never to go hunting again in the Black Hills, and we never did. *(Ewert)*

Aug 9

CHAPTER 13

Monday-Tuesday, August 10-11

Little Elk Creek to Boxelder Creek south of Nemo, with a layover

We were continually looking for trout in these streams,
which seemed as though made expressly for that fish. (Ludlow)

Even though Gen. Custer had scouted the country during the previous afternoon, he was apparently still unsure of the route. Leaving camp near present-day Wonderland Cave, the Expedition didn't travel far before the order came to halt again in a wide part of the Boxelder Creek valley, a little more than two miles south of present-day Nemo. It was in this area that the Arikara scouts held an Elk Dance that was well described by Private Ewert and Aris Donaldson. Distance traveled: 7.5 miles.

— Taking the trail —

U.S.G.S. MAPS: Deadman Mountain, Nemo, Piedmont

CAUTIONS: The roads are all paved or gravel.

TO START: *From Nemo*, drive north almost half a

mile to Forest Service Road 26 (often referred to as the Vanocker Canyon Road). Turn right and drive 4.1 miles to a pond on the left. You will see a good place to turn around partway up the hill ahead of you, on your right. The easiest thing to do is make the turn first, then pull off the road near the pond.

➥ We . . . camped early in a wide, grassy valley in the midst of Potsdam sandstone. *(Winchell)*

Though the hills on the right and left are barren, the narrow valley in which we are encamped is clothed with a carpet of rich, wavering grass, luxuriant in growth and excellent in quality. *(Calhoun)*

These descriptions of the previous night's campsite

create a bit of confusion. Was it a narrow valley as Calhoun says, or the wide one Winchell describes? Perhaps the two descriptions refer to different areas of the same camp, which we believe is crossed today by the road between Nemo and Vanocker Canyon.

> **1**   **44 15 11.7**   At the starting point, you are parked in **103 31 38.2**   front of a pond fed by a large spring mentioned in the journals in Chapter 12. (Note that today's paved road passes slightly east of the road shown on the old topographic map.) Standing here in 1874, you would have been within the camp of the night before.

➥ On the knolls on both sides of our camp are numerous fragments of rusty sandstone. Just below our camp, about a mile, is an outcrop of what appears like a fine-grained granite, somewhat schistose. *(Winchell, August 9)*

Winchell's journal entry contributes to our efforts to locate the August 9 campsite. (Ludlow did not record the latitude and longitude here.) If you have ever driven from Nemo Road down to Dalton Lake, you have passed through the granite outcrops seen by the geologist.

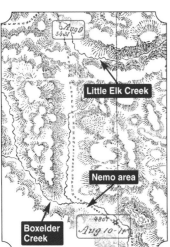

Expedition map
(1 inch = 3 miles)

Set or check your odometer at **Point 1** and drive south seven-tenths of a mile to the four-corner intersection. It is likely that the present-day road is on or close to Custer's route leaving the valley of Little Elk Creek.

2 44 14 35.7 Turn left on Dalton Lake Road and drive 103 31 40.3 three quarters of a mile.

A 44 14 47.1 The road passes the lower end of the pasture here, southeast of the August 9 camp. How far southeast? Continue driving and note how quickly you come to the granite outcrops described by Winchell.

The geologist placed the granite about a mile below camp. Did he mean from the edge of camp, or from headquarters? If the former, then the camp itself may have been a little further up the valley than is shown on our map.

If you keep going—just short of half a mile east from Point A—you will come upon the area of a possible photo site.

B 44 12 57.0 While this cannot be called a true match 103 30 43.0 for **Photo 850**, "Forsyth's Glen" (page 262), William Illingworth might have taken the picture in this general area. There are similar rock formations, and it is not that far from the site of Photos 848 and 849 (see next page).

There is nothing like keeping your engagements. "Punctuality is the life of business," wisely said Poor Richard. "Sixty days, Custer, shalt thou be absent and do all thy work," said Gen. Terry, "but on the sixty-first thou shalt rest from thy labors." And it was so. Six hundred hungry horses, 700 hungrier mules, and 800 dusty sunburnt, weather-worn soldiers joined in the benedictory "Amen." *(New York Tribune)*

The General could have been home five days early if he hadn't been turned back by the rugged gulches of the Black Hills, particularly to the northeast.

Leaving camp we turn south and come within a mile upon hills and ridges that are capped with limestone. *(Winchell)*

Return to **Point 2** and drive seven-tenths of a mile south on the paved highway.

3 44 14 03.5 Pull over briefly on the curve to orient your- 103 31 13.7 self for future reference. White Mansion is the large hill directly ahead, and over its right shoulder you can see Green Top in the distance. The Expedition continued in the vicinity of the current road, to the east of White Mansion. As you finish the curve, in about two-tenths of a mile, take note of the next limestone outcrop you see straight ahead. Continue exactly one mile from Point 3.

We are now engaged in finding a practicable route through the outlying mountains to the plains, and thence to Bear Butte. Have explored two valleys, but cannot find a good wagon-road. Will try another route to-day. Upon leaving camp at 4:30 a.m., we moved due south over a small hill into a fine valley, about half a mile wide, with a splendid stream of water running through it. *(Forsyth)*

The route was southerly, crossing a low ridge, and taking the head of a creek flowing a little east of south. *(Ludlow)*

Both Forsyth and Ludlow make it sound as if the Expedition reached a valley just a short distance from camp, and the engineer's map shows it happening after a little more than two miles. We believe that this is the valley beginning near **Point 4**, *along the lower portion of Vanocker Canyon road (FS 26). It is not half a mile wide at that point, however, nor could the stream be called "splendid." Forsyth's account seems to link the first valley with Boxelder Creek, which the command would soon encounter.*

4 44 13 21.9 At 2.4 miles from the spring on Little Elk 103 30 45.9 Creek, having crossed a divide, you have now come into the head of a grassy valley.

Take a moment to notice a prominent red sandstone bluff up the hill to your left, then drive another tenth of a mile to a pullout in front of a ranch gate on your right.

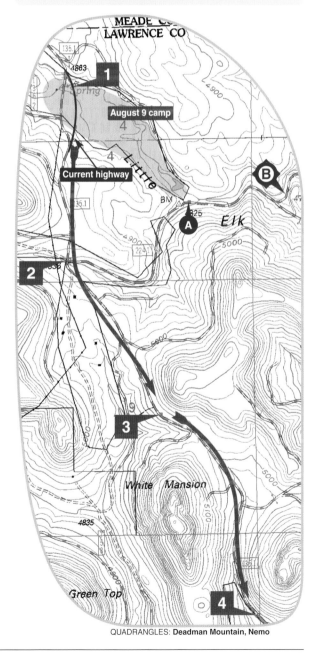

QUADRANGLES: **Deadman Mountain, Nemo**

5 **44 13 17.0** If you get out of your car here, you will be **103 30 39.6** able to see a limestone outcrop across the road behind you. Talus below the outcrop slopes down to the sandstone bluff you looked at a moment ago, much like the slope in Winchell's Figure 7 (below).

🖐 The limestone shows the same lithological characters as described where it was first met, in the upper portion of Floral Valley . . . . The sandstone is red and in heavy layers, and shows no fossils. . . . Figure 7 is a profile across the valley down which we pass, intended to show the relative positions of the outcropping belts . . . at the point near where we entered the valley. *(Winchell)*

It is interesting that the geologist linked the limestone in the Nemo area to formations all the way over on the Wyoming side of the Hills, north of Buckhorn. Winchell's Figure 7 (below) corresponds quite closely with the head of the valley at **Point 4** *on the map at right. The sandstone bluff on the east side of the road is shown to be level with the low hill you can see today across the valley. Even the elevations Winchell recorded with his "aneroid" (barometer) are within ten feet of the elevations above Point 4 as shown by contour lines on the topographic map.*

Winchell's cross-section is our primary reason for believing that the command passed to the east of White Mansion rather than moving straight south from Point 2 and traveling through the narrow gap between White Mansion and Green Top. If that were the case, White Mansion would have to be the limestone peak in Figure 7, and Green Top—which is actually 40 feet higher—would be absent from the drawing altogether. Note that the geologist specifically places his drawing "at the point near where we entered the valley." It is very likely that he was climbing the hills around Points 4 and 5 to make the measurements you see in the figure below.

🖐 We follow down one of the grassed valleys, with the high limestone ridge on our left, and the low sandstone hills on the right. Sometimes the limestone constitutes two parallel ridges, that to the right or toward the west rising somewhat higher than the other, owing to a southeasterly dip. *(Winchell)*

The geologist probably referred to what we call White Mansion, which is "toward the west" and higher

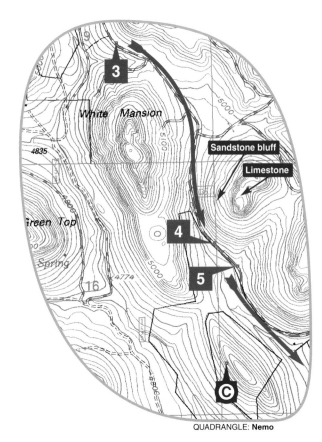

QUADRANGLE: **Nemo**

than the peak above **Point 5***. South of White Mansion are the low sandstone hills Winchell mentioned, one of which William Illingworth climbed the next day.*

The engineers returned to this area the following day, and the photographer probably joined the detachment. Across the valley from **Point 5** you can see a low saddle, south of which is the hill he climbed for a pair of pictures.

C **44 12 57.0** Illingworth recorded two views from this **103 30 43.0** site: **Photo 848**, "Red Sandstone in Elk Creek Valley" (page 258) and **Photo 849**, "Top of Custer Peak and Elk Creek Valley" (page 260).

Elk Creek? That's what members of the command called Boxelder Creek until they realized their mistake. Even so, the Boxelder is two miles south, at Nemo. Illingworth—who confused geographic place names in several of his titles—apparently thought the stream between Green Top and White Mansion was the head of Boxelder Creek.

Aug
10
11

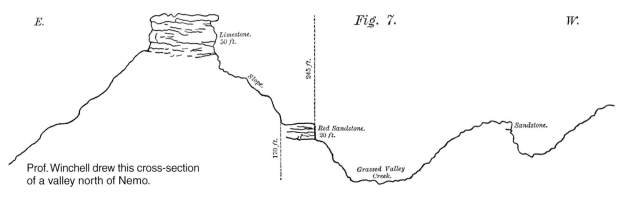

Prof. Winchell drew this cross-section of a valley north of Nemo.

Lovely indeed were the Black Hills, a charming solitude beyond the grace of pencil or pen. "I should like to stay here the rest of my life," said one enthusiastic officer. The wish found a few dittoes. But when the band one day . . . played with the best of intentions a wretched parody on "Home, Sweet Home," the charms of this delightful region had not so benumbed our affection that we could not recognize the sentiment concealed in the discord. I really believe there were some large drops in our tear sacs—for even soldiers have such an outfit—ready to roll down bronzed and dusty cheeks, had the imitation of the beloved air been more successful. At all events, we were ready to "About face." We hated the dreary march across the plains, but the Missouri River had in our imaginations an amiable flow, and we longed to watch it once more. *(New York Tribune)*

It is remarkable and characteristic of the hills that, in whatever direction we have wished to go, a creek-valley has always furnished a road. *(Ludlow)*

The engineer is revealed to be an optimist. He is talking about the Boxelder, but has forgotten that Custer "wished to go" straight to Bear Butte.

I placed the command in camp in a fine valley *[Little Elk Creek]* . . . and devoted the remainder of the day to a further search for a practicable route through the hills. The result decided me to to follow down a water course which led us first toward the south, and afterwards towards the east. *(Custer, referring to August 9)*

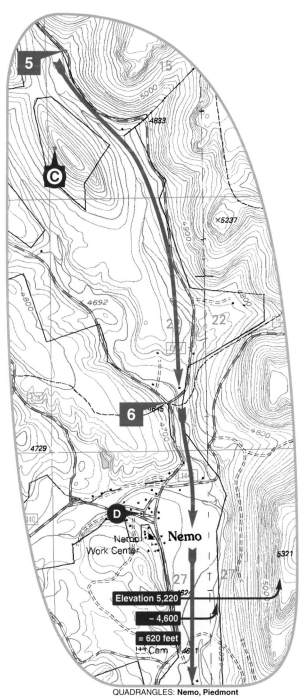

QUADRANGLES: **Nemo, Piedmont**

Drive another 1.6 miles south from **Point 5**, noting the continued appearance of limestone on the left as Winchell described. The valley also becomes wider until just before the point where you reach Nemo Road.

As you come up to **Point 6**, the intersection of Nemo and Vanocker Canyon Roads, you probably cross Custer's trail toward the narrow gap on your left between the valley and Boxelder Creek.

Boxelder Creek impressed the explorers when they came into the valley just above present-day Nemo.

Following down the valley, we found it enlarging to a broad fertile meadow luxuriantly grassed, through which wound the creek, a fine rapid stream 10 feet to 12 feet wide, flowing over a rocky bed. *(Ludlow)*

Marched through a most beautiful valley to-day; the stream the largest we have seen in the Black Hills. *(Grant)*

Turn left on Nemo Road and drive almost half a mile to the Nemo Store (**Point D**). You may already be familiar with the high precipice across from town. Now imagine climbing to the top—as the geologist did.

After passing down this valley toward the south about two miles, another shoulder slowly rises, dimly outlined along the base of the bluff on our left. . . . Thus the wall of rock becomes more precipitous. . . . I ascend the bluff on the east and take aneroid measurements of the ascent. The formations here seen are the same as mentioned this morning on entering the valley, but the wall of the bluff is much more precipitous, and affords a more constant exposure of the beds. *(Winchell)*

The new climbing area was two miles from the area of the cross section (opposite page). Winchell listed the height of each stratum he came to—conglomerate, talus, "brick-red" sandstone, more talus, and a 130-foot cap of limestone. The total height was 615 feet above the valley floor. Note how closely this figure agrees with the height of the cliff across from Nemo, as derived from contour lines on the map at left.

Off to the west from this bluff are rounded hills of iron-ore. This ore, being at so great a distance from other ore-beds, and in the midst of a timbered region, will at some day be very valuable, though it does not seem very pure, especially the surface fragments. *(Winchell)*

The ore works just fine as an ingredient of cement, as it turns out. Pete Lien & Sons of Rapid City quarries this ore along Nemo Road, north of **Point 7** *on the map.*

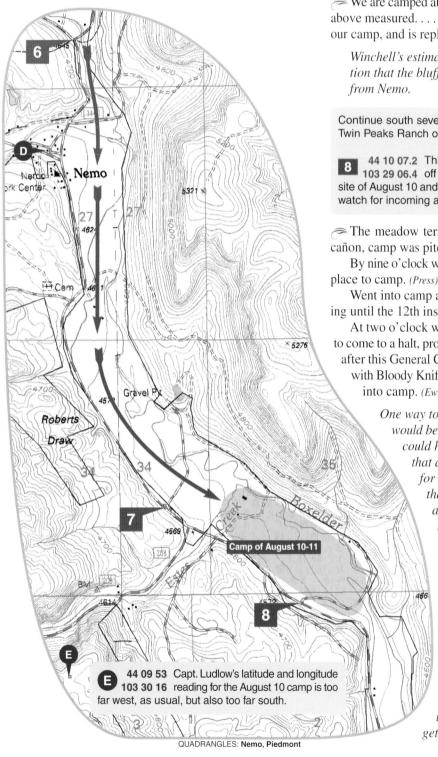

QUADRANGLES: **Nemo, Piedmont**

From the Nemo Store (**Point D**) drive 1.5 miles south on Nemo Road. Watch for a mining operation across the valley, and stop at a gated entrance on the left. (Be careful of incoming and outgoing traffic)

7 44 10 27.8 This is the entrance to the Pete Lien &
103 29 47.0 Sons quarry, where you will see hues of red that indicate the presence of iron. But this is roughly where the ore begins to "run out," as Winchell says.

We are camped about a mile and a half below the bluff above measured. . . . The iron-ore runs out suddenly near our camp, and is replaced by a talcose slate. *(Winchell)*

Winchell's estimate of distance is another confirmation that the bluff he climbed was the one across from Nemo.

Continue south seven-tenths of a mile to the entrance of Twin Peaks Ranch on the left.

8 44 10 07.2 This is probably the safest place to pull
103 29 06.4 off the road and observe the likely camp-site of August 10 and 11. But if the gate is unlocked, please watch for incoming and outgoing traffic.

The meadow terminating and the stream entering a cañon, camp was pitched. *(Ludlow)*

By nine o'clock we came to a halt, fortunately in a good place to camp. *(Press)*

Went into camp at 12 p.m., where we intend remaining until the 12th inst. *(Forsyth)*

At two o'clock we were ordered by an aide-de-camp to come to a halt, progress again being barred, and shortly after this General Custer, who had been scouting ahead with Bloody Knife, returned and ordered the command into camp. *(Ewert)*

One way to sort out the time differences would be to suggest that by 9 A.M. the wagons could have gone the 7.5 miles covered that day in the four hours they had had for travel. It is hard to believe, in fact, that it would take them nine hours, as Ewert seems to say. A better idea is that the wagons waited for word from Custer, which came about noon (not two), and that after camp was set up the General continued his explorations.

General Custer and myself made a careful exploration for 12 or 15 miles down the creek, and found a good wagon-road to the plains. *(Forsyth)*

Whenever camp was actually set up, it wasn't soon enough to avoid getting wet.

Before we could get our tents pitched however, a furious rain storm of an hour's duration set in giving us a good soaking. *(Ewert)*

We had a copious shower today. I have omitted to mention the fact that rains are copious and frequent, rendering irrigation unnecessary. *(Calhoun)*

> *The rain may have been copious and frequent during the summer of 1874, but that isn't what we normally expect in the Black Hills in August. Calhoun doesn't seem to have considered the possibility of an unusual weather pattern.*

 I being about 1/2 mile in advance of the train went fishing and enjoyed the rain all by my self, which was not at all agreeable. *(Power)*

We were continually looking for trout in these streams, which seemed as though made expressly for that fish, which requires an unfailing flow of cold pure water. There could be no finer trout-streams in the world than these were they once stocked. *(Ludlow)*

The valley was large, and the stream wide and deep, with sufficient fish to supply the entire camp. Most of us indulged our selves with the sport, and succeeded in capturing a good supply of the finny tribe. Those of the command who were not fond of fishing went hunting. *(Press)*

A great many deer killed and 3 elk—one with splendid antlers. *(Grant)*

A CELEBRATION FEAST

 In the evening I went over to the line of scouts tents as I had been informed that they intended to have an Elk Dance in celebration of the first elk having been killed by one of their number this day. *(Ewert)*

> *Private Ewert could have had an alternate career as a reporter or novelist. Here he gives us a vivid image of an American Indian ceremony along Boxelder Creek south of present-day Nemo, perhaps close to the mouth of Estes Creek.*

 A large fire had been built. By this, standing on the ground and propped up by sticks, were two sides of a once huge elk roasting slowly and watched with critical eyes by one of their number, who, no doubt, was cook and chef of the evening. Ranged on one side of this were about twenty Ree braves, naked except the customary breechclout, their bodies and faces made more hideous by the fantastic paintings they had adorned themselves with. They were seated in a half-circle, tailor fashion. Four of the older braves had small tin pans in front of them on which they beat with two little sticks, keeping good time. The one side of the fire was allowed their white brothers, the soldiers, who were also invited to participate in the dance and, I believe, one or two did really follow them in their fantastic evolutions during the evening. I noticed that General Custer, his two brothers, a number of officers and all the professors were present, which gave a significant aspect to the evening's proceedings. *(Ewert)*

The entertainment was in the edge of the pine forest, and around the bright camp fires. . . . They danced to the music of sticks beaten on frying pans and tin wash basins. It was perfect in time, but lacked everything else to charm. *(Pioneer)*

> *The learned botanist and kindly "Professor" Aris Donaldson proved in this case less able to appreciate another culture's art form than Theodore Ewert, the private from Prussia. Ewert displays a genuine interest in and even enjoyment of what he sees.*

 Soon after my arrival there, Rees commenced to chant their "hunt after the enemy" song. The professors of the tin pans commenced to beat a rapid gallop time and all the others sang in the time kept on the pans and I must confess that they were quite melodious. When the singing had got fairly started, one of the braves would proceed to illustrate the song; he would arise slowly from his seat and, crouching on the grounds, would cast his eyes in every direction as if searching for an enemy, his body in the meantime keeping a bobbing motion with the tin pans. Now he shades his eyes with his hands as if he discovered the object of his search. He then rises to his feet, his body bent close to the ground, his feet keeping time. He now imitates running after a Sioux; he draws his knife and tomahawk [and] imitates shooting with bow and arrow. Now he yells forth the war whoop of his tribe. Quicker beats the time on the tin pans, quicker are his motions, quicker come the war whoops. Ah! One of his tribe has heard him; he is answered. The exact counterpart of his war cry is sent back to him, faint at first, but louder and louder 'till another brave arises from the circle and falls in the rear of the first, keeping time like him with his feet, with his body bent precisely the same way, his every motion the same. The tin pans beat faster, the voices grow louder, the excitement commences to tell. Another arises from the circle and joins in the chase, another, and still another, 'till finally some twenty are in the circle, dancing, yelling and cutting down imaginary Sioux. Tomahawks and knives are handled carelessly and indifferently; revolvers are brandished in the air and war clubs used. *(Ewert)*

> *Compare Ewert's straightforward description to the view of the proceedings Donaldson left us.*

 We are apt to consider dancing as easy and graceful and lithe and fascinating. But in the Ree's dancing, all these were wanting, and everything else (except time) that could render it pleasing. They never straighten up; but keep the knees bent and body inclined forward, while the head is thrown up to stare around. Each one dances independently of all the others, except that they jostle against and stumble over one another. They jerk up their feet and stamp them on the ground as awkwardly and clumsily as bears, clowns or Calibans. They make no vocal symphonies, but grunt and whoop-howl and groan. Some wore trousers and others leggins and breech cloths. Some wore shirts and others only blankets. They were bare-foot, or else wore moccasins,

Like with a great number of whites in eastern cities, supper is the main attraction.

boots or shoes. On their heads were hats, or caps, or cloths, or only long, laughing black locks. *(Pioneer)*

Aris Donaldson was always comparing what he saw to what he already knew, and judging it harshly by those standards. Private Ewert was able to report what was in front of him, on its own terms.

⬱ Wilder and wilder the song. The dancers are sweating. Still they are in pursuit 'till at the end, the entire crowd gives a terrible triumphant yell, the Sioux are killed or captured, their chief is slain. Rees didn't lose a single brave. Hurrah! Hurrah! Big Injun me! Everybody is happy and the warriors resume their seats with a self-satisfied grunt that spoke as plain as words: "Well, if you palefaces ain't confident now that we are brave and fearless warriors, then you are hard to convince, and we give it up." *(Ewert)*

Strongly in contrast with the hideous dancing and music of the Indians, are the songs sung by the white men around our camp fires. "Fairy Bell," "Bonny Jean," "Lightly Row," "Over the Sea," "Poor Old Joe," and many others have been rendered in a style worthy of professional vocalists. *(Pioneer)*

It would be fun to know what the Arikara and Santee Sioux said about these songs among themselves.

⬱ Later in the evening the Santee's and still later the Fort Rice scouts came over and participated in the dancing and singing, but it is my humble opinion that the feast of roasted elk meat was the main drawing power with these gents. We were favored with about twenty of these dances during the evening; they all terminated in the same way, vis. Sioux got whipped every time. Ree didn't lose a warrior. Sioux remained a coward and Ree a big Injun all the evening. Every Ree inspired by his national pride and Ree enthusiasm, felt himself—for the time being at least—equal to ten or twelve of the hereditary enemy. If, however, any of these had appeared personally on the scene we would have had, I think, a much livelier tune than any played tonight, and not quite so much to our Ree scouts' liking. *(Ewert)*

With spirits high along the Boxelder, it was about to become clear that the Arikara scouts were harboring something of a grudge. They had not forgotten the Sioux village (Chapter 4) found where Deerfield Reservoir is now.

⬱ Bloody Knife also favored us with a dance (he must have been the star of the evening for he danced solo), also

a speech which the interpreter gave to us again. This is it nearly verbatim: "General Custer big chief — White warriors very brave — We have seen the chief and his warriors fight the Sioux on the Yellowstone last year and know them to be very brave — We are the chief's friends — The Sioux are the chief's enemies — They are also our enemies — They want to get our scalps — They want to burn the Ree and the white warriors at the stake — The chief of the whites had captured 27 Sioux — He had let them go — This was wrong — It was wrong to the Rees — It was wrong to the white warriors — It was wrong to the chief himself — The Ree warriors felt bad — They returned to Fort Lincoln without a single scalp — They had told their squaws that they would bring their belts full of scalps — Now they would be liars — He (Bloody Knife) hoped that the chief would never do this again." *(Ewert)*

Custer might have redeemed himself two years later if the Battle of the Little Bighorn had gone a different way. But Bloody Knife was among the first to die there, shot through the head while standing close to Major Marcus Reno in a grove at the south end of the village. It was later said that Reno lost his nerve at that moment, and led a panicked retreat to the high point now known as "Reno Hill," where surviving soldiers held out until late the next day.

⬱ Several of the Santees made speeches to the Rees. These were heartily applauded. Cold Hand, of the Fort Rice scouts, also made lengthy address to the providers of the elk supper, and this, judging by the applause and the many approving grunts with which it was received, must have been the masterpiece of the evening. Several quick Ugh! Ughs! from the kitchen caused the tin pans to start off again, and this time the cook took his dance all by himself, and he did his part of the programme right well. After he stopped he went to work on the meat and cut it up in two-pound pieces. All the scouts having been helped, he passed it to us, but all refused except a poor hungry looking fellow of Company "A" whose rations had, no doubt, been insufficient to still his hunger, and the way he demolished that two-pound piece of elk must have shamed any Indian on the place. It seems that it is with the Indians like with a great number of whites in eastern cities, supper is the main attraction, for no sooner had the last piece of elk disappeared than the dancers dropped out one by one, and a half hour later everything was quiet; sleep held possession of the camp; only the guards were awake. *(Ewert)*

Donaldson's detached perspective did allow for a sense of wonder over the unique venture in which he was involved.

⬱ The Santees sing the most charming of our Sunday school songs, and sing them well. Sunday school songs, sung by Indians, in the Depths of the Black Hills! *(Pioneer)*

On the 11th we remained in camp, and sent two companies forward to make a road for the next day. *(Press)*

"K" and "G" companies went on pioneer duty with orders to cut a road as far as possible in the direction of the open prairie, to encamp tonight where darkness overtook them, and to resume work the next morning when the command would leave this camp. *(Ewert)*

While the pioneers were going in one direction, Captain Ludlow was going in the other.

I returned to the camp of the day before with a surveying party, for the purpose of measuring a base line and locating with the transit the important elevations. *(Ludlow)*

Ludlow would be using the triangulation method, which requires a known "base line" between two observation points. The line acts as the base of a triangle, the other legs of which run from each observation point to a chosen landmark. If you know the exact length of the baseline, and the precise angles (measured by a transit) at which the landmark can be seen from each point, then geometry defines where the second and third legs of the triangle intersect. That intersection not only locates the landmark in relation to your baseline, but also in relation to other landmarks sighted during the triangulation.

A base of 3,200 feet was carefully laid out, whence two hills were located, from the summits of which Bear Butte, Harney, Terry, and Custer Peaks, and many minor hills could be seen, and their azimuths determined. Lieutenant Warren spent a week in camp in 1859 near Bear Butte. Regarding that as properly located, Harney, on Warren's map, is too far east by six or seven miles. *(Ludlow)*

In other words, the engineer assumed that Warren had a chance to accurately record the latitude and longitude of Bear Butte. With that as a starting point, Ludlow could then determine the true placement of Harney Peak—which Warren only saw from afar. Ludlow was also able to place Terry and Custer Peaks on his map with remarkable accuracy, even though he never went near them.

Where were the observation points? Green Top and White Mansion, about three miles north of Nemo, are the highest points near the previous camp—except for Flag-

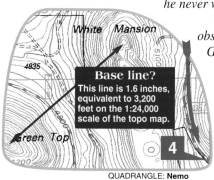

Base line?
This line is 1.6 inches, equivalent to 3,200 feet on the 1:24,000 scale of the topo map.

White Mansion
4835
Green Top
4

QUADRANGLE: **Nemo**

staff Mountain—and Green Top measures exactly 3,200 feet from the northern tip of White Mansion, as shown on the topographic map below.

William Illingworth may have joined Ludlow's detachment (see page 132). Both White Mansion and Green Top are seen in **Photo 848** *(page 258).*

The soldiers spent the day in washing their clothes and fishing. I saw some very fine fish which were caught in this stream. *(Calhoun)*

We found nothing but some small chub, and a species of sucker of perhaps a pound weight. *(Ludlow, August 10)*

That day, like all others, passed away, and "taps" reminded us that it was again time to commit ourselves to the arms of "Morpheus," which we did—some with our boots on, others without. *(Press)*

Remained in camp, preparing skins. *(Winchell)*

MYSTERIES OF THE TRAIL

For the record, there are three unexplained oddities concerning these days on the Boxelder. One has to do with the second baseball game in the Black Hills.

The men played the popular game of base ball. *(Calhoun)*

In his journal entry for August 11, Calhoun was the only one to mention the game other than Ewert—who seemed to place it in the next camp on the next day (Chapter 14). We will follow Ewert's lead for now, but Calhoun may have been writing daily entries in his journal that were more accurate about the date. It also makes sense that the game would be played on a layover day where plenty of space was available.

Lt. Godfrey & Escort went over to Bear Buttes and retd that P.M. *(Power)*

Lt. Godfrey did do some exploring down the Boxelder, but Ludlow and Winchell both talk about that trip two days later (Chapter 15). Fred Power is the only one to mention the Bear Butte trip, but notice his use of "that P.M." instead of "this," as if writing about the events at a later time. In the end, however, we don't know for sure whether Power was mistaken or the trip simply went unnoticed in the other journals.

About 4 o'clock this P.M., Private O'Gara Co. G, 7th Cavy., on duty in the Subsistence Department, returned from hunting and reports the immediate presence of a large body of Indians. *(Calhoun)*

No one else ever mentioned this report, and Calhoun didn't follow up. One immediately thinks of the pioneers out building a road, which O'Gara may have seen from afar. But your guess is as good as ours.

CHAPTER 14

Wednesday, August 12
Down Boxelder Creek to Norris Peak Road

He was obliged to crawl into a wagon
where his little life will soon be shaken out of him. (Ewert)

Even after two days of advance reconnoitering and a full day of road-building, the explorers covered only 10.4 miles between this day and the next—an odd development that no one ever explained. This was the day they finally figured out the name of the creek they were following; that Private James King became very ill; and that a solitary deer made a brave and wild dash through camp. Distance traveled: 5.7 miles.

— Taking the trail —

U.S.G.S. MAPS: Piedmont *(Optional: Pactola Dam)*

CAUTIONS: Roads are paved, but be wary of traffic.

TO START: *From Rapid City*, drive up Nemo Road 15.7 miles from the intersection of West Chicago and South Canyon Roads, to the entrance of Twin Peaks

Ranch on the right. *From the north*, go to Nemo and drive 2.2 miles further to the entrance of Twin Peaks Ranch on the left. *From the south and west*, take Highway 385 to Forest Service Road 208, near Trout Haven. Follow FS 208 all the way east to its end. Turn right and go six-tenths of a mile on Nemo Road to the entrance of Twin Peaks Ranch on the left.

This stream proved to be Elk Creek, the valley of which, as well as the stream itself, proving at least equal in beauty and extent to any passed through during our march. We camped twice on the stream, and as far as we proceeded down its course we had a most excellent road. *(Custer)*

By referring to Boxelder Creek as Elk Creek, Custer made a mistake that appeared in several other journal entries. From August 10, for example:

The engineer Sergeant informs me that this stream is called "Elk Creek." *(Calhoun, August 10)*

Calhoun was talking about Sergeant Becker (whom we met in Chapter 8) suggesting that the mistake

originated with Captain Ludlow of the Engineers. They were working with maps drawn in the 1850s that indicated where principal creeks left *the Black Hills. Portions of Elk Creek on the prairie are indeed at roughly the same latitude as the Nemo area, where the Expedition came upon Boxelder Creek. It would be understandable that the two were linked at first. But that changed as the command continued south.*

We have finally concluded that the stream upon which we have been encamped for the last three days is the Box Elder, although it runs in a more southerly direction, and heads higher than it is shown to do on the map. *(Forsyth)*

While the rest of the command followed the Boxelder on this morning, the geologist was drawn in another direction—this time by something other than rocks. Three more elk had been killed the previous day.

While the Command moves on down the valley to a chosen camping place, I go west and S.W. with a party of Santee Indians, according to arrangements last night, to skin an Elk that was killed yesterday by one of them, Jo Lawrence. Col. Ludlow *[his brevet rank]* also goes. The Indian killed three large stag elk and one of them I prom-

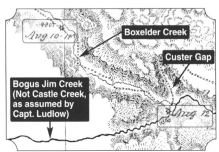

Expedition map
(1 inch = 3 miles)

Map labels: Boxelder Creek · Custer Gap · Bogus Jim Creek (Not Castle Creek, as assumed by Capt. Ludlow) · Aug 10-11 · Aug 12

Aug 12

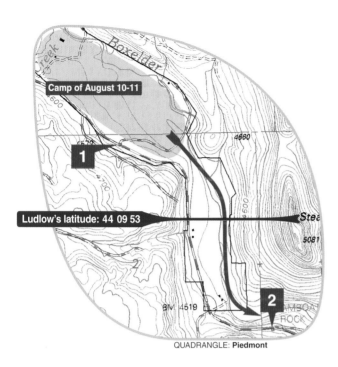

Camp of August 10-11

1

Ludlow's latitude: 44 09 53

2

QUADRANGLE: **Piedmont**

Because Capt. Ludlow's latitude readings were so consistently accurate—almost never wrong by more than a few hundred yards—his latitude for the August 10-11 camp (at left) is reason to question its location. But the *St. Paul Press* called the valley "large," and the location we show was on the confluence of two creeks (Boxelder and Estes), a common practice for the command. The enlarged detail from the Expedition map reproduced above is further evidence. Note the change in direction taken by Boxelder Creek just below the camp, where it turns almost straight south—just as it does on the topographic map at left.

The north-south portion of the valley (crossed by Ludlow's latitude) is now occupied by a private airstrip, which you will see on the left after about half a mile as you drive south from **Point 1**. It appears that the Expedition traveled on the far side of the creek to avoid a steep bluff you will cross just before **Point 2**—the entrance to the Steamboat Rock Picnic Ground—which is 1.1 miles from the Twin Peaks gate.

2 44 09 28.6 Turn left at the first entrance you come to
103 28 22.6 and stop at the first parking area (**Point 3**, next page). Go down to the creek, if you wish, and scout back upstream, where you might see evidence of an old ford. You will also notice a perilous ledge cut into the stone wall across the creek from the picnic ground. This was part of an extension of the Black Hills & Fort Pierre narrow gauge line that went as far as Piedmont in 1910.

This is a good place to get a feel for what it was like to take wagons down the valley of the Boxelder.

ised $15 for if he would let me have it, and have it skinned in my way. *(Winchell notebook)*

Make a detour to the southwest over a rolling wooded district about six miles from camp. . . . It is with the greatest difficulty that the Indians can be got to skin a mammal, except as they have been used to do from childhood; and as they are the best hunters, the collector for scientific purposes generally laments the loss to him of many valuable specimens. We found three fine specimens, two of which, in spite of injunctions to the contrary, they had beheaded, and all of which had been visited and gnawed by wolves during the night. *(Winchell)*

Those beheaded are ruined for my purpose, but Col. Ludlow wants one & Gen. Custer spoke for the other. I skin the one chosen and pack it to camp on my horse — i.e., the skin & head, walking & leading my horse about 8 miles. "Mose" *[a Moses Hunter was listed among the scouts]*—brother of the hunter who killed the elk—goes in advance and clears a road through the woods with a hatchet. The other heads are carried on horses by Indians. *(Winchell notebook)*

The only entire skin was secured for mounting, and will be placed in the museum of the University of Minnesota. . . . Where we skin the elks the rock is a very fine-grained, greenish chlorite slate. *(Winchell)*

1 44 10 07.1 This is the entrance to Twin Peaks ranch,
103 29 06.6 the safest place to pull off the road and observe the probable campsite of August 10 and 11. (If the gate is unlocked, please be aware of incoming and outgoing traffic.)

It would be interesting to know how far the geologist traveled from here. His estimates of distance often proved to be somewhat exaggerated when we could verify them, but a full six miles southwest from camp would have taken Winchell almost to present-day Pactola Lake.

Moving down the bank of the stream, crossing it now and then as it cuts into the bank on either side, we finally encamped . . . below our morning's resting place. *(Forsyth)*

Our march on this day, although a short one, was quite interesting; the scenery was very fine. We followed the stream, which was flanked on each side with bluffs composed of sand and lime-stone, and presented quite a picturesque appearance, though not so grand and imposing as that around "Custer Valley." *(Press)*

Custer Valley, along French Creek, was considered a beautiful park-like country. But when Fred Power used words like "grand" and "imposing," he was certainly thinking of Castle Creek Valley (Chapter 4).

When you are ready to leave, set or check your odometer at the lower entrance of the picnic ground. The next stop is the intersection of Norris Peak Road, 4.2 miles away. As you drive—particularly if you have traveled Nemo Road enough to take it for granted—try to look at the valley with fresh eyes, seeing it as it might have appeared to the first white men who came this way.

Our march . . . was through a beautiful valley flanked on each side by high bluffs that presented a beautiful appearance, and watered by quite a large stream. *(Power)*

On the lower bottoms of Elk *[Boxelder]* Creek, we

Aug 12

find white oak, birch, elm, ironwood, wild grapes, and wild hops. (These hops may be the same as the cultivated variety.) *(Pioneer)*

We find an agreeable change in the foliage along the creek,—elm taking the place of pine, and any quantity of hop vines, in full bearing, running all over them. *(Forsyth)*

One soldier could not enjoy any of these things. It was his next-to-last day alive.

☞ James King of "H" company [is] very sick; he fainted twice in the sun. Still, the brutes with us called doctors marked him for duty. He finally could not set on his horse any longer, but being unable to get admission into an ambulance (these being in use for the transportation of Negro servants, owls, rattlesnakes, etc.) he was obliged to crawl into a wagon where his little life will soon be shaken out of him. *(Ewert)*

Marched through the timber until we came to an open valley where we went into camp. *(Calhoun)*

Where we camped to-day is one of the most beautiful spots. *(Grant)*

4 44 07 49.3 The intersection of Nemo and Norris 103 24 43.8 Peak Roads has been moved slightly east since the last revision of the topographic map, and sees more and more traffic. Turn right on Norris Peak Road and pull to the side for a good view of the campsite. From here you can consider how this valley—"one of the most beautiful spots"—might have looked in 1874.

☞ This is indeed a delightful place. Excellent grazing. The consummation of real enjoyment. The whole command is in excellent spirits. The soldiers feel that they are fully remunerated for the manual labor performed by them, in beholding such a beautiful place. *(Calhoun)*

"Fully" remunerated? The young Calhoun (he was about to turn 29, on August 24) might have been getting carried away, and one could question whether he was speaking for the enlisted men.

☞ Just as we were unsaddling, a fine buck ran through camp, and no one dare shoot him for fear of hitting some of the men or horses. . . . After our chagrin had subsided, we really enjoyed his feat. *(Forsyth)*

We had no trouble on the following day to pass over the road built by "K" and "G" companies. Made eight miles and encamped in Genevieve Park. As "H" company was waiting for its wagons to come up, a deer was startled by some of the scouts in the woods behind us, and it came to within ten steps of the line, halted a second as if undetermined what to do, then gave a great bound or two and darted through the center of the company, some of the men being nearly run over. As it ran across the open portion of the park, Captain Hale of "K" started in pursuit, revolver in his hands and bareheaded. The deer got away. . . . The

Actives and Athletes played the second of their games today. The weather was splendid and the field good and the attendance large. *(Ewert)*

This is the passage in Ewert's diary that creates some confusion. In context it clearly refers to the day "following" the August 11 layover. His mileage for the day's march is wrong, but others got it wrong as well, and Ewert included the story of the deer that was also mentioned by Forsyth on this day. The problem lies partly in identifying the intersection of Norris Peak and Nemo Roads as Genevieve Park, which disagrees with the South Dakota Geographic Names: ". . . lying in the southern part of [Lawrence] County and including the present site of Nemo, was given this name by General Custer in honor of the wife of his engineer officer, Captain William Ludlow." That is an obvious reference to the large

QUADRANGLE: **Piedmont**

valley where the camp of August 10 and 11 was located—an area much more likely to be called a park and given a name than the small opening at the end of Norris Peak Road. Did the book get it right, then? It seems at least possible that Ewert confused dates and places if he worked on the diary at a later time, or that something was jumbled in transcribing, or that we are reading it wrong.

William Curtis may support the Nemo version.

☞ Elk Creek Valley was christened "Genevieve Park" because Colonel Ludlow's wife bears the name of Wordsworth's lady love. *(Inter-Ocean)*

This is in a dispatch dated August 15, when Curtis should have known better, but if he was still referring mistakenly to the Boxelder as Elk Creek, Genevieve Park would have to be the large valley south of Nemo.

The question is significant because it also bears on the location of the second baseball game, which is described in a separate paragraph that could have been placed in the wrong order. Again, the camp of August 10 and 11 was a much more likely site for the game, given the size of the valley and the added day of freedom—and the fact that Lt. Calhoun said the game was played on August 11 (Chapter 13).

The game was worthy of professional clubs, closely contested and well played. . . . One of the engineer party acted as umpire. At the 9th inning the score stood Athletes 11, Actives 9. The latter then went to the bat and gained one run, placing the score at 10. *(Ewert)*

The Athletes had already won at this point, and by today's rules the game would have ended.

The Athletes then went to the willow and managed, by some brilliant batting and playing, to add six runs to their score, giving us a score as above, 17-10. In the early part of the game McCort of "H," playing first base and having one of the Actives there to look after, did not attend to his duty properly and so received a "red hot one" from pitcher McCurry right square in the eye. (He should have caught it with his hands.) His friends advised him to give up playing for today. This, however, he refused to do. He tied a handkerchief over the injured eye and played the remainder of the game at right field. . . . The game was an excellent one for amateur players and deserves a much better record. The

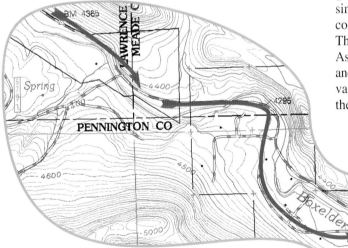

photographer took several views of this camp and vicinity, one picture of all headquarters with officers and professors in the foreground. He also took several private views. *(Ewert)*

Here is further apparent confirmation of "this camp" as the location of the baseball game. Several other accounts mention the group photograph (page 264) recorded by Illingworth the next morning.

This is a tantalizing passage because the group

*photograph is the only one we know of in this area, although the location of two other images remains unknown. One of them—***Photo 850***, "Forsyth's Glenn" (page262)—was Illingworth's last published view within the Black Hills. Numerically it follows the photos near White Mansion (page 132) and might have been taken in that area. But Ewert's diary raises the possibility that Forsyth's Glen could be somewhere not far from here, tucked away near Bogus Jim Creek and still in hiding after all these years.*

Arrived at Camp No. 33. The left wing camped on Elk [*Boxelder*] Creek, the right wing on a beautiful rivulet, running into Elk Creek. *(Calhoun)*

Camp was moved down the creek a few miles into a very pretty and luxuriant valley, at a point where another large creek joined it from the westward. Judging from its size and direction, this must be the Castle Valley Creek, upon which we twice encamped, (July 26–'7 and July 28) and the hills portion of what is called Box Elder on Warren's map. *(Ludlow)*

It is surprising and disappointing that Capt. Ludlow, who worked so hard to prepare an accurate map, would have made such an assumption. There is a large open space in the middle of his finished map representing about 12 miles of unknown and unexplored country. Across that white space is a single line connecting Bogus Jim Creek (which apparently was quite a bit larger at the time) with Castle Creek near Reynolds Prairie—based entirely on "must be."

We were cheered this evening in hearing some good singing by members of Co. H, 7th Cavalry. What a wide contrast to the mournful ditty of the barbarous red men. The songs sung by civilized men are full of inspiration. As these men gave vent to their vocal powers the very hills and dales all awoke, and transmitted the sound through the vast arena of nature. Such melodious notes should soothe the savage breast. *(Calhoun)*

The lieutenant would be among those who died with Custer at Little Big Horn.

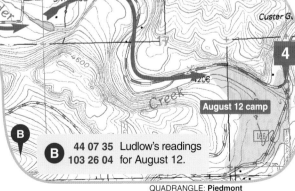

B 44 07 35   Ludlow's readings
103 26 04   for August 12.

Aug 12

4

August 12 camp

QUADRANGLE: **Piedmont**

CHAPTER 15

Thursday, August 13
Leaving the Boxelder through Custer Gap

The idolized son, the worshiped lover, the darling brother . . . lay here dead before us, killed by carelessness, murdered through neglect. (Ewert)

Officers and scientists gathered in the morning for a group portrait near the intersection of Nemo and Norris Peak Roads, after which the command passed through a narrow and providential cut in the limestone wall—the only escape available from the valley of Boxelder Creek—to reach a high plateau with a view of the prairie. Private James King died as the new camp was being prepared. Distance traveled: 4.7 miles.

Taking the trail

U.S.G.S. MAPS: Piedmont *(Optional: Pactola Dam)*

CAUTIONS: The roads are paved or gravel, but an optional two-hour hike will prove rewarding.

TO START: *From Rapid City,* drive 10 miles up Nemo Road from the intersection of West Chicago and South Canyon Roads. Turn left onto Norris Peak Road, and pull to the side as soon as possible. *From the north*, drive 7.8 miles south from Nemo and turn right onto Norris Peak Road. Pull to the side as soon as possible. *From the west and south*, go to Johnson Siding on Highway 44 and take Norris Peak Road all the way to the end. Find a safe place to pull over just before you reach Nemo Road.

☞ That night an order came around saying that the command would not move on the 13th until after 2 p.m., and that the officers would meet at headquarters next morning at 9. They met there and were photographed by Illingworth. *(Press)*

Yesterday afternoon and this morning was occupied with the necessary care of my elk skin. We break camp about 11½ o'clock, the morning having been passed by the command in preparing a road. *(Winchell notebook)*

Professor Winchell—in his private notebook—is the only one to give what could be the real reason for the delay, and it adds to the mystery of the short marches. Way back on Monday, remember, Forsyth wrote this:

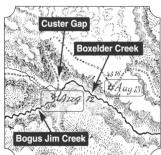

Custer Gap

Boxelder Creek

Bogus Jim Creek

Expedition map
(1 inch = 3 miles)

☞ General Custer and myself made a careful exploration for 12 or 15 miles down the creek, and found a good wagon-road to the plains. *(Forsyth, August 10)*

Road-builders went out the following day, as Ewert described at the time.

☞ "K" and "G" companies went on pioneer duty with orders to cut a road as far as possible in the direction of the open prairie. *(Ewert, August 11)*

Either the "good wagon-road" didn't work out, or two pioneer companies required two days to cut a road down the Boxelder. The summary table in Ludlow's report does list the arrival time in this camp as seven o'clock the night before—14 hours to cover 5.7 miles—which seems questionable, since no one complained of an arduous journey in the accounts. On the other hand, if it is true it raises yet another doubt about Ewert's reference to a baseball game on the Bogus Jim and Boxelder Creeks (Chapter 14).

☞ The photographer took several views of this camp and vicinity, one picture of all headquarters with officers and professors in the foreground. *(Ewert)*

Aug
13

General Custer reclines on the ground at the center of the group in this fascinating image (page 264), which was taken in front of his tent somewhere within the campsite that stretched along the Boxelder and Bogus Jim Creeks. If Illingworth did record other scenes here, they have so far not been discovered.

1 **44 07 49.3** This is the first stop, on Norris Peak Road **103 24 43.8** a few yards from Nemo Road. (Be alert for fairly steady traffic.) Set or check your odometer here and drive three-tenths of a mile east on Nemo Road, pulling off at the entrance to a primitive parking area on the left.

2 **44 08 01.7** The pullout is across the Boxelder from **103 24 36.2** an opening in a formidable limestone wall that otherwise would have prevented further travel.

We break camp about 11½ o'clock. *(Winchell notebook)*
. . . 12 o'clock (noon). *(Calhoun)*
. . . 12½ o'clock. *(Ewert)*
Started at 2 p.m., and crossing the Box Elder moved east up the dry bed of a creek, which has forced its way through the limestone bluffs that just here loom up along the east bank of the stream in a solid wall. *(Forsyth)*
. . . ascending a difficult ravine, in which some of the wagons capsized. *(Winchell)*

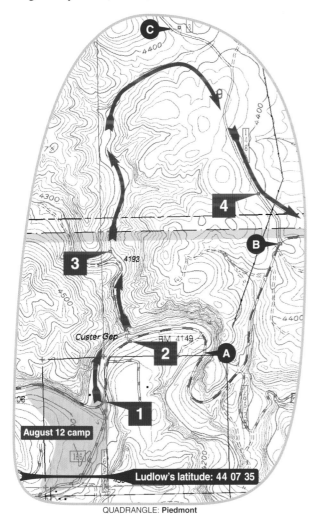

QUADRANGLE: **Piedmont**

This opening in the rocks was a great relief, as many thought we would have to turn back and travel in search of another outlet. *(Calhoun)*

This cut in the rock is still known today as "Custer Gap," and it truly was a remarkable stroke of fortune that it should appear at the last possible moment. The command might well have had to turn around and follow its trail back to Inyan Kara. Rapid and Spring Creeks would have been just as impassable for wagons as the Boxelder.

Continue four-tenths of a mile and pull over just beyond the bridge that crosses the Box Elder (**Point A**). From here you can see that the wagons could have gone no further down the creek—which will probably be dry when you see it.

The Box Elder sinks in its bed and disappears entirely, though we followed the dry bed down stream for several miles. *(Forsyth)*
Lieutenant Godfrey, with an escort, was dispatched down the creek, to determine its course and ascertain his position from bearings to Bear Butte and Harney when clear of the hills. *(Ludlow)*
Like all the other creeks on the east and south side of the Hills, it leaves the mountains through deep gorges and canons. The lovely parks and valleys of the interior are most effectually shut in. Only indomitable energy and zeal could ever find a way for a wagon train into or out of these secluded retreats. *(Pioneer)*

Lt. Godfrey must have gotten a late start, since he was included in the group photograph.

Continue one mile on Nemo Road (1.4 miles from Custer Gap) and turn left on Rolling Hills Road (Forest Service 149) at **Point B**. Then drive north 1.1 miles to a dirt trail on the left.

C **44 09 06.1** The unimproved trail that intersects here **103 24 20.1** has been blocked for vehicular travel by an earth berm after a hundred yards or so, but you may hike down the trail all the way to Custer Gap. This is of course an optional part of the day, and you should allow at least a couple of hours. But the narrow portion of the draw at the lower end will give you a much better appreciation of the difficulty the wagons faced in negotiating the gap.

3 **44 08 20.2** If you decide to make the hike, pay close **103 24 41.5** attention to this area, where today's trail has been cut into the hill above the drainage. Did Custer's pioneer crew create this detour? Perhaps it is one of the areas where wagons "capsized," as Winchell puts it.

Set or check your odometer at **Point C** and return south, keeping an eye on the head of the draw to your right. The wagon train turned in this area and came up to where Rolling Hills Road is today. Note that the road passes between high ground on the right and the heads of three draws on your left. This would have been the most logical route for the command.
Go seven-tenths of a mile to an old trail on the left.

Aug 13

4 44 08 31.5 An abandoned trail on the left angles to
103 23 57.8 the southeast, past the head of a draw,
almost on a line with a section
of Nemo Road (see arrows
on topo map). Altogether,
the combination of Rolling
Hills Road, the old trail and
Nemo Road bear a striking
resemblance to the enlarged
detail from Ludlow's map at
right. We believe the wagons
changed direction in this vi-
cinity, and the portion of Nemo Road between Points 5 and
6 is either on or at least very close to the Expedition's route.

Area of Point 4?

5 44 08 20.7 From here you can see the site that is now
103 23 25.5 marked as the grave of Private James
King, whose story will be told shortly. Note the location
before continuing seven-tenths of a mile. You will see a small
space where you can pull off on a bend in Nemo Road.

6 44 07 50.6 This is a high spot in the middle of the
103 22 52.1 open area, and may be very close to the
location of headquarters for this camp. Note that the center
of camp was located at the bottom of a "V" formed by the trail
on Ludlow's map. Also note that this bend is just a little more
than 100 yards north of Ludlow's latitude reading.

In any case, this is an excellent place from which to see
the open prairie beyond the Black Hills.

☞ A march of an hour *[for headquarters, not the wagons]*
up a gradual ascent and through a pine forest, brought us
to a beautiful park . . . from which we obtained a fine view,
in the distance, of our old acquaintance—the plains. *(Custer)*

We pass more easterly out of the valley in which we
camped, and find . . . a more open, level country, clothed only
with scattered small pines and turfed with good grass. *(Winchell)*

Then turning east and south through open timber and
a second growth of pine, emerged upon an open, rolling
park of great extent, where camp was made. *(Ludlow)*

☞ The following day we . . . encamped on a large plateau
on the outer range of hills above and in plain view of the
prairie. *(Ewert)*

The train-men now get the first view since entering the
hills, though many of the troops and citizens, not confined
to the line of march, have seen the plains from various parts
of the hills since we first entered them, some having been
down on to them. *(Winchell)*

*Anyone who has driven east on Nemo Road has seen
this view of the prairie. You have also, just possibly,
driven right through or near the location of the headquarters tents (**Point 6** on the map)—and without
doubt through the location of the camp itself.*

Continue a little more than two-tenths of a mile, turn left on
Seventh Cavalry Trail, and pull over to the side of the road.

D 44 07 42.9 Much or all of the housing to your left is
103 22 37.6 built on Custer's last camp in the Hills.

☞ The open prairie was visible, separated from us by a
wooded ridge, which, though not high, was deeply cut by
ravines. *(Ludlow)*

There is still one large ridge between us and the
plains. *(Winchell)*

The ridge Ludlow and Winchell refer to is plainly visible from
where you are parked. Look at the height straight ahead,
to the north, and follow its outline down toward your right.
This would be the barrier they had to surmount the next day.

Return to **Point B**, set or check
your odometer, and turn left onto
Nemo Road to "emerge" onto the
rolling, open country. Drive a little
more than three-tenths of a mile,
looking for a headstone in the private pasture on your right.

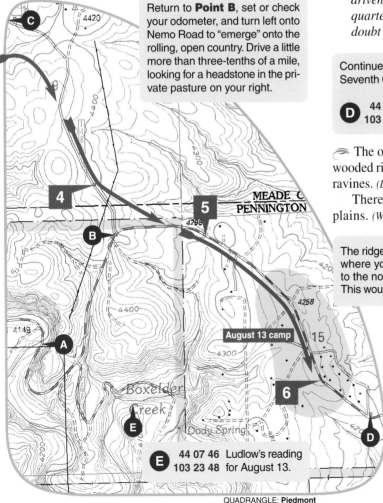

MEADE C
PENNINGTON

August 13 camp

E 44 07 46 Ludlow's reading
103 23 48 for August 13.

☞ General Forsyth, Lieut. Hodgson and myself
each took a party of men and went out to see if
we could find a road out of the Black Hills. All
returned having found a good road. *(Grant)*

Here we pitched our tents for the last time
in the Black Hills; nearly every one being loth
to leave a region which had been found so
delightful in almost every respect. Behind us
the grass and foliage were clothed in green
of the freshness of May. In front of us, as we
cast our eyes over the plains below, we saw

QUADRANGLE: **Piedmont**

Aug
13

nothing but a comparatively parched, dried surface, the sunburnt pasturage of which offered a most uninviting prospect to horse and rider, when remembering the rich abundance we were leaving behind. *(Custer)*

We had barely finished pitching our tents when the news was brought to our camp that our dear, good, honored and respected comrade, James King, had died; that, like Cunningham, he had been criminally neglected, pushed [and] crowded to his death by the two inhuman brutes with us called doctors. King, the quietest, best, most loved man in the command, inoffensive, good hearted, ever ready and willing to help and assist a comrade, noted for his sobriety, honesty and integrity, loved for all a man's sterling qualities, here lay before, having died for want of proper attendance. *(Ewert)*

The members of Company H, 7th Cavy, are exceedingly displeased at the conduct of the Medical officer of the left wing. *(Calhoun)*

That was putting it mildly. King was the second man from the same company to die of chronic diarrhea. John Cunningham had suffered greatly before his death three weeks earlier (Chapter 1), when assistant surgeons J.W Williams and S.J. Allen had been worse than useless—at least according to Ewert's account.

⌒ No wonder the curses came deep and direct from the heart against these two inhuman butchers. No wonder that the men of Company "H" cast threatening looks at the couple guilty of the loss of our friend and I am persuaded that had an opportunity presented itself they would [have] exacted full measure of the divine law: "Eye for an eye, Tooth for tooth and life for life!" Great God, poor King! Only a few more months and his term of service would have been cancelled, his plans for a successful and happy civil life already layed out, a widowed mother watching for him with loving, anxious eyes, the heart of a betrothed wife yearning for him daily, brothers and sisters counting the minutes 'till Jim, the idolized son, the worshiped lover, the darling brother should join them in June next. And now he lay here dead before us, killed by carelessness, murdered through neglect. *(Ewert)*

Private Ewert's outrage extended beyond the surgeons to a general sense of neglect that he felt was pervading the Army.

⌒ The men at the head of the government are ever making new laws for the stricter governing of the enlisted men of the Army. Would it not be as well, and a little more humane, if these would also see that the rank and file would get the most important of the few rights allowed them? Attendance when sick and competent doctors to prescribe for them? Have our Senators, Representatives and Generals no interest in the soldier? . . . Is his life less precious than that of a horse? The latter gets the attendance of a veterinary surgeon when sick; a man [is attended] whenever the drunken brute with us sees fit to visit him, and then only to tell him with an insulting, drunken stare that he is only "playing off"

Private King died far from home and family, but his grave was being carefully tended 127 years after the Expedition left him behind.

and needs no medicine. And so the sick man is fairly pushed into the grave. *(Ewert)*

If you have driven Nemo Road you have probably seen Private King's headstone, in a pasture on the far west side of the plateau. We have not been able to discover the basis for placing it there, or whether the location is accurate.

⌒ The body of King was sewn in canvass and was ordered to be interred this evening. To this Major Tilford objected. A man should not be buried two hours after death if he could prevent it, and if the commanding officer could not wait with the train in the morning 'till after the burial, he would keep only the companies comprising the left wing for that purpose. *(Ewert)*

Custer must have been in a hurry, as you will see in the next chapter. He was not present for the funeral that would be observed the following morning. You may wish to return to the grave site before you read descriptions of the services on this plateau at dawn.

⌒ The usual square was formed by the companies; Captain Benteen read the services [and] every eye in "H" company gave proof of the love we bore the deceased, of the respect we had for him. It was an impressive scene. *(Ewert)*

Just as the golden rays of the rising sun began to tint the tree-tops and gild the light clouds in the eastern sky, his body was laid away. . . . The trumpeter blew the call "Day is out, extinguish lights." King's day on earth was indeed out; but we trust that as bright and glorious celestial morning dawned upon his soul, as was that earthly morning which shown upon his comrades weeping around his grave. *(Pioneer)*

The hardest tasked remained still unfulfilled, and that is to inform King's mother of his death; we can guess that it will almost break her heart. . . . We can assure her that Jim has gone to a better life, he having always been an exemplary man and Christian. *(Ewert)*

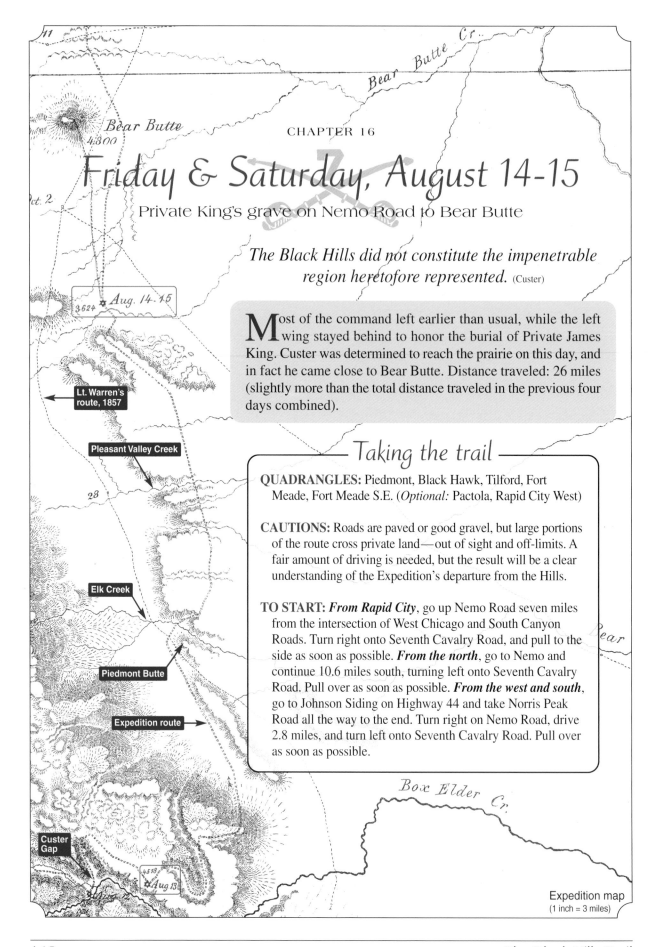

CHAPTER 16

Friday & Saturday, August 14-15

Private King's grave on Nemo Road to Bear Butte

The Black Hills did not constitute the impenetrable region heretofore represented. (Custer)

Most of the command left earlier than usual, while the left wing stayed behind to honor the burial of Private James King. Custer was determined to reach the prairie on this day, and in fact he came close to Bear Butte. Distance traveled: 26 miles (slightly more than the total distance traveled in the previous four days combined).

Map labels:
- Bear Butte Cr.
- Bear Butte 4300
- Oct 2
- Aug. 14-15 3624
- Lt. Warren's route, 1857
- Pleasant Valley Creek
- 28
- Elk Creek
- Piedmont Butte
- Expedition route
- Custer Gap
- 4518 Aug 13
- Box Elder Cr.
- Bear

— Taking the trail —

QUADRANGLES: Piedmont, Black Hawk, Tilford, Fort Meade, Fort Meade S.E. (*Optional:* Pactola, Rapid City West)

CAUTIONS: Roads are paved or good gravel, but large portions of the route cross private land—out of sight and off-limits. A fair amount of driving is needed, but the result will be a clear understanding of the Expedition's departure from the Hills.

TO START: *From Rapid City*, go up Nemo Road seven miles from the intersection of West Chicago and South Canyon Roads. Turn right onto Seventh Cavalry Road, and pull to the side as soon as possible. *From the north*, go to Nemo and continue 10.6 miles south, turning left onto Seventh Cavalry Road. Pull over as soon as possible. *From the west and south*, go to Johnson Siding on Highway 44 and take Norris Peak Road all the way to the end. Turn right on Nemo Road, drive 2.8 miles, and turn left onto Seventh Cavalry Road. Pull over as soon as possible.

Expedition map
(1 inch = 3 miles)

Aug
14
15

🖝 We broke camp . . . earlier than usual. (*Press*)
  Started at 4 a.m. . . . . (*Forsyth*)

And so it happened the Lieutenant Colonel of the 7th Cavalry did not wait in the morning with the command, and as he was leaving camp Companies C, G, K, M and H were marching to the solemn strains of the band to where the grave had been dug. (*Ewert*)

Private James King had died the night before of dysentery (Chapter 15), but Custer apparently was feeling too impatient to pay his respects. The rest of his command was already on its way.

A 44 07 43.3 This is the first stop, the intersection of 103 22 37.6 Nemo and Seventh Cavalry Roads. To visit King's grave, drive one mile northeast on Nemo Road.

B 44 08 20.7 Look for a fenced headstone in the pasture 103 23 25.5 on your left, honoring Private King.

🖝 In the grey twilight of the morning, the men with bowed heads, tears trickling down the sunburnt cheeks, the dead body suspended over the grave, the captain, with his grey hair, reading the service, the silence, all are impressed on my memory never to be erased. The three volleys were fired and Taps sounded and then the body was lowered, the grave was filled and a fire built over it and all that was mortal of our friend was left in peace, resting in the red men's country away from the hum and stir of civilization, alone on the highlands of the Black Hills. (*Ewert*)

Returning toward **Point A**, take note of the high wooded ridge about a mile in front of you. It was a barrier between the soldiers and the prairie.

🖝 Breaking camp before sunrise, we descend an easy slope toward the east, formed by the dip of the rock, when we come, within three-fourths of a mile, facing upon a north and south ridge formed by the Minne-lusa sandstone, capped with a few feet of the Carboniferous limestone. (*Winchell*)

From **Point A**, continue a quarter of a mile east and turn left on Potter Road at **Point C**. Go north five-tenths of a mile to Woodcrest Court on your left (not shown on the map).

2 44 08 08.8 Turn left here on Woodcrest Court and drive 103 22 19.9 two-tenths of a mile to the end of the road.

1 44 08 05.3 This is a cul-de-sac very close to where the 103 22 31.9 wagons passed. When you turn around you'll have a closer view of the ridge looming ahead.
  Follow the wagons back down the "easy slope" to **Point 2**. At the intersection you'll be looking straight into a drainage that wraps around the base of the ridge you were just observing. The wagons entered the drainage near here.
  Return to Nemo Road (Point C) and turn left. Drive a little more than a tenth of a mile to Palmer Road (**Point D**) and turn left again. Go half a mile to a cul-de-sac at the end of Palmer Road.

3 44 07 56.8 This is a continuation of the drainage, just 103 21 48.3 before it turns sharply to the south. Notice, as Winchell did, the rock formations that form the ridge.

🖝 Here we turn south to pass it. I make this sandstone to be about 75 feet. There is here, also, a thickness of about 20 feet of limestone overlying. The latter gives form and sharpness to the brow of the ridge. (*Winchell*)

A favorable road was found through the intervening ridge by making several abrupt turns among ravines filled with oak and hills covered with pine. (*Ludlow*)

We do not go far south, but turn to the north and northeast, climbing at last over this ridge. (*Winchell*)

The geologist's description of these first two or three miles dovetails very usefully with the southern loop

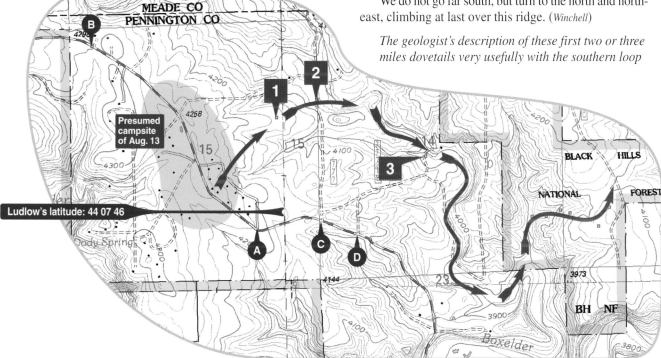

QUADRANGLES: **Piedmont, Blackhawk, Pactola, Rapid City West**

that appears on the Expedition map. Little else was written about these first few miles of travel, some of which took place in near-darkness. It was just the beginning of a long day and the men had their eyes set on home. But the Expedition map—backed up by the Winchell's account—suggests a trail that would have taken the wagons back toward present-day Nemo Road to get around the "intervening ridge."

At **Point 3** you are near the base of this ridge, which is clearly depicted in the enlarged section of Ludlow's map below. Note that the trail forms a "U" as it dips below the latitude of the campsite. The arrows on the topographic map show the "abrupt turns" described by Ludlow as the ravine winds south and east. While it is not  certain where the Expedition climbed out, the arrow leading to **Point 4** follows a very old trail up the side of a draw. At the top, you would be on the crest of the eastern extension of the ridge. The landscape between Point 4 and **Point 5** is a high rolling meadow, which Major Forsyth appreciated in his diary.

Forsyth's "long divide" corresponds most closely with the north rim of today's Ward's Canyon, starting at **Point 5**—probably close to where the wagon train made a 90-degree turn to the east that is shown on the enlarged section at right. The scale of the Expedition map indicates that the distance from the bottom of the loop to the sudden eastward turn is 1.7 miles—about the same as the distance on the topo map between the southernmost area of the drainage and Point 5.

It was on the 14th of Aug. that we climbed the last ridge of the eastward range of the hills. A deep pine-fringed cleft in the ridge opened a wide vista to our view. We were in a lovely harbor; a great ocean rolled miles away, until it melted into the blue sky in the far distance. So it seemed to us. But it was a great land ocean, lacking most what it best imitated—an abundance of water. *(New York Tribune)*

Traveled about 4 miles when we got once more on the open prairie. *(Calhoun)*

Soon after sunrise we were on the plains once more. *(Press)*

Moved directly east, across the outer range of mountains, finding a good road up on to their crest; thence across a very pretty, park-like country, and down a long divide. *(Forsyth)*

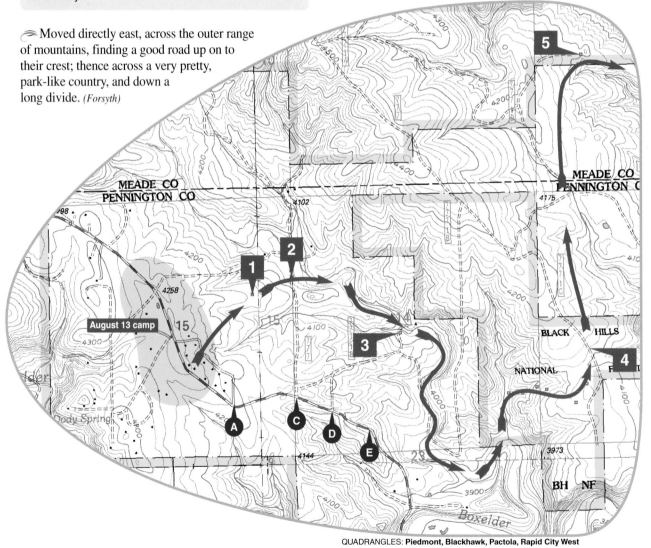

QUADRANGLES: **Piedmont, Blackhawk, Pactola, Rapid City West**

The Black Hills Trail

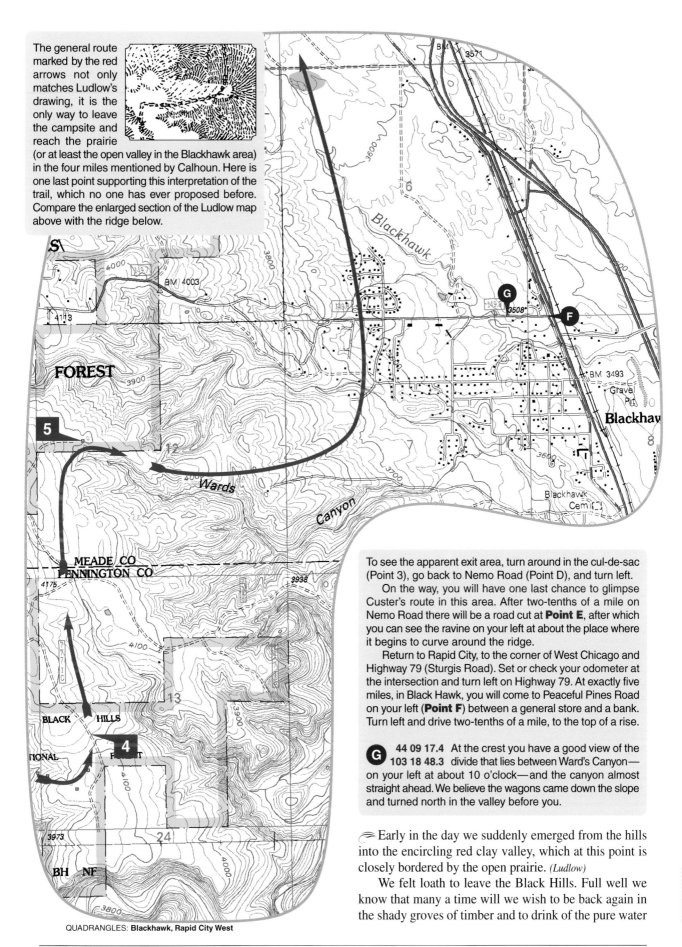

The general route marked by the red arrows not only matches Ludlow's drawing, it is the only way to leave the campsite and reach the prairie (or at least the open valley in the Blackhawk area) in the four miles mentioned by Calhoun. Here is one last point supporting this interpretation of the trail, which no one has ever proposed before. Compare the enlarged section of the Ludlow map above with the ridge below.

QUADRANGLES: **Blackhawk, Rapid City West**

To see the apparent exit area, turn around in the cul-de-sac (Point 3), go back to Nemo Road (Point D), and turn left.

On the way, you will have one last chance to glimpse Custer's route in this area. After two-tenths of a mile on Nemo Road there will be a road cut at **Point E**, after which you can see the ravine on your left at about the place where it begins to curve around the ridge.

Return to Rapid City, to the corner of West Chicago and Highway 79 (Sturgis Road). Set or check your odometer at the intersection and turn left on Highway 79. At exactly five miles, in Black Hawk, you will come to Peaceful Pines Road on your left (**Point F**) between a general store and a bank. Turn left and drive two-tenths of a mile, to the top of a rise.

G 44 09 17.4   At the crest you have a good view of the
103 18 48.3   divide that lies between Ward's Canyon—on your left at about 10 o'clock—and the canyon almost straight ahead. We believe the wagons came down the slope and turned north in the valley before you.

↝ Early in the day we suddenly emerged from the hills into the encircling red clay valley, which at this point is closely bordered by the open prairie. *(Ludlow)*

We felt loath to leave the Black Hills. Full well we know that many a time will we wish to be back again in the shady groves of timber and to drink of the pure water

Aug
14
15

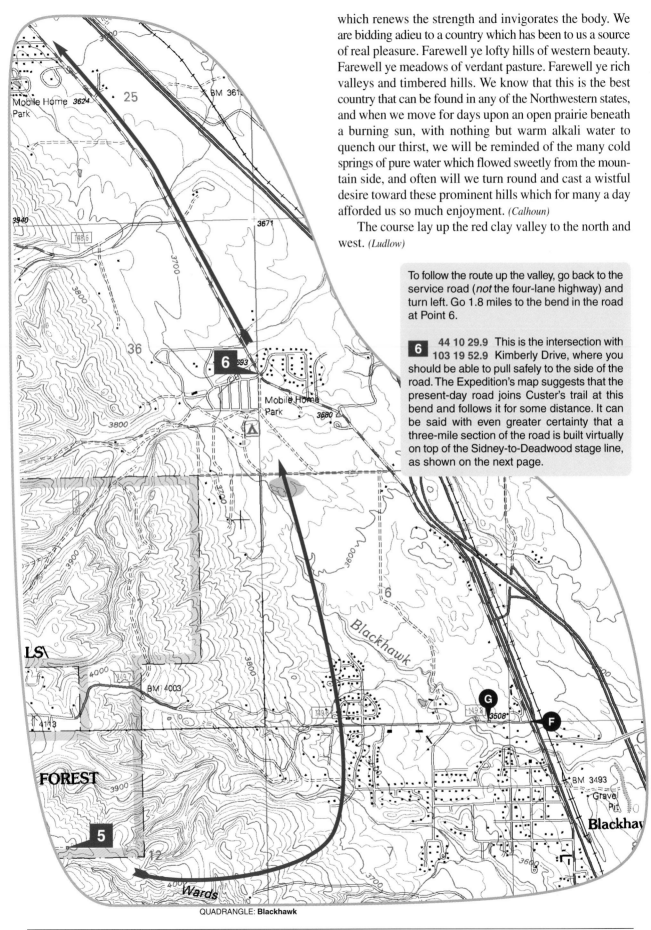

which renews the strength and invigorates the body. We are bidding adieu to a country which has been to us a source of real pleasure. Farewell ye lofty hills of western beauty. Farewell ye meadows of verdant pasture. Farewell ye rich valleys and timbered hills. We know that this is the best country that can be found in any of the Northwestern states, and when we move for days upon an open prairie beneath a burning sun, with nothing but warm alkali water to quench our thirst, we will be reminded of the many cold springs of pure water which flowed sweetly from the mountain side, and often will we turn round and cast a wistful desire toward these prominent hills which for many a day afforded us so much enjoyment. *(Calhoun)*

The course lay up the red clay valley to the north and west. *(Ludlow)*

To follow the route up the valley, go back to the service road (*not* the four-lane highway) and turn left. Go 1.8 miles to the bend in the road at Point 6.

6 **44 10 29.9** This is the intersection with **103 19 52.9** Kimberly Drive, where you should be able to pull safely to the side of the road. The Expedition's map suggests that the present-day road joins Custer's trail at this bend and follows it for some distance. It can be said with even greater certainty that a three-mile section of the road is built virtually on top of the Sidney-to-Deadwood stage line, as shown on the next page.

QUADRANGLE: **Blackhawk**

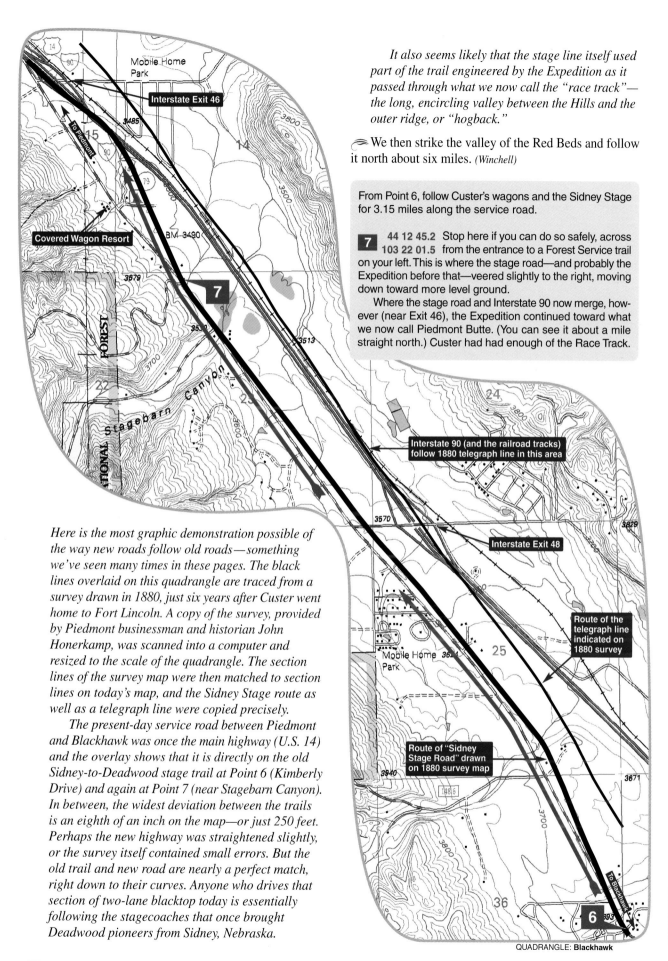

It also seems likely that the stage line itself used part of the trail engineered by the Expedition as it passed through what we now call the "race track"— the long, encircling valley between the Hills and the outer ridge, or "hogback."

We then strike the valley of the Red Beds and follow it north about six miles. (Winchell)

From Point 6, follow Custer's wagons and the Sidney Stage for 3.15 miles along the service road.

7 **44 12 45.2** Stop here if you can do so safely, across **103 22 01.5** from the entrance to a Forest Service trail on your left. This is where the stage road—and probably the Expedition before that—veered slightly to the right, moving down toward more level ground.

Where the stage road and Interstate 90 now merge, however (near Exit 46), the Expedition continued toward what we now call Piedmont Butte. (You can see it about a mile straight north.) Custer had had enough of the Race Track.

Mobile Home Park

Interstate Exit 46

To Piedmont

Covered Wagon Resort

BM 3490

FOREST

Stagebarn Canyon

NATIONAL

7

Interstate 90 (and the railroad tracks) follow 1880 telegraph line in this area

Interstate Exit 48

Route of the telegraph line indicated on 1880 survey

Mobile Home Park

Route of "Sidney Stage Road" drawn on 1880 survey map

To Blackhawk

6

Here is the most graphic demonstration possible of the way new roads follow old roads—something we've seen many times in these pages. The black lines overlaid on this quadrangle are traced from a survey drawn in 1880, just six years after Custer went home to Fort Lincoln. A copy of the survey, provided by Piedmont businessman and historian John Honerkamp, was scanned into a computer and resized to the scale of the quadrangle. The section lines of the survey map were then matched to section lines on today's map, and the Sidney Stage route as well as a telegraph line were copied precisely.

The present-day service road between Piedmont and Blackhawk was once the main highway (U.S. 14) and the overlay shows that it is directly on the old Sidney-to-Deadwood stage trail at Point 6 (Kimberly Drive) and again at Point 7 (near Stagebarn Canyon). In between, the widest deviation between the trails is an eighth of an inch on the map—or just 250 feet. Perhaps the new highway was straightened slightly, or the survey itself contained small errors. But the old trail and new road are nearly a perfect match, right down to their curves. Anyone who drives that section of two-lane blacktop today is essentially following the stagecoaches that once brought Deadwood pioneers from Sidney, Nebraska.

QUADRANGLE: **Blackhawk**

Moved north for about 6 miles, finding some beautiful springs. *(Forsyth)*

We traveled this morning fully 14 miles before we reached water when we arrived at a running stream. By the side of this stream was found three (3) springs hidden from view by the tall blades of grass. *(Calhoun)*

Custer's brother-in-law overestimates the distance, which was closer to ten or eleven miles from camp, but several sources mentioned these springs—which were, in fact, part of Custer's decision to leave the Race Track as soon as he found a good opportunity.

The numerous creeks in the hills reaching the prairie sunk beneath the gravel and shingle of their beds and disappeared; some of them reappeared briefly in the form of springs in the red clay valley, which was from two to three miles in width. On account of these springs and the occasional marshy ground, the trail broke through the low hills separating the valley from the prairie on the east. *(Ludlow)*

Continue almost one mile to Elk Creek Road (**Point H**) and stop at the intersection to survey the valley ahead on the right, where the Expedition crossed in front of Piedmont Butte.

Continue 1.55 miles to **Point I** and turn right on Deerview Road. In half a mile you'll pass Piedmont Cemetery on a small hill, where you may want to pause once again.

J 44 114 32.0   This will give you a good overall view of
103 23 08.4   the flanks of Piedmont Butte, which the wagons appear to have used to stay above Elk Creek.

On the south side of this hill, by the way (to your right), is the entrance to an old underground gypsum mine.

In the Red Beds I noticed the white gypsum to-day, that abounds in the same beds in the northern part of the hills,

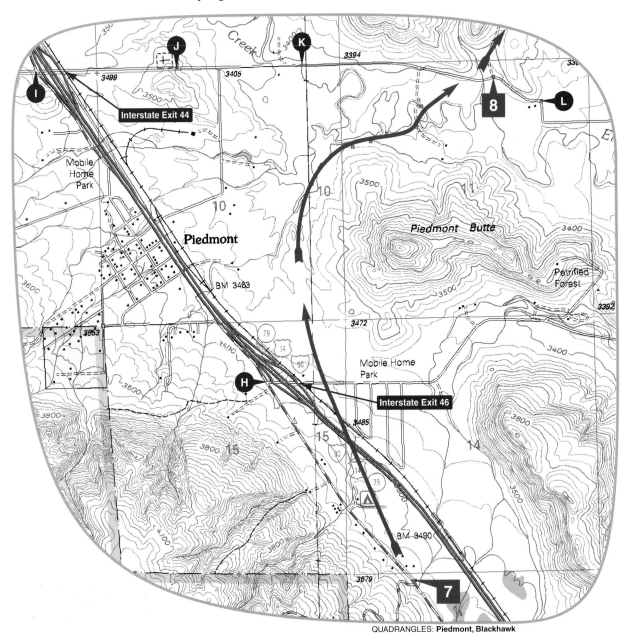

QUADRANGLES: **Piedmont, Blackhawk**

and which was also seen by Colonel Ludlow in the southern part. Thus it appears the gypsiferous character of these beds is nearly constant in the region of the hills. *(Winchell)*

As with the iron ore Winchell found near Nemo (Chapter 13), this mineral deposit would one day prove very useful. According to John Honerkamp's At the Foot of the Mountain, *U.S. Gypsum Company established a mine and mill in Piedmont in 1916 that produced plaster until 1948.*

Half a mile down Deerview Road you'll cross Elk Creek (**Point K**), and about seven-tenths of a mile after that there will be a driveway on the left. Stop beside the road.

8 44 14 28.6 The Expedition crossed Elk Creek somewhere in this vicinity and continued over
103 21 34.9 the shallow rise on your left, passing to the northeast and out onto the open prairie.

We cross Elk Creek and pass to the east of the ridge formed by the Dakota sandstone, reaching soon another known as the Bear Creek. *(Winchell)*

We reached Bear Creek which is indeed an excellent and large stream of running water. While the pioneer company were fixing a crossing the soldiers were busy fishing, a sport which proved satisfaction. I saw one soldier with 21 fish (some of large size) which he caught in about 40 minutes. *(Calhoun)*

There is no "Bear Creek" on today's maps. Winchell and Calhoun are referring to what is now called Morris Creek, which cuts through the hogback east of Tilford. While the Expedition map (page 146) got it wrong—referring to Elk Creek as Bear Creek— the geologist's report makes a direct link between Elk Creek and the exit route through the hogback. Morris Creek is the next major drainage to the north.

From **Point 8**, continue east less than three-tenths of a mile to a 90-degree right-hand turn (**Point L**). Pull to the left and stop in front of a ranch gate. This will give you a place to turn around after viewing the prairie over which the soldiers turned north.

The arrows on the topographic map are only approximations of the trail, based on the direction of travel shown on Ludlow's map (the section at right is twice its original size) combined with plausible routes through the topography. The actual route is virtually all on private land.

To pick up the trail north of Morris Creek, return to Interstate 90 and take the northbound ramp. Go four miles to the Tilford exit (No. 44, not shown) and turn east on Tilford Road. (Morris Creek will be on your right as you pass through the hogback.) Go exactly four miles from the exit ramp.

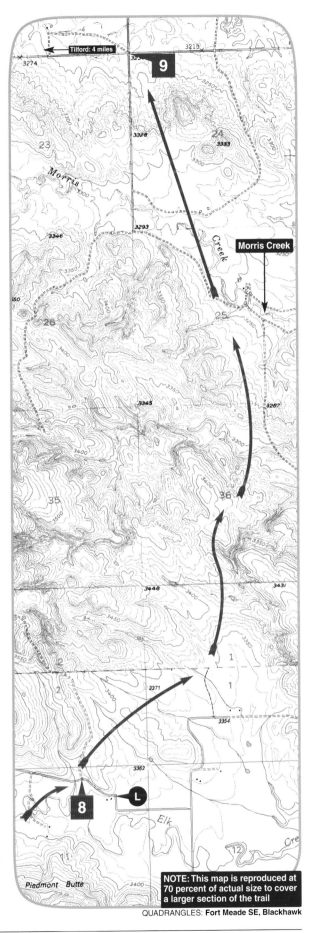

NOTE: This map is reproduced at 70 percent of actual size to cover a larger section of the trail

Aug
14
15

QUADRANGLES: **Fort Meade SE, Blackhawk**

From Private King's grave to Bear Butte

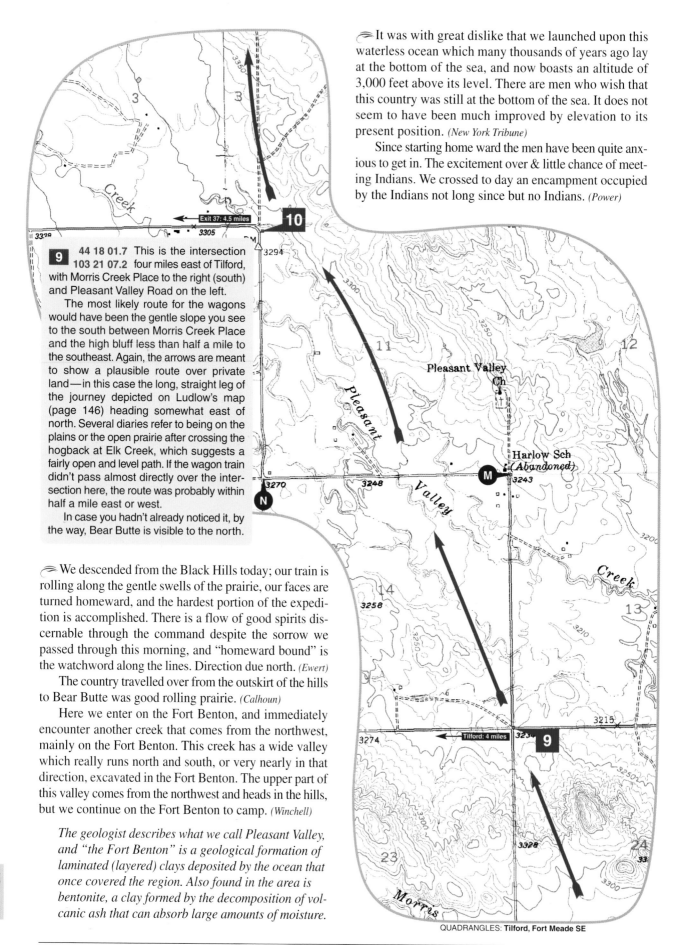

It was with great dislike that we launched upon this waterless ocean which many thousands of years ago lay at the bottom of the sea, and now boasts an altitude of 3,000 feet above its level. There are men who wish that this country was still at the bottom of the sea. It does not seem to have been much improved by elevation to its present position. *(New York Tribune)*

Since starting home ward the men have been quite anxious to get in. The excitement over & little chance of meeting Indians. We crossed to day an encampment occupied by the Indians not long since but no Indians. *(Power)*

9 44 18 01.7 This is the intersection 103 21 07.2 four miles east of Tilford, with Morris Creek Place to the right (south) and Pleasant Valley Road on the left.

The most likely route for the wagons would have been the gentle slope you see to the south between Morris Creek Place and the high bluff less than half a mile to the southeast. Again, the arrows are meant to show a plausible route over private land—in this case the long, straight leg of the journey depicted on Ludlow's map (page 146) heading somewhat east of north. Several diaries refer to being on the plains or the open prairie after crossing the hogback at Elk Creek, which suggests a fairly open and level path. If the wagon train didn't pass almost directly over the intersection here, the route was probably within half a mile east or west.

In case you hadn't already noticed it, by the way, Bear Butte is visible to the north.

We descended from the Black Hills today; our train is rolling along the gentle swells of the prairie, our faces are turned homeward, and the hardest portion of the expedition is accomplished. There is a flow of good spirits discernable through the command despite the sorrow we passed through this morning, and "homeward bound" is the watchword along the lines. Direction due north. *(Ewert)*

The country travelled over from the outskirt of the hills to Bear Butte was good rolling prairie. *(Calhoun)*

Here we enter on the Fort Benton, and immediately encounter another creek that comes from the northwest, mainly on the Fort Benton. This creek has a wide valley which really runs north and south, or very nearly in that direction, excavated in the Fort Benton. The upper part of this valley comes from the northwest and heads in the hills, but we continue on the Fort Benton to camp. *(Winchell)*

The geologist describes what we call Pleasant Valley, and "the Fort Benton" is a geological formation of laminated (layered) clays deposited by the ocean that once covered the region. Also found in the area is bentonite, a clay formed by the decomposition of volcanic ash that can absorb large amounts of moisture.

Aug
14
15

QUADRANGLES: **Tilford, Fort Meade SE**

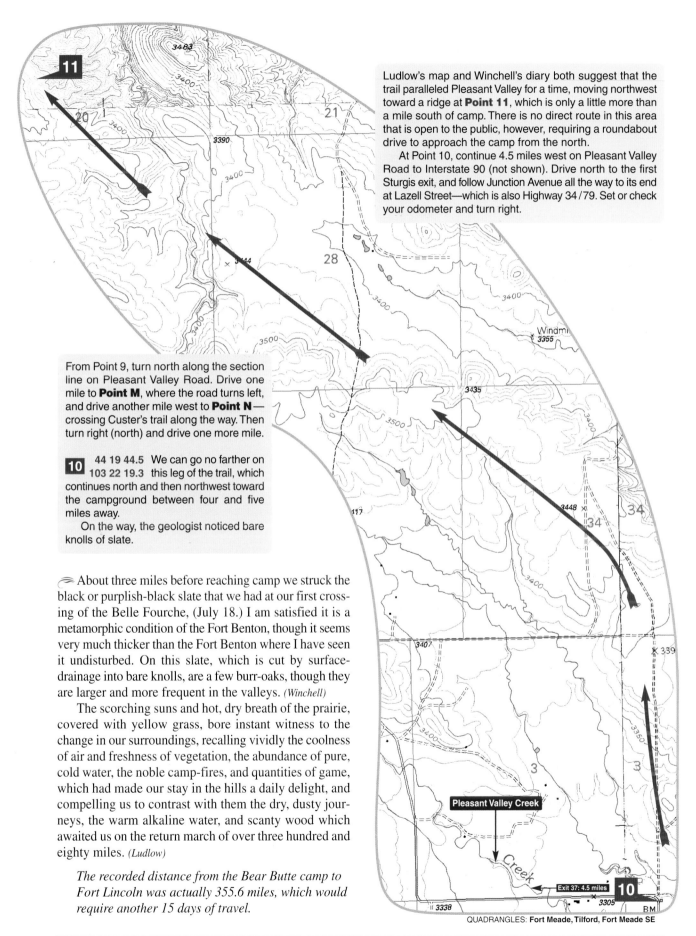

Ludlow's map and Winchell's diary both suggest that the trail paralleled Pleasant Valley for a time, moving northwest toward a ridge at **Point 11**, which is only a little more than a mile south of camp. There is no direct route in this area that is open to the public, however, requiring a roundabout drive to approach the camp from the north.

At Point 10, continue 4.5 miles west on Pleasant Valley Road to Interstate 90 (not shown). Drive north to the first Sturgis exit, and follow Junction Avenue all the way to its end at Lazell Street—which is also Highway 34/79. Set or check your odometer and turn right.

From Point 9, turn north along the section line on Pleasant Valley Road. Drive one mile to **Point M**, where the road turns left, and drive another mile west to **Point N**— crossing Custer's trail along the way. Then turn right (north) and drive one more mile.

10 44 19 44.5 We can go no farther on 103 22 19.3 this leg of the trail, which continues north and then northwest toward the campground between four and five miles away.

On the way, the geologist noticed bare knolls of slate.

☞ About three miles before reaching camp we struck the black or purplish-black slate that we had at our first crossing of the Belle Fourche, (July 18.) I am satisfied it is a metamorphic condition of the Fort Benton, though it seems very much thicker than the Fort Benton where I have seen it undisturbed. On this slate, which is cut by surface-drainage into bare knolls, are a few burr-oaks, though they are larger and more frequent in the valleys. *(Winchell)*

The scorching suns and hot, dry breath of the prairie, covered with yellow grass, bore instant witness to the change in our surroundings, recalling vividly the coolness of air and freshness of vegetation, the abundance of pure, cold water, the noble camp-fires, and quantities of game, which had made our stay in the hills a daily delight, and compelling us to contrast with them the dry, dusty journeys, the warm alkaline water, and scanty wood which awaited us on the return march of over three hundred and eighty miles. *(Ludlow)*

The recorded distance from the Bear Butte camp to Fort Lincoln was actually 355.6 miles, which would require another 15 days of travel.

QUADRANGLES: **Fort Meade, Tilford, Fort Meade SE**

Aug
14
15

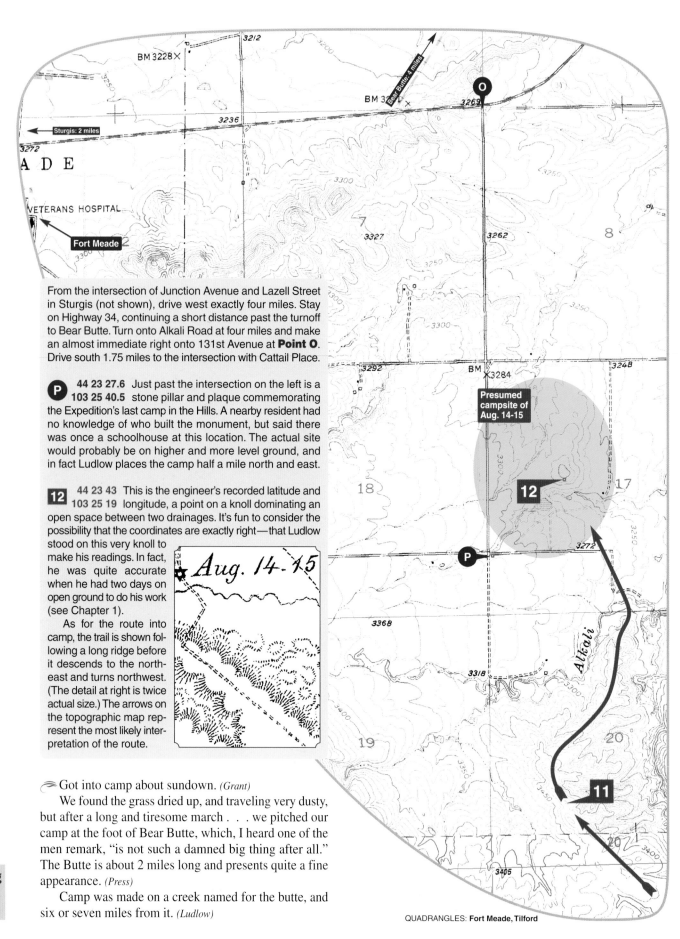

From the intersection of Junction Avenue and Lazell Street in Sturgis (not shown), drive west exactly four miles. Stay on Highway 34, continuing a short distance past the turnoff to Bear Butte. Turn onto Alkali Road at four miles and make an almost immediate right onto 131st Avenue at **Point O**. Drive south 1.75 miles to the intersection with Cattail Place.

P 44 23 27.6 Just past the intersection on the left is a
103 25 40.5 stone pillar and plaque commemorating the Expedition's last camp in the Hills. A nearby resident had no knowledge of who built the monument, but said there was once a schoolhouse at this location. The actual site would probably be on higher and more level ground, and in fact Ludlow places the camp half a mile north and east.

12 44 23 43 This is the engineer's recorded latitude and
103 25 19 longitude, a point on a knoll dominating an open space between two drainages. It's fun to consider the possibility that the coordinates are exactly right—that Ludlow stood on this very knoll to make his readings. In fact, he was quite accurate when he had two days on open ground to do his work (see Chapter 1).

As for the route into camp, the trail is shown following a long ridge before it descends to the northeast and turns northwest. (The detail at right is twice actual size.) The arrows on the topographic map represent the most likely interpretation of the route.

Aug. 14-15

⌐ Got into camp about sundown. *(Grant)*

We found the grass dried up, and traveling very dusty, but after a long and tiresome march . . . we pitched our camp at the foot of Bear Butte, which, I heard one of the men remark, "is not such a damned big thing after all." The Butte is about 2 miles long and presents quite a fine appearance. *(Press)*

Camp was made on a creek named for the butte, and six or seven miles from it. *(Ludlow)*

Aug
14
15

QUADRANGLES: **Fort Meade, Tilford**

A march of twenty-six miles gradually bearing northward brought us to the base of Bear Butte, at which point I concluded to remain one day before beginning our return march. *(Custer)*

Spent the day in getting off our letters to go to night by the Indian Scout. . . . I went down & had a good wash. Watered & fed "Coon" my horse. Retd., wrote to Lizzie & then managed ½ col for the press. Ate dinner rather earlier than usual. Fed & watered horse at 12, finished letter, took it over. *(Power)*

Went up the Butte this forenoon. Compared with the hills in the range, it is a pigmy, being only 1,140 feet above the level of the plains; but, standing alone as it does, it looms up quite grandly, especially when first seen by parties approaching the hills on this side. *(Forsyth)*

With Colonel Ludlow and an escort, we go about five miles north to this celebrated butte. . . . In ascending, Professor Donaldson and myself pass round to the northwest side, where we have the advantage of both shade and a strong northwest wind. . . . The remainder of the scaling party, having ascended from the southeast, approach the summit . . . along the same ridge. *(Winchell)*

*Custer himself did not climb Bear Butte. William Illingworth, meanwhile, went about three miles northeast of the camp (**Point Q**) to take his last picture in the Black Hills, **No. 851**, "Bear Butte near Custer Peak" (page 266). The site is now private land.*

Two of the correspondents, preparing dispatches for their newspapers according to very different styles and prejudices, considered the future.

It is useless for me to say that Custer's Black Hills Expedition has been a decided success throughout—the fact is well known by all, and may memories live in the hearts of the American people. Through the untiring energy of Gen. G. A. Custer, a Paradise hitherto unknown, rich in numerous minerals, has been made known to the world, and now all that remains to be done, is for Congress to open this beautiful land for settlement, and protect those who go there, from its present worthless inhabitants—the Indians. *(Bismarck Tribune)*

We wonder if there is an excitement in Chicago over the gold discoveries; if we won't meet an expedition coming out here as we go in; and then we go to thinking that if the people believe what we have told of the gold. That there is lots of gold here we are positive—that it lies both in and out of the lines that bound the Sioux reservation, and that with the pressure which certainly must be brought to bear on Congress, the whole country must soon be opened up to settlers. What a rush there will be here then; what a flood of humanity will flow in, washing out the treasure trove of these beautiful hills. One almost can regret there is anything to tempt such men as usually get the gold fever;

one thinks such a natural paradise as this should be set apart for poets, like William Cullen Bryant and Waldo Emerson, who "Can communion hold with nature." But with such inducements as are here displayed, there will be a rush next spring . . . . But it will not last long, the area is not very large, and 5,000 men will soon clean these gulches dry. *(Inter-Ocean)*

Deadwood alone was said to have a population of 5,000 at one point (although not many of them were miners). But if Curtis failed in the accuracy of his immediate prediction, his larger vision for the Black Hills may still resonate today.

The first who come will go away rich. Others will move on out into Wyoming or Montana, or somewhere else; but some will remain here, I hope, to cultivate these valleys, to cut this timber, and quarry this glorious building stone. *(Inter-Ocean)*

NOTE: This map is 50 percent of actual size

QUADRANGLES: **Fort Meade**

CHAPTER 17

Legacy of an Expedition

The beginning of the end for the Old West

The Expedition passed to the east of Bear Butte and crossed the Belle Fourche River on August 16, the first of five punishing days on the dry plains. Grazing would be very poor or burned off entirely by extensive fires, and several horses or mules were shot each day when they could no longer keep up. The command was forced to make one march of more than 35 miles (think of the men in the infantry) and averaged 30 miles a day before traveling far out of its way to stop for rest at the Little Missouri River. (See the map on page *x*.) Conditions began to improve after that, but not in time for Sergeant Charles Sempker. He died of dysentery on the 25th, the final casualty of the Expedition.

The larger casualty was peace with the Lakota Sioux, who called Custer's trail the "thieves' road." A chief named Fast Bear used that term the following year, when the Black Hills had already been invaded by hundreds of prospectors. We cannot say that the Expedition was *the* cause for the Lakota's loss of the Hills. It is clear now that it would have happened eventually, given human nature and the rumors of gold and the increasing population along the frontier. But the Expedition was still the *immediate* cause of the gold rush that ensued, and it played a key role in a series of events that would close out the frontier.

The first prospectors known to have followed Custer—literally—were members of the Gordon Party, who intersected his trail along the Boxelder that December and traced it back to French Creek. They had left Sioux City, Iowa, in October, just a few weeks after the Expedition's return to Fort Lincoln. There had been plans for a large exploring party, but the Army threatened to burn its wagons and arrest its leaders. Indeed, detachments began to patrol the routes to the Black Hills. Just 28 souls of the Gordon Party persisted, including Mrs. Annie Tallent and her young son Robert. Pretending to be settlers bound for the O'Neill Colony in Nebraska, they braved not only the Army patrols but the Lakota as well. Their efforts are memorialized in a reconstruction of the stockade they built that winter, not far from Permanent Camp.

The Army learned of their presence and sent three separate detachments into the Hills, finally evicting the prospectors who were still at the stockade in April 1875. The Army was making a legitimate effort to prevent a rush to the Hills, as was their duty under the Fort Laramie Treaty. A number of prospectors were caught and escorted out, and at least one party saw its wagons burned and its leader arrested, just as General Philip Sheridan had promised.

The motive for this diligence was in part pragmatic. Pressure was mounting on the government to negotiate the sale of the Black Hills, which would be much harder to do if the Lakota were aroused by trespassing miners. When it became clear that a second reconnaissance was needed to assess the value of the Hills more carefully—to know exactly what the government was negotiating for—the high-profile Custer was passed over in favor of Lieutenant-Colonel Richard Irving Dodge.

This would be called the Newton-Jenney Expedition, for its leaders Henry Newton and Walter P. Jenney. They and their 15 assistants, escorted by 400 soldiers, conducted a thorough geological exploration of the Black Hills from early June through the end of September in 1875. They even had help from some of the prospectors they encountered along the way, after Dodge let it be known that he had no interest in arresting them.

But the prospectors did create a problem for the government, which had already begun negotiations with the Lakota. Red Cloud, Spotted Tail and other chiefs had been invited to Washington in the spring to talk about selling the Black Hills. When the chiefs insisted on consulting with their people, they were sent back with assurances that a special commission would visit them in September. In the meantime, the Army made another attempt to clear the Hills of intruders. General George Crook met with the miners near the end of July and again on August 10. He said he would remove them by force, if necessary, but he worked out an arrangement that would protect their claims until after the purchase of the Black Hills—which everyone thought was imminent—if the miners left with him voluntarily. Only a few holdouts remained behind, deep in hiding.

As it turned out, none of these efforts would make a difference in the outcome of the commission's meeting with 20,000 Lakota on the White River in September. It did not go well. The young men had no interest in selling the Black Hills, while the older men named a price that the commission couldn't live with. It has been said that those who named the price were victims of bad advice about the value of the Hills, which was probably half true. The estimations of value were conservative, if anything, but it should have been clear that the government would balk at paying a spectacular price.

The failed meeting in Nebraska was another turning point in a rapidly deteriorating situation. The hostile bands might have reacted in pretty much the same way no matter what happened there, but President Grant's reaction was to withdraw all troops protecting the Black Hills. From that point on there was no official hindrance to the prospectors, who poured in by the thousands. Among them was Horatio

Nelson Ross—credited with making the first discovery on French Creek the previous summer—leading a large party from Bismarck. The gold rush was now at full bore.

Some prospectors paid the price, dying at the hands of passing Lakota, most of whom were gathering along the Powder and Yellowstone Rivers under Crazy Horse and Sitting Bull and Gall. The government suddenly decided to call in all the hunting parties early in 1876, ordering them to return to their respective agencies. It was an unreasonable order with a short deadline in the middle of a harsh winter. The government instigated the Sioux War that followed by labeling all those who did not return as hostile. Crazy Horse fought Crook on the Rosebud, and Custer had a reason to make his headlong attack at the Little Big Horn.

While the Black Hills Expedition was a real source of bitterness among the Lakota, it was not the only one. They saw the buffalo disappearing, and were angered by plans for building the Northern Pacific Railroad across their hunting grounds in Montana. "They had lost, in their own generation, everything," said Donald Jackson in *Custer's Gold*. "Custer did not die because he found gold in the Hills, but because he trapped himself by a foolish military move."

The Lakota and their Cheyenne allies must have been gratified to see Custer destroyed so completely that day on the Little Big Horn, but for them it was the classic case of winning the battle and losing the war. The voices of moderation were drowned out after June 25, and the Army went to work with renewed feeling. Most of the hostile forces were trapped at the end of October and forced to surrender. By then a new treaty commission had met with hand-picked chiefs at Red Cloud's Agency and dictated the terms under which they would surrender the Black Hills. Gone was the $6 million offered by the government the year before. The Lakota essentially gave up the Hills and all the gold they contained in return for the promise of rations.

The new treaty was ratified in February of 1877, legalizing the occupation of the Hills that had already taken place. Scattered bands of Lakota were still attacking miners that year, but gradually they gave up. Crazy Horse himself surrendered in May, only to be killed later that summer at Fort Robinson in Nebraska. Sitting Bull, having found refuge for a time in Canada, returned in 1881.

Cowboys, trappers and homesteaders are the most common inhabitants of the West in our collective imagination, but it was gold that moved the great populations. Railroads would begin to play a role, of course, but the gold had to come first. Otherwise who would have wanted to lay tracks across a nearly empty continent to the sleepy village of Yerba Buena, now known as San Francisco? The California Gold Rush put westward expansion into fast forward, and the Black Hills Gold Rush was its coda—at least in the continental United States. For a short time, people reading dime novels about the Wild West could go to Deadwood and see the real thing.

It was an odd era of overlap between the Old West and what we think of as the modern age. While the hostile Lakota were gathering in Montana in 1876, Alexander Graham Bell was tinkering in a lab in Massachusetts. It was on March 10 that he said, "Watson, come here. I want you." Custer missed reading about the telephone by only a month or two, and in 1879 a phone line was installed between Lead and Deadwood—so one town could warn the other of impending floods. The phonograph was nearly two years old by then, and the first two gas-powered cars were built ten years later in Germany, in 1889.

There was an encore for the old days, of sorts, when the Ghost Dance raised hopes among some of the Lakota that they could return to the life that had been taken from them. That hope was destroyed forever in 1890 by soldiers on horseback at Wounded Knee, just 13 years before the first airplane flew at Kitty Hawk. There would be no turning back.

Part II: Rediscovering the Illingworth photographs
by Paul Horsted

Introduction to the Black Hills Expedition photo sites

When you realize you have finally found an 1874 Black Hills Expedition photo site, after perhaps weeks of searching, there is a feeling of great excitement—and a strange sense of expectation. You look at the same rock, stump or tree shown in the photograph of 128 years ago, and in a way it seems as if the photographer has just left. You almost expect to look down and see a discarded bottle of developing chemicals or some other evidence of his visit to the site. The evidence, of course, is the photograph itself.

This book is the culmination of the most intriguing project I have worked on in 20 years as a photographer in South Dakota. Tracing the trail of the Black Hills Expedition and its photographer, William Henry Illingworth, has given me a tangible personal connection with this fascinating, tragic, defining period of our region's history. Discoveries made along the way, such as realizing that a rock formation in one of Illingworth's photographs can be seen from my own front yard, only intensified my interest in finding and re-photographing his Black Hills views, and in learning all I could about the Expedition of which he was an important part.

The question asked most often about the photography project is: "How did you find the 1874 photo sites?" The answers to that question are as varied as the photographs themselves. Research, technology, help from knowledgeable people, a little luck, and miles of hiking were all part of the equation. Several photo locations near Custer, S.D., are well-known locally, and landowners across the Black Hills region helped us with clues or directions to others. Many of the sites were first documented by Dr. Donald R. Progulske in the ground-breaking 1974 book *Yellow Ore, Yellow Hair, Yellow Pine* (see bibliography, page 284).

Joe Sanders and Jack McCulloh of Rapid City, who had been researching the Expedition for a decade before I became interested in it, showed me several of the sites, or were able to point at the right mountain range or valley. And Ernest Grafe's analysis of journals and the Expedition map led directly to finding one of the most significant previously undocumented photo sites, where Gen. Custer was photographed with the grizzly bear he and others had killed (pages 254-257).

Even with help, some photo sites were found only after days or even weeks (in a few cases, months) of searching on foot, combined with further study of the original photographs and other Expedition documents. Some of the sites documented in *Yellow Ore* (and in Progulske's later book, *Following Custer*) had virtually become lost again, because the technology of the 1970s made it difficult to precisely record the photo site locations. Maps in earlier publications provided a good starting point, but they couldn't be as precise as the Global Positioning System (GPS) we now have available.

We used computer technology in several cases to enhance details not visible in the 1874 photos as they are normally printed. Two unknown photo sites were found this way, using prints ordered to our specifications from the South Dakota State Historical Society. And we used the Internet to solve the mystery of two additional photos long thought to be from the Expedition, but which were actually taken in Minnesota or Wisconsin (pages 269 and 276).

Illingworth took some 50 views (plus near-duplicate negatives at some locations) in the Black Hills area. Two of these views remain unfound, while another is uncertain. For each missing view, however, we have evidence that narrows down the location, and we share what we know in the following pages. Perhaps in time these elusive sites will be located, though they may have been altered beyond recognition by changes in the Black Hills.

It should also be noted that we chose to focus on the Black Hills area photo locations only (which proved to be a large enough task). However, the eight known views Illingworth took as the Expedition traveled hundreds of miles across the plains *between* the Black Hills and Ft. Lincoln are also reproduced in this book, and their modern counterparts may be part of a future project.

I took most of the modern photos on or near the dates Illingworth did (in July or August) although lighting challenges sometimes caused delays. Tree growth had thrown the foreground of several photo sites into deep shadow, while the background was still in bright light—a difficult situation for the landscape photographer. I waited for cloudy skies to shoot those locations in an effort to soften the light and produce a good matching photograph.

Some of the modern matching photos were relatively easy to create once the locations were found. Others were complicated by the changes of more than 125 years, including erosion, mining, cattle grazing, highway and railroad building, and, most of all, the massive, widespread growth of pine trees due to the suppression of forest fires. Comparing the 1874 and modern photographs shows, in nearly every case, many more trees growing now over vast areas of the Black Hills. These trees tend to be smaller and growing closer together, and they are a fire hazard that grows (literally) worse every year. But that's another story.

The exact placement of Illingworth's camera and tripod could often be determined using such foreground clues as rock formations, tree stumps, snags, and even live trees still visible in the modern scene. Illingworth often used such foreground elements to enhance the three-dimensional effect of his stereoviews. But some photos contain few such clues, leaving only the distant background as a reference. These locations are less precisely established.

I have a great admiration for William Henry Illingworth. Although his later life was unhappy, at the time of the Expedition he seems to have been at the peak of his career and his art. His energy shows in the mountain heights he climbed to take some of his photographs, and in the number of artistically excellent photos he made in a short time, using very primitive equipment and processes.

I hope you will enjoy following Illingworth's footsteps through the Black Hills, and that as you stand in his place, you too will be surprised by the changes, and amazed by the similarities, as I was at each photo site.

Looking at the photo pairs

W.H. Illingworth took most of the views in this book as "stereographs," or stereoviews as they are now commonly known, using the "wet plate" photographic process. After setting up his camera at a photo site, he coated a glass plate with chemicals in a nearby dark tent or wagon and put the plate in his camera. After making the exposure, he had to develop the plate immediately and store it in a way that protected the glass from breaking until he returned home.

His camera had two identical lenses, each recording the view from a slightly different angle to produce two separate images on the same glass plate negative. (An example of a 19th-century stereo camera can be seen on page 272.) When these side-by-side negatives were printed and mounted on a card for use in a stereopticon viewer, they created the illusion of a three-dimensional image (similar to Viewmaster™ images popular in the 1950s-60s).

In this book, the term "stereoview" refers to the actual card produced by Illingworth, with two nearly identical images. When an image has been printed from only one side of the stereograph negative, we call it a "photograph" or a "photo." The word "view" may apply to either a single photo or a stereoview, or to the scene photographed.

For each pair of photos on the following pages, I have noted briefly what we've learned from studying the 1874 photos, and how that may relate to the modern view. In some cases the 1874 photo illuminates an event or description in the trail guide, or vice versa. Cross-referenced page numbers allow you to read more about these instances if you wish. The specific date of most of Illingworth's photos can be determined by careful reading of Expedition documents. This date is noted beneath each photo along with the title and series number (when known) as published by the photographer following the Expedition.

The direction of view has been provided for each photo pair, below the lower left corner of the modern version. Below the lower right corner you will see a Photo Location reference to a page number in the trail guide. There you will find a symbol marking the photo site on a topographic map. If it is on public land, you will also find GPS coordinates for the site and sometimes specific directions leading you there. GPS coordinates are not supplied for sites on private land. We ask you to respect the landowner's rights; do not visit these sites without their explicit permission.

If you find your way to an 1874 photo site, please tread lightly; you are truly "standing in history" there. Enjoy the experience, and try to leave absolutely no trace of your visit. Remember that picking up rocks, breaking branches, or even moving dead wood changes the visual environment and interferes with future research—not to mention the enjoyment of those who will follow you in decades, and even centuries, to come.

— Paul Horsted

Below: Paul Horsted makes an exposure at Illingworth's photo site on the peak of "Beaver Mount" (pages 216-217). **Preceding pages:** Illingworth made this panoramic photograph and three other views from a rock outcropping above the Permanent Camp (see others, pages 248-253).

©BILL GOEHRING

DEVEREAUX LIBRARY ARCHIVES

No. 807, View from our first camp in the Hills, looking north

July 20, 1874

The location of this photo site eluded current and past researchers for many years. One clue we have when seeking these sites is the numbering system used by W.H. Illingworth on many of his stereoviews, which generally places the photos in the order they were taken. In this case, the photo's title and its number implied that it was taken well up in the Black Hills, presumably after number 806,

a known location along the Expedition's route (page 170). Here, however, the photographer changed the order for some reason, as we know he took this photograph three days and many miles before the next published view, number 805.

Illingworth was also mistaken about the direction of this view, which is actually looking east.

Camera direction: **East**   Photo location: **Point C, Page 19**

During research on the Expedition camp near Alladin, Wyo., a local
landowner showed the authors the exact location of this site (see page
19 for details), one of many times we were assisted by helpful residents of
the region while working on this project. The distinctive rock in the foreground
was a key element in determining the precise photo site. Illingworth often composed his stereoviews with such a rock or other object in the foreground; this
technique enhances the three-dimensional effect when viewing the scene in
stereo, in addition to giving us a valuable reference point when trying to locate
the 1874 photo point. In this case, with extensive growth of trees, this reference was essential.

View from our first camp in the Hills, looking north   165

No. 805, Inyan Kara – altitude 6600 feet

July 23, 1874

We can date this photo to July 23, 1874, the only time the Expedition's photographer would have seen a sunrise at the camp near Inyan Kara Mountain. The Expedition arrived here July 22, but left again before daybreak on July 24. Illingworth's shadow, and that of his tripod and camera, are visible in the foreground. The photographer changed lenses and also took a close-up view of the mountain from the same position (see next photo spread). The actual elevation of the mountain is now established at 6368 feet.

Camera direction: **Southwest**

Photo location: **Point I, Page 26**

B y scouting the location in advance, we were able to replicate the photograph on July 23, 2000, at 7:26 a.m. The foreground ridge has eroded, and Ponderosa pine trees have spread across the mountain and into the valley below.

No. 805. Inyan Kara—Altitude 6600 feet.

No. 805, Inyan Kara – altitude 6600 feet

July 23, 1874

This view and the previous wide-angle view of Inyan Kara were both published by Illingworth on similar card stock, with the same series number (the titles vary; on the back of the card the title says 6000 feet rather than 6600 as shown here). He took this photo from the same position, apparently changing lenses to obtain a closer view of the mountain. As with several of Illingworth's Black Hills views shown in this book, we reproduce here the stereoview in the format published and sold by the photographer after he returned to his St. Paul studio.[1] If you have a stereoviewer, you can appreciate these views in their three-dimensional form. If you need a stereoviewer and cannot locate one, check our web site, www.custertrail.com.

Camera direction: **Southwest**

Photo location: **Point I, Page 26**

A fascinating example of the longevity of dead wood can be seen at this photo site. At lower left, an enlargement from Illingworth's photograph shows the roots of a tree which had tipped over perhaps decades before the photographer arrived. The same roots are visible in the current scene (photographed separately with a telephoto lens, lower right). Several pieces of dead wood seen in the 1874 photographs can still be found at the photo site today.

No. 806, Floral Valley

July 24, 1874

Now located on private land, this site shows the famous valley where Custer's soldiers picked the flowers which grew with "such beauty, such variety, such profusion!" (pages 34-37). This green and fertile valley was a welcome change from the hot, dry plains the Expedition had traveled in the weeks before arriving in the Black Hills.

A few faint wagon tracks are visible in this view, possibly left by Illingworth's dark wagon or from lead vehicles in the wagon train, which was soon to pass through the valley.

Camera direction: **Southeast**

Photo location: **Point D, Page 34**

The foreground of this location seems to have eroded and is much steeper than it appears. Stumps remain where trees have been logged in the past, but young pines are growing rapidly in their place. "Floral Valley" is still a green and inviting area.

No. 808, Castle Creek Valley, near the divide

July 26, 1874

This view and others that follow indicate that Illingworth was ahead of the wagon train, apparently traveling with Custer's advance party just behind the Indian scouts. Several men on horseback are visible at center right, but the wagons would have been behind the camera, possibly several miles back down the trail. The Expedition is about to proceed up the valley into the distance; the next photo site is located to the left of the rock outcropping just visible at upper left.

Camera direction: **Southeast**

Photo location: **Point E, Page 48**

Because of man-made changes here, this was a difficult photo location to match with a modern photo. A road (FS 110) has been cut through the slope where the explorers paused in 1874, leaving a very steep embankment where Illingworth once placed his camera.

Castle Creek Valley, near the divide

No. 809, Wagon train passing through Castle Creek Valley

July 26, 1874

In one of the most famous views Illingworth made during his career, the Expedition's wagons (coming toward the camera) stand in a line, backed up in Castle Creek Valley. The wagons are nearly stationary due to a delay of several hours as a bridge was built in the valley off camera to the left (details in trail guide, pages 48-49). The delay gives Illingworth time to take this view and the next. Illingworth's dark wagon can be seen parked alone just to the right of the train; we believe he used a horse or mule to haul his equipment to this location, as he must have done for other locations where a wagon could not be driven.

Careful study of Illingworth's photograph reveals that part of his developing tent is visible in the upper left part of this scene. A dark cloth lies across what appears to be a folding white canvas box. This portable darkroom would have been essential when the dark wagon was not parked nearby to prepare and then develop his "wet plate" negatives at each location photographed.[2]

Camera direction: **Northwest**

The current scene reveals a fascinating example of dead trees or "snags," which have been standing since 1874 or longer. Note the several burned stumps from 1874 which can still be seen in the present view. The small photo at left shows how the modern view looked in July of 2000, completely blocked by tree growth; later that summer the U.S. Forest Service, in consultation with the authors, trimmed back some of the growth so that the middle and background could be photographed and studied. The ancient stumps were carefully avoided during this process.

Wagon train passing through Castle Creek Valley

No. 810, Castle Creek Valley, looking east

July 26, 1874

Illingworth moved a few hundred yards south along the ridge from his previous location and took this view of the Castle Creek Valley, apparently before the main wagon train had proceeded this far (or it would be seen in the photograph). Tracks visible on the valley floor may be those of advance wagons or Custer's "ambulance" which was often ahead of the train. The tracks could also be from travois, the long poles dragged behind a horse which were used by Indians to transport their belongings. The Expedition had been following Indian trails here and a Sioux village would be discovered several miles down the valley on the day this photo was taken (Chapter 4).

Camera direction: **Southeast**

Photo location: **Point G, Page 48**

The current scene shows a tree-choked view (similar to the one which existed at the previous location before some trees were removed). This was one of the most difficult photos to match. The rock outcrops seen in the middle distance of the 1874 view are still there, but they are hidden by trees. The foreground has apparently eroded a great deal. We chose an overcast day to shoot the photo in an effort to show as much under the tree canopy as possible.

Castle Creek Valley, looking east

No. 811, Lime Stone Peak and Castle Creek Valley

July 26, 1874

The hill Illingworth called Lime Stone Peak towers above the valley where the photographer was apparently set up and ready to work as the first wagons rolled into this campsite just above the present town of Deerfield. He was to take seven photographs of or near this camp over the next day or two.[3]

Camera direction: **Northwest**

Photo location: **Point K, Page 53**

The tracks at right, where a wagon once passed, are from a truck which was spraying weeds on this Forest Service property the day before the matching photo was taken. The cliffs of "Lime Stone Peak" are now covered with a thick growth of pine trees.

No. 812, Sioux Camp in Castle Creek Valley

July 27, 1874

We assume Illingworth made this photo, and the following views, a day after the previous photo, which had been taken in late afternoon. From a grassy hill northwest of camp, he created this excellent view of the Expedition camp, clearly showing tents all set up and wagons parked. Interestingly, he scratched the title "Buffalo Mount" on the original glass plate negative of this photo, but when it was published as a stereoview, the title became "Sioux Camp," possibly in reference to tipi poles and still-smoldering fires left by recent Indian visitors to this valley.

Camera direction: **Southeast**   Photo location: **Point L, Page 55**

I n the current scene, with more than 100 years of fire suppression, pine trees
have sprouted and matured on the formerly open valley and hill. The little town of Deerfield is just visible at the end of the valley.

DEVEREAUX LIBRARY ARCHIVES

Untitled

July 27, 1874

As far as we have been able to determine, this view was not published as part of Illingworth's set, thus no title or number is known. However, stereoviews of the photographer's Black Hills work are scarce, and it is possible he printed this view under one of the other titles around this camp, such as "Lime Stone Peak in Castle Creek Valley." The location is a few dozen yards from the previous photo site, looking north away from camp.

Camera direction: **North**

Photo location: **Point M, Page 55**

Unlike many of Illingworth's other views, this image was not framed with a large boulder or other object, which makes replicating it in a modern photo difficult. The alignment of foreground and background hills appears to be a close match here, but a convenient "window" in the trees was selected to allow a view of the prominent rock outcropping.

No. 813, Camp in Castle Creek Valley

July 27, 1874

Setting up his equipment on another high hill, Illingworth made this view and the next from within a few feet of each other, overlooking the camp where the Expedition stopped for an extra day. The layover gave the soldiers an opportunity to do laundry, and some of their clothing can be seen laid out to dry on the bushes at lower left.

Camera direction: **West**

Photo location: **Point N, Page 55**

Tracks from weed sprayers crisscross the pasture where Custer's camp once stood. This valley is now U.S. Forest Service property, and is open to the public for hiking, fly fishing and other activities.

No. 814, Headquarters in Castle Creek Valley

July 27, 1874

Composing another view of camp, Illingworth turned his camera to the left from the previous photo. (He may have just turned it on the tripod, or possibly moved a few feet to avoid trees.) "Headquarters," Custer's tent, is in the line of tents at upper right, behind a tipi framework apparently left by Indians who were in the area earlier. (See page 51 for an enlarged view of this feature.) Illingworth's dark wagon is also visible, behind the left end of the center row of tents. Other wagons are parked in rows in the foreground.

Camera direction: **Southwest**

Photo location: **Point N, Page 55**

Ⅰn the current view, trees have grown from the cliffs at the top of the photo, and have crept down into the valley as well. Stands of aspen visible in 1874 have now been succeeded by a pine and spruce forest.

DEVEREAUX LIBRARY ARCHIVES

Lime Stone Peak in Castle Creek Valley

July 27, 1874

The titles and numbering system Illingworth used on his published stereoviews contain several irregularities, as has been noted. Early versions of
his stereoviews have a number and a title, while what seem to be later versions contain only a title, possibly so he could use the same card stock for
different views of an area. The authors have seen an example of the above scene
numbered as 816, but because Illingworth would have passed this location
at least once or twice between earlier locations, we have placed it here in the
sequence. This view shows the same peak as on page 182.

Camera direction: **North**

Photo location: **Point O, Page 55**

The slope of the hillside, in alignment with the background peaks and hills, indicates this view is within a few feet of Illingworth's original camera location.

Lime Stone Peak in Castle Creek Valley

No. 816, Lime Stone Peak and Castle Creek Valley

July 26 or 27, 1874

Moving to a position very close to where No. 811 was taken as the wagons rolled in, Illingworth either made this view after camp had been set up on July 26, or returned to this location about the same time the following day. Both views appear to be late-afternoon photographs.

Camera direction: **Northwest**

Photo location: **Point P, Page 55**

The succession of the forest can plainly be seen here; aspen spread out in an open area (in 1874 and the present), and are gradually crowded out by pine and spruce.

No. 817, Elk Horn Prairie

July 28, 1874

The Expedition moved north from its Castle Creek Valley camp, apparently led here by Sioux Chief One Stab, whom Custer had surprised and captured the day before (Chapter 4). The Expedition crossed what is now known as Reynold's Prairie, coming to a pile of elk horns stacked by earlier Indian visitors at the high point of the prairie. Then, realizing they were going the wrong way, the Expedition returned to the Castle Creek Valley, camping just a short distance below their prior camp, where Deerfield Lake now lies. Note what appears to be a sego lily or a prairie rose growing at the bottom center of the photo. Both wildflowers are still found in this area.

Camera direction: **Northwest**   Photo location: **Point C, Page 60**

In the modern view, a deer is just visible passing along the tree line as this exposure was taken. The exact site of the elk horn pile (of which no visible trace remains) is difficult to determine, as background clues are now obscured by trees, but the authors believe this location is within 50 feet of the camera's placement in 1874. This site is now private property.[4]

No. 818, Gorge near Elk Horn Prairie

July 28, 1874

As the title states, Illingworth took this photo of a gorge somewhere near Elk Horn Prairie, and, it could be guessed, near his previous photo site. A horse, likely Illingworth's, is tied to a tree at right in this nondescript Black Hills valley.

This scene has been difficult to pinpoint in the modern time; unlike many of the other views, it contains no foreground or background features such as rocks or other landmarks which would help identify a certain location.

Camera direction: **East**

Photo location: **Point D, Page 62**

The photo above shows a valley just a few hundred yards below Illingworth's previous photo site. This view is similar to the one shown in the 1874 photo, but is by no means an exact match. Although it is not obvious due to brush and tree growth, this valley has been reshaped by extensive mining activity along its course. Because of this change (and because Illingworth's photo looks like almost any Black Hills valley), we could be standing on the exact site and not be able to prove it with a new photograph.

It is also possible that Illingworth's gorge is one of the valleys now flooded by Deerfield Lake (formed when a dam was built in the 1930s), which of course we have not been able to explore for possible photo sites. The Expedition camped in the valley where the lake now lies following their visit to Elk Horn Prairie, so Illingworth could have had time to make a photograph there.

DEVEREAUX LIBRARY ARCHIVES

No. 819, Harney's Peak at 10 miles distance, altitude 9200 feet

July 30, 1874

After a couple of rough days of travel, having come miles from their last camp, the Expedition arrived within view of Harney Peak enroute to the present town site of Custer. Illingworth made this view of the mountain top, just barely visible over the distant range of hills. One version of the title for this view says "9400 feet." The actual height of Harney Peak has now been determined to be 7,242 feet.

Camera direction: **Northeast**

Photo location: **Point A, Page 74**

As with other photos that have no obvious foreground clues, the exact location of this scene cannot be absolutely determined. Based on the background, and the known route of the Expedition, we believe this view is within a quarter mile of the 1874 camera position. This "window" in the thick tree growth along this ridge was the only location we found where a similar view could even be made.

The triangular slab of granite in the distance is just above the present Highway 16/385, about half a mile north of Crazy Horse Memorial, which would be visible just to the right of the scene shown here.

Harney's Peak at 10 miles distance, altitude 9200 feet

No. 820, Pulpit Knob, altitude 8700 feet

July 30, 1874

This site, and the next four, are all located in an area about six miles north of the town of Custer. To take these photos, Illingworth departed from the wagon train's known route by several miles. We believe that he and others, including N.H. Winchell, the Expedition geologist, were drawn by the large rock formations they could see in the distance, and moved toward them as the Expedition rolled toward French Creek (Chapter 7). However, since Illingworth's photo numbering is not always in order, it's also possible that this photograph and those following were taken a day or two later, after the Expedition had set up camp and was making forays into the surrounding territory.[5]

The altitude in Illingworth's title is about 2000 feet too high for this rock formation.

Camera direction: **East**

Photo location: **Point B, Page 74**

In contrast to 1874 images of mule-drawn wagons and explorers on horse-back, in this modern view a sight-seeing helicopter prepares to land at its base and motorcycles roar down Highway 16/385, which cuts across the background. A closed private road crosses the foreground. The actual photo site is on U.S. Forest Service land, but you must have permission to cross the private property between it and the highway, or find another route around on public land. However, many features of the 1874 photo can be seen without leaving the highway.

Pulpit Knob, altitude 8700 feet

No. 821, Pulpit Knob, altitude 8700 feet

July 30, 1874

Setting up his tripod and camera on what seems to have been a barren hill-top at the time, Illingworth made this view (titled the same as his previ-ous one) and the next two photos from almost exactly the same spot, by turn-ing his camera, and possibly moving it a couple of feet, from the southeast to the north. These locations are on private land, but the land forms shown in 1874 can be seen from nearby Highway 385, including "Pulpit Knob."

Camera direction: **Southeast**

Photo location: **Point C, Page 74**

©PAUL HORSTED

This was a difficult site to "see" at first, even when we were looking right at it. Illingworth often used a wide-angle lens, and here that made foreground rocks appear larger than they really are. We walked past this site several times before identifying it, in part because of a screen of trees which now obscures distant reference points.

No. 822, Gold Quartz Mountain, altitude 3600 feet

July 30, 1874

B y turning his camera from the previous view, Illingworth was able to frame
this shot through a "V" of foreground rocks. We don't know how the elevation for "Gold Quartz Mountain" was determined in 1874; it is adjacent to
"Pulpit Knob," so it is possible the number shown is a typographical error.
The elevation of this area is around 6600 feet.

Camera direction: **Northeast**

Photo location: **Point C, Page 74**

As with the previous photo site, trees now block the formerly open view of a nearby mountainside. The foreground rocks, too, are at first difficult to identify as the ones in Illingworth's photo. This site, like the ones before and after, is on private property.

No. 823, Turkey Rock

July 30, 1874

This unusual rock formation, sticking up at the end of what was once a barren ridge, must have drawn Illingworth's attention immediately and could be the reason he set up at this location in the first place. As mentioned, he took this and the previous two views from nearly the same tripod location by merely swinging his camera around or moving it slightly, a labor- and time-saving technique he used several times during the Expedition.

No glass plate negative is known to exist of this scene, but one print, which is probably unique, was found in the Minnesota Historical Society archives. Stereoviews of this image also survive.

Camera direction: **North**

Photo location: **Point C, Page 74**

A s in the other modern photos taken here, the hillside behind Turkey Rock is now obscured by a tall stand of Ponderosa pine. Foreground rocks remain in remarkably similar positions, but they are gradually being buried by a rain of pine needles from the trees overhead.

No. 824, Illingworth Valley, near Harney's Peak

July 30, 1874

Perhaps looking for a measure of immortality, Illingworth named this view after himself. The photo location had never been documented previously; as a fairly average view that could be of just about any Black Hills area, it didn't offer many landscape clues to its location.

By obtaining a much darker than normal print, the authors were able to bring out the distant mountains shown in the computer-enhanced view reproduced here. The distinctive mountain at center was recognized as one you can see as you approach Hill City from the south. By backtracking from there, the authors eventually were able to pinpoint the photo location on a mountain top not far from the previous photo sites.

Camera direction: **North**

Photo location: **Point D, Page 74**

The hillside where Illingworth placed his tripod appears to have been obliterated by a large mine that is now abandoned. We estimate the modern photo was taken within 50 yards of the 1874 site. Highway 16/385 is just visible at center left, passing through "Illingworth Valley." We had literally been driving through this scene for months before we found where the camera stood.

This location is on U.S. Forest Service land, a steep hike up from Highway 16/385 or the nearby Mickelson Trail.

(Untitled) "Drinking Party"

July 31, 1874

This fascinating photograph documents a champagne party held by Lt. Col. Joseph Tilford on July 31. Custer had taken a detachment and left early in the day to climb to the top of Harney Peak. Due to several delays, he did not return until 1 a.m. the morning of Aug. 1. Back in camp, Expedition accounts tell us of a champagne supper beneath "a large tarpaulin stretched under the pine trees" (see page 83 in the trail guide). Quite recognizable at this party are Lt. Col. Fred Grant, son of then-President Ulysses Grant, at right, and Col. Frederick Benteen, fourth from right. Others present at this party, according to Expedition accounts, included Capt. Owen Hale, Lt. Benjamin Hodgson, Capt. Thomas McDougall, and Lt. Frank Gibson. Although stereoview examples of this photo are known to exist, Illingworth did not make it part of his Black Hills stereograph set.[6]

The Illingworth Photographs

Camera direction: **Southeast**

Photo location: **Point L, Page 83**

The modern location of this photo site is based on several thin but supporting threads of evidence. From diary accounts, we believe the 1874 photo was taken July 31, and from Col. Ludlow's map we know the Expedition was camped on that date at the junction of French and Laughing Water Creeks, on the present townsite of Custer. A search for rocks like those in the foreground was inconclusive, but there is a ridge of granite with similar characteristics that meets the north end of 8th St. Using a computer to sharpen and darken the background of the 1874 photo (normally it is much lighter) allowed us to see a flat, gently sloping hill in the distance. If you stand at the corner of 8th and Montgomery Streets in Custer and look to the east and southeast, you can see such a hill. Try to imagine this view without all the trees and houses which now fill the valley. Laughing Water Creek is just half a block away here, running beneath the street at center left, and the height above what would have been an open field is similar to that shown in the 1874 photo. Montgomery Street, however, has cut through the ridge which used to stretch down into the field, and it is this cut which we believe was once the site of a champagne party during the Expedition.

No. 825, The Granite Range from Turkey Rock

Aug. 1-5, 1874

The title of this view is initially confusing; it turns out the location is several miles from Turkey Rock, and Illingworth was apparently referring to a granite range that runs to this area from Turkey Rock, a landscape feature not apparent in the present day.

This view and the next three were taken within a short distance of each other, near the summit of a prominent hill located in what is now the Norbeck Wildlife Preserve of the Black Hills National Forest, an area closed to vehicles but open to hiking. Valleys below this hill run down to the Expedition's Permanent Camp, and provided reasonably easy access, probably by wagon and on horseback, for Illingworth and his equipment. There's not enough information to precisely date all photos taken during this period, but all views in the range of Nos. 825-846 would probably have been made between Aug. 1-5, 1874.

Camera direction: **Northwest**

Photo location: **Point I, Page 81**

Comparing this view with the 1874 scene dramatically shows how pine trees can grow on a base of what appears to be solid rock, when fire has been suppressed for more than 100 years.

Great care was taken to align foreground rocks to match the 1874 photo. Notice the "thumb" at lower left; the tip of this thumb, apparently missing in the modern view, is actually another rock twenty feet back in the shadows.

The Granite Range from Turkey Rock   211

No. 826, Organ Pipe Range

Aug. 1-5, 1874

This site is just a few feet above the previous one; it provides a stunning view of the "Organ Pipe Range," now known as the Needles of Custer State Park.

Camera direction: **North**   Photo location: **Point I, Page 81**

Foreground rocks provide reference points for replicating the view from 1874, clearly indicating the location of Illingworth's tripod and camera. This photo site, like the one before and the two after it, is about 4 miles northeast of the town of Custer.

827   Organ Pipes and Harney's Peak.

No. 827, Organ Pipes and Harney's Peak

Aug. 1-5, 1874

This image apparently survives only as a stereoview published by the photographer; no glass plate negative is known to exist. Here, Illingworth
clearly just turned his camera to the right from the previous photo to capture
a view of the "Organ Pipes," which are now called the Cathedral Spires. Illingworth may have believed he was looking at Harney Peak here, but the mountain is in fact hidden behind the distant rock formations.

Camera direction: **Northeast**

Photo location: **Point I, Page 81**

The Needles Highway of Custer State Park runs near the top of the distant ridge nearly 2 miles away; one of the parking areas there is just visible at top center. Much of the area shown is in the Norbeck Wildlife Preserve of the Black Hills National Forest, and is open to the public, though mostly closed to vehicles.

As with all the photo sites and trail locations shown in this book, if you visit this historic site, please leave it exactly as you found it. Don't move any rocks, carve into wood, break off branches, or throw anything over the cliff. These sites provide a link to our past, and by treading lightly you can help preserve them for the future as well.

No. 828, From top of Beaver Mount over Agnes Park

Aug. 1-5 1874

That Illingworth had little fear of heights can be seen by climbing to this platform of rock at the very summit of this small mountain, a few yards above the site where he took the three preceding views.

Camera direction: **Southwest**

Photo location: **Point J, Page 81**

The large foreground rock seen in the 1874 view has fallen off the cliff and now lies in the woods below. At top and upper right, you can see valleys which lie just east of the town of Custer; the city itself is hidden behind the mountain at upper right. This mountain appears in several of Illingworth's other views taken later from the other side; see pages 220, 222 and 230.

If you climb to this area, use extreme caution. It would be easy to fall at several points along the way, and the rocks are not entirely stable.

No. 829, Flora Park

Aug. 1-5, 1874

Moving down to lower elevations, Illingworth composed this shot two miles up a valley from the Permanent Camp. "Flora" was the name of Illingworth's wife at the time of the Expedition, and we can guess this view was named for her.

Camera direction: **Southeast**

Photo location: **Point M, Page 92**

The foreground rocks visible in Illingworth's photograph can still be seen,
now shaded by tall pine trees and covered with pine needles. Core samples taken from these mature trees by the U.S. Forest Service indicate that none
are old enough to have grown from the sapling visible in the center of the 1874
photo.

This view and the next one are just inside Forest Service property adjacent to private land.

No. 830, Head of Golden Valley

Aug. 1-5, 1874

Moving his camera a few yards and turning it in the other direction, Illingworth captured this view of a valley with a mountain at its head; this mountain is called "Grant's Peak" in the next photo in the series, and can be seen from the other side in the view on page 216.

Camera direction: **Northwest**

Photo location: **Point N, Page 92**

Although the photo site is on U.S. Forest Service land, the valley below, where a horse stands beyond the fence, is on private property. The mountain is there, hidden now by mature pine trees; the point of rock at lower left confirms we are standing within inches of Illingworth's camera location (see page 227 for an alternate view of the mountain in the present day).

DEVEREAUX LIBRARY ARCHIVES

No. 831, Grant's Peak

Aug. 1-5, 1874

This granite outcropping was apparently named after then-President Ulysses Grant, or possibly after his son Fred, who was on the Expedition. This is the same mountain shown in the previous view, from another location a few hundred yards away. Note the interesting mature trees, which have apparently been victims of intense fire that burned below as well as in the crowns. A young stand of "dog hair" pine is growing up from beneath.

Camera direction: **North**

Photo location: **Point L, Page 92**

Careful study of the land form alignments on the distant mountain led us to this location that is believed to be within yards of Illingworth's photo site. The mountain is hidden by forest here, but the short granite ridge in the middle distance, more visible in this photo than in Illingworth's view, points to this area. Someday, when fire or logging thins this area, it will be possible to designate a more precise location.

An alternate view of the hidden mountain, now known locally as Castle Peak or Courthouse Rock, can be seen on page 227.

No. 832, Sunshine and Shadow Mount

Aug. 1-5, 1874

Three soldiers (one nearly hidden in the trees at left) pose in this unusual scene. The one at right may be Lt. Col. Fred Grant. (Compare this view to the "Drinking Party" on page 208 and see if you agree.) The date of this photo is open to question; Illingworth's number places it among many photos we know were taken Aug. 1-5, but it may have been taken as early as July 30, when some members of the Expedition, including the photographer, were in this valley north of Custer as the explorers arrived in the area.

Camera direction: **Northeast**

Photo location: **Point H, Page 76**

©PAUL HORSTED

Without good foreground references, specifying the location of this photo site is not easy. But careful alignment with the angle of rocks in the mountainous background indicates it is this area, just off the Mickelson Trail (a former railroad line) north of Custer. Mining and the building of the railroad nearby have re-arranged some of the hillside shown here.

No. 833, Godfrey Peak

Aug. 1-5, 1874

Illingworth made this interesting and elusive view of a solitary granite peak (probably named for Lt. Edward Godfrey of the Expedition), located at the end of a grassy plain and framed by lower ridges. Where he made the photo is not known for certain at this writing. Its number places it in the middle of a group of 27 images (820 through 846) which were all taken within five miles of Custer, so it seems likely this view is within that radius as well. Many weeks over a period of three years were spent in search of this location, with the results shown on the opposite page. None is a good match for the 1874 view. It's very possible this apparently barren peak is now covered with pine trees, or that this view was taken elsewhere in the Black Hills and inserted in the numbered series here, as we know Illingworth did in at least one other instance (page 164).

The modern photos here show possible candidates for the view of "Godfrey Peak." Our best guess (upper left) is that it shows the Buckhorn Mountain area from the southeast, though not necessarily from the angle shown here. Buckhorn is the most prominent mass of granite near Custer, and it would be surprising if Illingworth did not point his camera at it at some time. Another possibility is a granite dome now known locally as Castle Peak or Courthouse Rock (upper right, seen from the south). This is the same rock which Illingworth photographed as

"Grant's Peak" from four locations, so unless he was confused about the area's geography, or didn't think anyone would notice, this mountain could perhaps be eliminated. A third possibility is Crazy Horse Memorial (bottom, seen from the southwest along Hwy. 16/385), located only two miles north of the preceding numbered site (No. 832) and visible from nearby. Illingworth could have been in the area and turned his camera toward the mountain from some location perhaps now overgrown with trees.[7]

No. 834, Genevieve Park

Aug. 1-5, 1874

Following his pattern of taking two or more photos in a small area, Illingworth set up for this view as well as another one just a few yards away. "Genevieve" was the name of Capt. William Ludlow's wife.

Camera direction: **Northwest**

Photo location: **Point P, Page 92**

Located on private land, the foreground rocks of this photo site are now surrounded by pines that have spread down into the valley. Soil levels, built up by pine needles and other decaying vegetation, are gradually burying the rocks here.

No. 835, Agnes Park

Aug. 1-5, 1874

At this location, Illingworth made not only a stereo photograph (lower left), but also a panoramic view (top) using the entire plate, which measured 4.5 x 8 inches. This photograph, taken from a slightly different position, is reproduced using a unique and recently discovered print made from the original glass plate negative in the 1920s. This is the first time it has been published in nearly 75 years. The panorama shows "Grant's Peak," seen on page 222, from another angle, as well as the Harney Peak range in the distance. The glass plate original has apparently disappeared, but approximately 70 other Illingworth negatives survive at the South Dakota State Historical Society in Pierre.

Another remarkable feature of this view is the soldier crouching in the shadows at lower right holding a rifle. (He is seen in an enhanced enlargement below the original.) The soldier has not been identified, and we can only guess at Illingworth's reasons for posing him there.[8]

Camera direction: **North**

Photo location: **Point O, Page 92**

Now on private land, the photo site is surrounded by trees, and the foreground rocks are slowly disappearing beneath a mantle of pine needles. Illingworth appears to be following a pattern of naming the pastures in this area after women. "Agnes Park" was named after Agnes Bates, a friend of Gen. Custer's wife, Libbie, according to Expedition accounts.

836 Golden Valley Gulch.

No. 836, Golden Valley Gulch

Aug. 1-5, 1874

Working closer to camp, Illingworth was apparently documenting the area where gold was first found during the Expedition, along a stretch of French Creek near where it is joined by Willow Creek in this valley.

Camera direction: **West**

Photo location: **Point J, Page 92**

©PAUL HORSTED

Homes now sit along the edges of "Golden Valley Gulch," and America Center Road cuts across the scene. Note that Buckhorn Mountain is visible in the distance in this photo, but not in Illingworth's. His wet plate process did not penetrate haze very well, and distant details were often lost, as seen here.

A forest fire in the early 1960s has left barren hill tops in the middle distance, an unusual area where fewer trees are seen now than in the 1874 photograph.

No. 837. Golden Park, where Gold was first found.

No. 837, Golden Park, where Gold was first found

Aug. 1-5, 1874

Just a few hundred feet from the previous site, Illingworth made this image, shown as the stereoview he later published. Four men are visible in the distance near French Creek, very close to the site where gold was discovered about three miles east of the present town of Custer. It is not known who they are, but perhaps they include Horatio N. Ross and William T. McKay, the Expedition miners credited with discovering gold here.

   The men are more visible in the enhanced enlargements at right; details are limited by the distance from the camera.

Camera direction: **Northwest**

Photo location: **Point K, Page 92**

The original photo site has been eradicated by the construction of Highway 16A east of Custer. This photo was taken from approximately the same height, just above the highway, and is probably within a few feet of Illing-worth's location, based on careful comparison of the rock formations on Calamity Peak across the valley. This small mountain was the scene of the next three photographs in Illingworth's series.

Golden Park, where Gold was first found

No. 838, Looking west from Granite Knob

Aug. 1-5, 1874

As he did earlier in his series, Illingworth climbed a mountain (the "Granite Knob") to take three photographs, of which this is the first. "Granite Knob" was the name given by the Custer Expedition to the mountain now known as Calamity Peak. Here, Illingworth set up near two dead trees at right. (Note the second tree trunk to the right of the prominent dead tree.)

Camera direction: **West**

Photo location: **Point D, Page 86**

In the modern view, one of the dead trees is still standing, although it now leans against a cliff that drops into a little canyon below. The other tree has fallen but is still lying there, out of sight.

Magnification of the photos reveals several larger trees in the background, and one small tree at extreme upper right, which appear to be the same ones in both photos. As unlikely as this may seem, it is supported by the next photo site.

Looking west from Granite Knob

No. 839, Looking east from Granite Knob

Aug. 1-5, 1874

Illingworth climbed higher to a reach a view of the Permanent Camp, which is spread across the valley in the distance. A pine tree frames the scene at right in this view which is really looking southeast.

Camera direction: **Southeast**

Photo location: **Point E, Page 86**

Most interesting in the modern view is the same tree from the 1874 photograph visible at right. A core sample taken by the U.S. Forest Service verified that this tree is more than 250 years old, despite its relatively small diameter. A log is also visible in both photos lying against the granite at center left. Careful comparison of the backgrounds shows that the Expedition's wagon road running along the line of tents is in the same position as the current road, which was the main route through the area before Highway 16A was built. Stockade Lake, a man-made body of water created in the late 1930s, is now visible at upper left in the modern photo.

Looking east from Granite Knob

No. 840, Spectre Canon

Aug. 1-5, 1874

Moving to a lower position on "Granite Knob" a few dozen yards away from the previous photo site, Illingworth set up this shot framed by a spectre-like rock formation, upper left, that looms over Illingworth's "canon" or canyon.

Camera direction: **Southeast**

Photo location: **Point F, Page 86**

Although it is not apparent from the 1874 photograph, we found that Illingworth stood on a narrow fin of rock, with a cliff about 20 feet high on either side. (See author biography on back cover flap for another view of this site.) The tree visible at center left is not the same tree as in 1874, since it is not visible in a 1972 photograph of the area.[9] However, the small tree at center right, clearly visible in the middle distance in the 1874 photo and just barely visible in the modern scene, is apparently the same tree.

Visiting the three photo locations on Calamity Peak requires climbing to heights; use caution and be prepared if you venture into this isolated and rugged Forest Service area. The easiest approaches to the mountain require crossing private property; please obtain permission from landowners before doing so.

No. 841, The Organ Pipes & Golden Valley

Aug. 1-5, 1874

Illingworth composed another view of the "Organ Pipes," now known as the Cathedral Spires, which lay to the north of the Permanent Camp. This Golden Valley is different than the Golden Valley he photographed earlier, though the two could be said to connect. The valley floor shows wagon tracks, possibly made by Illingworth's dark wagon as he took photos here and in another valley to the east. One track is clearly visible at right and others can be seen along the left side of the valley. The main wagon train did not pass here.

Camera direction: **North**

Photo location: **Point Q, Page 92**

A considerable amount of searching on foot was required before this site, partially hidden by trees, was found on private property. The location is relatively isolated, alone in this valley about half a mile and over a ridge from the next site in Illingworth's series.

No. 842, Turret Rock

Aug. 1-5, 1874

One of Illingworth's least intriguing views, this photo depicts a small rock outcropping north of the Permanent Camp. As far as is known, this view survives in the present day only as part of the stereoview set published by Illingworth. No glass plate negative or regular prints could be found.

W.H. Illingworth: A Biography
by Don Schwarck

During the latter half of the 19th century, a few intrepid photographers ventured into the relatively unknown West to bring back images of mysterious frontier wonders, and sometimes of their fellow explorers. They hauled bulky cameras and equipment on pack mules or in wagons and recorded their images on fragile panes of glass using a combination of volatile chemicals (the "wet plate process"), all of this under unpredictable conditions far removed from their comfortable studios back home. And they had to race the clock, developing their glass plates immediately in light-tight tents or dark wagons. Strength, dogged determination and a working knowledge of chemistry—not to mention an artist's eye and extreme patience—were the hallmarks of these pioneering photographic artists, one of whom was William Henry Illingworth.

He was born in England on September 20, 1842, immigrating to the United States with his family in the late 1840s. They settled first in Philadelphia, then moved west in 1850 to St. Paul, Minnesota. It was his father's desire that young William follow in his footsteps as a clock maker, but by the age of 20 Illingworth had chosen a different course.[1]

During the summer of 1862 Illingworth spent two months learning the basics of photography in Chicago, and went to Philadelphia early the next year for additional training.[2] The St. Paul Pioneer announced his return: "Wm. Illingworth . . . [has] graduated in the profession of photography . . . [and] is prepared to execute pictures in the highest style of art and on the most reasonable terms. . . . [He] has opened one of the best Photographic Galleries in the city, and warrants perfect satisfaction in the execution of his pictures."[3]

William married Catherine Gunnuh on September 26, 1863, and their son, William J., was born a year later. Looking for a better opportunity, or perhaps less competition, Illingworth moved his young family to Red Wing, Minnesota, and opened a studio in 1865.[4] The venture did not last, however, and they were back in St. Paul by the summer of 1866, in time for Illingworth to be enthralled by the excitement surrounding Captain James L. Fisk's immigrant expedition to the newly opened Montana gold fields. Leaving his wife and young son behind, he joined the excursion at its departure point in St. Cloud, Minnesota.

It was here that Illingworth associated himself with George Bill [deBill].[5] Illingworth's interest did not lie in

A Life of Obscurity, a Legacy of Distinction

William Henry Illingworth
1842-1893

gold, but in the recognized commercial prospects of photographing the expedition. A series of scenic western stereopticon cards (stereoviews) could generate a steady income, as the St. Paul Weekly Press predicted: "If Illingworth and Bell [sic] are as successful in getting up their photographic representations as they expect to be on this tour, their pictures will be in large demand, and their labors meet with a handsome reward."[6] The public was eagerly seeking out these stereoviews, which consisted of nearly identical photographs taken by a twin-lens stereo camera, and mounted side by side on a card (see accompanying photographs). In a stereo viewer they produced a three-dimensional effect of depth and realism that captivated the public in an era before motion pictures. The stereoviews from this period are still fascinating to look at today.

The 27 stereoviews produced by Illingworth and Bill over the next two months proved to be among the most important ever taken during the early years of Western expansion.[7] But their value to history did not translate into profits for Illingworth. He reestablished a studio in his father's watch shop at St. Paul, where he and Bill tried to publish the Fisk Expedition views.  They lacked the necessary production and marketing expertise, however, and ultimately sold the negatives to John Carbutt, a successful Chicago publisher of western views. Carbutt credited himself as the photographer, a common if unfair practice of the times whenever negatives changed hands.[8]

Illingworth's wife Catherine died the year after the Fisk Expedition, in 1867, leaving him alone with a three-year-old son. He married a woman named Celisia in 1869, but they suffered repeated domestic problems and were divorced in 1871. He was married a third time the following April, to Flora Leonard. This, too, was an unhappy union, but it would last until she divorced him in 1888.[9]

Illingworth continued to pursue his photography during this difficult period. City directories indicate that he moved his studio at least three times between 1866 and 1874. He also ventured out of St. Paul, spending considerable time (circa 1870-1873) with construction crews building the Northern Pacific Railroad and its various branches. The series was titled "Stereographs of Minnesota & Dakota," and many of the early views show NPRR crews laying track. The series also includes images of steam engines, railroad stations and infant towns along the line in Minnesota.[10] Illingworth also traveled as far as the eastern edge of what would become the state of South Dakota; his photographs of the Big Sioux Falls (circa 1870) are among the earliest views of that landmark.[11]

The Black Hills Expedition

It is not known exactly how or why Illingworth was selected as the photographer for the Black Hills Expedition by Captain William Ludlow, its Chief Engineer. Illingworth's studio was located in downtown St. Paul, as was the U.S. Army's departmental office. His name had also appeared in recent newspaper accounts of a photographic trip he made to England.[12] Illingworth's experience with the Fisk Expedition and his growing reputation as a landscape photographer undoubtedly played a part as well.

In any case, Capt. Ludlow and Illingworth entered into a verbal agreement[13] stipulating that the government would provide the photographer with "a complete apparatus for taking stereoscopic views."[14] The photographer's outfit, in addition to camera, lenses and tripod, consisted of "a light proof tent, several pounds each of collodion, iron sulfate, potassium cyanide, silver nitrate, alcohol, nitric acid, and varnish, a set of developing trays, a set of scales and weights, and a box of glass squares far too fragile for so much wagon transportation."[15] Ludlow also provided Illingworth with an assistant, a horse and forage, and a photographer's dark wagon procured through the Quartermaster's Department—the same wagon used by William Pywell on the Yellowstone Expedition during the summer of 1873. Ludlow placed Illingworth on the muster rolls as a teamster, which enabled him to draw a daily ration and receive $30 a month in wages.[16]

For his part, Illingworth seems to have agreed to deliver six complete sets of printed pictures from the Expedition, which Ludlow was to use to accompany his official reports later that fall.[17] Most important to Illingworth's future

profits, though, was the provision that he would "remain in undisturbed possession of the negatives."[18]

Illingworth's activities are mentioned often by the journalists and others who wrote about the Expedition. (See the trail guide in this book for more examples.) The first impression he made, however, was not with his camera but with his rifle. Writing from the Prospect Valley Camp of July 15, A.B. Donaldson of the *St. Paul Pioneer* said, "Antelopes have been hunted more or less everyday since we started. Mr. Illingworth is entitled to the laurel for his success. He brings in more game than any other man [and] keeps our mess of seven all the time supplied."[19] Fred W. Power,[20] reporting for the *St. Paul Daily Press*, told his readers: "Mr. Illingworth [the] photographist, . . . prov-

ing conclusively that he can use a rifle as good as a camera, . . . has had the good fortune not only to get some good pictures but also to prove himself to be one of the best shots on the expedition, which is considerable to say, as we have several. Gen. Custer, Capt. French, Lieuts. McDougall and Hodgson, are all considered fine marksmen."[21]

While the quality of Illingworth's work was understood and admired, the first of his photographs to be seen outside the Black Hills was of another hunter—Custer himself. The General and several others had killed a grizzly bear while scouting ahead on August 7. By the time the wagon train came up he had the animal draped across a rock outcrop, displayed for the entire regiment to see, and Illingworth was setting up his camera. Custer wrote about the event in a letter to his wife Elizabeth, and included a view that Illingworth apparently printed and mounted in the field. "Our photographer has obtained a complete set of magnificent stereoscopic views of Black Hills scenery," Custer told his wife, "so I will not allude to the beautiful scenery until I can view it with you by aid of the photographs. I send you one of his stereoscopic views, which will show you that at last I have reached the highest round in the hunter's ladder of fame. I have killed my Grizzly after a most exciting hunt and combat. Col. Ludlow [his brevet rank], Bloody Knife and Private Noonan 7th C[avalry] are with me in the group. We constitute the hunting party. Is not the picture superb? The grizzly was eight feet in height. I have his claws."[22]

The letter and photograph went out with other dispatches from Bear Butte, where the command was poised for its march home across the plains. The Expedition reached Fort Abraham Lincoln on August 30, but first paused about 10 miles west, just before crossing the Heart River. "The

---

Opposite page, left: A portrait of W.H. Illingworth. (Paul Horsted Collection)
Right: A typical stereo camera of the 19th century, with two lenses. (Bob Kolbe Collection)
This page, above: The "dark wagon" Illingworth used on the Black Hills Expedition. (Devereaux Library Archives)
Left: The back of a gallery portrait by W.H. Illingworth announces his award for "Best Photographs and Stereoscopic Views" in 1873. (Minnesota Historical Society)

STEREOGRAPHS OF THE BLACK HILLS.
—o—

800　Our first crossing of an Alkali Valley
801　Camp at Hiddenwood creek.
802　Index Butte at Hiddenwood creek.
803　Cannon-Ball River.
804　Ludlow's Cave, 450 feet deep.
805　Inya Kara, altitude 6,000 feet.
806　Floral Valley.
807　View from our first camp in the Hills, looking north.
808　Castle creek Valley near the Divide.
809　Wagon Train passing through Castle creek valley.
810　Castle creek valley, looking east.
811　Limestone Peak and Castle creek valley.
812　Sioux camp in Castle creek valley.
813　Camp in Castle creek valley
814　Headquarters in Castle creek valley
815　Limestone Peak in Castle creek valley.
816　Limestone Peak in Castle creek valley.
817　Elk Horn prairie.
818　Gorge near Elk horn prairie.
819　Harney's Peak at 10 miles distance, altitude 9,400 feet.
820　Pulpit Knob, altitude 8,700 feet.
821　Pulpit Knob altitude 8,700 feet
822　Gold Quartz Mountain, altitude 3,000 feet.
823　Turkey Rock.
824　Illingworth Valley, near Harney's Peak.
825　The Granite Range from Turkey Rock
826　Organ Pipe range.
827　Organ Pipes and Harney's Peak.
828　From top of Beaver Mount over Agnes Park.
829　Floral Park
830　Head of Golden Valley.
831　Grant's Peak, 1,000 feet high.
832　Sunshine and shadow Mount.
833　Godfrey Peak.
834　Genevieve Park.
835　Agnes Park
836　Golden Valley Gulch.
837　Golden Park, where gold was first found.
838　Looking West from Granite Knob.
839　Looking East from Granite Knob.
840　Sweet Cañon.
841　The Organ Pipes and Golden Valley.
842　Turret Rock.
843　Permanent Camp in Agnes Park.
844　Granite Knob and Harney's Peak.
845　Gold Mountain Range and Headquarters.
846　Permanent Camp in Agnes Park.
847　Our first Grizzly, killed by General Custer.
848　Red Sandstone in Elk Creek Valley
849　Top of Custar Peak and Elk Creek Valley.
850　Forsyth's Glen.
851　Bear Butte near Custer Peak.
852　Custer's Expedition.
853　Our Wagon Master.
854　Custer's Expedition.

Comprising some of the most beautiful Scenery in America. The Hills situated as they are in latitude 40 about in rugged grandeur; on the South and East sides the Limestone Walls and a mile Pinnacles rising to the mormons height of 4,865 feet, and enclosing the Hills in such a manner so as to make it almost an impossibility to penetrate the interior with conveyances, there being but two openings on the East side and three on the South. The North may be considered the easiest route and, should it be so thought, you will your way in almost any direction, through the beautiful fertile Valleys and delightful Parks, the latter looking more like being attended and cultured, than a wild and uncivilized region, magnificent trees, rich grass lands, extending for miles.

The Gold was found on the South and north sides, and in the vicinity of "Harney's Peak." The Gold region extends about fifty miles square, amid scenery so hauntingly grand, and for mineral wealth, no Territory can exceed the Hills.

The Views, in all, number 55. None genuine unless bearing my name on each end of the Stereo. Card.

W. H. ILLINGWORTH.

PAUL HORSTED COLLECTION

---

photographer took several negatives of the command and train on a flat, level piece of prairie," Private Ewert wrote in his diary.[23] Shooting from a small rise, Illingworth made one of the most important photos of his career, dramatically capturing the entire regiment as it posed in marching formation.

In all, he had made more than 70 wet plate negatives during the Expedition. Eager to begin printing these plates, Illingworth immediately left Ft. Lincoln for home. The September 3 edition of the *St. Paul Daily Press* trumpeted his return: "Mr. Illingworth has taken no less than sixty different views . . . . Many of them are described as possessed of remarkable beauty. Copies of these will be taken without delay, and there can be no doubt that a large demand will be discovered for them in all portions of the United States."[24] Through an agreement Illingworth had made before the expedition, the publishers Huntington & Winne were advertising and selling complete sets of "Stereographs of the Black Hills" within a week of his return,[25] despite a fire that swept through their gallery on September 9,

destroying all of their equipment and nearly all of their negatives. Fortunately, the Black Hills negatives were not in the publisher's gallery at the time.[26]

Illingworth was less efficient when it came to the six sets of views that Captain Ludlow was expecting for his reports. The engineer made several unsuccessful efforts to obtain copies, and was finally ordered by his commander, General Alfred Terry, to sue the photographer. Ludlow had Illingworth arrested by a U.S. Marshall on November 24 and charged with "embezzling . . . [and] misappropriating and applying to his own use and benefit . . . sixty glass plates of photographic negatives."[27] The Black Hills negatives were confiscated and Illingworth was forced to post a $500 bond for his release.[28]

The case was dismissed four days later when a judge determined that the glass and chemicals used to produce the negatives belonged to Illingworth, and that the government had no claim to them.[29] It was also learned in court that Illingworth had prepared a set of views for each of the Expedition's command officers, effectively completing his obligation.[30]

The most serious blow for Ludlow, however, was finding out that General Custer had been undermining his previous efforts. Ludlow's outrage is evident in a letter he wrote to Custer on November 28, the same day the suit was dismissed: "This case went to trial before the U.S. Commissioner, when to my astonishment the defense glibly showed that Illingworth looked entirely to you as the person with whom his contract was made, that he was only obliged to furnish you with pictures, that you had not stipulated for any copies to be furnished the Govt [Government] and more than all—to clinch his defense that he had showed you my demand for the negatives as being Govt property and that you had entrusted him to pay no attention to it."[31] Ludlow reminded Custer that "the photographer was furnished with the Govt. outfit . . . . which I purchased with Engineer funds. . . . Illingworth therefore went out under his arrangements with me."[32]

The lawsuit and Ludlow's letter suggest a relationship between Illingworth and the General that is not generally known. In fact, Custer had a portrait made in Illingworth's St. Paul studio on November 8, 1874, as he passed through the city on his way to Fort Lincoln—only 16 days before the trial.[33]

Life after the Expedition

Most of Illingworth's 30-year career still lay ahead of him in 1874. He would specialize in regional scenic stereographs, accumulating more than 1,600 negatives.[34] The majority of his views, a series called "Stereographs of Minnesota Scenery," featured landscapes of the rock formations and waterfalls along the St. Croix River and north shore of Lake Superior. St. Paul's wharves and levees also drew Illingworth's attention, as shown by his numerous views of paddlewheel steamers and other traffic on the Mississippi River. His studio portrait work included St. Paul's pioneer citizens in addition to the Sioux and Chippewa Indians who inhabited the area. Although he was a good por-

The Illingworth Photographs

trait artist, the majority of his work during this time was done out-of-doors, and it might be assumed he preferred outdoor subjects over portraiture.

Illingworth's photo wagon must have been a common sight in the streets of St. Paul as he recorded many images of the city's prominent buildings. One stereoview of Ft. Snelling also captured his wagon parked at a ferry landing. Painted on the side of the wagon was:

> W. H. Illingworth, St. Paul, Minn.
> Landscape Photographer
> Buildings Photographed to Order[35]

During the height of his career Illingworth aligned himself with several of the large publishing houses in St. Paul, freeing him from the tedious printing, mounting and trimming of thousands of stereocards. His stereoviews of the era were published and distributed at various times by Flower & Hawkins, Illingworth and McLeish, Burrit and Pease, and by Huntington and Winne. Illingworth, meanwhile, would have more time to pursue the activity he appears to have liked best—creating photographs in the field.

But the popularity of stereo photographs was already beginning to decline, a trend that continued into the 1880s. Illingworth's productivity and his business slowly waned, aggravated by his excessive drinking. After his divorce in 1888, Illingworth was alone, alcoholic and in failing health, and may have sold much of his equipment for living expenses and liquor. He is said to have asked a nearby shopkeeper for a drink on the day before his death, but is also reported to have finished up some darkroom work that day. On March 16, 1893, he placed his favorite hunting rifle to his left temple—possibly the same rifle he had so enjoyed using in the Black Hills—and pulled the trigger.[36]

William Illingworth died as a rather obscure photographer from St. Paul who nevertheless had joined and documented two of the more important expeditions into the American West.

The legacy

A St. Paul journalist, photographer and historian named Edward Bromley had tried to purchase Illingworth's glass negatives as early as 1880. Illingworth had refused, clinging to his best source of continued income. Some years after his death, however, his son sold the entire collection of more than 1,600 negatives to Bromley. In 1919 Bromley offered most of the Black Hills Expedition negatives to the South Dakota State Historical Society for the sum of $60. Short on funds, State Historian Doane Robinson had to wait nearly a year before the money was appropriated, but he completed the transaction, and the negatives have resided in Pierre ever since.[37] The thin glass plates had survived a journey of 880 miles by wagon, riding in the slots of a simple pine box, but that was just the beginning. They continue to survive, after more than a century and a quarter of time and chance.

William Henry Illingworth may have reached his zenith with the Black Hills views. Many of them continue to be

reproduced in books and magazines, particularly No. 809, "Wagon Train passing through Castle Creek Valley"; No. 847, "Our first Grizzly, killed by General Custer"; and Nos. 852 and 854, "Custer's Expedition." Illingworth's life may have ended unhappily, but with his "first photographs of the Black Hills" he left us a priceless legacy.

Don Schwarck is a past editor of the Little Big Horn Associates Newsletter, and a former board member of the LBHA, serving as Chairman in 1996-97. He has collected original stereoviews for nearly 20 years, amassing a collection of more than 200 Illingworth views. He is a commissioner for his local historical society, and works as an Earth Science teacher and track coach in his hometown of South Lyon, Michigan.

Opposite page: The back of an Illingworth *Stereographs of the Black Hills* stereoview lists the title of every view in the 55-card series. Some versions of the stereoviews have only a descriptive paragraph about the Black Hills on the back, while others are blank.

This page, above: Illingworth's stereoview No. 803, "Cannon Ball River," from his *Stereographs of the Black Hills* set. (Minnilusa Pioneer Museum)

Below: Illingworth's view of "Index Butte at Hiddenwood Creek" was taken as the Expedition crossed the plains enroute to the Black Hills. (Devereaux Library Archives)

Above: The glass plate negative of this view is in the archives of the South Dakota State Historical Society and was previously thought to have been taken during the Black Hills Expedition. As this book was going to press, the authors located a stereoview by W.H. Illingworth showing the same location from a slightly different angle, entitled "Dalles of the St. Croix." The St. Croix is a river on the Minnesota-Wisconsin border, and this appears to be another example of one of Illingworth's other negatives being mixed in with the Black Hills set, as was the case with "Fairy Falls" on page 268. (Devereaux Library Archives)

Below: W.H. Illingworth made two views of the Missouri River near Ft. Lincoln, most likely before the Expedition began. After returning from the Black Hills he is known to have hurried home to St. Paul to begin printing his stereoviews. These river views were not published as part of his Black Hills set. (Devereaux Library Archives)

Opposite page: Three of Illingworth's Black Hills photographs were reproduced as engravings in the Sept. 12, 1874, issue of *Harper's Weekly,* a popular newspaper of the time, along with a short article describing the Expedition. (Paul Horsted Collection)

CAMP WHERE GOLD WAS FIRST DISCOVERED—CUSTER GULCH ON THE LEFT.

THE BLACK HILLS EXPEDITION.

No expedition since the war has attracted more attention or excited more interest than the one which left Fort Abraham Lincoln, Dakota, on the 2d of July, to explore the Black Hills. This region of country, lying in the southwestern part of Dakota, and extending some distance into Wyoming, and slightly indenting Montana (as shown in the map printed in a recent number of the *Weekly*), has, until this summer, in its interior been entirely unexplored by the white man. Previous expeditions have skirted the hills, but never penetrated them, and we have been dependent on the reports and traditions of the Indians for the little we have known of them. The hostility of the Indians has defeated any attempts to explore the country by civilian parties.

The present expedition was entirely a military one, and consisted of ten companies of the Seventh cavalry, two companies of infantry, and three pieces of artillery, in all about 700 soldiers, with the addition of a train of 120 wagons, and about as many teamsters, the whole under command of Major-General GEORGE A. CUSTER. Colonel FREDERICK D. GRANT, the President's oldest son, accompanies the expedition as aid to General CUSTER. The scientific corps consists of Colonel WILLIAM LUDLOW, U. S. Engineer Corps; W. H. WOOD, assistant; Professor N. H. WINCHELL, geologist; Professor A. B. DONALDSON, assistant; GEORGE B. GRINNELL, paleontologist; L. H. NORTH, assistant; Dr. J. W. WILLIAMS, chief medical officer, botanist.

The expedition reached the Black Hills about the 20th of July, after a march of eighteen days, mostly over an arid, treeless, desert country. General CUSTER, in spite of the prophecies of his Indian guides, who declared the thing impossible, succeeded in penetrating to the very interior of the hills with his wagon train, and by sending off detachments of cavalry here and

ORGAN-PIPE RANGE.

there, has succeeded in exploring and mapping the hills through their entire length and breadth. The country is found to be of great scenic beauty, as shown by our illustrations on this page, and is luxuriant in vegetation, abundant in game, timber, and good water. Thousands of acres of fertile land invite settlement. The country, however, is a part of the Sioux Reservation, and can not be opened to the whites until the government shall make some satisfactory arrangement with the Indians.

On the 31st of July gold was discovered along the banks of a creek on which the expedition was encamped, the best pans yielding from five to ten cents' worth of gold, equivalent to fifty dollars a day to the man, if the yield should prove as good as promised.

We present a view taken on the spot, showing the camp near which gold was discovered. A portion of Custer Gulch, as it was named by the miners, is seen on the left. The Organ-pipe Range was so called by the party from the peculiar shape of the tall granite range found near the park. A camp view of the principal park in the hills gives some idea of the size of the expedition. This site was selected for the permanent camp, and from this point detachments radiated for several days.

THE CAMP IN THE PARK.

THE BLACK HILLS EXPEDITION.—[FROM PHOTOGRAPHS BY W. H. ILLINGWORTH.]

rth Photographs *(pages 162-269)*

publish a stereoview in the photo pair section of this book, it generally means no regular print could be obtained for publication because the negative is not known to survive in the present day. Almost all the known surviving glass plate negatives of W.H. Illingworth's Black Hills Expedition views are in the South Dakota State Historical Society collection; there are about 70 of these, several of which are near-duplicates of others. We believe there may be additional glass plate negatives from the Expedition in other private or public collections. Please contact the authors if you have any information about other original negatives from the Black Hills Expedition, or of original prints (stereoviews or otherwise) from those negatives.

2. Dave Rambow, a naturalist for the Minnesota Dept. of Natural Resources, is a modern-day wet plate collodion photographer who uses the same techniques 1870s-era photographers did; he helped identify the object in this photo as Illingworth's portable dark tent.

3. It's possible the long smooth pole in the foreground, which looks out of place, is actually a tipi pole. A complete tipi skeleton can be seen in enlargements of No. 814, which shows an area a few dozen yards from this photo site, and several accounts mention remnants of earlier Indian camps in this valley. Also, while this is almost certainly the first photograph Illingworth took of this camp, the order of the remaining photos is subject to question, as his own numbering system shows inconsistencies here.

4. Ivan Reynolds, grandson of the man who homesteaded Reynolds' Prairie (Elk Horn Prairie), told the authors that his uncle had elk horns along his driveway at a nearby ranch in the 1930s. It is not known whether the horns were from this pile.

5. The present-day Tenderfoot Gulch winds from just below the site of No. 819 to the area shown in this view. It's tempting to speculate that Illingworth used this valley as a travel route, but there is no other evidence of this. Down in the gulch, the rocks shown here and in No. 819 would have been lost to view, and Expedition diaries, such as geologist N.H. Winchell's, seem instead to suggest travel across the open prairie area a mile or so to the south.

6. A complete chapter could be written about this photograph and possible related events. One item not addressed in the caption is the question of the mysterious figure standing in the back of the scene. Some have speculated that this could be "Aunt Sally," Sarah Campbell, the black woman who was the only female known to have accompanied the Expedition. Aunt Sally is, however, described as a very large woman ("a huge mountain of dusky flesh" is how a newspaper reporter described her) which does not appear to fit the physique of the figure in back. Extreme enlargement of the photograph seems to show the outline of a beard on this figure in white, which would point to, perhaps, an enlisted man in a serving jacket. Someday, when the original negative of this view (held in the collection of the South Dakota State Historical Society) can be digitally scanned and enhanced, it may be possible to draw out facial details in the shadowy figure which are not visible in a regular print.

7. Locations for the new photographs are as follows. The photo of Buckhorn Mountain in the distance was taken near the junction of Hwy. 16A and America Center Road, about three miles east of Custer. The photo of Castle Peak/Courthouse Rock was taken from from Hwy. 16A about one mile east of Custer, straight south of the sewage treatment plant. The photo of Crazy Horse was taken from near Hwy. 16/385, about one mile north of Custer. There are other granite formations near Crazy Horse which could also be the mysterious "Godfrey Peak," but none seems to be a good match.

8. The "crouching soldier" photograph was apparently printed for the first time on page 268 of the November 1929 issue of *The Black Hills Engineer,* published by the South Dakota State School of Mines, in an article about the Black Hills Expedition by editor and school president Cleophas C. O'Harra. The soldier was not mentioned in the photo caption, and he is so well hidden in the shadows that he may not have been noticed in the small reproduction size of the 1929 magazine. The authors didn't notice him until an enlargement was made from the original contact print.

O'Harra was an enthusiastic researcher of the Black Hills Expedition, and the prints he had made from the original glass plate negatives (in 1920 and 1924 according to dates on the reverse), provide a glimpse of the condition of the fragile negatives at that time. In the 80 years since, at least two plates have been lost (including the "crouching soldier" plate), while others have cracked or broken, but the majority survive in good condition at the South Dakota State Historical Society.

9. See page 87 in Dr. Donald R. Progulske's book, *Yellow Ore, Yellow Hair, Yellow Pine* (see bibliography, page 284).

10. This location probably has more visitors than any other photo site shown in this book; it is well known in the Custer area and is publicized by the campground you can see in the photograph, as well as by this book, of course. All the more reason to be sure to pack out your picnic leftovers and anything else you may have carried up with you. Please try to leave the site exactly as it was when you arrived; don't pick up or throw rocks or other debris over the edge, and don't break branches from live or dead trees.

11. The ten sources of identifications for this photograph do not all agree with each other, and some identify only a few people. However, taken together they provide a comprehensive list, and there remain only 6 of the 38 men who cannot be identified with near certainty. One problem with past published lists is that they were not always clear about which name goes with which person.

We are fortunate that C.C. O'Harra (see Footnote 7) contacted surviving members of the Black Hills Expedition in the 1920s and 1930s, and that two of them, Charles Varnum and Luther North, left partial lists of names clearly identifying these men, and others they recalled. O'Harra's notes also include a typed name list from W.A. Falconer, identified as an early settler of Bismarck, N.D., which confirms several other sources for many names. As far as we know, these lists have not been published before.

The sources are:

a. Expedition member Charles Varnum, via O'Harra Collection, Expedition Correspondence, Devereaux Library Archives, South Dakota School of Mines and Technology, Rapid City, S.D.

b. Expedition member Luther North, ibid.

c. W.A. Falconer, ibid.

d. C.C. O'Harra's own list, apparently drawn up from his research and the sources listed above. One document attached to the list indicates that the group photograph was published in the Feb. 26, 1928, *St. Paul Pioneer Press,* listing several identifications with which O'Harra disagreed. O'Harra Collection, Expedition Correspondence, Devereaux Library Archives, South Dakota School of Mines and Technology, Rapid City, S.D.

e. A typed list apparently dating to the 1920s or 1930s, as it contains a reference to Lt. (then Col.) Varnum and Lt. (then Brig. Gen.) Godfrey, as well as Dr. Grinnell. The list says they "are the only survivors" in the photograph following the Little Big Horn and other conflicts of the Indian wars. The list has a number of names and several "unknowns." South Dakota State Historical Society Archives, Black Hills Expedition and Illingworth file, Pierre, S.D.

f. Charles A. Windolph, a survivor of the Black Hills Expedition and

Camera direction: **Southwest**

Photo location: **Point K, Page 81**

With careful study of the foreground rocks, it was possible to locate the photo site almost exactly. Several trees from the 1874 photo are visible in the modern scene, most notably the tree on the left shoulder of "Turret Rock."

No. 843.   Permanent camp in Agnes' Park.

No. 843, Permanent Camp in Agnes Park

Aug. 1-5, 1874

Returning to camp, Illingworth made these and several other views shown on the following pages, a historical treasure trove which defines the layout of tents and wagons and offers glimpses of life in camp. As he did in several other locations we know of, Illingworth made two nearly identical stereo images here; note how a small pine tree has appeared in the half-stereo view at bottom. (Or

was it removed from where it originally grew for the other photo?) In the stereoview above, he chose to publish the version without the small tree.

Illingworth also took a panoramic view of the camp from this photo location (see pages *iv-v*). This could have been done with another camera, or more likely by replacing the two stereo lenses he normally used with a single lens.

Camera direction: **South**

Photo location: **Point G, Page 86**

©PAUL HORSTED

The same foreground rocks (which are not as large as they seem in the photos) are easily found at this site located on U.S. Forest Service property just a few yards off America Center Road. The 1874 campsite is now the location of private homes, horse pastures and two campgrounds.

No. 844, Granite Knob and Harney's Peak

Aug. 1-5, 1874

Crossing the camp, Illingworth climbed a granite outcrop to take this and three more views. This photo shows the same line of tents as seen from the reverse angle in the previous photo. Part of "Granite Knob" (now known as Calamity Peak) is visible at left, as is the Harney Peak range in the hazy distance.

Camera direction: **North-Northwest**

Photo location: **Point B, Page 85**

On a clear day, the photo site affords a beautiful view of the Harney Peak range as well as the location of the Permanent Camp in the foreground (the valley below is mostly private property). To visit this site, which is on Forest Service land, drive a little more than 3 miles east of Custer on Highway 16A, and turn right onto Lower French Creek Road. Drive a quarter mile and find a safe place to park near the intersection with Stockade Lake Drive. (Be advised that you may need a South Dakota State Park entrance license to stop in this area, which is in Custer State Park; licenses are available at the entrance station a little farther up Highway 16A.) Walk to the west side of Lower French Creek Road, where you should be able to see a logging road a few yards up in the trees. Follow this road, which was once the main highway through this area.

If you have a GPS receiver, set the coordinates of the photo site as your "go to" point. After passing through a gate flanked by large rock pillars you will be on U.S. Forest Service property. Walk another 50 yards or so, then leave the road and begin a short but steep climb to a solitary granite peak on your left; you might see a path others have used. The hike up to the vantage point will take 20-30 minutes. At the top is a nice place to rest, have lunch, and ponder the changes that have taken place in the Black Hills since W.H. Illingworth set up his camera on this rock more than 125 years ago — not far from where you're sitting.[10]

From here you can see that Highway 16A now cuts through the site of Custer's camp. And today there is a public campground across the valley where you can camp very close to where Custer and his men once staked their tents.

No. 845, Gold Mountain Range and Headquarters

Aug. 1-5, 1874

Illingworth apparently just rotated his camera on its tripod to take this view of another area of camp from the same position used for the previous photo. We believe, in confirmation of the title, that Custer's distinctive headquarters tent is visible here; it's in the center of the line, the pointy-topped tent at center right. This tent, unlike any others in the camp, is clearly seen in the photos on pages *xii* and 254.

The Illingworth Photographs

Camera direction: **Northwest**

Photo location: **Point B, Page 85**

A Forest Service road cuts through the area where Custer's tent once stood, but the view is remarkably similar to what Illingworth saw in 1874. The round granite knob at left center on the horizon is the face of Crazy Horse Memorial, just barely visible in the afternoon light.

Gold Mountain Range and Headquarters

No. 846, Permanent Camp in Agnes Park

Aug. 1-5, 1874

This photo shares the same title as one Illingworth took across the valley (No. 843). The last view he apparently took at this location, and at this camp, it is similar to one taken earlier (No. 844 on page 248), but Illingworth apparently moved the camera a short distance and changed to a telephoto lens.

The photographer also made a single-plate panoramic view from this angle, (see pages 160-161), giving us an excellent visual record of this historic site.

Camera direction: **North**

Photo location: **Point B, Page 85**

We cannot be certain about the angle of foreground rocks in this scene. A close look at Illingworth's photo shows there are several planes of rock formations, some out of focus, and some at a greater distance than they first appear and now obscured by trees. Clearly he was very close to this area on a granite outcrop overlooking the campsite, but as mentioned he appears to have moved a few feet from the location of his previous two views.

847- Our First Grizzly, killed by Gen. Custer and Col. Ludlow.

No. 847, Our First Grizzly, killed by Gen. Custer (and Col. Ludlow)

Aug. 7, 1874

The Expedition had been covering ground quickly since leaving their Permanent Camp, on the way home now. Illingworth apparently took no photos for two days, until he composed this famous view. Gen. Custer is surrounded by his chief scout Bloody Knife, his orderly Pvt. John Noonan, and his chief engineer, Capt. William Ludlow (who had a brevet rank of Colonel), all of whom apparently shot at and killed the grizzly bear shown here. Illingworth made two different plates of this scene (see next spread), only min-utes apart. He originally published one of them through the firm of Huntington & Winne with the full title as shown; later versions of this stereoview, such as the one on the back cover of this book, do not include the words "and Col. Ludlow." Perhaps Illingworth changed this wording after Ludlow had him arrested a few months after the Expedition for failing to deliver copies of the photos he had taken. (See Illingworth biography, page 274, for the complete story.)

In an uncropped print directly from the original negative used by Illingworth to make the stereoview on the opposite page, we can now see the entire image. Behind the hunters, in addition to Custer's tent, is a line of parked wagons (including Illingworth's box-shaped dark wagon at right). Other wagons are moving toward camp at upper right. Also more visible is a dog, likely one of Custer's hounds, lying to Bloody Knife's right.

Our First Grizzly, killed by Gen. Custer (and Col. Ludlow)

The photographer made a second view of the men and their bear. We can't be sure, but this one appears to have been the second photo taken based on the additional wagons now visible arriving in camp. The lighting has not changed enough to be a definite clue, and Custer and Bloody Knife have barely moved from their original positions.

In any case, this second view gives us a slight but significantly clearer view up the valley, where a long line of wagons curls out of sight. This was critical in attempting to verify the modern location of this photo site.

Other interesting details can be seen in the background of the two versions. Elk antlers, picked up by soldiers along the trail, lie on top of wagons (this view) and on the ground (previous view). Note how Illingworth's time exposure of several seconds causes the movement of arriving wagons in the middle to leave a long white blur. But the sharpness of the rest of the photo even reveals grasshoppers on the snout of the deceased grizzly bear. Diary accounts mention a large number of grasshoppers in this valley (page 113).

Camera direction: **South**

Photo location: **Point H, Page 112**

The authors believe that this site, located on private land, is the actual location of the grizzly bear photo. Earlier studies and tradition had placed the photo and campsite near Nahant, two miles north. Several clues, and the geography of the modern scene, convince us otherwise.

The Expedition's map, when compared carefully with a modern map, points to this area, as do written descriptions (see pages 111-112). The angle of light in a 4:20 p.m. photograph taken just one calendar day later than the 1874 photograph (Aug. 8, in 2001) is correct. The height of the foreground, the angle of the rocks there, and the arrangement of the background all match very well.

This valley contains examples of nearly all the changes that have taken place since the Black Hills were settled, and we believe the foreground rocks would be identical if not for the railroad building, logging, mining and cattle grazing that have occurred on or within 1,000 feet of this site in the 127 years between 1874 and the day this photograph was taken.

Our First Grizzly, killed by Gen. Custer (and Col. Ludlow)

No. 848, Red Sandstone in Elk Creek Valley

Aug. 11, 1874

Illingworth set up on a barren ridge looking north for this and the following view, taken from almost exactly the same position. Fire had clearly burned through this area not many years before the Expedition arrived. The two prominent peaks are now called Green Top (left) and White Mansion. The small pine tree between the two rocks may have been placed there (or removed) by Illingworth as he had done once before (page 246); it should also be visible in the next view, but has disappeared.

Camera direction: **Northwest**

Photo location: **Point C, Page 132**

©PAUL HORSTED

The unique oval rocks Illingworth chose for his foreground give us a precise location aid on this ridge north of Nemo. Tremendous growth of trees in the area is the most obvious change at this photo site. The "Red Sandstone" is also clearly visible in the modern view.

No. 849, Top of Custer Peak and Elk Creek Valley

Aug. 11, 1874

Moving his camera a couple feet forward, Illingworth also turned it a little to the west for a second view from this vantage point, attempting to capture an image of Custer Peak. The mountain is lost in distant haze, but the shadow of Illingworth and his camera can be seen in the foreground.

At the time this and the previous view were made, journal accounts indicate that members of the Expedition believed they were in the Elk Creek Valley; a day or two later they realized it was actually the Boxelder Creek drainage. Illingworth's title, however, remained.

Camera direction: **West**

Photo location: **Point C, Page 132**

Custer Peak is the distant mountain near the top center of this modern view.
A forest has sprung up in the formerly open valley below.

Top of Custer Peak and Elk Creek Valley

STEREOGRAPHS OF THE BLACK HILLS.
Photographed by W. H. Illingworth.

PUBLISHED BY W. H. ILLINGWORTH.
No. EAST SEVENTH STREET, ST PAUL, MINN.

MINNILUSA PIONEER MUSEUM

No. 850. Forsyth's Glenn.

No. 850, Forsyth's Glenn

Aug. 11-13, 1874

Apparently named for brevet Brig. Gen. George "Sandy" Forsyth, second in command on the Expedition, this view shows a stream meandering beneath a sharp cliff. It is one of three sites we could not definitely locate in the modern Black Hills landscape, despite searches of several likely areas. At the time this photo was probably taken (based on its number in Illingworth's series), the Expedition was searching for a route out of the rugged Black Hills, attempting to return to the plains and begin the journey back to Ft. Lincoln. Illingworth may have had time to explore some of the canyons and water-courses being searched for exit routes. Our best guess is that this could be along the watersheds of the Boxelder or Little Elk Creek. Or Bogus Jim Creek. Or Estes Creek.

Camera direction: **Northeast**

Photo location: **Point B, Page 131**

©PAUL HORSTED

We do not claim that this location is Illingworth's, but it is as close as we could get to a matching view in two summers of searching. We found several areas along the Expedition's known route which could possibly be the 1874 photo site, but natural and man-made landscape changes may have altered these areas beyond recognition. At this location near an Expedition campsite, about 25 feet of the cliff has been blasted away to make room along Little Elk Creek for Dalton Lake Road. The road is hidden behind brush at the center of the photo.

(Untitled) Expedition group photo

Aug. 13, 1874

This fascinating print shows officers and civilian members of the Black Hills Expedition and was made at the Custer Gap campsite. Several accounts (pages 142-143) discuss the picture being taken in front of Custer's tent in the morning (and one, Ewert's Diary, mentions other photos being taken by Illingworth at this camp, although none are now known). The identification lists on the opposite page have been gathered from ten sources, some dating to the 1920s when a few people in the photograph were still alive to provide names. (The penciled-in numbers in the photo above are from one such source.) When sources were split on identity or spelling, both versions are noted.[11]

The authors are interested in viewing other original prints of this photograph that could help our research; please see page *vi* for contact information.

1. Capt. William Ludlow **2.** Capt. George Yates **3.** 1st Lt. Thomas Custer **4.** 2nd Lt. George Wallace **5.** 1st Lt. James Calhoun **6.** 2nd Lt. Henry Harrington **7.** Dr. A.C. Bergen, asst. surgeon **8.** Boston Custer, Forage Master, or Capt. Thomas French **9.** 1st Lt. Donald McIntosh **10.** William Curtis, Chicago *Inter-Ocean* correspondent (holding a hammer).

11. Luther North, assistant to Grinnell **12.** George Bird Grinnell, naturalist **13.** Aris B. Donaldson, botanist and correspondent for St. Paul *Pioneer* **14.** 1st Lt. Algernon Smith (see #31) **15.** Major John W. Williams, asst. surgeon **16.** Major George "Sandy" Forsyth **17.** Brevet General George Custer **18.** 1st Lt. Thomas McDougal (or McDougall)

19. Bloody Knife, chief scout **20.** Major Joseph Tilford **21.** Lt. Col. Frederick Grant **22.** Capt. Thomas French **23.** 2nd Lt. Charles Varnum **24.** Capt. Myles Moylan **25.** 2nd Lt. Julius Gates (see #34) **26.** Capt. Verling Hart **27.** Capt. Lloyd Wheaton **28.** Newton Winchell, geologist **29.** 1st Lt. Edward Mathey Men in background not identified by any known source.

30. 2nd Lt. Benjamin Hodgson (see #35) **31.** Capt. Louis Sanger or 1st. Lt. Algernon Smith (resembles #14) **32.** Capt. Owen Hale **33.** 2nd Lt. George Roach **34.** 2nd Lt. Julius Gates (see #25; also note elk head above left elbow) **35.** 1st Lt. Josiah Chance or 2nd Lt. Benjamin Hodgson (see #30) **36.** Capt. Frederick Benteen **37.** 1st Lt. Edward Godfrey **38.** 1st Lt. Frank (or Francis) Gibson

©PAUL HORSTED

A careful look at Illingworth's group photo reveals no obvious rocks or other landmarks that point to an exact location in the pasture near Bogus Jim and Boxelder Creeks, where the group photo was made. We know from diary accounts that the photo was taken in mid-morning; study of light and shadows in the photo indicates the subjects were facing east at that time. The photograph at left shows an area on private land that may or may not encompass the group photo site, on a rise now enclosed by trees. If other 1874 photos are any guide, this area would have had fewer trees during the time of the Expedition.

DEVEREAUX LIBRARY ARCHIVES

No. 851, Bear Butte

Aug. 15, 1874

The Expedition camped a few miles south of this prominent landmark for two nights, as the wagons were refitted for travel across the plains. Illingworth took this view from the prairie south of Bear Butte Creek, just barely visible as a line in the middle distance. This is his last known photo in the immediate vicinity of the Black Hills, although he did make a few more exposures out on the prairie during the weeks of travel back to Ft. Lincoln (see pages *i, ii-iii, xi, xii,* and 1 for examples).

Camera direction: **North**

Photo location: **Point Q, Page 157**

The former open prairie has been turned into a hayfield, and cottonwood trees and a ranch have sprung up along Bear Butte Creek since Illingworth set up his camera on what is now private property. Bear Butte is almost barren after a fire, started in the campground near the base of the mountain, burned off most of the trees in 1996.

A mystery solved

Date Unknown

For at least 80 years this striking photograph of a waterfall was assumed to have been taken during the 1874 Expedition, because the original glass plate was included in a collection of Illingworth's Black Hills Expedition negatives purchased by the South Dakota State Historical Society in 1920. The authors, as well as earlier researchers, spent many hours and days looking for this site, mainly in the northern Black Hills along the Expedition's known route. Although there are similarities of terrain in some areas of the Hills, no such site could be found.

Fairy Falls, near Stillwater.

Modern technology helped solve this mystery when the authors found the stereoview above on the Minnesota Historical Society web site. Also taken by Illingworth, it bears the title "Fairy Falls, near Stillwater." It shares several similarities with the view on the opposite page, such as the shape of the granite blocks near the top of the falls, the white tree trunk at the top left side of the falls, and the odd white patches on the ground (now believed to be snow). There is also a man (previously assumed to be a soldier on the Expedition) dressed in a suit and wearing a derby hat, sitting at upper left of the waterfall on the opposite page; he also poses at center right of the waterfall on this page.

We are convinced that the two photos are of the same site, probably taken the same day. Illingworth operated a studio in St. Paul before and after the Black Hills Expedition, and took hundreds of views in the surrounding area. In this case, one of his Minnesota negatives somehow got put in the box with the Expedition photographs, and the rest is history. (As this book was going to press, another Minnesota photo site was "discovered" in the Black Hills negatives; see page 276.)

"Fairy Falls" is a known location on private land in present-day Stillwater, Minnesota, according to the local historical society. The stream no longer flows there as it once did, due to changes in the local environment.

the Battle of Little Big Horn, spent his later years in Lead, S.D. Ralph Cartwright, a neighbor and a Custer researcher, left a large collection of papers at the Hearst Library in Lead, including a copy of this photograph with a few names noted by Windolph. Ralph G. Cartwright Collection, Phoebe Hearst Memorial Library, Lead, S.D.

g. A little-known book apparently published by "Mole & Miller" in Pierre, S.D., in the 1940's included a number of the Illingworth views of the Black Hills. The group photograph was published with a partial identification list; the original plate from this book is in Paul Horsted's personal collection.

h. Little Bighorn Battlefield National Monument has two copies of this photograph in its archives. One apparently came from Libbie Custer's estate, with an attached hand-written list identifying 18 of the men in the photograph (as well as a scrawled note that appears to read, "Yellowstone Expedition probably"). This is the photograph reproduced in our book, complete with penciled-in numbers keyed to the list (#19 is the tent).

i. There is an identification list for this photograph on page 205 of the book *Prelude to Glory* by Herbert Krause and Gary D. Olson. (See bibliography on page 284.)

j. There is another identification list for this photograph on pages 114-115 of the book *Custer in Photographs* by D. Mark Katz. (See bibliography on page 284.)

Biography of W.H. Illingworth *(pages 272-277)*
by Don Schwarck

1. Minnesota Historical Society, Minnesota Photographers File, Illingworth Vertical File.

2. Ibid.

3. *The Saint Paul Pioneer*, Wednesday, July 1, 1863. page 4, col. 2.

4. Minnesota Historical Society, Minnesota Photographers File, Illingworth Vertical File.

5. *St. Paul Weekly Press*, June 7, 1866.

6. Ibid.

7. Taft, Robert, *Photography and the American Scene*. Dover Publications, Inc., Mineola, New York, 1964, page 276.

8. Minnesota Historical Society, Minnesota Photographers Biography File, Illingworth Vertical File. The negatives are believed to have been lost when the Great Chicago Fire consumed Carbutt's studio in 1871.

9. Ibid.

10. Flower & Hawkins of St. Paul published these views. The series is a mixed collection of some very early images with scratched-in negative numbers ranging from the 250s through 270s that show the track-laying and trestle-building crews. Others numbered in the 520s through the 550s show steam engines, railroad stations and buildings in towns along the line. Evidently Illingworth combined views from two time periods to create this series.

11. Personal conversation by publisher with antique photo collector and historian Bob Kolbe of Sioux Falls, S.D., Dec. 20, 2001.

12. *St. Paul Daily Press*, March 26, 1874, page 2.

13. Ludlow to Chief of Engineers, Jan. 12, 1875, RG 77, National Archives.

14. Ludlow, William, Captain of Engineers, *Report of a Reconnaissance of the Black Hills of Dakota, Made in the Summer of 1874*. Government Printing Office, Washington, D.C., 1875, page 8.

15. Jackson, Donald, *Custer's Gold: The United States Cavalry Expedition of 1874*. University of Nebraska Press, Lincoln, Nebraska, 1966, page 60.

16. Ludlow to Chief of Engineers, Jan. 12, 1875, RG 77, National Archives.

17. Ibid.

18. Ibid.

19. *St. Paul Pioneer Press*, July 28, 1874, page 55.

20. The mysterious identity of the *Saint Paul Daily Press* correspondent calling himself "Power" has been sufficiently cleared up in "'Distance Lends Enchantment to the View': The Black Hills Expedition Diary of Fred W. Power," Buecker, Thomas R., ed. *South Dakota History*, published by South Dakota State Historical Society, Pierre, S.D.; Vol. 27., No. 4 (Winter 1997), pages 202-208.

21. *St. Paul Daily Press*, August 15, 1874. Also in *Prelude to Glory*, page 85.

22. Letter from Custer to Libbie, Bear Butte, Aug. 15, 1874. Custer's Black Hills letters are in the Marguerite Merington Collection, New York Public Library.

23. Carroll, John M., & Frost, Lawrence A., eds., *Private Theodore Ewert's Diary Of The Black Hills Expedition Of 1874*. CRI Books, Piscataway, New Jersey, 1976, page 80.

24. *St. Paul Daily Press*, Sept. 3, 1874, page 4.

25. Ibid., Sept. 6, 1874, page 4.

26. Ibid., Sept. 10, 1874, page 4.

27. Ibid., Nov. 24, 1874, page 4.

28. Ibid.

29. Ludlow to Chief of Engineers, Jan. 12, 1875, RG 77, National Archives.

30. *Minneapolis Tribune*, November, 28, 1874.

31. Letter written Nov. 28, 1874, from Captain William Ludlow to General George Custer, Merington Collection, New York Public Library.

32. Ibid.

33. Katz, D. Mark, *Custer in Photographs: A Photographic Biography of America's Most Intriguing Boy General*. Custer Battlefield Museum Publishing, Garryowen, Montana, 1985, page 118.

34. Minnesota Historical Society, Photographers Biography File, Illingworth File.

35. Illingworth's wagon and the signage quoted can be seen under magnification in a view of the fort, which is located near St. Paul. A scan of this stereoview was provided to the publisher by collector and dealer Richard Wood of Juneau, Alaska.

36. The *St. Paul Dispatch* of March 17, 1893, contains an account of Illingworth's movements the day before his suicide. It was gleaned from neighbors who lived above his shop and home, and from other people the reporter interviewed in the neighborhood. Illingworth's lodgings are described, and there is a graphic description of his suicide.

37. Letters describing the transaction between Bromley and Robinson are in the Black Hills Expedition photo file, South Dakota State Historical Society Archives, Pierre, S.D.

Summary table of daily instrumental observations, with deduced altitudes, the latitude and longitude of each camp, distances traveled, &c.

Date.	Location.	Start.	Arrive.	Max.	Min.	No.	Total.	Mean.	Evening.	Morning.	Feet.	Latitude.	Longitude.	Day's march. Miles.	Total distance. Miles.	Heights of peaks above sea-level, in feet.
1874. July 2	Buck Creek	8.00 a.m.	8.45 p.m.	94	79	3	260	86.6	27.66		2,169	46 40 50	101 03 08	15.1	15.1	
3		8.00 a.m.	3.00 p.m.	98½	83	3	273	90.6	27.85		1,939	46 35 55	101 06 43	14.1	29.2	
4	Dog's Teeth Creek	5.00 a.m.	3.00 p.m.	102	64	5	434	86.8	27.74		2,090			14.7	43.9	
5	Creek "where bear winters"	5.00 a.m.	11.30 a.m.	78	59	5	342	68.4	27.56		2,251			16.9	60.8	
6	Cannon Ball River	11.30 a.m.	1.00 p.m.	94	60	5	392	78.4	27.36		2,392	46 19 52	101 47 43	12.9	73.7	
7	Cedar Creek	1.00 p.m.	10.00 a.m.	82	67	4	308.5	77.1	27.32		2,459	46 03 00	102 06 07	30.4	104.1	
8	Hidden Wood Creek	10.00 a.m.	10.00 p.m.	84½	46	4	305	76.8	27.45		2,608	45 57 20	102 45 01	39.0	143.1	
9	Grand River	4.00 a.m.	4.30 p.m.	100	45	5	384	67.5	27.57		2,305	45 54 58	102 45 42	19.0	162.1	
10	do	4.30 a.m.	2.30 p.m.	83	4	5	270	76.8	26.50		2,439	45 49 10	103 01 43	9.7	171.8	
11	Cave	4.45 a.m.	4.00 p.m.	90	6	6	476	79.3	26.61		2,825	45 35 00	103 26 46	24.0	196.8	
12	do	2.30 p.m.	4.00 p.m.	56	4	5	374	74.9	26.50		3,439	45 49 10	103 28 09	1.0	197.8	
13	Sage Brush Camp	4.50 a.m.	3.00 p.m.	87	62	5	405	81.0	26.61		3,925	45 42 14	103 26 10	15.5	213.3	
14, 15	Prospect Valley	4.45 a.m.	2.00 p.m.	90	63	5	386.5	67.3	26.76		3,189	45 35 50	103 38 50	11.0	224.3	
16	Border Camp	1.00 p.m.	2.00 p.m.	78	58	5	357.5	76.4	26.57		3,271	45 28 56	103 47 25	13.0	256.8	
17	Bad Lands	5.00 a.m.	8.30 a.m.	82	56	5	382	76.4	26.39		3,488			30.0	274.5	
18, 19	Belle Fourche	2.00 p.m.	2.15 p.m.	84	4	4	338	76.4	26.38		3,858	44 58 10	104 02 39	17.7	292.0	
20	Red Water Valley	4.45 a.m.	4.30 p.m.	93	5	5	388	71.5	26.14		3,654	44 48 05	104 15 27	18.3	310.3	
21	Inyan Kara Camp	8.30 a.m.	4.30 p.m.	78	37	26	2,644.6	69.1	25.71		5,318	44 30 18	104 14 33	14.3	324.6	Inyan Kara, 6,500.
22, 23	Floral Valley	2.15 p.m.	5.00 p.m.	88	50	26	1,811.5	82.3	24.85		4,226	44 13 00	104 15 57	22.2	346.8	
24	do	4.45 a.m.	5.00 p.m.	91	73	16	1,333.3	83.3	24.09		5,734	44 13 01	104 14 13	11.0	357.8	
25	Castle Valley	4.30 a.m.	5.00 p.m.	88	62	11	842.7	76.6	23.73		6,459	44 12 40	104 03 34	11.0	369.3	
26, 27	do	4.45 a.m.	5.00 p.m.	86	1	1	86	86.0	23.73		6,136	44 08 35	103 51 30	14.0	383.3	
28	Indian Camp	4.45 a.m.	2.00 p.m.	66	11	11	591.2	53.7	24.03		6,923	44 01 45	103 53 20	10.0	393.3	
29		4.45 a.m.	2.00 p.m.	88	9	9	846	71.8	23.92		6,903	44 00 52	103 48 27	15.0	408.3	
30, 31	Permanent Camp	3.00 p.m.	3.00 p.m.	83	46	12	805	74.6	24.25		5,488			10.2	418.7	
Aug. 1–5		1.00 p.m.	1.00 p.m.	70	4	4	268	67.0	24.50		5,664	43 46 10	103 33 02	13.5	422.2	Harney's Peak, 9,700.
6		9.30 a.m.	9.30 a.m.	71	65	2	136	68.0	23.53		6,768	44 08 33	103 45 50	16.2	445.4	
7		7.30 a.m.	7.30 a.m.						23.55		5,877	44 15 10	103 38 08	3.5	461.6	
8		7.45 a.m.		89	63	2	152	76.0	24.49		5,633			14.7	476.3	
9		4.55 a.m.	5.30 p.m.	72	6	6	416	69.3	24.61	24.49	5,481	44 09 53	103 30 16	7.5	483.8	
10, 11		5.00 a.m.	2.00 p.m.	57	46	6	961	53.2	24.96	24.61	4,361	44 07 35	103 26 01	7.7	491.3	
12		4.45 a.m.	2.00 p.m.	90	5	5	355	52.3	25.64		4,518	44 05 46	103 23 19	5.7	497.0	
13		4.45 a.m.	7.00 p.m.	88	14	14	1,100	78.5	25.45	24.96	3,694	44 23 43	103 28 02	4.7	501.7	
14, 15	Bear Butte Camp	12.00 m.	6.00 p.m.	90	11	11	1,849	77.1	26.30	25.58	2,889	44 47 35	103 28 19	29.5	557.2	Bear Butte, 4,500.
16		4.45 a.m.	7.00 p.m.	86	14	14	730	78.6	26.87	26.30	3,067	45 09 30	103 25 41	28.2	565.4	
17		7.00 a.m.	7.30 p.m.	84	10	10	786	73.7	26.75	26.30	3,675	45 31 05	103 23 35	30.2	615.6	
18		6.00 p.m.	7.00 p.m.	62	11	11	791	71.7	26.27	26.85	3,285	45 09 35	103 52 35	35.3	650.9	
19	Prospect Valley	7.00 a.m.	7.15 p.m.	79	22	22	1,534	69.7	26.63	26.27	3,023	46 08 30	103 51 30	29.9	680.8	
20, 21		5.30 p.m.	7.20 a.m.	66	15	15	1,058	69.7	26.59	26.84	3,256	45 42 20	103 42 54	28.5	709.3	
22	Little Missouri River	7.00 a.m.	5.00 a.m.	61	16	16	1,070	66.9	26.28	26.59	2,554	46 34 55	103 29 25	19.0	728.3	
23	Little Missouri River	7.20 a.m.	7.15 p.m.	84	11	11	1,132	66.3	27.13	26.63	2,718	46 44 45	103 07 51	24.7	753.0	
24	Heart River	5.00 a.m.		81	11	11	751	68.3	27.00	26.85	2,779	45 09 40	103 02 45	17.7	770.7	
25	Little Missouri River	7.15 p.m.		75	16	16	1,910	67.4	26.90	26.27	2,965	45 09 20	102 45 06	38.2	802.9	
26	Young Men's Buttes	5.00 a.m.		59	13	13	829	63.8	27.15	27.35	2,608	45 03 20	103 01 28	32.0	835.1	
27		4.45 a.m.		58	11	11	1,307	68.3	27.33	27.00	2,394	46 06 30	103 23 35	28.8	865.6	
28		4.45 a.m.		87	64	4	751	66.5	27.23	27.25	2,608	45 52 30	102 15 49	17.1	880.9	
29	Little Muddy Creek	4.45 a.m.	12.00 m.	64	13	13	795	66.3	27.30	27.35	1,998	46 34 55	102 15 49	17.1	902.9	
29	White Fish Creek	4.45 a.m.	5.00 p.m.	69	13	13	865	62.4	27.82	27.55	1,998	46 32 00	101 16 18	16.0	856.0	
30	Fort Abraham Lincoln	4.30 a.m.	10.50 a.m.	78	20	20	1,507	75.3	27.65	27.80	2,211	46 46 10	100 50 57	27.3	883.3	

RECONNAISSANCES.

		Distance.	Total.
Colonel Ludlow	July 31	30 }	136 miles.
	Aug. 3 to 5	100	
	Aug. 10	16	
Lieutenant Godfrey	July 27	8 }	104 miles.
	July 31	20	
	Aug. 2 to 5	70	
	7	6	

			Distance.	Total.
July 25	Mr. W. H. Wood		10	28
July 27	do		18 }	
July 27	Sergeant Becker		11	
July 31	do		11 }	322 miles.
July 27	Sergeant Wilson		16	
	do		16 }	32

Wagon-train traveled .... 883.3 miles.
Reconnaissances, traveled .... 322.0 miles.
Total .... 1,205.3 miles.
Camps 47

CHIEF ENGINEER'S OFFICE, *Saint Paul, Minn., April 23, 1875.*

O

The official report published in 1875 included a table of measurements and readings that add a great deal to our understanding of the Expedition's experiences and accomplishments. (Paul Horsted Collection)

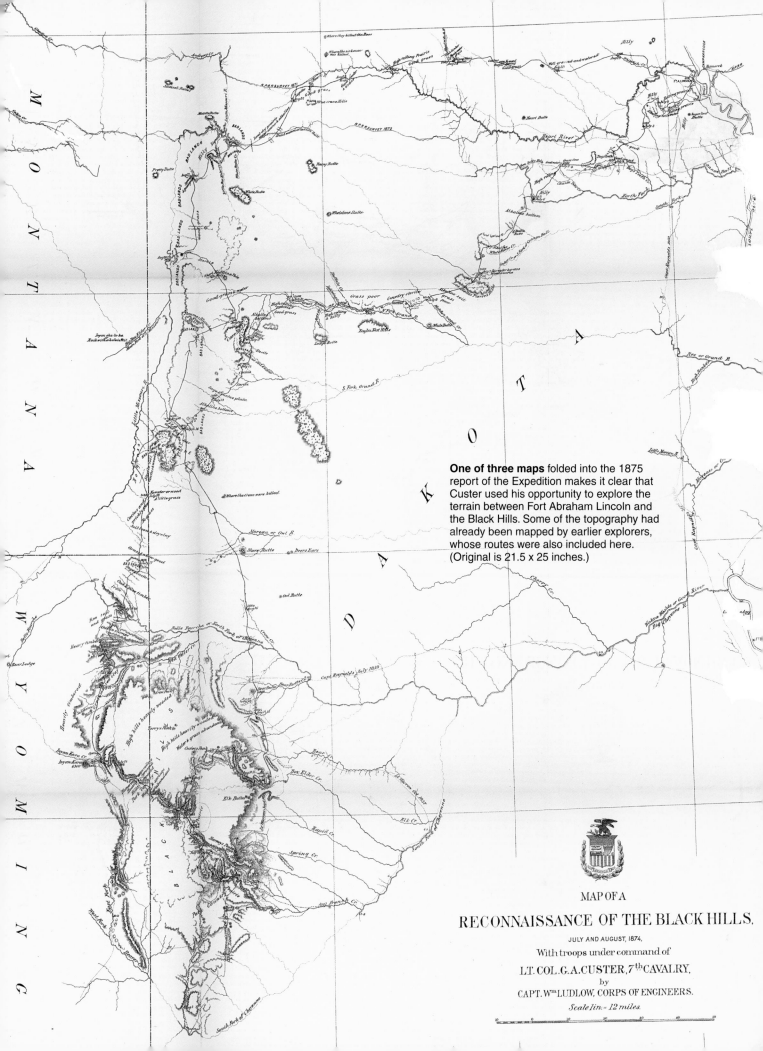

One of three maps folded into the 1875 report of the Expedition makes it clear that Custer used his opportunity to explore the terrain between Fort Abraham Lincoln and the Black Hills. Some of the topography had already been mapped by earlier explorers, whose routes were also included here. (Original is 21.5 x 25 inches.)

MAP OF A

RECONNAISSANCE OF THE BLACK HILLS,

JULY AND AUGUST, 1874,

With troops under command of

LT. COL. G. A. CUSTER, 7th CAVALRY,

by

CAPT. Wm LUDLOW, CORPS OF ENGINEERS.

Scale 1 in. = 12 miles.

MAP OF
THE BLACK HILLS
From a reconnaissance by
Capt. WILLIAM LUDLOW Corps of Engineers,
1874
And maps of WARREN and RAYNOLDS.
Scale 1in = 3miles

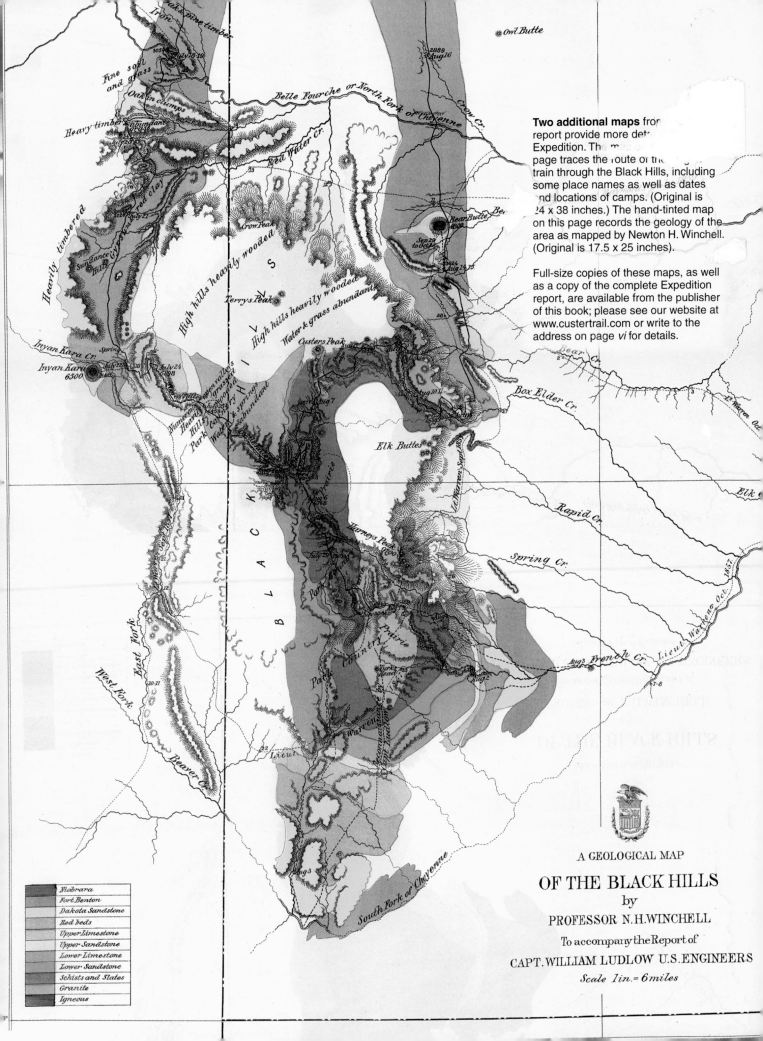

Owl Butte

Belle Fourche or North Fork or Cheyenne

Red Water Cr.

Crow Peak

Terrys Peak

High hills heavily wooded

High hills heavily wooded

Water & grass abundant

Bear Butte

Custers Peak

Elk Buttes

Box Elder Cr.

Rapid Cr.

Spring Cr.

Harneys Peak

Inyan Kara Cr.

Inyan Kara
6500

Beaver Cr.

West Fork

East Fork

Bear Cr.

Park Country Prairie

Warren

South Fork of Cheyenne

French Cr.

Two additional maps from report provide more det... Expedition. The map o... page traces the route of the... train through the Black Hills, including some place names as well as dates and locations of camps. (Original is 24 x 38 inches.) The hand-tinted map on this page records the geology of the area as mapped by Newton H. Winchell. (Original is 17.5 x 25 inches).

Full-size copies of these maps, as well as a copy of the complete Expedition report, are available from the publisher of this book; please see our website at www.custertrail.com or write to the address on page *vi* for details.

	Niobrara
	Fort Benton
	Dakota Sandstone
	Red beds
	Upper Limestone
	Upper Sandstone
	Lower Limestone
	Lower Sandstone
	Schists and Slates
	Granite
	Igneous

A GEOLOGICAL MAP

OF THE BLACK HILLS

by

PROFESSOR N.H.WINCHELL

To accompany the Report of

CAPT. WILLIAM LUDLOW U.S. ENGINEERS

Scale 1 in. = 6 miles

Dakota Histo... ...121-162.

Bodmer, Karl. *Karl Bodmer ...* introduction by William H. Goetzmann; annotations by David C. Hunt and Marsha V. Gallagher. Lincoln: University of Nebraska Press, 1984.

Buecker, Thomas R., ed. "'Distance Lends Enchantment to the View': The 1874 Black Hills Expedition Diary of Fred W. Power," *South Dakota History*, Vol. 27, No. 4 (Winter 1997), 197-260.

Carroll, John M., and Frost, Lawrence A. *Private Theodore Ewert's Diary of the Black Hills Expedition of 1874.* Piscataway, New Jersey: Consultant Resources Incorporated, 1976.

Cartwright, R.G. Collected papers archived in the Phoebe Hearst Public Library, Lead, South Dakota.

Casey, Robert J. *The Black Hills and Their Incredible Characters.* Indianapolis: Bobbs-Merrill Company, Inc., 1949.

Danker, Donald F., ed. *Man of the Plains: Recollections of Luther North, 1856-1882.* Lincoln: University of Nebraska Press, 1961.

Fielder, Mildred. *Railroads of the Black Hills.* New York: Bonanza Books, 1964.

Frost, Lawrence A., ed. *With Custer in '74: James Calhoun's Diary of the Black Hills Expedition.* Provo, Utah: Brigham Young University Press, 1979.

Grafe, Ernest, and Horsted, Paul. "In Illingworth's Footsteps: Rediscovering the First Photographs of the Black Hills," *South Dakota History*, Vol. 31, Nos. 3 & 4 (Fall/Winter 2002), 289-316.

Grinnell, George Bird. *Two Great Scouts and their Pawnee Battalion.* Lincoln: University of Nebraska Press, 1973.

Honerkamp, John R. *At the Foot of the Mountain.* Piedmont, South Dakota: Self-published, 1978.

Jackson, Donald. *Custer's Gold.* New Haven: Yale University Press, 1966.

Katz, Mark D. *Custer in Photographs: A Photographic Biography of America's Most Intriguing Boy General.* Garryowen, Montana: Custer Battlefield Museum Publishing, 1985 and 2001.

Kime, Wayne R., ed. *The Black Hills Journals of Colonel Richard Irving Dodge.* Norman: University of Oklahoma Press, 1996.

Krause, Herbert, and Olson, Gary D. *Prelude to Glory: A newspaper accounting of Custer's 1874 Expedition to the Black Hills.* Sioux Falls, South Dakota: Brevet Press, 1974.

Ludlow, Capt. William. *Report of a Reconnaissance of the Black Hills of Dakota, Made in the ...* Washington, D.C.: Government Printi...

McGillycuddy, Dr. Valentine T. "First Su... ...Black Hills," *Motor Travel* (September and ... ...11-14, 18-21.

... ...W. *Making the Grade: A century of Black ... ...ailroa...* Rapid City, South Dakota: Self-publish... ...1985.

...Harra, Cleophas C. ...lected papers, archive... of the ...Devereaux Library, Sou... Dakota School of Mines & Technology, Rapid City, South L...

———. "Custer's Black Hills Expediti... ...874," *The Black Hills Engineer*, Vol. XVII (Novembe... 1929), 220-286.

———. "The Discovery of Gold in the Black Hills," *The Black Hills Engineer*, Vol. XVII (November, 1929), 286-299.

Palais, Hyman. "A Study of the Trails to the Black Hills Gold Fields," *South Dakota Historical Collections*, Vol. XXV (1951), 215-62.

Parker, Watson. *Gold in the Black Hills.* Lincoln: University of Nebraska Press, 1966.

———, and Lambert, Hugh K. *Black Hills Ghost Towns.* Chicago: The Swallow Press, 1974.

Power, Fred W. Diary kept during the 1874 Black Hills Expedition. In the collection of Kirk Budd.

Progulske, Donald R. *Yellow Ore, Yellow Hair, Yellow Pine: A Photographic Study of a Century of Forest Ecology.* Photography by Richard H. Sowell. Brookings: Agricultural Experiment Station, South Dakota State University, 1974.

———, with Shideler, Frank J. *Following Custer.* Brookings: Agricultural Experiment Station, South Dakota State University, n.d.

Reiger, John F. *The Passing of the Great West: Selected Papers of George Bird Grinnell.* Norman, University of Oklahoma Press., 1985.

Sneve, Virginia Driving Hawk, ed. *South Dakota Geographic Names.* A revision of South Dakota Place Names, University of South Dakota, 1941. Sioux Falls, South Dakota: Brevet Press, 1973.

Spring, Agnes Wright. *The Cheyenne and Black Hills Stage and Express Routes.* Lincoln: University of Nebraska Press, 1948.

Taft, Robert. *Photography and the American Scene.* Mineola, New York: Dover Publications, 1964.

Tallent, Annie D. *The Black Hills: Or, the Last Hunting Ground of the Dakotahs.* Introduction by Virginia Driving Hawk Sneve. Sioux Falls, South Dakota: Brevet Press, 1974.

Urbanek, Mae. *Wyoming Place Names.* Boulder: Johnson Publishing Company, 1967.

Winchell, Newton M. Field notebook containing entries dated during the Black Hills Expedition of 1874. Archives of the University of Minnesota, Minneapolis.

Windolph, Charles. *I Fought with Custer: The story of Sergeant Windolph.* As told to Frazier and Robert Hunt. New York: Charles Scribner's Sons, Ltd., 1947.